DON'T BELIEVE A WORD

DON'T BELIEVE
A WORD

The Surprising Truth About Language

DAVID SHARIATMADARI

First published in Great Britain in 2019 by Weidenfeld & Nicolson
an imprint of The Orion Publishing Group Ltd
Carmelite House, 50 Victoria Embankment
London EC4Y 0DZ

An Hachette UK Company

1 3 5 7 9 10 8 6 4 2

Illustration credits: p. 78 IPA Chart,
http://www.internationalphoneticassociation.org/content/ipa-chart,
available under a Creative Commons Attribution-Sharealike
3.0 Unported License. Copyright © 2015 International Phonetic
Associa   137, Benjamin Lee Whorf edited by John B. Carroll
and Stu   ed Writings
of Benja   Institute of

A CIP catalogue record for this book
is available from the British Library.

ISBN (hardback) 978 1 4746 0843 5
ISBN (trade paperback) 978 1 4746 0844 2
ISBN (ebook) 978 1 4746 0846 6

Typeset by Input Data Services Ltd, Somerset

Printed and bound in Great Britain by Clays Ltd, Elcograf S.p.A.

www.orionbooks.co.uk

For Arfa'

CONTENTS

INTRODUCTION

Is anything quite so familiar, yet so mysterious as language? It fills our lives, often from the moment we wake up, to last thing at night. Most of us use it without thinking about it. But most of us also have only the vaguest idea of what it really is, and how it works.

It is something close – closer than anything, really: in our lungs and on our lips.* But it remains far from our grasp in terms of understanding. It is the box of magic tricks inside every one of us. It is also an inescapable trap: we can only think and talk about language by using it. Language is deployed to wonder about itself, to scrutinise itself, to praise and deplore itself. No surprise, then, that amateur explorers sometimes feel as though they are lost in a hall of mirrors.

Even so, it remains an obsession. Today, an ordinary Tuesday, I searched Google News for 'words' and 'language'. Among the hundreds of headlines from around the world:

> From 'titanic success' to 'Mad Max': how language
>   around Brexit changed
> The murky linguistics of consent

---

* And if you're a signer, in your hands. Sign languages are just as expressive and sophisticated as spoken languages.

Danish minister to migrants: learn the language or pay for
     your own interpreter
10 German words becoming extinct thanks to English
Climate change can also transform language
How the left's war on words manipulates your mind
The generation who can't remember life before mobiles
     are not just social media obsessed, they speak their own
     language. From 'kitten-fishing' to 'adulting', here's how
     to speak millennial!

There appears to be an almost insatiable appetite for linguistic debate. A fascination driven in part, perhaps, by the
lack of satisfying explanations. Why *do* millennials speak
their own language? Do the words they choose reflect the
fact that they are superficial, lazy, addicted to technology?
How can you protect a language against outside influence?
Does the language we use to talk about climate change, or
Brexit, change the way we think about them? Are words
responsible for directing our thoughts, or is it the other way
around? Who decides what a word actually means?

There are good reasons language is such a battleground
and source of frustration: it is also a source of delight, of
self-esteem and solidarity. Great poets and writers – the
ones who can shape language in elegant and startling
ways – are loved by millions and can find themselves richly
rewarded. Song lyrics capture the spirit of the times and
stay with people their whole lives. Lullabies are imbibed
with mothers' milk, and words and stories we associate
with childhood are intimately linked to our sense of self.
Language is used for social differentiation: think of all the
effort people go to in order to expunge the 'wrong' kinds
of words or sounds from their speech. Conversely, there's
pride in local language, in 'slang', in words that are markers

of identity. Imagine you're homesick in a far-off country, surrounded by strangers. What's the feeling you get when you overhear someone speaking your language – not only that, but in your accent, from precisely your part of the world?

Something as precious as this is bound to be fought over.

And puzzled over. Our curiosity about language has given rise to a bewildering variety of explanations, from myth, to folklore, to theory. That theory – linguistics – represents our most advanced attempt at decoding this familiar, mysterious thing. Experts' views are far from settled. But the arguments are better informed than they've ever been.

The journey towards this state of enlightenment began thousands of years ago. The Hebrew Bible represents the starting point for Western understanding of language. Adam, the first man, was given the power to create words: 'Now the Lord God had formed out of the ground all the wild animals and all the birds in the sky. He brought them to the man to see what he would name them; and whatever the man called each living creature, that was its name' (Genesis 2:19). Later, when Adam's descendants challenged his power by building the Tower of Babel, God said: 'If as one people speaking the same language they have begun to do this, then nothing they plan to do will be impossible for them. Come, let us go down and confuse their language so they will not understand each other' (Genesis 11:6–7).

The idea that we all once spoke in the same way is found across cultures. The ancient Greeks thought that there was perfect linguistic unity under Zeus. But then his son Hermes taught humans their many languages, and they began to fight. The Aztecs believed that only one man and one woman survived a great flood in a hollowed-out tree. They had children, who were all dumb, until a dove came down and taught each one to speak differently.

The sheer variety of languages was obviously a preoccupation. Listening to people say things you can't understand is a uniquely strange and maddening experience. You might be able to interpret emotion and tone, but otherwise it is an undifferentiated mishmash of syllables, and you are frozen out. Mutual incomprehension serves nobody well. It must, therefore, be the result of a mistake, or a sin. How much easier would things be if we all understood each other? (It makes sense that 'to speak the same language' has become an idiom suggesting recognition, empathy and co-operation.)

The many things languages have in common were equally intriguing. Over the centuries, scholars, traders and conquerors noted similarities among words that could not have been coincidental. An English judge in India, William Jones, made these observations explicit in a famous lecture to the Asiatic Society of Bengal in 1786. Jones had identified correspondences between Sanskrit, Greek and Latin, among other languages, and recognised them as a 'family', theorising that they must have evolved from a common 'ancestor'. For example, the Sanskrit for 'foot' is *pāda*, in Latin it's *pes*, in ancient Greek it's *poús*. These 'related' languages were later given the label 'Indo-European', and their hypothetical common ancestor named 'Proto-Indo-European' (the Proto-Indo-European for 'foot' is *pốds*). The family includes siblings such as German and Dutch, as well as more distant cousins like Spanish and Nepali. The parents are the older, classical languages. But what does it mean for languages to be mothers, sisters or daughters to one another? Is each one as separate as an individual human being, 'born' at a particular moment in time and in turn giving birth to its own offspring?

The family-tree analogy is tempting, but obscures some

important facts. As the linguists of the nineteenth century pored over data from those connected Indo-European languages, they began to understand that the biological model didn't always fit the evidence. The skin around languages was permeable: they tended to bleed into one another. And it gradually became clear that 'a language' can only ever be a snapshot, a single slice of time in the history of a community of speakers.

The attention of scholars turned from language history to language in the present. What were the relationships between different components of language? What was its structure? There seemed to be several interlocking layers. First, sounds – 'phonemes' (like 'b', 'd' and 'g') – then groups of sounds – 'morphemes', which built words (like 'mis-', '-ness' and '-ing'). These layers were called 'phonology' and 'morphology'. Morphemes and words carried meaning, which was itself another layer, called 'semantics'. The order of words in a sentence followed certain rules of 'syntax'.[*] Those rules allow us to work out the difference between, say, 'Joni kicked the elephant' and 'The elephant kicked Joni'. In English syntax, the 'subject' (often the doer in the sentence) usually comes before the verb, which precedes the 'object' (often the thing that has something done to it).[†]

Complexity in one area, say morphology, could be balanced out by simplicity in another, say syntax. So words might have special endings to indicate the role they play in the sentence, but then it wouldn't really matter what order

---

[*] For definitions of the linguistic terms used throughout the book, see the Glossary.

[†] Subjects aren't always the 'doer' – for example, in sentences like 'the milk tastes off' – but this interpretation is a reasonable starting point.

you put them in. In Latin, you can say *taurus agricolam fugat* or *agricolam taurus fugat* and they both mean 'The bull chased the farmer'. We know that the farmer (*agricola*) is the one being chased in both sentences, because it has the ending '-*m*'.* According to this view, strongly associated with the Swiss linguist Ferdinand de Saussure, language is a balanced 'system' where 'everything holds together'.

One puzzle in particular became the focus of much twentieth-century linguistics. How do children learn language? The process appears natural and inexorable. None of us remembers doing it. There doesn't seem to be conscious effort involved, at least not the kind that learning a second language as an adult takes. So much so that linguists call it 'acquisition' – babies seem to acquire their mother tongue in the way you might acquire the ability to walk. One idea, popular until the 1960s, was that language could be viewed as 'verbal behaviour'. Children are simply 'conditioned' to produce certain words and sentences according to the feedback they receive. If they say 'milk' and the result is that they are fed, then they will use that word in the same situation again. This is 'positive reinforcement', analogous to a rat in a laboratory pressing a lever it knows will dispense food. If a hungry child says 'klim' and the mother stares at it, confused, then it will not use that combination of sounds to try to get milk in future. This is 'punishment'. There is no need to look for explanations in the mind of the baby; all that's necessary is to observe how it behaves and the reinforcement it receives.

------

* These are called 'case endings'. In some languages, the relationships between words are labelled with 'cases'. Those relationships include that of the subject and the object to the verb. The subject takes the 'nominative' case, and the object the 'accusative' case. In the example above, '-*m*' is the accusative case ending.

One scholar disagreed. In a 1959 review of B. F. Skinner's book *Verbal Behavior*, Noam Chomsky wrote that children's responses to the linguistic environment in which they find themselves are 'genetically determined and mature without learning'. In other words, babies bring something pre-cooked to the table. Language is acquired not simply through positive reinforcement of behaviour, but because a blueprint for language already exists in the brain of the infant. 'The fact that all normal children acquire essentially comparable grammars of great complexity with remarkable rapidity suggests that human beings are somehow specially designed to do this.' They are not like rats – which no one would say are 'designed' to press levers.

Chomsky's review of Skinner's book initiated a paradigm shift in linguistics. From that time on, many mainstream linguists saw the search for the blueprint as a core aim of the field. There was less focus on describing and categorising the various external features of language – phonemes, morphemes, words – or delving into how meaning is communicated. Instead, attention was paid to the internal – what it means for an individual to know a language, how structure is stored in the synapses.

It was syntax, apparently, that could provide this window into the brain. The ultimate prize was to uncover the 'universal grammar' – the common rule or set of rules underlying all grammars. To account for the fact that languages, as we all know, can be wildly different, grammar was divided into two layers: surface structure and deep structure. Surface structure includes all of the quirks of individual languages, built up somewhat haphazardly over centuries of use. Deep structure is the boiled-down version, the far simpler set of instructions that yoke all languages together, and is the same for all of us because we all grow the same kind of brain.

Crucially, it must account for what Chomsky describes as the 'basic property' of language – 'that a language is a finite computational system yielding an infinity of expressions'. That's to say, there is no limit to the number of novel sentences that can be dreamed up. I would bet that the sentence 'David told his editor, "I won't write about 4,000 indigo elephants in the year 2019"' has never been uttered or written before. Yet, clearly, an infinite number cannot all be stored in the brain; instead, there must be a finite rulebook that can be used to generate all possible sentences.

Chomsky has single-mindedly pursued this position – that there exists an innate, genetically determined blueprint which accounts for the structure of all languages – ever since the 1950s. His theory has undergone its own evolution, from the complex 'rewrite rules' of his early work to the extraordinarily simple 'minimalist programme', and the use of a single rule – known as 'Merge' – to explain the basic property of human language. This work, which we will explore in more detail in Chapters 4 and 9, can seem distant from the world of human communication. That much Chomsky admits: 'language can of course be used for communication, as can any aspect of what we do: style of dress, gesture, and so on . . . [but] the overwhelming use of language is internal – for thought'.

Chomsky has always had his critics, but it feels as though a major change is gathering pace in academic linguistics. More and more, scholars are abandoning the idea that the shape of language is ultimately determined by a structure in our brain that evolved separately from other cognitive systems. In particular, Chomsky's account of language acquisition is being called into question. The process appears to be much more like regular learning than we thought. And much of the structure of language can be explained not by appealing to a hidden blueprint, but by observing what tends to happen to languages over time, given certain external and internal constraints. These ideas have been called 'usage-based' theories, and they put the emphasis back on language in the real world.

There is still much to argue over in linguistics: the data is so diverse that a lot of theories can be put forward to explain it. This is perhaps where it differs from the hard sciences, in which there are more incontrovertible facts and settled explanations. But that's not to say that the couple of centuries of serious work on linguistics haven't got us any closer to understanding language. Apart from anything else, the efforts of linguistic fieldworkers – the people who go out and record obscure and not-so-obscure languages – mean we have more empirical evidence than ever before on which to base those theories. We can now say a lot about how and why language changes; about its structure; about how meaning is conveyed in a conversation; about the extent to which the language you speak influences the way you think; about whether animals can communicate in language-like ways; about how language is shaped by social and political facts; about language and the brain.

And yet not much of this knowledge seems to have reached the wider public. Despite all the heated disputes, theorising and counter-theorising, for most of us our understanding of language is still largely based on folklore, instinct or hearsay. Someone told me recently that a variety of British English spoken in Birmingham (known as Brummie) is the only accent in a minor key. This idea has the air of a scholarly explanation. But what does it mean? People don't speak in musical keys, which require you to stick to certain notes and avoid others. Speaking pitch is much less constrained than that, and will of course vary greatly even among people who share a dialect. I suspect what people really mean when they say this is that Brummie sounds gloomy to them. But that can only be a matter of association – perhaps because Birmingham, as a former centre of manufacturing industry, is sometimes (unfairly) perceived as grim and grimy. As we shall see, linguistic variations carry social weight in the form of either stigma or prestige. These variations could include differences in vowel quality – Brummie 'woide' instead of 'wide' – or patterns of intonation. (It's been suggested that in yes–no questions, which for speakers of southern British English often rise at the end – 'Do you want a cup of tea?' – instead have a rise-fall-rise pattern in Brummie. Falling tones could be associated more with sadness than with happiness. Minor keys are associated with sadness too, but it doesn't follow that falling intonation in questions gives you an accent 'in the minor key').

Cod explanations like this seem to crop up a lot in discussions about language, whether among friends or in the media. They usually slip by unchallenged, in a way that wouldn't be the case if someone suggested, for example, that moonlight is made of rainbow dust. You could say that this is because knowledge of how language works, as opposed to knowing how to speak a language, isn't very important. Most of us are perfectly capable of using language as a tool. Isn't that enough? When you're doing DIY, you don't worry about what metal the hammer is made of and how it was manufactured.

But language is different. We shouldn't settle for just knowing how to use it. To understand it is to understand what it means to be human. As we've seen, speech is deeply entwined in all aspects of our lives. It's not hyperbole to say that linguistics is the universal social science. It intrudes into almost every area of knowledge: psychology, sociology, neuroscience, anthropology, literature, philosophy and computing.*

Wherever we are, language is. Most of what we do, we do using language. Ignoring its workings seems foolish. And this isn't just a question of satisfying intellectual curiosity.

Earlier I suggested that listening to people speak a language you can't understand is a strange and maddening experience. It can be more than that. It can be the origin of prejudice and hostility. If you are unable to talk to someone, it's hard to appreciate how much you have in common.

When I was nineteen, I arrived at university and took a course in Arabic. I didn't want to. I wanted to learn Farsi, my father's language, but the rules said you couldn't study that on its own from scratch. I had to take another language too, and Arabic was the obvious choice (Farsi borrows around 30 per cent of its vocabulary from Arabic). I may have been a reluctant student, but what happened over the following weeks and months was a revelation – and one I've never told anyone about, because it's embarrassing to admit to prejudice, however vague, and however young you were at the time. My perceptions of the Arab world, insofar as I thought about it at all, had been shaped by news reports of violence in Palestine and in Lebanon, of the Lockerbie bombing, of hijackings and the war waged by Iraq on Iran. I wasn't alone in this: when baddies in movies weren't English, they were Arabs. If I pictured an Arab in my head, he was an angry man, jabbing his finger and shouting guttural syllables at a news camera. At the same time, I thought the script was beautiful – but then scripts don't have an accent.

---

* If that's not enough, professional linguists must have some knowledge of anatomy (albeit an incomplete slice, from the diaphragm to the brain) and also of physics, which is important in the study of phonetics.

The sound of a human voice has a unique emotional resonance, and the resonance here was bad.

But as I began to chip away at the edifice of Arabic grammar, to learn about its elegance and precision, something changed in my attitude to Arabs and the Arab world. I found myself spellbound by Arabic morphology – the way that words are built up – and I still find it astonishing today. Every word in Arabic, unless it's been borrowed from another language, is based on a set of three, or more rarely four, consonants. This is the scaffolding around which the word is built. So you have, for example, 'k-t-b', which is the root that has to do with books and writing. *Maktab* means 'office', *kitaab* is 'book', *kataba* is 'to write', *kaatib* is 'a scribe', *aktubu* means 'I write', and so on. The roots can be used to build verbs which take up to ten forms: *kataba* is form I, *kattaba* form II, *kaataba* form III. Skipping ahead, form X is *istaktaba*. Any root can be made into a verb using these patterns: so, form II of the root 'm-l-k', which has to do with owning or possessing, would be *mallaka*, form III *maalaka* and form X *istamlaka*. Each of these forms has its own 'flavour' of meaning. Form II is often a causative verb: *kattaba* means 'to make someone write something', *mallaka* means 'to make someone the owner of something'. Form III is often about doing the action to or with someone else. So *kaataba* means 'to correspond with someone'. Form III of 'm-l-k', *maalaka*, doesn't actually exist (not all roots take every possible form). Form X often involves asking for something or thinking something should be done. *Istaktaba* is 'to ask someone to write something'. *Istamlaka* is 'to take possession of something'.

This was my first experience of a non-Indo-European language, and it overturned my assumptions about what language was. Everything that had seemed natural and obvious to me – like the way you look up a word in the dictionary – turned out to be a quirk of the languages I was used to. (In Arabic you have to pick out the root consonants and look the word up under that entry. *Istaktaba* doesn't come under 'i' but under 'k'.) The formal kind of Arabic I was studying seemed a lot more sophisticated than English in many ways, and my main feeling was one of respect, awe even.

I'm not saying it was the verbs that did it, but they were a way in. Of course, I was learning much more about the Arab world in general; but in terms of establishing a human connection, there was something fundamental about getting to grips with the language. Arabic was no longer scary-sounding. Learning it had offered me a more accurate picture.

People are now more exposed to foreign languages than ever before. Sadly, we're not better linguists – far from it, in many cases. But as we move about modern cities and fly abroad for business or pleasure, we hear foreign accents and incomprehensible words far more often than our ancestors did. There is a risk that we fall back on our instinct to dis-identify with these people, to judge them as being not like us, or worse, not quite human. Understanding the mechanics of language – not necessarily understanding the words, but appreciating that here is a complex mode of expression with layers just like our own (phonemes, morphemes, words and syntax) – can help check this instinct.

If you are a native English speaker, you're also now more likely to be exposed to more people who speak your language with some degree of difficulty. You may find their speech laborious, or their accents grating. You may fall into the trap of thinking that they are slower or less intelligent than you because they struggle with English prepositions (on, over), phrasal verbs (do up, tie down), or definite and indefinite articles (the, a). Perhaps if you knew what these things were, and how they are not laws of nature but idiosyncrasies of your own language (many others lack articles, don't use phrasal verbs, and the number of prepositions varies hugely), you might not.

You don't have to be multilingual to have an interest in linguistics. But if you are curious about the mechanics of your own language, it's possible you'll dip your toes in another – just to see what it's like. The experience may be frustrating, but it will also be fascinating. In related languages, you will discover words that seem similar, and might therefore be descendants of a common ancestor (we call these 'cognates', like the Latin and Greek for 'foot').* You might come across false friends – words that seem as if they should mean one thing, but actually mean another (*actuellement* in French means 'at the moment', not 'actually'). You might stumble over sounds that seem unnatural to you – or that you can't even tell are different. (The 'u' sound in the words *tu* 'you' and *chou* 'cabbage' are distinct to French ears, but hard for the English to pin down. Perhaps now you can sympathise with Japanese speakers who find it hard to distinguish between 'l' and 'r'.)

All this might get you wondering what languages are, how they got that way, and what it all means. When it comes down to it, we all speak at least one language, so

---

* Sometimes all is not what it seems. I remember learning that the Farsi for 'better' is *behtar* and the word for 'bad' is *bad*, and assuming that, since both languages are Indo-European, these were cognates. In fact, the similarities are thought to be merely coincidence, or, as the Online Etymological Dictionary puts it, an 'accidental convergence' of sounds. A knowledge of the history of the languages concerned is needed to establish true relatedness.

these questions are relevant to everyone, polyglot or no. The aim of this book is to help answer some of them and to cut through the fallacies and folklore that cloud our understanding. Each chapter takes a common claim about language and deconstructs it, using linguistic knowledge. But these myths are simply the jumping-off point for a much deeper examination of the subjects at hand, which I hope amounts to a course in the beauty and intrigue of language. I have chosen not to use technical chapter headings like 'historical linguistics', 'semantics' and 'pragmatics', partly because those words are opaque to many, and I want to spread linguistic knowledge without alienating anyone. It's also because I don't always agree with the priority given to certain aspects of language in traditional academic linguistics, or the divisions between areas of study. For example, while most of the chapters have something to say about language change and meaning, only one really touches on syntax, the focus of lots of late-twentieth-century linguistics. Instead, I've tried to tackle questions that most of us start off with when we think about language. Initial wonderings are a good signal of what might be important in a field of study. Why does language change? What is meaning? Can you think without language?

By the end of the book, you'll have the beginnings of a rounded understanding of language. My view, which is different to Chomsky's, is that language is fundamentally a social phenomenon. Its structure does not derive from an internal blueprint, but from the general cognitive abilities of a social species, and external factors which include principles of interaction, the vagaries of history, and certain patterns that tend to emerge in complex systems which are subject to constraints of one sort or another. It is best understood as a tool for communicating, shaped by the way our brains and bodies are (which gives rise to some of the common properties of language), as well as by the particular culture we find ourselves in (which accounts for some of the differences). You could make an analogy with tools for eating: in the Far East, culture and context gave rise to chopsticks; in other countries knives and forks are used. Both fulfil the requirement of bringing food to the mouth. Similarly, the need for effective communication is shared by all human beings – but there are many different solutions to the problem.

I start with a subject that attracts a lot of attention: the idea that language is going to the dogs, or that standards are slipping. I'll show you why that argument makes no sense because of what we know about the way language evolves. I'll also have a go at explaining why I think those wedded to this view seem unable to admit that they're wrong.

Have you ever used the word 'decimate' to mean 'lay waste to' or 'destroy', only to be told that its Latin derivation shows that it *really* means to kill or eliminate one in ten of something? The idea that the origin of a word, or etymology, is a guide to its true meaning is false, as I show in Chapter 2. In the process of explaining the 'etymological fallacy', we get a lesson in the enchanting way meaning evolves. A word's history can tell us about earlier stages in our culture – such as when 'engine', in the absence of machines, meant any cunning product of the human mind (sharing a root with 'ingenuity'). It can illuminate tendencies in human thought or behaviour – for example, the likelihood that words to do with seeing become ones to do with understanding ('Is that clear?'). But it's how a word is used now that matters: as Ludwig Wittgenstein explained nearly seventy years ago, there's really no other way of making sense of meaning.

In Chapter 3 we'll learn about influences on the way you speak that are beyond your control. You might be able to pick the words you use – unless you stub your toe, or hit your thumb with a hammer, when it becomes more difficult. But do you really control how you sound, or do others make that call for you? We are constantly adapting our speech to the people around us, or the ones we aspire to be like. Our accents are subtly shaped in unexpected ways by the social milieu in which we operate. Why do some people 'sound gay'? Why do British pop stars sing in American accents? We can all think of examples of people who try to change their voices to fit in, or get on. But you're changing your voice too, whether you know it or not.

Have you ever wondered why animals can't speak – or if there are any that can? I look at some of the evidence in Chapter 4. Doctor Dolittle is just a fantasy, isn't it? Well, one scientist had daily conversations with her parrot for more than a decade, and demonstrated in carefully designed experiments that he had language abilities similar to those of a small child. Dolphins have accents. Birds have grammar. So what is it that makes human communication different from monkey howls and whale calls?

There is no linguistic topic more beloved of the internet than so-called 'untranslatable words', the subject of Chapter 5. These are the magical objects that make us believe there are kinds of meaning we just can't access, because we don't speak the right language. Do they really exist? Does the world really look different to speakers of Mandarin, Malay, Portuguese and Dutch? The answer is yes and no. No word is completely untranslatable, but no word is easily translatable either. Luckily, one linguist has invented a kind of skeleton key for all the world's languages. If you want to know the precise difference between 'happiness' in English and *Glück* in German, she can tell you what it is.

In Chapter 6, we ask what might seem like a bizarre question: do languages even exist? It's less bizarre once you understand that, for example, there's no hard border between German and Dutch. And that the difference between a dialect and a language doesn't necessarily have much to do with linguistic facts. Our concept of what constitutes a language is less scientific and more dependent on politics and power than many of us realise.

In Chapter 7 I ask whether what you say is what you mean. You might think the answer to that is obvious. But we often say things that, on the face of it, bear very little relation to the message we want to convey. 'It's cold in here' doesn't literally mean 'Please close the window', but it might do in a particular context. How do our brains get from what is said to what is meant, and why do computers seem to have such a hard time doing the same?

Language is political. Language is social. As such, you'd expect that it is also often a vehicle for chauvinism, for racial pride and prejudice. Are certain languages better than others? Lots of speakers of lots of languages would have you believe so. But they can't all be right. In Chapter 8 we look at whether some languages really are more complicated, faster or richer than others.

Finally, in Chapter 9, we'll turn to Chomsky's ideas about language. His belief that it's hardwired into the human brain, formed at the very beginning of life, has crossed over into the mainstream. Steven Pinker's 1994 book *The Language Instinct* encapsulated it, and his title embodies an idea that seems to have stuck. But linguists today are unearthing more and more evidence that, although language is only possible because of the way our brains have developed, it's not a specialised 'organ' as Pinker and Chomsky claim.

Instead it comes into being because of capacities evolved for other purposes.

If language isn't an instinct, what is it? We'll find out – and we'll also have fun along the way. This is a subject that most of us have wondered about, but the ivory-tower nature of much academic linguistics means few of the explanations have filtered through. You could argue that common know-ledge of language is at the level that common knowledge of physics was before Galileo, when people thought the sun went around the earth. And the reason this continues to be the case is a failure – ironically – of communication. I want to help remedy that, and in attempting to do so I will draw on the painstaking work of hundreds of professional linguists far more accomplished than me, whose insights deserve to be brought to a wider audience.

I hope that this book will change the way you think about a fundamental daily activity, one in which we all – not just the nerds and pedants – have a stake. So let's begin.

CHAPTER 1

Language is going to the dogs

The twenty-first century seems to present us with an ever-lengthening list of perils: climate change, financial meltdown, cyberattacks. Should we stock up on canned foods in case the ATMs snap shut? Buy a shedload of bottled water? Hoard prescription medicines? The prospect of everything that makes modern life possible being taken away from us is terrifying. We'd be plunged back into the Middle Ages, but without the skills to cope.

Now imagine that something even more fundamental than electricity or money is at risk: a tool we have relied on since the dawn of human history, enabling the very foundations of civilisation to be laid. The doomsayers admit that this apocalypse may take some time – years, decades, even – to unfold. But the direction of travel is clear.

I'm talking about our ability to communicate. To put our thoughts into words, and use those words to forge bonds, deliver vital information, learn from our mistakes and build on the work done by others. Without complex, rich, subtle language, without clear, precise speech and writing, there would be no cities, no philosophy, no science, no shoulders to cry on, no political organisation, no arguments to win or lose, no love letters, no jokes, no understanding. No humanity.

Any threat to this apparatus is deeply alarming. If they took it seriously, governments would be setting up task forces, the UN would be calling for collective action, scientists would be labouring to come up with possible solutions. But none of this is happening. As things stand, it's left to a few heroic individuals to raise their voices in warning about the dangers of doing nothing, like Marie Clair of the Plain English Campaign.* 'There is a worrying trend of adults mimicking teen-speak. They are using slang words and ignoring grammar,' she told the *Daily Mail*. 'Their language is deteriorating. They are lowering the bar. Our language is flying off at all tangents, without the anchor of a solid foundation.' If this is the case now, what will things be like in a generation's time? We must surely act before it's too late.

But young people are only too readily picking up bad habits. 'Text-speak', which is 'creeping beyond . . . smartphones and into pupils' everyday language', the English lecturer Anne Merrit wrote in the *Daily Telegraph*, 'looks like a simple decline in proper language skills, born out of a digitally literate culture that has grown too comfortable in an age of abbreviations and spellchecks.'

That decline is something the Queen's English Society, a British organisation, has been trying to prevent. Though it is at pains to point out that it does not believe language can be preserved unchanged, it nevertheless worries that communication is at risk of becoming far less effective. 'We do not want the language to lose its fine or major distinctions,' the Society says on its website. 'Some changes would be wholly unacceptable as they would cause confusion and the language would lose shades of meaning.'

---

* Founded in London in 1979, the Plain English Campaign describes itself as 'an independent group fighting for plain English in public communication' that opposes 'gobbledygook, jargon and legalese'.

With a reduced expressive capacity, English would no longer be up to the task of describing the world around us, or the world inside our heads. Research, innovation and the quality of public discourse would suffer. We'd be facing a breakdown in shared knowledge of language – a rusting of the key that allows us to unlock the message contained in someone else's speech or writing. The columnist Douglas Rushkoff put it like this in a 2013 *New York Times* op-ed: 'Without grammar, we lose the agreed-upon standards about what means what. We lose the ability to communicate when respondents are not actually in the same room speaking to one another. Without grammar, we lose the precision required to be effective and purposeful in writing.'

On the other hand, our laziness and imprecision are leading to unnecessary bloating of the language – 'language obesity', as the British broadcaster John Humphrys described it. This 'is the consequence of feeding on junk words. Tautology is the equivalent of having chips with rice. We talk of future plans and past history; of live survivors and safe havens. Children have temper tantrums and politicians announce "new initiatives".'

It is frightening to think where all this might lead. The slump in language, if it's as dangerous as has been suggested, ought to lead to a slump in human effectiveness.

The bad old days

But there's something perplexing about claims like this. By their nature, they imply that we were smarter and more precise in the past. Seventy-odd years ago, people knew their grammar, and knew how to talk clearly. And if we follow the logic, they must also have been better at organising, finding things out and making things work.

John Humphrys was born in 1943. Since then, the English-speaking world has grown more prosperous, better educated and more efficiently governed, despite an increase in population. Most democratic freedoms have been preserved and intellectual achievement intensified. Information has become far more accessible, news media have proliferated and the technological advances have come thick and fast.

Linguistic decline is the cultural equivalent of the boy who cried wolf, except the wolf never turns up. Perhaps this is why, even though the idea that language is going to the dogs is widespread, nothing much has been done to mitigate it: it's a powerful intuition, but the evidence of its effects has simply never materialised. That is because it is unscientific nonsense.

Here we bust our first myth: there is no such thing as linguistic decline, so far as the expressive capacity of the spoken or written word is concerned. We need not fear a breakdown in communication. Our language will always be as flexible and sophisticated as it has been up to now. Those who warn about the deterioration of English haven't learned about the history of the language, and don't understand the nature of their complaints – which are simply statements of preference for the way of doing things they have become used to. The erosion of language to the point that 'ultimately, no doubt, we shall communicate with a series of grunts' (Humphrys again) will not, cannot, happen. The clearest evidence for this is that warnings about the deterioration of English have been around for a very long time.

In 1785, a few years after the first volume of Edward Gibbon's *The History of the Decline and Fall of the Roman Empire* had been published, things were so bad that the poet and philosopher James Beattie declared: 'Our language (I mean the English) is degenerating very fast.' Some seventy years before that, Jonathan Swift had issued a similar warning. In a letter to Robert, Earl of Oxford, he complains:

> From the Civil War to this present Time, I am apt to doubt whether the Corruptions in our Language have not at least equalled the Refinements of it; and these Corruptions very few of the best Authors of our Age have wholly escaped [. . .] . . . most of the Books we see now a-days, are full of those Manglings and Abbreviations. Instances of this Abuse are innumerable: What does Your Lordship think of the Words, Drudg'd, Disturb'd, Rebuk't, Fledg'd, and a thousand others, every where to be met in Prose as well as Verse?

Swift would presumably have thought that *The History of the Decline and Fall*, revered as a masterpiece today, was a bit of a mess. He knew when the golden age of English was: 'The Period wherein the *English* Tongue received most Improvement, I take to commence with the beginning of Queen *Elizabeth's* Reign, and to conclude with the Great Rebellion in [Sixteen] Forty Two.'

But the problem is that writers at *that* time also felt they were speaking a degraded, faltering tongue. They had particular concerns about the importation of new, foreign words. In 1589 the critic George Puttenham wrote, in *The Arte of English Poesie*: 'We find in our English writers many words and speeches amendable, and you shall see in some many inkhorn terms* so ill-affected brought in by men of

---

* 'Inkhorn terms' means words derived from classical sources which, from the sixteenth century onwards, 'were being used by scholarly writers but which were unknown or uncommon in ordinary speech', as etymologist Michael Quinion puts it. For example: 'ingenious', 'capacity', 'mundane', 'celebrate' and 'extol'. Some of them caught on; many, such as 'illecebrous' (attractive or alluring), did not.

learning as preachers and schoolmasters: and many strange terms of other languages by secretaries and merchants and travellers, and many dark words and not usual nor well sounding, though they be daily spoken in Court.' That was halfway through Swift's golden age. Just before it, in the reign of Elizabeth's sister, Mary, the Cambridge professor John Cheke wrote with anxiety that 'Our own tongue should be written clean and pure, unmixed and unmangled with borrowing of other tongues.'

This concern for purity – and the need to take a stand against a rising tide of corruption – goes back even further. In the fourteenth century Ranulph Higden complained about the state English was in. His words, quoted in David Crystal's *The Stories of English*, were translated from the Latin by a near-contemporary, John Trevisa: 'By intermingling and mixing, first with Danes and afterwards with Normans, in many people the language of the land is harmed, and some use strange inarticulate utterance, chattering, snarling, and harsh teeth-gnashing.'

That's five writers, across a span of 400 years, all moaning about the same erosion of standards. And yet the period also encompasses some of the greatest feats of English literature.

It's worth pausing here to take a closer look at Trevisa's translation, for the sentence I've reproduced is a version in modern English. The original is as follows: 'By commyxstion and mellyng furst wiþ danes and afterward wiþ Normans in menye þe contray longage ys apeyred, and som vseþ strange wlaffyng, chyteryng, harrying and garryng, grisbittyng.' As you can see, if we go back as far as the fourteenth century, the 'English' being used is so different from our own as to need translation – which is strange, given all the appeals we've seen to the purity of earlier stages in the language. For those who worry about language deteriorating, proper usage is best exemplified by the speech and writing of a generation or so before their own. The logical conclusion is that the generation or two before that would be even better, the one before that even more so. As a result, we should find Trevisa's language vastly more refined, more correct, more clear and more effective. The problem is, we can't even read it.

Hand-wringing about standards isn't restricted to English. The fate of every language in the world has been lamented by its speakers at some point or another. In the thirteenth century, the Arabic lexicographer Ibn Manzur described himself as a linguistic Noah – ushering words into a protective Ark in order that they might survive the onslaught of laziness. Elias Muhanna, a professor of comparative literature, describes one of Manzur's modern-day counterparts: 'Fi'l Amr, a language-advocacy group [in Lebanon], has launched a campaign to raise awareness about Arabic's critical condition by staging mock crime scenes around Beirut depicting "murdered" Arabic letters, surrounded by yellow police tape that reads: "Don't kill your language."'

The linguist Rudi Keller gives similar examples from Germany. 'Hardly a week goes by,' he writes, 'in which some reader of the *Frankfurter Allgemeine Zeitung* doesn't write a letter to the editor expressing fear for the future of the German language.' Gustav Wustmann addressed those readers' great-grandparents in 1891: 'Language is today so quickly transformed that it has become decayed and rotten. Ineptitude and sluggishness, bombast, foppery* and grammatical errors are increasing.' His book *Allerhand*

---

* In case you're wondering what the rather colourful words 'ineptitude', 'sluggishness', 'bombast' and 'foppery' sound like in German, these are Keller's translations of *Unbeholfenheit*, *Schwerfälligkeit*, *Schwulst* and *Ziererei* respectively.

Sprachdummheite (*All Kinds of Language Blunders*) was reprinted fourteen times over the next seven decades. But in 1929 Thomas Mann won the Nobel Prize in Literature. Are we to assume that the language he spoke and in which he wrote was degenerate? As Keller puts it, 'for more than two thousand years, complaints about the decay of respective languages have been documented in literature, but no one has yet been able to name an example of a "decayed language".' He has a point.

The hard truth is that English, like all other languages, is constantly evolving. Unlike biological evolution, it happens quickly. Some linguistic changes occur when new speakers learn the language and unwittingly reinterpret the rules that govern its use; changes like that only take a generation to become established. There are many sources of change, though: the influence of other languages or the cultural dominance of one dialect over another (take American English and its British counterpart, for example). Certain changes set off chain reactions – and some sound changes are natural tendencies that most languages exhibit over time.

It's the speed of the change, within our own short lives, that creates the illusion of decline. Because change is often generational, older speakers recognise that the norms they grew up with are falling away, replaced with new ones they aren't as comfortable using. This cognitive difficulty doesn't feel good, and the bad feelings are translated into criticism and complaint. We tend to find intellectual justifications for our personal preferences, whatever their motivation. If we lived for hundreds of years we'd be able to see the bigger picture. Because when you zoom out you can appreciate that language change isn't just a question of slovenliness: it happens at every level, from the superficial to the structural.

Any given language is significantly reconfigured over the centuries, to the extent that it becomes totally unrecognisable. But, as with complex systems in the natural world, there's often a kind of homeostasis: simplification in one area can lead to greater complexity in another. What stays the same is the expressive capacity of the language. You can always say what needs to be said.

Time, like an ever-rolling stream

Frequently, these changes are unexpected and revealing. They shed light on the workings of our minds, mouths and culture. Let's look at some examples.

One common driver of linguistic change is a process called 'reanalysis'. This can happen when a language is learned for the first time, when babies begin to talk and construe what they hear slightly differently from their parents. In the abstract it sounds complex, but in fact it's straightforward: when a word or sentence has a structural ambiguity, what we hear could be an instance of A, but it could also be an instance of B. For years A has held sway, but suddenly B catches on – and changes flow from that new understanding.

Take the words 'adder', 'apron' and 'umpire'. They were originally 'nadder', 'napron' and 'numpire'. 'Numpire' was a borrowing from the French *non per* – 'not even' – and described someone who decided on tie-breaks in games. Given that 'numpire' and those other words were nouns, they often found themselves next to an indefinite article – 'a' or 'an', or the first-person possessive pronoun, 'mine'. Phrases like 'a numpire' and 'mine napron' were relatively common, and at some point – perhaps at the interface between two generations – the first letter came to be seen as part of the preceding word. The prerequisite for reanalysis is that communication is not seriously impaired: the reinterpretation takes place at the level of the underlying structure. A young person would be able to say 'where's mine apron?' and be understood, but they'd then go on to produce phrases like 'her apron' rather than 'her napron', which older folk presumably regarded as idiotic.

Reanalysis can be made more likely when changes have occurred elsewhere in the language. The verb 'to like' originally meant 'to be pleasing to'. Which is to say that if I was expressing a preference, I would have come up with something like 'chips like me' – meaning 'chips are pleasing to me'. The verb, crucially, agrees with the plural 'chips'. If it agreed with 'me' it would be 'likes'. But me is not the subject, the doer in the sentence, it is the object, the thing that has something done to it.

Keep that in mind when you consider the sentence 'The king liked pears' in Old English.

Tham cynge licodon peran
To-the king were-pleasing pears

At this stage in the language, case endings were more common than they are now. They gave you more information about a noun's relationship to other parts of the sentence, and were often stuck onto the end of the noun. 'Tham' displays a 'dative' case ending '-am',* so we can gloss it as 'to the' rather than just 'the'. This is an unambiguous

---

* Remember (see footnote on p. 6) that case endings are attached to words to indicate their relationship to other words in the sentence. The 'nominative' case indicates the subject of the verb, 'accusative' its object. 'Dative' is just another case that usually indicates the indirect object – the 'beneficiary', if you like, of the verb. In English, the preposition 'to' performs the same function.

structure – there's no way of misinterpreting what the subject of the sentence is. It's pears.

At some point, the language lost dative endings, among other changes. Now we just have:

The king liceden peares
The king were-pleasing pears

We still know that pears are the subject of the sentence, as the verb 'liceden' takes the plural form and there's only one king. But if this plural marking also falls away, the whole thing is likely to be reanalysed:

The king liked pears

The underlying structure, or, to put it another way, the 'feeling' that the verb 'liked' belongs to pears, rather than the king, disappears. And since most sentences in English follow the pattern subject-verb-object, that's how this sentence is reinterpreted. 'To like', which once meant 'to be pleasing to', now means 'to find something pleasing'. A fine distinction is completely lost – speakers have disregarded rules of grammar, and the meaning of a verb has fundamentally changed. Stalwarts of the Queen's English Society should by rights be up in arms every time they read the word 'like'.

Change often takes the form of grammaticalisation: a process in which a common phrase is bleached of its independent meaning and made into a word whose sole function is grammatical. One instance of this is the verb 'to go', when used for an action in the near future or an intention. There is a clue to its special status in the way we've started saying it. We all inherit an evolutionarily sensible tendency to expend only the minimum effort needed to complete a task. For that reason, once a word has become a grammatical marker, rather than something that carries a concrete meaning, you don't need it to be fully fleshed out. It becomes 'phonetically reduced' – or, as some would have it, pronounced 'lazily'. That's why 'I'm going to' becomes 'I'm gonna', or even, in some dialects, 'Imma'. But this change in pronunciation is only evident when 'going to' is grammatical, not when it's a verb describing real movement. That's why you can say 'I'm gonna study history' but not 'I'm gonna the shops'. In the first sentence, all 'I'm going to'/'I'm gonna' tells you is that the action (study history) is something you intend to do. In the second one, the same verb isn't simply a marker of intention, it indicates movement. You can't therefore swap it for another tense ('I will study history' vs 'I will the shops').

'Will', the standard future tense in English, has its own history of grammaticalisation. It once indicated desire and intention. 'I will' meant 'I want'. The closely related German verb for want is in fact *willen*. We can still detect this original English meaning in phrases such as 'If you will' (if you want/desire). Since desires are hopes for the future, this very common verb gradually came to be seen simply as a future marker. It lost its full meaning, becoming merely a grammatical particle. As a result, it also gets phonetically reduced, as in 'I'll', 'she'll' and so on.

Evidence of grammaticalisation exists in every language. Take the French negative marker, *pas*. It is now formally part of French grammar, but was originally just a descriptive word used for emphasis (it survives as a regular word, meaning 'step', in other contexts). One might say '*Je n'y vais pas*' – 'I'm not going [even] a step there' – but, as with many markers of emphasis, it became routine, was used all over the place, and ended up being bleached of independent meaning. '*Je ne t'aime pas*' – 'I don't love you' – has nothing to do with steps.

Phonetic reduction often forms the first part of a cycle, a sort of engine that keeps language in a constant state of flux. It's nicely illustrated by another example from French, starting with an earlier stage in that language, one that we are in the habit of regarding as a different language altogether: Latin. In the classical language, *hoc* meant 'this'. Later on, the phrase *ecce hoc* (something like 'this here') began to be used again and again and, as you would expect, it got condensed, becoming just *ce* in French. But the tendency to reduce frequent phrases is always balanced by the need for emphasis – saying what you mean so it really stands out. The two pull against one another in a linguistic tug-of-war. So, to *ce* was added *là*, meaning 'there' (itself a squashed form of the Latin *illac*). Modern speakers have in turn condensed even *celà* into *ça*, which, etymologically, corresponds to *ecce-hoc-illac*, or 'this-here-there'. The word has puffed in and out like an accordion.

Human anatomy makes some changes more likely than others. The simple mechanics of moving from a nasal sound ('m' or 'n') to a non-nasal one can make a consonant pop up in between. Thunder used to be 'thuner', and empty 'emty'. You can see the same process happening now with words like 'hamster', which often gets pronounced with an intruding 'p'. Linguists call this 'epenthesis'. It may sound like a disease, but it's definitely not pathological laziness – it's the laws of physics at work. If you stop channelling air through the nose before opening your lips for the 's', they'll burst apart with a characteristic pop, giving us our 'p'.

The way our brain divides up words also drives change. We split them into phonemes, building blocks of sound that have special perceptual significance,* and syllables, groups of phonemes. Sometimes these jump out of place, a bit like the tightly packed lines in a Bridget Riley painting. Occasionally such cognitive hiccups become the norm. Wasp used to be 'waps'; bird used to be 'brid' and horse 'hros'. Remember this the next time you hear someone 'aks' for their 'perscription'. What's going on there is metathesis, and it's a very common, perfectly natural process.

Sound changes can come about as a result of social pressures: certain ways of saying things are seen as having prestige, while others are stigmatised. We gravitate towards the prestigious and make efforts to avoid saying things in a way that's associated with undesirable qualities – often just below the level of consciousness. Some forms that become wildly popular, such as Kim Kardashian's vocal fry,† though prestigious for some, are derided by others. One study found that 'young adult female voices exhibiting vocal fry are perceived as less competent, less educated, less trustworthy, less attractive, and less hireable'.

Changes in culture can also result in changes in language. The internet wasn't the first invention to usher in new vocabulary. Throughout history, new technologies have been accompanied by novel words. Where an interaction between two cultures takes place, a word can be imported along with a product. Today, for example, English terms

---

* We'll learn more about phonemes in Chapter 3.

† Vocal fry, also known as 'creaky voice', is produced when the vocal folds of the larynx vibrate more slowly than normal. This gives rise to a distinctive sputtering or 'creaky' sound. It is an integral feature of languages such as Danish, Vietnamese and Burmese, but in English it's optional. In Chapter 3 I'll set out how these optional features can become socially significant. Creaky voice has come to be identified with women, and with Kim Kardashian, who apparently uses it a lot.

associated with computer culture – 'computer' itself, 'email', 'internet' and so on – tend to be adopted by other languages (French attempts to come up with their own equivalents have been mixed: *courriel* for 'email' – a blend of *courrier* and *électronique* – has failed to vanquish its opponent, but *ordinateur* for 'computer' has become the norm). Many words for technical innovations or unfamiliar trade goods reached the English language in this way: 'orange', 'saffron', 'sugar' and 'coffee' from Arabic and Persian via various Romance languages; 'algebra' and 'algorithm' ultimately from Arabic; 'piano', 'opera' and 'violin' from Italian. The influence of other languages can be seen more subtly, in the form of words called 'calques' – literal translations. From German philosophy we get 'worldview', which imports the phrase *Weltanschauung*. 'Brainwashing' comes from the Mandarin *xǐ nǎo*, used to describe a technique allegedly employed during the Korean War. From down-at-heel French street commerce we get 'flea markets' – *marchés aux puces*.

Other aspects of our culture are thrown into sharp relief by language change: through history, words linked to women have often undergone a process of pejoration – they move from being a neutral label into something more stigmatised. 'Hussey', 'a brazen or immoral woman', developed from 'housewife', and 'slut' originally meant merely a servant girl. Taboos around sex also play their part. 'Rooster' has been gradually gaining in popularity as the correct way to refer to a male chicken over the once far more common 'cock', now avoided because it sounds risqué.

All this is merely a glimpse of the richness of language change. It is universal, it is constant, it throws up extraordinary quirks and idiosyncrasies despite being governed by a range of more or less regular processes. Anyone who wants to preserve some aspect of language which appears to be changing is fighting a losing battle. Anyone who wishes people would just speak according to the norms they had drummed into them when they were growing up may as well forget about it. But what about those, like the Queen's English Society, who say they merely want to ensure that clear and effective communication is preserved; to encourage good change, where they find it, and discourage bad change?

The problem arises when deciding what might be good or bad. There are, despite what many people feel, no objective criteria by which to judge what's better or worse in communication. Take the loss of so-called major distinctions in meaning bemoaned by the Queen's English Society. The word 'disinterested', which can be glossed 'not influenced by considerations of personal advantage', is a good example. Whenever I hear it nowadays, it's used instead to mean 'uninterested, lacking in interest'. That's a shame, you could argue: disinterest is a useful concept, a way (hopefully) to talk about public servants and judges. If the distinction is being lost, won't that harm our ability to communicate? Except that, of course, there are many other ways to say 'disinterested': unbiased, impartial, neutral, having no skin in the game, without an axe to grind. If this word disappeared tomorrow, we'd be no less able to describe probity and even-handedness in public life. Not only that, but if most people don't use it properly, then the word itself has become ineffective. Words can't really be said to have an existence beyond their common use. There is no perfect dictionary in the sky with meanings that are consistent and clearly defined: real-world dictionaries are constantly trying to catch up with the 'common definition' of a word. The simultaneous exact agreement of millions of people has never been easy to achieve, if it's possible at all; so why do we assume that it could be found in the realm of language? But here's the clincher: 'disinterested', as in 'not interested', has actually been around for a long time. The blogger Jonathon Owen cites the *Oxford English Dictionary* as providing evidence that 'both meanings have existed side by side from the 1600s. So there's not so much a present confusion of the two words as a continuing, three-and-a-half-century-long confusion.'

As we've seen, there is no evidence for the claim that language is going to the dogs. On the contrary, there's a lot of evidence to suggest that the kinds of changes that get complained about the most are perfectly normal, and when they've happened in the past it hasn't hampered our ability to communicate. In fact, the redundancy of language – the rough-around-the-edges nature of speech, which allows it to be bent and twisted in all sorts of ways – is what makes it nimble, able to maintain its expressive power, even as tastes, culture and society change.

The generation gap

So what is it that drives the language conservationists?

Younger people tend to be the ones who innovate in all aspects of life: fashion, music, art. Language is no different. Children are often the agents of reanalysis, reinterpreting ambiguous structures as they learn the language. Young people move about more, taking innovations with them into new communities. Their social networks are larger and more dynamic. They are more likely to be early adopters of new technology, becoming familiar with the terms used to describe them. And they get more involved in pop culture – perhaps because they are still trying on identities, sampling lifestyles and manners until they figure out what fits. At school, on campus or in clubs and pubs, groups develop habits, individuals move between them, and language change is the result.

What this means, crucially, is that older people experience greater linguistic disorientation. Though we're all capable of adaptation, many aspects of the way we use language, including stylistic preferences, have solidified by our twenties. If you're in your fifties, you may identify with many aspects of the way people spoke thirty to forty-five years ago.

This is what the author Douglas Adams had to say about technology. Adapted slightly, it could apply to language too:

1. Anything that is in the world when you're born is normal and ordinary and is just a natural part of the way the world works.
2. Anything that's invented between when you're fifteen and thirty-five is new and exciting and revolutionary.
3. Anything invented after you're thirty-five is against the natural order of things.

Based on that timescale, formal, standard language is about twenty-five years behind the cutting edge. That equates to the time when people now aged forty-five had a lot of their language preferences fixed. But if change is constant, why do we end up with a standard language at all? Well, think about the institutions that define standard language: universities, newspapers, broadcasters, the literary establishment. They are mostly controlled by middle-aged people. Their dialect is the dialect of power – and it means that everything else gets assigned a lower status. Deviations might be labelled cool, or creative, but because people generally fear or feel threatened by changes they don't understand, they're more likely to be called bad, lazy or even dangerous. This is where the 'standards are slipping' narrative moves into more unpleasant territory. It's probably OK to deviate from the norm if you're young, as long as you're also white and middle class. If you're from a group with fewer social advantages, even the forms that your parents use are likely to be stigmatised. Your innovations will be doubly condemned.

The irony is, of course, that the pedants are the ones making the mistakes. To people who know how language works, pundits like Anne Merritt and Douglas Rushkoff only end up sounding ignorant, having failed to really interrogate their views. What they are expressing are stylistic preferences – and that's fine. I definitely have my own, and can easily say 'I hate the way this is written'; or even 'this is badly written'. But that's shorthand: what's left off is 'in my view' or 'according to my stylistic preferences and prejudices, based on what I've been exposed to up to now, and particularly between the ages of five and twenty-five'.

Mostly, pedants don't admit this. I know, because I've had plenty of arguments with them. They like to maintain that their prejudices are somehow objective – that there are clear instances of language getting 'less good' in a way that can be independently verified. But, as we've seen, that's what pedants have said throughout history. George Orwell, a towering figure in politics, journalism and literature, was clearly wrong when he imagined that language would become decadent and 'share in the general collapse' of civilisation unless hard work was done to repair it. Maybe it was only conscious and deliberate effort to arrest language change that was responsible for all the great poetry and rhetoric in the generation that followed him – the speeches 'I Have a Dream' and 'We Choose to Go to the Moon', the poetry of Seamus Heaney or Sylvia Plath, the novels of William Golding, Iris Murdoch, John Updike and Toni Morrison. More likely, Orwell was just mistaken.

The same is true of James Beattie, Jonathan Swift, George Puttenham, John Cheke and Ranulph Higden. The difference is that they didn't have the benefit of evidence about the way language changes over time, unearthed by linguists from the nineteenth century onwards. Modern pedants don't have that excuse. If they're so concerned about language, you have to wonder: why haven't they bothered to get to know it a little better?

CHAPTER 2

A word's origin is its true meaning

Words have meanings – that's why they're useful. But how do we know what a given word *really* means? Is it possible you've been using some of them wrongly all this time? I'm not talking about common mistakes like saying 'pacific' instead of 'specific'; there's not much argument over the fact one is the name of an ocean and the other an adjective meaning 'particular'. If you've mixed them up, you're confusing sounds, not meanings. I'm referring to the 'hidden', 'original' or 'true' meanings of words of which you simply may not have been aware. Let me explain.

'Lucifer Our Lord'* is a phrase you might have expected to hear before dinner at Aleister Crowley's house, and not in a text from your mother. But there are those who believe that every 'lol' you've thrown into casual chat is not a shorthand for 'laugh out loud' but has, in fact, invoked Satan. Not on purpose, you protest. But still, you typed it, and the responsibility is yours. Ignorance is not generally

---

* Since we're going to be talking about word origins, Lucifer is the Latin translation of a Hebrew word used in the Book of Isaiah, said to be an epithet of the king of Babylon. The Latin means 'light-bearer' and was the name of the Morning Star, Venus. Theologians interpreted the passage containing Lucifer as a parable about the devil, so it became one of his alternative names.

considered a valid defence: if the true meaning of 'lol' is what some say it is, then you've unwittingly performed an act of devil worship.

In 2012 an image explaining the demonic derivation and bearing the warning 'Do not use LOL ever again!' was posted on the website Reddit, and spread across cyberspace. Whether it was the authentic work of a concerned Christian, or a spoof all along, remains a mystery. It has nevertheless taken on a life of its own: at the time of writing, Google Trends data shows consistent use of the search term 'does lol mean Lucifer Our Lord?' over the past six years. Internet users are presented with some 1,500,000 results to help them make up their minds. We have to assume that some of those asking are genuinely curious: could they have mistaken the true meaning of lol, even while using it to express something completely innocent?

The idea that a word you use one way can mean something else is hardly restricted to the more conspiracy-minded corners of the internet. The 'Lucifer' meme is an example of a 'backronym'. This, according to Oxford Dictionaries, is an acronym invented to match a word, 'either to create a memorable name, or as a fanciful explanation of a word's origin'. An example of the former is Apple's LISA computer, named after Steve Job's daughter, but justified by the label 'Local Integrated Software Architecture'. It's done consciously, as an in-joke or a marketing tool.

It's the 'fanciful explanations' that are more mischievous. These yarns are the linguistic equivalent of fake news. And, unfortunately, they're just as popular. So the origin of the ancient word 'fuck' is described as being short for 'Fornication Under Consent of the King'. The story goes that hanging up a sign on your door with those initials on it was a way to show the world your sex life had the royal seal of approval.

Backronyms are absurd, but when it comes to spreading misinformation, they may not be the worst offenders. After all, they're easy to spot. Most people will only fleetingly entertain the idea that 'golf' comes from 'Gentlemen Only, Ladies Forbidden', however much it might seem like the cap fits. Golf is hundreds of years old, but, with one or two exceptions, acronyms only arose over the last century.* They're part and parcel of the bureaucratisation of work and public life and the use of advanced technologies. Government and international agencies produce them: NASA, INTERPOL, UNESCO. So do scientists, like the teams behind Radar and Lasers (not everyone realises that these are in fact acronyms: they stand for Radio Detection and Ranging, and Light Amplification by Stimulated Emission of Radiation). All of these are recent, in linguistic terms. Fun as it might seem, there's no way that 'fuck' and 'golf' fall into the same category.

As accounts of hidden or original meaning, backronyms at least hint at their own implausibility. Far more insidious are explanations that rely on the same idea of 'true sense', but instead of spurious glosses like 'Lucifer Our Lord', use real etymological information to persuade you.

Original sin

I've already mentioned the word 'decimate'. It's often used as a synonym for 'lay waste to' or 'ruin'. Say it enough and sooner or later someone will tell you that, strictly speaking, it means 'to destroy one in ten' of something, because it's

---

* One very aged acronym is Tanakh, the collective name for the Jewish scriptures. The word is formed from the names of the Hebrew letters at the start of each of its components: the Torah, Nevi'im and Ketuvim (Ta, Na, Kh).

from Latin, and the Romans used to execute every tenth soldier in a unit as a form of collective punishment. Well, sort of. In fact, the English word 'decimation' is first recorded in the fifteenth century. Back then, however, it meant 'to tithe': to take 10 per cent in tax for the Church. The sense of punishing is first recorded a century later, and our friends at Oxford Dictionaries say it was retrospectively applied to descriptions of the Roman practice. The details of the derivation are one thing. But what are we actually saying when we 'correct' someone in this way? Not only is the 'one in ten' meaning redundant, since it refers to nothing in contemporary life; underlying it is a premise that gets increasingly bizarre the more you examine it.

Let me introduce you to the etymological fallacy. This is the notion that a word's origin reveals you its true meaning. You might imagine, given its fancy name, that it's a rare beast – the preserve of librarians and Latin teachers. But it's surprisingly common. Think for a moment whether anyone has said to you, about a familiar term you've just used in your native language, 'What that actually means is . . .'. Unless you've just mentioned the 'specific ocean', they're probably going to tell you something they've heard about the word's backstory – its etymology. What it used to mean in the past.

Age often equals authority and value. We talk about 'old masters', 'ancient wisdom', things having 'stood the test of time'. It's a rule of thumb that many believe should extend to words. No less a forward-looking organ than *The Economist* has in its style guide the statement that 'transpire' means 'to exhale'. Why? Because it consists of the Latin prefix *trans*, meaning 'across', and a form derived from the verb *spirare*, 'to breathe'. Despite what you may have thought, it doesn't mean 'become evident', let alone 'happen'. The *Economist* definition, however, makes it pretty much unusable: if you said 'I transpired with relief', people would look at you as though you were crazy, pretentious, or both.

An educationalist might tell you that she is in the business of 'drawing out' a child's talents ('educate' comes from the Latin *ex*, 'out', and *ducere*, 'to lead'). A professor of government will note that parliament is above all a place for debates (via French *parlement*, from *parler*, 'to speak'). Some politicians will tell you that economics is the art of household management (*oikos*, from which we get 'eco', means 'home' in ancient Greek). These explanations may be the speaker's preferred way of thinking about the subject at hand; it's obvious from some of them that they can be used to marshal political arguments too. But a word's origins do not reveal underlying meanings. The appeal to etymology can in fact be a form of deceit. The politician should say 'I believe that managing a country's finances as though it's a household is good economics', rather than pretend that this is a truth borne out by the pedigree of the word itself.

Just how crazy can the etymological fallacy get, taken to its logical conclusion? If you believe that a word's origin is its true meaning, then you're in a pickle when it comes to 'treacle'. This word is derived from the Greek *thēriakē*, which means 'a sticky concoction of spices and resins'. So far, so good. But *thēriakē* in turn comes from *thērion*, which means a 'wild or venomous beast'. *Thēriakē* was a kind of medicine used to offer relief from the effects of bites and stings. Things that bite and sting include dogs, snakes and other wild or venomous beasts. Is 'wild beast' really the true meaning of 'treacle'? Of course not.

Treacle is no freak occurrence. There are literally thousands of surprising semantic developments that undercut the appeal to etymology. 'Litter', in the sense of rubbish, goes back to Latin *lectus*, meaning bed. It came to be used, by extension, to refer to the sometimes messy materials making up bedding, particularly straw (hence a 'litter' of animals born on straw). 'Passion' comes from Latin *passio*, meaning suffering or martyrdom, in reference to Jesus Christ. 'Junket' ultimately derives from *juncus*, the Latin word for rush or reed. *Jonquette* meant a basket made from rushes, and it was used in Wycliffe's fourteenth-century English translation of the Bible to refer to the basket in which Moses was placed as a baby. In the fifteenth century it came to mean a cream cheese served on a mat made of rushes, and then any kind of sumptuous feast – which is how we get the contemporary meaning of an extravagant celebration or trip.*

Examples like this raise the problem of where you decide to pause and say 'No further; this is where the true meaning lies': is 'litter' *really* 'straw' (fifteenth century), or 'bed' (first century)? Does 'silly' *really* mean 'happy' (thirteenth century) or 'innocent' (sixteenth century)?

We are now in a position to dismiss the idea that a word's origin is its true meaning. But it would be a mistake to stop here just because we've bust our myth, shown that etymology is pointless. On the contrary: we will shortly see just how captivating the history of a word can be. The point is that its value doesn't lie in explaining language *as it is now*.

---

* Sol Steinmetz collected these and many other unexpected etymologies in his book *Semantic Antics*. Language nerds might enjoy the etymology of the word 'glamour' and its close relationship to 'grammar'. The former once meant 'enchantment' or 'spell', and developed from 'gramarye', which signified 'occult learning', and before that simply learning in general. Both modern words are ultimately derived from the Old French *gramaire* – the study of language and letters.

But first: if etymology can't do that, what can? How should we start to think about what words mean?

Talking sense

This question has preoccupied thinkers for as long as we have written records. Plato tells us that his teacher, Socrates, wondered whether the way a word sounded told us how it should be understood (an idea now seen as far-fetched, outside the realms of onomatopoeia: words which mirror the physical qualities of the things they describe such as 'splash' and 'thwack').

Nearly 1,000 years later, in AD 400, St Augustine wrote about his own experience of learning language (how did he remember, you might well ask). His account appears to offer a common-sense view of meaning. 'When grown-ups named some object and at the same time turned towards it, I perceived this,' he said. 'And I grasped that the thing was signified by the sound they uttered, since they meant to point it out ... In this way, little by little, I learned to understand what things the words, which I heard uttered in their respective places in various sentences, signified. And once I got my tongue around these signs, I used them to express my wishes.'

That seems about right: words stand for things in the real world. Apple, flower, water. Once a child has learned to associate sounds with different objects, he or she can ask for them. It follows that if you want to know the meaning of a word, you should ask someone to point to whatever it refers to. You don't have to perform an Augustinian feat of memory to understand this. If you've ever learned a second language you'll be familiar with the idea, albeit in reverse. 'What's the French word for this?' you say, pointing at a glass full of water. '*L'eau!*' '*Bah, merci.*' But sometimes we use different words to refer to the same thing.

Imagine you're in the countryside with little St Augustine. Over in a field you see an equine animal, point to it and say 'horse'. Simple word, simple explanation. Except that, as with many even apparently basic words, there are several other options. And I'm not talking about names for different kinds of horse, like 'stallion', 'mare' or 'foal'. I mean words that refer to exactly that equine animal, like 'steed', 'mount' and 'gee-gee'. Augustine would have been confused if each time someone pointed at a horse they said either 'horse', 'steed', 'mount' or 'gee-gee'. They mean the same thing, but they're obviously different. The things we associate with certain words contribute a lot to their 'feel'. When you hear 'steed', what do you picture? Probably a medieval knight on a caparisoned animal. 'Mount' brings professional show-jumping to mind. 'Gee-gee' conjures a world of gambling.

So what is the 'feel' of a word, and how can you distinguish it from the thing being pointed at? One way to answer this question is to imagine that names have both a 'sense'* and a 'reference', which together make up the meaning. 'Steed', 'mount' and 'gee-gee' have different senses (ways in which they are presented) but the same 'reference', that of an equine animal.

---

* Gottlob Frege, the German philosopher who first thought to differentiate sense and reference, used the following example to help his readers understand: it's clear that 'the Morning Star' and 'the Evening Star' have very different meanings. But they refer to exactly the same object – Venus, seen at dawn and at dusk. The difference, then, lies in their senses, the way Venus is presented to the hearer or reader. (You'll remember from earlier in the chapter that the Latin name for the Morning Star happens to be Lucifer.)

Unfortunately, the problems just keep coming. I know the meaning of the word 'apple' because I've been shown lots of examples of them, each time linked to a fairly consistent sequence of sounds. My idea of 'apple' is now pretty clear: I will not mistake a peach or a pear for one. But what about 'angry'? You might think it's possible to point out 'angry'. Maybe Augustine saw his older brother screaming and looked questioningly at his mother. She said 'he's angry', and the association was formed. But what if all there was to go on was a screwed-up face and tears? Or just silence. 'He's angry', she might say again, but it looks different. How are we supposed to tell that particular emotional state apart from 'sad' or 'jealous'?

As we can see, the more abstract those concepts become, the harder it gets: how is Augustine expected to learn about 'regret', 'nostalgia', or 'randomisation'? Concepts, of course, are not naturally occurring, like apples. They are, in fact, created by cultures. Even concepts that we assume have boundaries defined by nature – for example, 'anger' – appear not to, as the emotion researcher Lisa Feldman Barrett has demonstrated.* We have our own ways of dividing up the spectrum of sensation and feeling, and other cultures may do it quite differently. Words divide an analogue world into digital chunks.

More than that, they can actually be 'concept-forming',

---

* Feldman Barrett argues that emotions are not natural entities, reflecting clearly defined physiological or neurological processes. She writes: 'Research has not revealed a consistent, physical fingerprint for even a single emotion. When scientists attach electrodes to a person's face and measure muscle movement during an emotion, they find tremendous variety, not uniformity. They find the same variety with the body and the brain. You can experience anger with or without a spike in blood pressure.'

according to the linguist Geoffrey Leech (who also provided the 'steed', 'mount' and 'gee-gee' examples above). The word 'babysitter', he pointed out, refers to something more than just someone who sits with a baby. It 'institutionalises' a new role: that of a family member, friend or professional who looks after your child while you are out. You might ask which comes first, the concept or the word? It's a bit chicken and egg: an increasingly familiar set of circumstances calls out for a shorter, more convenient way of describing them, and the label distils that phenomenon into a concept. Regardless, the fact of naming has its own real-world effects. Babysitting becomes a more easily accessible idea as a result of its handy label; people may then decide to try to earn some extra money 'babysitting', whereas without this clearly defined role it might not have occurred to them to do so. Importantly, this doesn't mean that languages without a word for 'babysitter' can't conceive of such a job. It just means it's less normal, less available, less a widely recognised part of everyday life.

Incidentally, it's relatively rare to be able to pinpoint the moment of naming. One clear-cut example, which sheds some light on the chicken-and-egg problem, is the word 'podcast'. Here's Ben Hammersley, writing in 2004 for the *Guardian*: 'MP3 players, like Apple's iPod, in many pockets, audio production software cheap or free, and weblogging an established part of the internet; all the ingredients are there for a new boom in amateur radio. But what to call it? Audioblogging? Podcasting? GuerillaMedia?' A journalist's brainstorm gave birth to a new word, and it caught on. Before you knew it, media organisations had 'podcasting' departments. Young people started thinking: I want to make podcasts when I grow up.

Sometimes, as with 'anger' or 'regret', it's difficult to

establish what a concept-word points at. But there are other kinds of words where it is, in principle, impossible. What does 'this' refer to? Or 'that'? Or 'then'? How do you define 'there' or 'here'? Try it – it's not easy. Dictionaries have a duty to define words, so it's worth looking at how they fare. Merriam-Webster defines 'this' as 'the person, thing, or idea that is present or near in place, time, or thought'. If Augustine's mother pointed at something and said 'this', maybe he'd understand. But maybe he'd mistakenly take her to be referring to the object itself – and start calling apples 'this' whenever he saw them. After all, 'this' can refer to anything. Are we therefore to understand that the meaning of 'this' is infinite? That would be a very strange notion; which makes you wonder whether there's something fundamentally wrong with the way we've chosen to look at things. We may now start to believe that the idea of a 'word' 'meaning' something is itself misleading.

First it's important to ask what a word actually is. Perhaps it's the smallest unit of meaning. But it turns out there are smaller ones. The British linguist Frank Palmer points out that bits of words can be meaningful too: '-ump' seems to signify a roundish mass in words such as 'bump', 'lump', 'hump' and 'stump'. Similarly, 'sl-' suggests something liquid or lubricated: it's what the words 'slide', 'slither', 'slip' and 'slush' have in common. Not only that: whole words can be more or less meaningless, at least when out of context: what does 'is' mean in a sentence like 'The sky is blue'? (Many languages just leave it out: in Arabic you say *as-samaa' zarqaa'* – the sky blue.)

If it's not meaning that makes a word, perhaps it's just a unit that occurs by itself in writing. It's a fact that all multi-syllabic words in English have a single primary stress, a syllable that's emphasised above all the others. '*em*phasised', for example, or 'a*bove*'. So in a phrase with several words, there would be several primary stresses – '*several pri*mary *stress*es'. But what about '*shoe* polish', '*pass*port office' or '*bagg*age handler'? They have only one primary stress. So a 'word' can actually be formed of two words.

Second, we must tackle the meaning of 'mean'. 'The whole language is a machine for making falsehoods', says Hugo Belfounder, the philosopher in Iris Murdoch's 1954 novel *Under the Net*. He is talking about the way in which the structure of language – in his view, a kind of net over the world of experience – throws up problems that we take to be problems with the way the world is. In fact they're problems with the way language is.

Here's why: our working theory is that the meaning of a word is the thing it points to (be that a concrete object or a concept). Implicit in this is the idea that a word 'has' a 'meaning'. But, as Palmer says: 'If this is so, it is obviously legitimate to ask what kind of entity meaning is, and to look for it either in the world or in people's minds. But to say that a word has meaning is not like saying that people have legs or that trees have leaves.' We are fooled, Palmer writes, by the verb 'have' and the fact that 'meaning' is a noun. As a result, we end up looking for some 'thing' that actually *is* meaning. To put it another way, the role these words play in the sentence makes them liable to be confused with completely different kinds of words that happen to play the same role. I have legs. Words have meanings. But is the 'have' in the first sentence the same as the 'have' in the second? Obviously not. We are under the net.

It's possible that our search for the meanings of words has been a bit of a wild-goose chase, then. If we want better answers we're going to have to approach the subject from a different angle.

Use it or lose it

The ideas Murdoch put into Belfounder's mouth were inspired by Ludwig Wittgenstein, an Austrian-Jewish philosopher who fled the Nazis and ended up in Cambridge. In his early work he wrote that language painted a picture of reality: words and sentences corresponded to facts in the world, a bit like colour and brushstrokes represent what the eye sees. This is very similar to Augustine's idea that words point to or stand in for things. Later on, however, Wittgenstein completely changed his mind – or, at least, realised how limited that explanation was as an account of natural language.

Take the word 'slab'. According to Oxford Dictionaries, this is 'a large, thick, flat piece of stone or concrete, typically square or rectangular in shape'. So far, so straightforward. A concrete noun in every sense. By saying 'slab' you are referring to a real, solid, heavy thing. But what if you said 'slab!'. Still the same word. Has the meaning changed?

Wittgenstein imagined a builder and his assistant. They are on a construction site, surrounded by blocks, pillars, slabs and beams. When the builder needs a slab, he shouts 'slab!' and his assistant obliges. So 'slab' here means something like 'At this moment, I need a slab, and I want you to fetch me one. You will do so in the manner we have agreed.' The assistant wouldn't actually have to know that 'slab' referred in general to large pieces of stone or concrete. He could simply have been taught that in this situation, for these purposes, 'slab' is a command to seek out a particular one from among the four types of building block he has learned about. As Wittgenstein wrote, he had been taught the 'rules' of a language 'game'.

This broadens our horizons a little bit. 'Slab!' is not a

symbol standing in for an object. It's more like a signal to follow a set of instructions. Let's go back to the word 'this'. Could we see 'this' as a little manual, an algorithm, instead of a simple symbol? Every time you hear the particular set of sounds 'th-i-s', you become aware of the fact that your attention is being drawn to something near the speaker. 'I can't open this', your friend says, and you look around for clues: they're carrying an object in their hands. It's a jam jar with a lid. 'This' must refer to the jam jar. So the algorithm for 'this', the set of instructions the word encourages us to obey, could be written out as follows: 'find something physically close, or an idea that has recently been referred to. That is probably what the speaker means.' 'This' is a prompt to do something with your eyes and your brain. You could say the same for 'here' (find the location of the speaker), or 'then' used as a time phrase (find the time the speaker is referring to; it has probably already been referred to more specifically).

Which leads us to Wittgenstein's crucial insight. Although he had it seventy years ago, it's hard to find a better account for the many different ways in which we deploy words: 'The meaning of a word is its use in the language.'

'Slab!' is an example of word-as-tool. Its meaning, in the context of a building site, was to get someone to do something that would help build a wall. Wittgenstein described a few other situations where language might be used in different ways, and called them all 'language games'. These games can involve giving orders, cracking a joke, requesting, thanking, cursing, greeting, praying. What does the word 'knock' mean? When you read a sign that says 'Please knock', you understand it as a request – aimed at anyone who wants to get in – to bang your knuckles on a door to alert the person inside. When you say 'knock knock' you're signalling that you're about to make a joke. When you say 'knock it off' you're warning someone that you're irritated with them. 'The meaning of a word is its use in the language.'

Wittgenstein's mantra helps us understand 'this'. It explains how 'regret' might be different from a similar word like 'remorse' – look at the way they are used, with 'remorse' cropping up more often in the context of crime or really serious wrongdoing. It helps us understand the difference between the meaning of 'baby' in 'baby, sit!' and 'babysit'.

When he talked about the 'use' of words in language games, Wittgenstein had something relatively specific in mind: an attempt to influence the situation at hand, to perform an action with the word in a particular situation. But we can take his explanation and run with it. Because, applied generally, it gives a far better account of meaning than the etymological fallacy. 'Decimate' means what we use it to mean. If you want to understand it, look at how it is applied. 'Dilemma' sometimes means a difficult choice between two things, as per its etymology, but mostly it doesn't. It means what people use it to mean: a tricky decision. We've already seen that change in language is inevitable. Now we can begin to understand why words in particular are so mutable: the way they are used is what matters. 'Treacle' is found in cake recipes and encountered in supermarkets. It's not a term zookeepers and conservationists use when talking about venomous reptiles.

Down the toilet

So, back to etymology. If it's not a guide to meaning, what is it good for?

Not much, according to some academic linguists. In his introduction to *Semantics*, Frank Palmer interprets 'etymology' literally (it is derived from the Greek *etymon*, or 'true sense'), taking the fallacy to be all there is. 'Etymology for its own sake is of little importance, even if it has curiosity value ... the chief difficulty is that there can be no "true" or "original" meaning since human language stretches back too far.' We have to agree with the latter – but the former seems absurd.

It's worth asking at this point why etymology is so seductive. For most people it represents their first (and frequently only) encounter with linguistics. As we know, words are at once completely prosaic – we use them every day, mostly without thinking – and rather mysterious. As a result it's natural to ask where they come from. We weave stories around their origin, both patently false ('lol' and 'golf') and more plausible ('decimate' and 'educate'). That curiosity shouldn't be dismissed: it's a knocking at the door of linguistics. If they shut it in people's faces, the guardians of knowledge about language risk closing off a route to both enlightenment and wonder. As a result, people seek their wonder elsewhere – in false accounts of how language works.

In any case, it isn't right to see etymology as some poor relation to 'proper' linguistics. An attempt to explain why the meanings of words change is an attempt to explain how the mind works, how language works and how society works. Perhaps this is why it has been deemed out of bounds. Those subjects are huge – for many, to use the phrase beloved of academic papers, 'beyond the scope' of what can be made precise and scientific. Too bad: that's what most people actually want help understanding. Since Palmer wrote that passage, a number of linguists have recognised this. The study of 'semantic change' has become more respectable. Some light has been shed on how it happens, and why.

Take the word 'toilet', a mundane word we don't even really like saying. It conjures, after all, the most basic human operations – ones we prefer not to think about and which are redolent* of some rather unpleasant aspects of ourselves. 'I'm going to the toilet', we might say several times a day. In Wittgensteinian terms, it's a means of excusing ourselves to perform essential bodily functions.

But 'toilet' also refers to a concrete object – a porcelain bowl with a flush handle. And the journey of the word 'toilet' to that particular point of reference has been quite remarkable. It has been buffeted by almost all the forces that can send a word careening this way and that through the territory of meaning. As the linguist Elizabeth Closs Traugott explains, it was first borrowed into English from French, in the sixteenth century. Back then it meant a 'piece of cloth, often used as a wrapper, especially of clothes'. Randle Cotgrave's French-to-English Dictionary of 1611 translates *toilette* as 'a toylet', indicating that the word had already come into English. He continues: 'the stuffe which drapers lap about their clothes; also a bag to put night-clothes and buckeram or other stuffe to wrap any other clothes in'.

This meaning shifted as the century wore on: it began to refer to a cloth spread over a dressing table, in front of a mirror. In 1683 the *London Gazette* reported that a 'toilet of blew velvet with a gold and silver fringe' had been stolen. It was sometimes spelled 'twilet' and even 'twilight'. In a hundred years or so it had changed again, referring more commonly now to the dressing table itself; in 1789 Edward

---

* From the Latin intensive form *re* plus the verb *olere* – 'to emit a smell'.

Gibbon remarked that his book about the Roman Empire 'was on every table and almost on every toilette'.

At the same time, the meaning was extended in various ways: 'to do one's toilet' was to get dressed, made up and perfumed (hence the now incongruous-seeming 'toilet water', a fresh-smelling fragrance). In the nineteenth century, your 'toilet' was used to refer to your manner of dressing, as in 'elegant toilet'. For some, the dressing table became the entire room, particularly if it had bathing facilities. It was also used as an adjective to describe the various implements you'd find there: a toilet-sponge, a toilet-basket, a toilet-pail. The latter is 'a tin pail for holding slops in a bedroom' – toilet is approaching its current destination. It was in America, finally, that it began to be used commonly as a synonym for lavatory: the room or cubicle containing a toilet.

In toilet's shift from innocuous to noxious we have several important clues about how the world and human nature influence language. First of all, a borrowing occurs. A French word jumps into the English language, very likely because of trade and politics – the term was one used by the professional class of drapers. France was close enough to England for its wares to be sold there, and for merchants to come and go. Not only that, but political upheaval in France, including the religious persecution of Protestants, resulted in the migration of skilled workers, such as weavers of fine cloth, many of whom settled in the Spital-fields district of London. They brought their terms of art with them.*

---

* Borrowing linked to a new technology or fashion originating in another country can be seen in the recent past too, with such familiar examples as 'Kalashnikov' (Russian, 1970) and 'latte' (Italian, 1989).

Next, the meaning of that word begins to evolve. It moves beyond the draper's workshop into people's homes. This could have been because a new habit of spreading a piece of cloth over a dressing table became fashionable and the draper's word piggy-backed along with it. An alternative explanation is that an existing habit got a fancy new name. Now, as then, the use of a term from abroad, and particularly a country like France, richer and more powerful at the time than England, lent a certain cachet to its user. If you wanted to appear sophisticated, you might say 'toylet' rather than the more banal 'cloth'.

In any case, the 'toylet' is now on the dressing table. What happens next illustrates a key mechanism of semantic change: the shift of meaning from one conceptual area into an adjacent, overlapping one. The 'toilet' becomes the dressing table itself. Some linguists like to think of this as metaphorical change. Others prefer to use the term metonymy, 'the substitution of the name of an attribute or adjunct for that of the thing meant'. We know that it reflects a universal feature of human cognition since it is found in all languages. Examples include the German word for 'leg', *Bein*, which originally meant 'bone'. Or the Spanish *boda*, 'wedding', with its origin in the Latin *vota*, meaning 'marriage vows'. We also see the meaning of 'toilet' being extended hugely, into all sorts of domains related to preparing oneself for the day or to going out. Clothes, scent, washing, make-up. The word has exploded. In doing so it embodies another common process – generalisation.

Some surprising words in the history of English have undergone generalisation. 'Arrive' once meant 'come to shore', the second part cognate with French *rive*, meaning 'bank'. Now, of course, it means to 'come anywhere'. 'Dog' once meant a particularly powerful canine, with 'hound' being the more general term. The word 'salary' ultimately derives from the Latin *salarium*, and is cognate with the modern word 'salt'. Why? Because the *salarium* was the portion of money allocated to Roman soldiers specifically for salt, from which it was generalised to a stipend, and to pay in general. In Spanish the word for 'gentlemen', which you find on the outside of toilets, is *caballeros*. This is cognate with the English 'cavalier', which makes you think of a man on a horse (compare the French word for the animal, *cheval*) – and that's what *caballero* once meant. From a fine, upstanding figure of a man on horseback came the polite expression for any man of quality.

Central to the mechanism of generalisation is the attention paid to a quality common to both situations: in 'salary' something being handed out, in *caballero* a noble demeanour. In the case of 'toilet' the common quality is: 'you do it when you're getting ready to present yourself to the world'.

'Toilet' now has a particular semantic flavour: privacy, preparation, ablution. As a result it finds itself in dangerous territory, for anything with these associations risks being sucked into a particularly strong evolutionary vortex – that of the taboo, a word that deserves its own detour.

That which must not be mentioned

'Taboo' is a word that entered the English language via the explorer Captain James Cook. It's from the Tongan language, and means something considered sacred and therefore to be avoided or treated specially. A host of rules surrounded the higher-ranking members of Tongan society – for example, eating their leftover food was forbidden. Tonga's main island, Tongatabu, is probably so named because of its sacredness as the home of the great chiefs. 'Taboo' also encompassed different kinds of superstitions, such as not wearing a necklace when pregnant because it invoked the idea of the baby's umbilical cord getting wrapped around its neck. Respecting superiors and warding off bad luck are hardly unusual, which is possibly why 'taboo' is such a successful borrowing: it wraps up a very familiar human experience into a short, memorable package.

A taboo can be a forbidden action, or a forbidden object. It can also, of course, be a forbidden word. Forbidden is relative: some taboos are stronger than others. 'Fuck' is worse than 'shit'. But blurting out either might be forgiven as little more than a loss of self-control. Racial epithets like the N-word are subject to more powerful taboos because they indicate an entire belief system seen as unacceptable.* Even these are dependent on context, however: a black person is free to use the N-word, which conveys a completely different meaning in his mouth – just as a Tongan woman who wasn't pregnant wouldn't have had to worry about wearing a necklace.

There are many examples of culture-specific taboos. Hand-holding among heterosexual male adults is taboo in the West, but normal in many Arab countries. In Japan and China slurping your noodles is fine, while in Europe and America eating noisily is considered bad manners. But there are some taboos that are widespread. These include

---

* You'll notice that I've chosen to use an abbreviation, rather than spell out the word concerned. Taboos are not anthropological curiosities, confined to museums – they are real and have meaning. This one is all the more powerful because of the egregious history of the epithet and the fact that discrimination against black people continues. Since I'm not black, I'm not free to use the word as I please. That is a taboo I am happy to respect.

ones related to sex, religion, death, disease, danger* and defecation.

Taboo subjects are usually dealt with in language via euphemism, which attempts to circumvent the stigma of whatever is being referred to. It's a losing game, though – and one that promotes an accelerated form of change. If a subject is stigmatised, and a word is understood to refer to it, then that word is going to get stigmatised by association. This means that a new word has to be dreamed up to re-place it – but then that gets stigmatised too.

This is the vortex into which 'toilet' was sucked. 'Lav-atory', the usual word in nineteenth-century American English, was itself originally a euphemism, having meant simply a place for washing. But it had been contaminated by association, and a new, more delicate word was needed. 'Toilet', suggestive of gentility, nose-powdering and delight-ful smells, sounded just right.

Now, of course, it's really only got one meaning – and that's the functional one. Even this has become awkward in conversation, particularly in American English, which seems

---

* The word for 'bear' has been euphemised in many languages be-cause of a taboo around invoking the deadly animal directly. Instead it is named for one or other of its typical qualities. In Lithuanian it is *lokys* – 'one who licks'; in Russian it is *medvedev* – 'honey eater'; the English is derived from a word that once meant 'the brown one'. The linguist Larry Trask has pointed out that the same is true of 'fox', which is given innocuous names like *Garcia* in Spanish (a common surname) or *Renard* in French (a given name). These etymologies are a direct connection with an earlier form of society whose people dwelled closer to nature than we do. Taboos of this kind arose either because of fear (the animal was lethal, or a threat to well-being), awe (the animal was worshipped), the avoidance of a jinx in hunting (saying the animal's name might somehow alert it) or a combination of the three.

to have a particularly strong taboo around bodily functions (another euphemism). Instead, 'restroom' or 'bathroom' are used. The stigmatised use of 'toilet' has effectively limited its meaning. From having rather large and productive scope, its meaning has shrunk to that porcelain bowl with its flush handle, or the room that contains it.

This is 'narrowing', and is another frequent pathway of change. The word 'deer', in Old English 'deor', once referred to any animal. (Its Indo-European roots suggest a meaning akin to 'breathing creature'.) Now, of course, it can only be used for the thing with antlers. 'Meat' originally meant 'food', but can now only be used to refer to animal flesh. Its former, wider meaning is evident in Shakespeare. In *Romeo and Juliet*, Mercutio says: 'Thy head is as full of quarrels as an egg is full of meat' (Act 3, Scene 1). In the King James version of the Bible, God announces that 'I have given every green herb for meat' (Genesis 1:30). 'Fowl', which once meant any kind of bird, has narrowed to mean a bird kept domestically, or used for meat. But its early, broader application can again be seen in the Bible: 'Behold the fowls of the air: for they sow not, neither do they reap, nor gather into barns; yet your heavenly Father feedeth them' (Matthew 6:26).

Through the history of the word 'toilet', we've learned about trade, geopolitics and domestic life in the sixteenth century. We've learned about a universal cognitive trait (that concepts can bleed into one another) which gives rise to a powerful linguistic tendency (change via metonymy). We've seen that this change can result in two further kinds of semantic change: generalisation and narrowing. And we've learned the perturbing effect of taboos on language evolution, as well as something about the strength of the defecation taboo in the Anglo-Saxon world. It's hard to credit that anyone could dismiss a panorama of language and society like this as being of 'little importance'.

It is the 'and society' part which foxes some linguists. They are trained to deal with the structure of the language system, rather than the tentacles it extends into culture (and vice versa). But while this might make linguistics more amenable to scientific modes of analysis, it doesn't help non-specialists grasp what kind of thing language is, and how it works.

Power to the people

Language is a uniquely complex phenomenon. It is both a cognitive and a cultural system, with contributions from at least four areas: our brains, the rules of interaction, patterns of collective behaviour and the idiosyncrasies of particular cultures. Linguists have tended to focus on brains: what it means for people to have knowledge of a language. But that purism becomes hard to maintain in the study of language change – because change is something that involves lots of people, not to mention accidents of history.

We've already seen that the nature of thought gives rise to particular kinds of changes, like the gradual shift of meaning from one concept into another. How those concepts are used in real conversations explains another very strong tendency: what Traugott has called 'subjectification', where meanings become infused with opinions. Words like 'evidently', once denoting 'according to the evidence', are now rarely used in a non-subjective way ('evidently, you're not listening to me' = 'I think you're not listening to me'). 'Possibly', 'obviously' and 'apparently' follow the same pattern. Such exchanges only happen between people, and must be governed by something like rules of interaction.

And then there are patterns of collective behaviour: the sometimes unexpected structures that evolve when thousands of speakers make the same kinds of judgement, which the linguist Rudi Keller has called 'the invisible hand in language change'. This is a stage beyond an exchange between two people. You can think of the resulting patterns as being a bit like the network of paths that form in the lawn on a university campus, as hundreds of people walk from lecture to lecture. At some point everyone goes to the canteen, digging a particularly deep furrow in the grass. At the end of the day they make their way to the university gates, digging another. The criss-crossing lines can look as though they were made by design, but they weren't.

Keller takes the example of the pejoration (getting-worse) of word meanings. This is usually seen as the result of everyone disapproving of the thing the word refers to: the negative association that builds up means it can no longer be used neutrally. One example is 'knave', which once just meant 'boy', but now signifies an untrustworthy cheat. As we've already seen, words that apply to women undergo pejoration: compare 'master' to its once neutral equivalent 'mistress', used to refer to the lover of a married man. Or 'sir' to 'madam', which can mean a cheeky woman, or one in charge of a brothel.

But what if laws of chivalry meant that, rather than thinking 'denigrate her', most adults pursued the strategy 'praise her'? In other words, women were to be exalted wherever possible. Keller argues that thousands upon thousands of interactions in which a slightly more gallant word for 'woman' was used would result in the neutral words not seeming good enough. The result? The pejoration of words involving women. According to this view, 'huswif' ('housewife') became 'hussy', not because of denigration but because people kept using a better word, like 'lady', instead. It's an intriguing idea; whether or not it's correct in this particular case, it's a good illustration of a pattern that results not from individual brains but from collective linguistic behaviour.

And then there's culture – including the influence of fashion and of great thinkers, the knock-on effects of political upheaval, the impact of art. These can leave their imprint on words too.

The Norman invasion of 1066 certainly left an indelible mark on the English language. William the Conqueror, together with a host of noblemen, soldiers and merchants, descended on the Anglo-Saxon kingdom and changed its government, laws and hierarchy. They brought with them Norman French, a Romance language with a vocabulary and grammar very different from Old English, with its Germanic roots. That period bequeathed English a bounty of new words* which we now call 'Latinate'. These often coexist with Old-English-derived alternatives, resulting in pairs like 'hard' and 'durable'; 'go' and 'proceed'; 'buy' and 'purchase'. As a result, you can try to speak or write entirely in 'Germanic English'. But it's tough. And there are plenty of words related to technology or scholarship that simply don't have Anglo-Saxon equivalents. This has led various adventurous writers to attempt to fill in the gaps. The word 'Anglish' describes a form of English shorn of non-Germanic vocabulary, and was coined by the journalist Paul Jennings in the 1960s. Its apotheosis comes in the form of 'Uncleftish Beholding', a 1989 essay by the science-fiction writer Poul Anderson. 'Uncleftish' is the Anglish for 'atomic', an

---

* Some fragments of unaltered Norman French have been preserved in the legal system: examples include 'bailiff' and 'jury'.

etymological calque, or form-for-form copy of the Greek-derived word. (In Greek, *a-* equals 'un-', *-tom-* comes from the verb *temnein*, meaning 'to cut/cleave', and *-ic* from the Latin stem *-icus*, meaning 'characteristic of', corresponds to 'ish'. An atom was once thought to be a particle that could not be divided – cut up – any further.) 'Beholding' is constructed in the same way, and is Anderson's word for 'theory', which comes from the Greek *theoria* (contemplation, speculation). 'Uncleftish Beholding' makes for curious reading to modern English speakers. Here's a quotation:

> Most unclefts link together to make what are called bulk-bits. Thus, the waterstuff bulkbit bestands of two waterstuff unclefts, the sourstuff bulkbit of two sourstuff unclefts, and so on. When unlike clefts link in a bulkbit, they make bindings.

Bulkbits are 'molecules'; *waterstuff* is 'hydrogen'; *sourstuff* is 'Oxygen' (compare the German *Sauerstoff*); *bindings* are 'compounds'.

Anglish, which started as a joke, has developed into something of a cult. There is a reddit page conducted entirely in it, and even an attempt at an Anglish encyclopaedia. It has a particular cultural feel, bringing to mind simple living and no-nonsense practicality – a result of the stripping-away of languages we associate with urbanity and learning: French, Latin and Greek. Reinstate them and you have a more complete picture of English's distinct history and, if you like, its take on the world.

As we'll see in more detail in Chapter 5, Anna Wierzbicka has devoted her career to the creation of a metalanguage which eliminates the particular biases of English and allows a far more accurate translation of words than is usually the case. With fellow linguist Cliff Goddard, she uses 'happiness' to illustrate the cultural values encoded by words – values which can be teased out by their history.

In my copy of the *Oxford Etymological Dictionary*, there is no entry for 'happy' or 'happiness'; instead the explanation of those words falls under 'hap', first attested in the thirteenth century, meaning 'chance', 'luck' – or simply an event (hence 'happen'). At this point it's neutral – like 'fortune', rather than 'good fortune'. 'Happy', meaning 'prosperous', comes along in the fourteenth century, whereas 'having a feeling of contentment' begins to creep in later, in the sixteenth. After that, as Wierzbicka and Goddard explain, an even greater semantic shift takes place.

To illustrate this, they compare English 'happiness' with German *Glück*, which is the usual translation. 'We can say that until the eighteenth century, happiness and *Glück* both referred to "very good feelings" which cannot endure, and which most people experience rarely or not at all.' The transience and rarity of happiness might be compared to the modern meaning of 'bliss' – intense, fleeting pleasure. Bliss isn't an everyday thing.

The story of these two words began to diverge because of an important philosophical split in the German- and English-speaking worlds. 'The whole idea of "the greatest happiness of the greatest number"', Wierzbicka and Goddard say, 'popularized by Jeremy Bentham . . . was based on the assumption that what people want and need is not some peak experiences, which can be achieved rarely and only by a few, but "good" experiences . . . which can become the goal of social and political endeavours. As a result of the success of this idea, the very meaning of the word happiness changed.' The knock-on effects of this philosophical change – cemented in a new use of the word 'happiness' –

are hard to understate. Thomas Jefferson used it in this way, rather than in the traditional sense of a fleeting, intense experience, when he framed the American Declaration of Independence. 'Life, liberty and the pursuit of happiness' pointed to sustained contentment rather than the possibility of good fortune, the chance, if fate permitted, of a brief burst of pleasure.

Meanwhile, *Glück* remained more or less where it was. In 1949 Sigmund Freud talked of *Glück* as being 'only possible as an episodic phenomenon ... We are made that we can derive intense enjoyment only from a contrast and very little from a state of things.' The translation of *Glück*, even in this passage, as 'happiness' can seem incongruous to English readers brought up on the Jeffersonian concept.

The etymology of 'happiness', then, helps us understand an important cultural shift. While telling us nothing of the 'real' meaning of the English word today, it lets us see it in proper perspective, and can be used as a tool to interrogate the usefulness of that concept – which is vitally important in the case of a 'cultural key word', as Wierzbicka labels it, like 'happiness'. Instead of being a self-evident, natural emotion, 'happiness' is revealed to be a cultural object of the Anglo-Saxon world. It suddenly seems like a mistake to leave an awareness of its history to hobbyists and pedants.

Isaiah Berlin wrote that 'words, by connecting passions with things, the present with the past, and by making possible memory and imagination, create family, society, literature, history'. He quotes Johann Herder, who argued that to speak and think is to 'swim in an inherited stream of images and words'. Wierzbicka and Goddard say: 'there is a very close link between the life of a society and the lexicon of the language spoken by it'. If this is even remotely true, then the 'curiosity value' of etymology is nothing less than the value of an inquiry into the history of the ideas, habits and practices of society. You don't get much curiouser than that.

CHAPTER 3

I control what comes out of my mouth

It's 1962, Saks department store, New York City. A man in a jacket, white shirt and tie pads the softly carpeted shop floor. He pauses near a display of scarves until he catches the eye of an immaculately dressed female employee. 'Excuse me, where are the women's shoes?' 'Fourth floor,' she replies. 'Excuse me?' 'Fourth floor.' 'Thank you ma'am,' he nods. The employee turns to another customer. The man scurries round the corner, pulls out a notebook and spends a few minutes scribbling, before walking down to the second floor.

It could be a scene from a Patricia Highsmith novel, or *Mad Men*. But truth can be nerdier than fiction. If you'd been to Saks at all that November, the chances are you would have noticed this same man flitting up and down the stairway. He repeated his little performance sixty-seven times. And in S. Klein, on Union Square, seventy-one times. In Macy's, on Herald Square, he did it 125 times. It's a wonder he wasn't marched away by security. What was he up to?

This wasn't a foot fetish, or a piece on conceptual art: it was the pursuit of linguistic knowledge. The man in the white shirt was William Labov, a PhD student at Columbia University, and he was trying to figure out why people pronounced certain words like they did.*

Since deciding to speak is a voluntary act – you can hold your peace, or say your piece – it's easy to imagine that what comes out of your mouth is always under your control. Sure, you need to use words that are widely understood and put them more or less in the conventional order. But that still leaves a lot of room for manoeuvre. Within those constraints you can ask for a pint of milk or deliver the Gettysburg Address. You are the master of all you convey.

But is that the whole story? We all know that people speaking the same language can sound quite different. Not only from South Africa to Australia or Great Britain. Not just from one region to another: the American South to California, or Liverpool to London. Even in the same city there will be fine gradations of accent, grammar and vocabulary. And geography is far from being the only factor in determining how someone speaks.

Perhaps the most striking thing about these many differences is how they shape our speech when we're not paying attention. They are, by and large, unconscious. We might strain to eliminate certain tendencies – like the glottal stop at the end of words such as 'what' and 'taught' in British English, or pronouncing '-ing' as '-in'. Or we might strain to incorporate the markers of right and proper diction, the clipped, clear pronunciation of every letter on the page. But 'strain' is the operative word. It's not easy to erase the default settings of your own speech without a great deal of

---

* The description isn't my own invention. In his seminal work, *Sociolinguistic Patterns*, Labov writes: 'The interviewer in all cases was myself. I was dressed in middle-class style, with jacket, white shirt and tie, and used my normal pronunciation as a college-educated native of New Jersey.'

practice, as those who have undergone dialect coaching or tried to speak like a native in a foreign language know.

Linguistics gets social

We make adjustments to the way we talk all day long, without really thinking about it. Our speech becomes clearer and more deliberate during a presentation at work. Our regional accent resurfaces on the phone to a friend from home. We tidy up our language for the bank manager, but maybe untidy it a little in front of a nightclub bouncer. None of these shifts require strain. If they did, talking to people would be a daily obstacle course. Language somehow lines up behind broader social goals: we want to demonstrate empathy, secure someone's co-operation, or even push them away. Without consciously willing it, the shapes of our vowels and consonants change depending on the situation we're in.

Labov needed the salespeople to say 'fourth floor' because it contained two instances of 'r' – the variable that split New Yorkers down the middle. At the time he was working, many of the city's inhabitants still left the 'r' out, saying something like 'fawth flaa'; before the Second World War, that had been the neutral standard. But increasingly people were adding the 'r', particularly at the end of a word, after a vowel (as in 'floor'). As we've seen, language changes all the time. In the year 1400, words such as 'bite' and 'time' were pronounced more like 'beet' and 'team'. 'Moon' was pronounced somewhere between 'moan' and 'mourn'. It's hard to work out why sound shifts like this happen. Is it laziness? Is there something in the structure of the language that makes certain patterns more likely? Is it fashion? Do people copy each other? Is it completely arbitrary?

Labov had a hunch that many sound changes occur for social reasons. He picked up on a sense that 'r'-dropping was increasingly seen as gauche, low-class, inner-city. The 'better' pronunciation – the one associated with education and wealth – was to keep the 'r's in. If that were the case, the spread of 'r'-full words could be said to have a social cause. If 'r'-full pronunciation was somehow aspirational, a trait associated with the 'right' class of people, you would expect it to squeeze out other pronunciations over time.

The task Labov set himself was to prove that 'r' had a social value. In order to get as clear a picture of normal speech as possible, he needed to catch people more or less unawares, then note down, sound by sound, exactly what they were saying. But he also had to find a way of homing in on a notoriously slippery variable: class. There is perhaps no sharper indicator of class – and of what class someone would like to be a member of – than what they buy. And New York City, with its dazzling array of stores catering to every conceivable taste, was the perfect place to do fieldwork. At the top of the pile was Saks Fifth Avenue, right opposite the Rockefeller Center, a few blocks down from Tiffany & Co. Fur coats, expensive jewellery, French perfume. One step down was Macy's, near the commuter hub of Penn Station, and on the bottom rung was S. Klein, where, Labov tells us, in contrast to the deep carpets of Saks, there is a 'maze of annexes, sloping concrete floors, low ceilings; it has the maximum amount of goods displayed at the least possible expense'.

He couldn't very well approach customers in these stores and expect them to talk to him; he'd quickly be dismissed as a weirdo. But salespeople are there to help you, and wouldn't question a stranger asking for directions. Labov was fairly sure that the employees' backgrounds and aspirations

would be closely aligned to the status of the stores themselves. Saks, for example, would likely discriminate against
lower-class workers, in order to maintain its own prestige.
To 'fit in' you'd need a certain look and a particular way
of speaking. All that remained was to find out what goods
were stocked on the fourth floor in each of the venues, and
tailor the question accordingly.

After a total of 264 'interviews', the pattern was unmis-
takable: rates of 'r'-dropping were inversely correlated with
the status of the department store. In Saks, 'fourth floor'
rang out. In Klein, 'fawth flaa' was the order of the day.
Labov had found a close proxy of social class, eliciting examples of a key linguistic variable in a natural environment
where subjects weren't aware their pronunciation was being
tested. 'R' really did give something away. His hunch that
it was riding a wave of social prestige – and would soon
become the standard – turned out to be correct.

What's really interesting about the department-store study
is that the results were probabilistic: there was no guarantee of getting an 'r' at the end of 'floor' in Saks, or failing
to find one in Klein – just a greater likelihood. And Labov
was careful to elicit examples of both casual and deliberate
speech – that's what the second 'Excuse me?' was for. The
first, casual encounter went on 'almost below the level of
conscious attention', he writes. With the request to repeat,
Labov forced employees to think about the words they were
saying, which he believed might make them more likely to
use what they regarded as the 'correct' pronunciation. In
Saks, 'r' was used less in casual than in deliberate speech,
though the difference wasn't stark; employees there had
more linguistic 'security', as Labov put it – they didn't feel a
need to prove themselves. In Macy's, there was a bigger shift
between casual and deliberate speech: 'It would seem that

r-pronunciation is the norm at which a majority of Macy employees aim, yet not the one they use most often.' Klein had the biggest shift of all, from using 'r' 5 per cent of the time to 18 per cent.

The difference when conscious attention was brought to bear seemed to be exaggerated for less linguistically secure speakers. Labov called this phenomenon 'hypercorrection': if people are aware of the negative social value of a pronunciation, when they're concentrating they try to avoid using it (even then, they don't always succeed). Crucially, though, the class differences are still there even when the speaker is barely paying attention. If you work all day at Klein, and go home to a tenement on the Lower East Side, the way the people around you speak gets under your skin and into your mouth. The same goes if you work at Saks and live in a smarter part of the city. In other words, when you say something you send out social signals. You can't help it. If you're lucky, the way you speak sends out the right ones. If you're not, there's only a limited amount you can do about it.

Sounds important

We've already seen how words are imbued with sense through a kind of collective negotiation. It's how they are used in real-life communication that establishes their meanings. Because these meanings are constantly being slightly renegotiated in millions of exchanges between millions of speakers, they judder and shift out of place, very often evolving in quite unexpected directions.

Speech comes with another layer of meaning, however, which is just as unstable and far less amenable to conscious control than our choice of words. What you say is an extraordinarily complex package of information. At the heart of this is the idea you want to convey. For example, you might want someone to lend you some money. The precise phrasing you use will tell us something about the dynamics of the situation you're in. 'Look, the trouble is, I'm a bit short at the moment', 'I'm very sorry to ask, but is there any way I could borrow ten pounds?' and 'Give me ten pounds' all indicate slightly different kinds of relationship between two speakers. That's not all, though. The manner of speech tells us something too. And it can operate at the level of individual sounds, not just choice of words. That's the difference between 'Give me ten pounds' and 'Gisa tenner', and it's basically a social one.

To learn about how linguists treat sounds requires a little bit of technical vocabulary. We are used to thinking of the building blocks of words as 'letters', but orthography – correct spelling, as decided by convention – is often at odds with the sounds we actually produce. What we are used to thinking of as the individual consonants and vowels of the alphabet are not always individual consonants and vowels in the specialised way linguists use the terms. 'Th' in 'the', for example, is a single consonant – a voiced dental fricative, to be precise. But in modern English spelling it has two letters.* Not only that, but these same two letters are used to represent different sounds: 'th' in 'the' is not the same as 'th' in 'thought' – that's a *voiceless* dental fricative.†

---

* It once had one: 'þ', which looked so similar in early print to a 'y' that it was mistaken for it – as in the London pub name 'Ye Olde Cheshire Cheese'.
† 'Voice' is the name linguists give to the vibration of the vocal folds. 'Voiceless' consonants like the 'th' in 'thought' are produced without this vibration, whereas voiced ones like the 'th' in 'the' are produced with it.

Forget spelling. Instead, linguists use a special method of transcription: they take a word and break it down into sound units called phonemes. In British English, 'thought' actually has just three phonemes: one consonant (the voiceless dental fricative spelled 'th'), one vowel (an open-mid back rounded one spelled 'ough') and another consonant (a voiceless dental 'stop' spelled 't'). By convention, when writing out phonemes linguists enclose the notation in slash marks, so the whole word is transcribed as /θɔːt/.

THE INTERNATIONAL PHONETIC ALPHABET (revised to 2015)

CONSONANTS (PULMONIC)   © 2015 IPA

	Bilabial	Labiodental	Dental	Alveolar	Postalveolar	Retroflex	Palatal	Velar	Uvular	Pharyngeal	Glottal
Plosive	p b			t d		ʈ ɖ	c ɟ	k ɡ	q ɢ		ʔ
Nasal	m	ɱ		n		ɳ	ɲ	ŋ	N		
Trill	ʙ			r					R		
Tap or Flap		ⱱ		ɾ		ɽ					
Fricative	ɸ β	f v	θ ð	s z	ʃ ʒ	ʂ ʐ	ç ʝ	x ɣ	χ ʁ	ħ ʕ	h ɦ
Lateral fricative				ɬ ɮ							
Approximant		ʋ		ɹ		ɻ	j	ɰ			
Lateral approximant				l		ɭ	ʎ	L			

Symbols to the right in a cell are voiced, to the left are voiceless. Shaded areas denote articulations judged impossible.

CONSONANTS (NON-PULMONIC)   VOWELS

Clicks	Voiced implosives	Ejectives
⊙ Bilabial	ɓ Bilabial	' Examples:
ǀ Dental	ɗ Dental/alveolar	p' Bilabial
ǃ (Post)alveolar	ʄ Palatal	t' Dental/alveolar
ǂ Palatoalveolar	ɠ Velar	k' Velar
ǁ Alveolar lateral	ʛ Uvular	s' Alveolar fricative

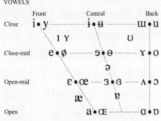

Vowels and consonants in the international phonetic alphabet, along with the technical terms used to describe them. Phonemes are represented by a range of symbols, many of which look similar to regular English letters. However, they don't always have the value you'd expect if you're an English speaker. 'Pulmonic' means produced with air from the lungs. Non-pulmonic consonants, like the clicks found in the Khoisan languages of southern Africa, are much rarer.

Phonemes are also an important part of the meaning of a word. One of the ways linguists determine whether sounds are phonemes is by seeing whether swapping them around interferes with meaning. Take the word 'map', and the phonemes /m/ and /n/. If I substitute the latter for the former, the word changes its meaning, and we have 'nap'. 'Map' and 'nap' are described as a 'minimal pair' which provides evidence for the phonemic contrast between /m/ and /n/. (Minimal pairs which establish the phonemic contrast between 'p' and 'b' include 'pat' and 'bat', 'park' and 'bark', and so on.) Now, imagine 'm', but long and drawn out, like 'mmmmmm'. This is definitely a different sound, but is it a separate phoneme? No. Because if you say 'mmmmmm-map', it sounds strange, but the meaning remains the same.

Differences like this – changes in the sound that aren't phonemic but are still clearly perceptible – are instead called 'phonetic'. Linguists use 'narrow' phonetic transcription (traditionally indicated by square brackets) to note down every aspect of the sounds in the word they're listening to, not just the phonemic information. This might include the 'height' of the tongue in the mouth when producing a vowel, its level of breathiness or creakiness, the amount of 'aspiration' in a consonant, the extent to which the 'r's are rolled.* The word 'pull' can be transcribed broadly as /pʊl/ and, with more phonetic detail, as [pʰʊəl]. Narrow transcription

---

* What is phonetic in one language might be phonemic in another, and vice versa. In English, whether or not you roll your 'r's makes no difference to the meaning of a word. In Spanish, the rolled 'r' and non-rolled 'r' are separate phonemes. The only difference between the word *perro* /pero/ (dog) and *pero* /pero/ (but) is the rolling of the 'r' in the former. Just to confuse you further, although 'r' is not often rolled in English, the symbol for a rolled 'r' – /r/ – is often used to transcribe English, even though the unrolled /ɹ/ would be more accurate.

is particularly useful in linguistic fieldwork, when the aim is to document a dialect very precisely, or to record the sounds of a rare language, perhaps for the first time.

Phonemes aren't just an invention – they're a discovery. They are the units of sound into which the brain breaks down words. We know this because of speech errors, like so-called Spoonerisms, where the initial phoneme of one word is substituted for the initial phoneme of the following word (the classic example, attributed to the Oxford academic William Archibald Spooner, is 'You have hissed all my mystery lectures!'). These errors happen naturally and regularly regardless of level of education or literacy, and are evidence that phonemes are separate in mental terms, capable of being hived off and swapped around.

What's more, researchers have demonstrated that infants – who have not yet learned any language – can tell the difference between phonemes. The proof comes via a technique called the 'high-amplitude sucking paradigm'. One way a baby registers something new in its environment is by changing the rate at which it sucks. A new stimulus will make a baby with a dummy in its mouth suck harder and faster in a way that can be easily measured with special equipment. When babies a few months old were played a series of syllables in which the initial phoneme gradually changed into another, they started sucking harder when the boundary was reached – when 'r', for example, became 'l'. Adult speakers of, say, Japanese are often unable to recognise this difference, having been habituated to a language which doesn't make the same distinction.* And it's not just

* These two consonants are known by linguists as 'liquids', and they contrast with 'stops' like 'k' or 'd' which completely obstruct airflow. In 'r', the tip of the tongue curls up towards the roof of the mouth without making contact, letting air escape around

because the babies in the sucking experiment were being raised in homes where English was spoken. We know from other work that infants are able to recognise distinctions made by languages they've never heard. In other words, we are all born with the ability to recognise the phonemes of all the world's languages, and we gradually whittle these down to those of our own.

It's phonetic, rather than phonemic, differences that are absolutely crucial when it comes to social signalling. Make phonemic changes (the difference between, say, 'fourth floor' and 'fourth door'), and you could be drastically mis-interpreted. Make phonetic changes (the difference between 'fourth floor' and 'fawth flaa'), and you'll be understood. But the quality of that change might say something about your class, age, gender or other aspects of your background. These sound changes don't cost anything in terms of meaning: they are 'free' to move across a range of values so long as they don't tip over into another phoneme. It is this 'free variation', once thought to be inconsequential, which Labov decoded.*

---

it. In 'l' the tip of the tongue is pressed against the ridge behind the teeth, and air escapes on either side (to reproduce these sounds, don't say the names of the letters, but try saying 'arrive' then 'alive' while concentrating on what your tongue does). In the Japanese liquid closest to English 'r', the tip of the tongue 'taps' the roof of the mouth briefly, resulting in a sound somewhere between the two English consonants.

* Not all phonetic differences are 'free variants' (itself now a dis-puted term given the fact that very few variations are truly 'free' in the sense of completely unmotivated, whether by class or other factors). A phoneme is an abstraction, standing for a group of sounds that may be perceived as being one and the same but which have different *realisations*, or 'allophones'. Where a phoneme sits in a word can affect its realisation. Here's an example: in English, a /p/ at the beginning of a word is 'aspirated' – pronounced with a burst of air, signified by a superscript 'h' – as in [pʰʊəɬ] for 'pull'.

Before he went to New York, Labov had spent a summer on an island off the coast of Massachusetts. Martha's Vineyard is now known as a playground for the rich and famous – a beautiful, green getaway for East Coast urban elites, dotted with holiday homes and golf courses. Before that, however, it was a rough-and-ready fishing community. When Labov visited in 1961, the gradual change towards a tourism-oriented economy was already under way. It was another change that caught his eye, though: the way in which islanders pronounced certain vowels bucked the broader New England trend. The sounds he was interested in were combinations of two vowels – called 'diphthongs' – like the ones in the words 'house' and 'night' (here again spelling is deceptive, because the diphthong /aɪ/ is represented by a single letter, 'i'). In standard dialects, the beginnings of these sounds are 'low' (another word for 'open') – they are pronounced with the jaw down and the tongue set low in the mouth. Vineyarders were 'centralising' them, moving the tongue up slightly, making the vowels sound more like 'huwse' and 'nueet'. The funny thing was that a generation earlier, those centralised diphthongs had been dying out. By 1960, they had largely gone on the mainland, where they were considered a throwback to an earlier time. What was behind their newfound popularity in Martha's Vineyard, even as the pace of gentrification accelerated?

It's important to note here that Labov thought the quality of diphthongs, while 'salient for the linguist, [was] not for most speakers; it is apparently quite immune to conscious distortion, as the native Vineyarders are not aware of it, nor are they able to control it consciously'.

When it comes after an /s/, however, it is 'unaspirated': 'spit' would be transcribed [spɪt]. Phonetic differences determined by context in this way are 'positional' or 'contextual variants'.

But this quirk definitely had a non-random distribution, and Labov wanted to discover what motivated it. He looked for answers in the social context in which the speakers found themselves, and their attitudes. Sixty interviews later, what he found was that centralisation was greatest among those who lived on the island year-round, who had traditional occupations and were in their thirties and forties. It was 'closely correlated with expressions of strong resistance to the incursions of the summer people'. It was found in younger people who had determined they wanted to stay on the island, not those whose ambition was to seek a career elsewhere. In other words, this was a marker of loyalty to the Vineyard, of authenticity, of giving the finger to the 'incomers': it said I'm a Vineyarder, born, bred and proud.

Here, then, was an instance of differentiation rather than striving to fit in. A group of speakers in a very specific set of circumstances were distancing themselves from the prestigious norm, rather than trying to emulate it. Their values were the reverse of the hordes of well-to-do tourists who descended on them every summer. Unlike the aspirational workers of Macy's, they were engaged in a race to the bottom – a desire to identify with the values of the older, poorer men who worked in the docks and went out to sea to earn their livelihoods. But again, they weren't consciously manipulating their vowels. This was another case of language lining up behind broader social goals: to be true to one's roots, and to mark oneself out as someone who belongs, rather than a mere visitor. If that was your aim, your vowels would magically follow suit.*

---

* Sometimes, however, people make a very conscious decision to use language to differentiate themselves. The psychologist Paul Ibbotson quotes research by the anthropologist Don Kulick which found that in Papua New Guinea people deliberately changed the

Karma chameleons

The roots of these kinds of subtle changes in language go deep. Human beings are a social species: we survive and thrive as co-operative groups rather than as individuals. Our lives are conducted through our relationships with others, and as a result we have evolved the ability to display our orientation towards our fellows in hundreds of tiny ways. Sometimes the group with which we are most closely associated comes into conflict with others, and we need to show how we differ from them. Though these abilities evolved over hundreds of thousands of years, they are as much in evidence now as when we were hunter-gatherers. Being able to quickly and precisely read myriad social signals and utilise the information to your advantage – whether they're messages sent via clothes, hair, posture, possessions or language – is a talent that might mean you're labelled 'savvy', a 'good judge of character' or even 'a smooth operator' or 'a manipulator'. It will determine your status, and your success. A failure to take social signals into account might lead to the charge that you're 'awkward', 'tactless', 'gauche' or 'bad with people'. You might end up lonely, frustrated, or involved in a conflict you would have preferred to avoid. It follows, then, that transmitting the right social signals at the right time is a valuable trait.

Some believe that they eschew style, and the social signals they send are 'neutral' – they don't follow fashion and don't have a noticeable accent. This is an illusion, and is as absurd

---

way they spoke in order to be less like nearby groups. 'One community [of Buian-language speakers], for instance, switched all its masculine and feminine gender agreements, so that its language's gender markings were the exact opposite of those of the dialects of the same language spoken in neighboring villages.'

as saying 'I don't have a posture'. As Penelope Eckert, who studied linguistic subcultures in American high schools, puts it:

> The world is full of people who think they don't have an accent – that everyone else, or certainly every other region, has an accent, but that their own way of speaking is 'normal' ... But the fact is that everyone has an accent – after all, we all have to pronounce the phonemes of our language some way or another. Some people, however, are in a position to define their own way of pronouncing those phonemes as 'normal'. Indeed, part of what constitutes power in society is the ability to define normality – to get others to view one's own style as unremarkable, as not a style at all.*

This process of reading social cues – and transmitting them – is such a fundamental part of human interaction that we rarely consciously manipulate the variables, such as vowel height or consonant quality, except in cases of hypercorrection and self-consciousness. If we experience the adaptations we make at all, it is as a 'feeling': of wanting to connect with someone, being particularly at ease in their company. Or, as a sense that we need to put up our guard. We might 'bristle' at them, and change our demeanour in all sorts of ways: tensing up, avoiding eye contact, speaking in coldly neutral tones. These alterations are part of a whole. The social goal is the driving force; the language (and other

---

* Saying that someone else 'has an accent' can sometimes just amount to saying they are 'different' – and language might not have much to do with it at all. Donald L. Rubin found that subjects listening to the speech of *the same woman* perceived it to be more 'accented' when they believed her to be Asian rather than white.

resources) mould themselves accordingly. Similarly, some-where at the boundary of awareness, we might adopt an open or an unfriendly posture towards someone, without consciously directing the position of our hands, elbows and shoulders.

The social psychologist Howard Giles developed Commu-nication Accommodation Theory to provide a framework for understanding how we alter our speech when we interact with others. Using variables including accent, rate, volume, pitch, word choice and even syntax, we either converge, diverge or carry on regardless (something Giles calls 'main-tenance'). There's another dimension to add to convergence and divergence: upwards and downwards. The posh sales-people at Saks probably converged upwards to their even posher clientele. Depending on how they were feeling, the customers might have haughtily diverged upwards, or con-verged downwards to meet the salesperson in the middle. Or they might have spoken without any adjustment at all – a sure sign of linguistic security. The proud islanders of Martha's Vineyard diverged downwards in conversations with visitors, towards a norm they believed captured the authenticity of the place. Similarly, in one study quoted by Giles and colleagues, when English-sounding people were heard describing Welsh as a 'dying language with a dismal future', Welsh participants diverged by 'overwhelmingly broaden[ing] their accents'.

So why does accommodation occur? We've already seen that language is just part of a whole system of social signalling, and this signalling is what enables humans to co-operate where they need to, and differentiate when neces-sary. As a result, accommodation gives us a better chance of thriving and surviving. Of the two tendencies, convergence and divergence, the former most likely exerts the stronger influence. Psychologists Tanya Chartrand and John Bargh have noted a 'chameleon effect', whereby human beings engage in 'nonconscious mimicry of the postures, mannerisms, facial expressions and other behaviours' of the people they are interacting with, in such a way that their 'behaviour passively and unintentionally changes to match that of others' in their social environment. This seems to be a fundamental rule of interaction – it would be surprising if it didn't apply to language as well; and, as we have all noticed at some point in our lives, it does. It's hard to maintain your own regional accent if you move away. After years living in Britain, Madonna ended up sounding more *Downton* than Downtown. She was vilified for it, but it's human nature. Brits who move the other way find themselves parroting standard American patterns of pronunciation and stress, saying 'tomayto' and 'crois*sant*' instead of 'tomahto' and '*crois*sant'.* As well as the chameleon effect, there's evidence

----

* In other words, you sound more like the people you hang around with a lot, or identify with. This might go some way towards explaining why some people, usually men, are said to 'sound gay'. It used to be thought that stereotypical gay male voices mirrored those of straight women, particularly in terms of pitch – an idea linked to the cultural association of homosexuality with femininity. Experimental evidence has refuted this. But that doesn't mean there aren't specific phonetic variations associated with gay men. These include an affrication (adding a hiss at the end) of 't' and 'd', the dentalisation (movement towards the teeth) of 's', 'z' and 'n', and a stretching-out of 'sibilant' consonants such as 's' and 'z'. If you view gay men as a group similar to the Vineyarders – a collection of people with a shared identity, who spend time with one another – you'd expect this to be reflected in their patterns of speech. These sounds are not intrinsically gay; they just happen to have been chosen from among the many variables available for social signalling. Their selection is arbitrary. Over time, they will become strongly associated with gay men, and, since this is a stigmatised

that convergence is sometimes necessary just to be understood. Experiments have shown that imitating an accent
can help you understand it better when you hear it again.
It must also make it easier for those with that accent to
understand you.

In some cases, an inability to converge can be bad for
you. Giles and colleagues note that 'members of ... stig-
matized ethnolinguistic groups who fail to accommodate to
the standard language tend to garner more negative evalu-
ations'. This certainly includes those who tend to default to
African American Vernacular English (AAVE), occasionally
referred to as Ebonics. This way of speaking is strongly
associated with middle- and working-class black people in
the United States, and is routinely denigrated as 'lazy' or
'incorrect'.

More rarely, divergence can be lethal. When, in 1937, the
Dominican President, Rafael Trujillo, wanted to ethnically
cleanse his country of Haitians, he is said to have asked those
carrying out his orders to use a linguistic test to identify
them. In Dominican Spanish the word for parsley, *perejil*,
is spoken with a rolled 'r'. Haitians, who spoke French or
creole, found this pronunciation difficult. Soldiers carried
sprigs of parsley around with them and asked confused
civilians to tell them what it was. If they produced a French
'r', they were shot dead, on the assumption that they were
Haitian. Thousands were executed this way and the events
passed into history as the 'Parsley Massacre'.

A strange footnote to the story of sociolinguistic prestige and convergence comes from the annals of pop music.
Think of an early Beatles single – 1962's 'Please Please Me',

---

group, they will be identified by others – often in order to ridicule
them – as 'sounding gay'.

for example. When John, George and Paul growl 'Come on', do they sound British to you? When pronouncing the vowel in 'on', their tongues are shifted towards the front of the mouth, reflecting American pronunciation. Think of almost any Rolling Stones song, regardless of date. Mick Jagger's singing voice sounds nothing like his southern-British-accented speaking voice. Think of the 'can't' in 1965's 'I Can't Get No Satisfaction'. It's fronted, as with the Beatles' 'come on'. Think of the 'You make a grown man cry' refrain in 'Start Me Up', from 1981. It's a bluesy drawl.* Since the beginning of British pop, artists have tended to adopt features of American pronunciation, including rhoticity – pronouncing 'r's – which they wouldn't use in conversation.

The obvious assumption is that British pop started out trying to emulate an American export. There was no British equivalent and the Beatles, Stones and others adopted norms for pop singing which happened to be American.† A possible bonus was that they wouldn't be seen as alien by potential purchasers of their records in the United States. But as pop culture diversified, the picture changed. A backlash gathered pace in the late 1970s, with punk channelling the home-made, bottom-up impulse to wreck the system. Had Sid Vicious tried to sound American he would've been seen as inauthentic – something that was anathema to the punk ethos. English folk singers also kept their natural accents, perhaps because they identified with a separate native British folk tradition.

------

* Interestingly, in more self-consciously 'British' songs in the Stones' repertoire, like 'As Tears Go By' and 'She's a Rainbow', the American accent disappears.

† The linguist Franz Andres Morrissey has argued instead that some of the relevant accent features are more 'sonorous' and therefore easier to sing and to understand.

Nevertheless, an American accent has become the standard; those whose British accents make it unmolested into their recordings are seen as outliers. Outlier status can of course become lionised, as we saw in Martha's Vineyard – and a whole swathe of indie bands, from the Smiths to Blur and the Arctic Monkeys (the latter even wrote a song about musical phoniness, 'Fake Tales of San Francisco'), sing proudly in British English. But for those who don't need to make a play of authenticity, an American twang remains the norm. As talent shows like *The Voice* and *The X Factor* demonstrate, the convention has become pervasive, such that when ordinary people get up and sing pop music, even their own compositions, they unconsciously bend towards it. The rules of the genre have become so familiar that they're invisible.

Language on the brain

So far, in looking at aspects of speech that are outside our conscious control, we've focused on healthy adult speakers. We have seen how their social environment and aspirations can affect the kinds of sounds they produce. Unfortunately, there's a category of people for whom control of language slips beyond their grasp for very different reasons. These include people who have suffered brain damage, usually as the result of a stroke. During a stroke, blood supply to parts of the brain is interrupted, often due to a blood clot or haemorrhage. The area subject to injury, described as a lesion,* ceases to function.

Neurologists have known for years that damage to

---

* Lesions can also be due to a tumour, or other problems such as infection.

certain parts of the brain affects language, through observation of language-impaired patients and examination of their brains post-mortem. Most obviously, language problems occur when the left half of the cortex – the outer layer of the brain containing the 'little grey cells' – is damaged. So-called 'left-hemisphere dominance' for language occurs in 95–99 per cent of right-handed people and 70 per cent of left-handed people (the left hemisphere controls the right-hand side of the body and vice versa). One interesting effect of left-hemisphere dominance is that there is a right-ear advantage for speech sounds. When two different words are played at exactly the same time and volume in either ear, you remember only the one played in the right ear. If you're unlucky enough to need an operation to remove a tumour which involves work around your left hemisphere, doctors will awaken you once they're inside (the brain itself has no pain receptors, so you don't feel anything) and keep you talking to make sure they're not damaging your ability to speak.

Those with language problems following a brain injury are said to suffer from aphasia. But not all aphasics are the same. Broadly speaking, they fall into two camps: those who have trouble producing speech, and those who have trouble understanding it – known as expressive and receptive aphasia respectively. In order to check which type of aphasia they're dealing with, speech therapists ask patients to describe a picture as best they can. One that's commonly used is the 'cookie-theft picture', which is a simple line drawing showing a woman absent-mindedly doing the washing-up. Water overflows from the sink, while behind her a boy teeters on a stool he has used to reach into a cupboard containing a cookie jar. A girl stands beneath him, her hand outstretched to receive a cookie. The psycholinguist

Sergey Avrutin records a typical response by someone with expressive aphasia:

> Wife is dry dishes. Water down! Oh boy! okay. Awright. Okay ... Cookie is down ... fall, and girl, okay, girl ... boy ... um ...

One of the most famous expressive aphasics in history, Tan, was a patient of the nineteenth-century French doctor Paul Broca, who named the area of the brain that often seemed to be damaged in such cases (for a long time, they were said to have 'Broca's aphasia'). Broca described him thus: 'He could no longer produce but a single syllable, which he usually repeated twice in succession; regardless of the question asked him, he always responded: *tan*, *tan*, combined with varied expressive gestures. This is why, throughout the hospital, he is known only by the name Tan.'

In contrast, according to the neuroscientist Kathleen Baynes, quoted in Pinker's *The Language Instinct*, a patient with receptive aphasia described the cookie-theft scene like this:

> First of all, this is falling down, just about, and is gonna fall down and they're both getting something to eat ... but the trouble is this is gonna let go and they're both gonna fall down ... but already then ... I can't see well enough but I believe that either she or will have some food that's not good for you and she's to get some for her, too ... and that you get it and you shouldn't get it there because they shouldn't go up there and get it unless you tell them that they could have it. And so this is falling down and for sure there's one they are going to have for food and, and didn't come out right, the uh, the stuff that's uh, good for, it's not

good for you but it, but you love it, um mum mum . . . and
that so they've . . . see that, I can't see whether it's in there
or not.

Linguists are interested in these kinds of patients, because
they seem to offer evidence for the location of different aspects of linguistic ability in the brain. In expressive aphasics,
the area of the left hemisphere responsible for grammar –
called Broca's area – may appear to have been 'knocked
out'. Although people with this condition are more disabled
in terms of language production, their comprehension is
often good. In receptive aphasics, a second region of the left
hemisphere, called Wernicke's area after another nineteenth-
century physician, is often affected. These patients retain
the capacity for grammar and correct, fluent pronunciation, but often produce meaningless strings of words, and
have a lot of trouble understanding the things that are said
to them.

The 'geographical' approach to language in the brain,
though appealingly neat, is likely to be an oversimplifica-
tion. For one thing, we don't know whether it's a question
of different types of knowledge actually being stored in
Broca's and Wernicke's areas, or of these parts of the brain
being necessary merely for the execution of those capacities.

There is one area of 'healthy' language on which aphasia
has shed clear light, though. In 1874 the great neurologist
John Hughlings Jackson wrote a paper called 'On the
Nature of the Duality of the Brain'. It looked at the different contributions of the left and right hemispheres, and
was among the first investigations to suggest that the left
hemisphere might not be responsible for all aspects of language. Indeed, he observed that 'the right hemisphere is the
one for the most automatic use of words, and the left the

one in which automatic use of words merges into voluntary use of words'.

What he'd noticed was that patients with severe expressive aphasia were at times able to produce single words, shriek or interject and, most strikingly of all, swear. One twentieth-century analysis of recurring words produced by otherwise severely language-impaired English patients recorded the use of 'bloody hell', 'bloody hell bugger', 'fuck fuck fuck', 'fuck off', 'cor blimey' and 'oh you bugger', alongside less colourful but equally 'automatic' phrases such as 'funny thing funny thing', 'it's a pity pity pity' and 'now wait a minute'. In contrast to the rest of their speech, these words are produced fluently and with completely normal intonation and stress.

Hughlings Jackson explained this phenomenon by arguing that the left hemisphere controlled 'propositional' speech, while the right was in charge of 'non-propositional' language. A proposition, a statement that expresses something about the world that can be judged true or false, is produced when someone thinks and actively selects the appropriate words. The sentence just before this one expresses a proposition. Non-propositional speech would include exclamations like 'ouch' or 'bloody hell' or stock phrases used without thinking, like 'good evening'.

Hughlings Jackson's intuitions about the differences between the hemispheres were by and large borne out by modern researchers. In the 1970s, psychologists began to talk of the 'analytic' left hemisphere, contrasting it with the 'holistic' right. The left hemisphere was better able to break things down, to segment them, to assemble rule-bound sequences like propositional sentences. The right, in contrast, operated by grasping things all at once, as wholes, or 'gestalts'. This didn't just apply to language. Experimenters working with trained musicians found that they recognised melodies better in the right ear (which connects to the left hemisphere). Ordinary people showed the opposite pattern: a left-ear (and therefore right-hemisphere) advantage. This, they argued, indicated that experienced performers broke melodies down into their constituents as a matter of course, while the rest of us hear music more naively – as a seamless whole, without mentally identifying its component parts. There is also evidence that the right hemisphere is involved in assessing some of the emotional components of language, such as tone. Patients with right-hemisphere damage may appear to speak normally from the point of view of grammar and understanding, but they can sound 'flat' and fail to identify jokes or moods correctly in others. Some have even compared communication difficulties following a right-hemisphere stroke to those seen in people with autism or Asperger's syndrome.

Of course, it doesn't really make any sense to talk about the left hemisphere behaving in one way and the right in another. In reality they work together, and the myriad connections between different parts of the brain ensure that both 'analytic' and 'holistic' processing occur and are integrated, giving rise to the richness of our experience of the world.

However, for some people the 'split brain' is in fact a daily reality. In the 1960s, a group of epilepsy patients became the subject of some intriguing experiments. What they had in common was a severe form of the illness for which drug treatments had failed. All that was left was the 'nuclear option' of severing the nerves that connect the two hemispheres, with the aim of stopping the electrical frenzy of a seizure spreading. This last-resort surgery meant that in many cases the two halves of their brain became completely

cut off from one another. But, rather than being left profoundly disabled, or having to deal with dramatic changes
in their ability to think or speak, they seemed to recover
and be able to live mostly normal lives. Some of them even
said they felt just like they did before. It was only in the
laboratory that it became evident they were like no other
human beings on earth.

The scientists studying them were aware of the effects
of left-hemisphere damage on language, and of Hughlings
Jackson's ideas about the non-propositional nature of the
right side of the brain. Now here was a chance to see exactly
how each side performed linguistic tasks when cut off from
the other. The important thing was to be able somehow to
channel stimuli only to one or other hemisphere, without
any cross-contamination. A device called a tachistoscope allowed them to do this. Split-brainers were placed in front of
a screen, on which words or pictures flashed up. (It's crucial
at this point to remember that each hemisphere is in charge
of the *opposite* side of the body.) By asking them to focus
on a dot in the dead centre of the screen at all times, the
experimenters ensured that everything that flashed up on
the left side of the visual field was only processed by the
right hemisphere, and vice versa.

This resulted in some extraordinary findings. When words
like 'car' or 'tree' flashed up in front of the right eye (and
therefore the left hemisphere), subjects had no problem re-
peating the word back. When the word 'pan', for example,
was presented to the left eye (and therefore the right hemisphere), something different happened. The split-brainers
would deny having seen anything at all. But when asked
to close their eyes and let their left hand draw whatever
it wanted, they would draw a pan. Only when they then
looked at that with both eyes were they able to name it. In

other words, the right hemisphere had been unable to read the word, but nonetheless knew what it was and could represent it non-verbally. These findings showed that the right hemisphere was specialised for visuospatial tasks, and the left for language and problem-solving – but that the right did have some understanding after all.

In another test, patients were shown two pictures, one only to the left hemisphere and one only to the right. They were then asked to choose an appropriate, related picture from among a range placed on the table in front of them. One patient's left hemisphere was shown a chicken claw, while his right hemisphere was shown a snowy scene. Among the related pictures were a whole chicken and a snow shovel, clearly the correct associations for the flashed images. And, as expected, the patient picked the shovel with his left hand (his right hemisphere, remember, had seen the snow scene) and the chicken with his right hand. Then something bizarre happened. When he was asked why he'd made that choice, he said, 'Oh that's simple. The chicken claw goes with the chicken, and you need a shovel to clean out the chicken shed.' But no one had mentioned a chicken shed! Researcher Michael Gazzaniga, in his report of the experiment, says: 'Here, the left brain, observing the left hand's response, interprets that response into a context consistent with its sphere of knowledge, one that does not include information about the . . . snow scene. We called this left-hemisphere process the "interpreter".' In other words, the right hemisphere saw the snow scene, and picked out the shovel to go with it. But, having no knowledge of this context, the isolated left hemisphere created a story to make the choice of the shovel fit with what *it* knew.

Another of Gazzaniga's subjects, a young man known as PS, slowly acquired a very limited language capacity in his right hemisphere in the year or two after his operation. This was seen as a function of his brain's plasticity – its ability to adapt to the new situation by changing the distribution of linguistic ability. His test results were perhaps the most remarkable of all the split-brainers. In one experiment PS's right hemisphere was presented with a picture of a solitary man holding a gun. He haltingly responded 'gun' and 'hold-up'. After a second, he began to speak more fluently: 'He has a gun and is holding up a bank teller. A counter separates them.' But there was no bank teller and no counter. Why had PS first identified the picture successfully, but then gone on to describe things that weren't there? Gazzaniga and his colleagues were led to the inescapable conclusion that his right hemisphere had managed, with difficulty, to blurt out the correct words to describe the picture. His left hemisphere, despite not having seen any image, 'heard' those words and began to weave a plausible story around them. It was the great interpreter in action.

The split-brain patients offered a weight of evidence that language mainly resides in the left hemisphere. Certainly, it seems, syntax, understanding of plurals, the possessive, active and passive sentences and so on are left-brain abilities. However, the fact that a handful of these patients were able to demonstrate some capacity in the right hemisphere means the situation isn't completely cut and dried. Indeed, as the researcher Eran Zaidel put it, 'the level of competence of most components of right-hemisphere language falls between that of three- to six-year-old normal children'. And then there are those swearing aphasics. Why should swear words alone be almost perfectly preserved when the left hemisphere is badly damaged?

Linguistic analysis of swearing in normal people strongly suggests that these words are different from everyday language. For a start, they don't obey the same grammatical rules. 'Fuck', for example, can be used literally, as a verb. But when it's deployed as a bona fide swear word it simply *appears* to be a verb, while performing a rather different function. With a normal verb, like 'tell', it's possible to modify it using adverbs, time phrases and so on. So I can say 'Tell me', but also 'Tell me precisely' or 'Tell me by midday'. I can say 'Fuck me!' as an exclamation, but I can't say 'Fuck me precisely' or 'Fuck me by midday' without reverting to the literal meaning. 'Fuck me!' is an emotional signal rather than an example of propositional speech.

Swear words are preserved when the left hemisphere, the seat of language, is damaged, but the 'mute' right hemisphere is intact. They are uniquely emotional, uttered almost automatically in situations of surprise, anger or fear. They are linguistically different. Could it be that these words represent a separate kind of language altogether?

According to one view, emotional expressions, including swear words, have more in common with the cries of animals than with propositional speech. They form a link back to the howls and exclamations of primates, vocalisations that show others that the speaker (or howler) is angry, or perceives danger. From an evolutionary perspective, these vocalisations are obviously useful, particularly to social animals. The brain regions that mediate anger and fear don't sit in the left hemisphere of the cortex, but in the limbic system, a more primitive part of the brain that evolved before the cortex. These areas are not affected by the kinds of stroke that give rise to aphasia, and there is evidence that swearing involves an interaction between the limbic structures known as the basal ganglia and the right hemisphere. As a result, swearing is preserved in aphasics for whom only the left hemisphere is damaged.

The basal ganglia are not immune from strokes, however. One seventy-five-year-old patient who suffered lesions in this area showed an interesting pattern of language disruption: he was no longer able to utter many automatic, learned-by-rote phrases. He couldn't say familiar prayers or sing well-known songs. And, startlingly, he no longer swore. In fact, he couldn't say in what kind of situations different swear words might be used, and 'couldn't complete a curse'. The basal ganglia are believed to be important in the 'automatic execution of learned motor plans', and that would include highly practised verbal formulae.

One group of people who famously find themselves unable to control what comes out of their mouths are those who suffer from Tourette's syndrome. Not all Touretteers exhibit coprolalia* – the tendency to swear loudly and involuntarily at inappropriate moments – but it's one of the best-known symptoms of the illness. Scientists now believe that Tourette's results from a dysfunction of the basal ganglia, with involvement of the right hemisphere too. Sufferers are somehow unable to prevent the dramatic emotional vocalisations, but the rest of their speech is generally undisrupted. Again, it's hard to escape the conclusion that two quite separate systems are at work here, one automatic, the other voluntary.

It takes a village

Despite the fact that we tend to think of speech as being entirely within our conscious control, it's clear that language is a system so complex that complete mastery of

---

* The physician Gilles de la Tourette, after whom the syndrome is named, invented this term using the Greek words for 'dung' (*kopros*) and 'to speak' (*lalein*).

the message is beyond even the most skilful manipulator.

When we speak, we are not merely spitting out code to be deciphered, like some kind of human telex, blank and neutral. We also serve up a welter of inadvertent information. Even robots are forced to conform to this rule. Siri cannot be accentless, genderless or devoid of register. Americans know her as a friendly but firm, formal voice, using a prestige version of the English language derived from a post-war East Coast dialect. Likewise, when I speak I transmit information about my social class, my geographical origin, that I am probably male, what my age is, my health, whether or not I am under the influence of drugs, how I perceive my status in our interaction and my emotional state (I might be unable to stop myself swearing if I am angry or frightened). Some of this I can deliberately alter. A great deal of it I cannot.

It is strange to realise quite how much of what I communicate is involuntary. I might start out with the intention of sending an unambiguous message, but how others receive it will depend on a whole host of factors: whether they are more or less powerful than me, whether we are of the same ethnicity, whether I want to pull closer to them, psychologically or socially, whether I want to push them away. The salesclerks at Saks Fifth Avenue wanted to impress, to align themselves with the social standing of the store. The way they pronounced their 'r's fell into line with this social aim, often without them realising. The young people of Martha's Vineyard, if they wanted to stay on the island and despised incomers, identified with the fishermen, beacons of authenticity in a rapidly changing environment. Their vowels centralised as they did so, again without them necessarily being aware of it.

All of this underlines the fact, once more, that language

is not simply a system in the head, a piece of software complete all by itself, every so often taken out into the world and deployed in a way that has neatly circumscribed effects. It is a collective endeavour, a process of negotiation, a phenomenon whose structure emerges only when we interact with others.

The fact that we rarely think of it in quite those terms may be down to linguists' own version of the mind-body problem. This is the set of difficulties that arise when you consider the mental and the physical to be distinct, an idea associated with the philosopher René Descartes. According to this view, our thoughts and feelings, our ideas about the world, exist in a realm separate from the squishy matter of our bodies, the blood and the nerves and the sinew. In reality, the two are inseparable.

In linguistics, the great imagined separation is that between *langue* and *parole*. It was articulated most clearly by the father of the modern academic discipline, Ferdinand de Saussure. He used *langue* to describe an abstract system, the set of rules and the lexicon which combine in the brains of speakers to give rise to *parole*, which is language as it is put into practice. Parole is imperfect, often idiosyncratic. It is the raw material that linguists use to sketch out the boundaries of langue, which is, in theory, a crystalline ideal, 'English', 'French' or 'Spanish'. Underlying the very many different individual languages that people actually speak is a further ideal, the basic linguistic competence that we are supposedly born with: the genetically defined principles of language, which give rise to a set of parameters within which real languages range. For some modern linguists, this internal linguistic competence is the only object of real interest, and the only one amenable to truly scientific analysis. They believe that studying parole, in all its wildly complex variation

and imperfection, its socially and culturally influenced mani-
festations, is likely to get you into all sorts of trouble.

The division between langue and parole, or competence
and performance, has often hindered our ability to see language for what I believe it is: a medium that is formed as it is
used, a structure that is built by feedback effects, a road that
is paved at the same time as we walk it. We have seen how
the meaning of words operates this way: they are not stored,
airtight, in the heads of human beings or in dictionaries, but
thrashed out between people, in real time. Dictionaries are
always struggling to keep up. The meaning of individual
sounds follows a similar pattern. The height of vowels and
the precise articulation of consonants carry information,
and the nature of that information subtly changes as those
sounds are put out into the world.

That is not to say, however, that language only exists
externally. That would simply turn the langue–parole
arrangement on its head, rather than dissolve the boundary. We navigate the world using our brains, and social
interaction is no different. The way our brains are built
determines how we speak. The equipment can break down,
and as a result our capacity for effective communication can
be ruined. Aphasics find themselves hobbled when it comes
to making themselves understood in the usual way. Their
ability to deploy propositions is often hugely compromised;
but because communication is not entirely propositional,
they can still express themselves. Their ability to swear,
for example, may be preserved, since it appears to rely on
different parts of the brain than the rest of language. They
may convey emotion and frustration in the tone and pitch
of their speech, unless the emotional parts of their brain
are also damaged. And they will still transmit information
about likely gender, age and so on.

John Donne's phrase 'No man is an island entire of itself' is true of most aspects of life. In terms of language, it means we determine only part of what we communicate. Perhaps the illusion of autonomy is important to our sense of pride. But it's as well to be reminded that even in speech, the very fount of our self-expression, we're subject to forces we cannot entirely control.

CHAPTER 4

We can't talk to the animals

Language seems so natural to us humans that it's hard to come to terms with the fact it is ours alone. It does not feel consciously devised, artificial, but as much part of the order of things as trees growing or birds singing. But no other species seems to have anything like it.

Perhaps that's why, as children, it takes a while for us to understand that we can't talk to animals the way we talk to our family and friends. We cling to the idea that the creatures we encounter must understand us, or even have their own language. It is a strangely tenacious fantasy, and one that adults indulge: we hardly question the replacement of human characters with walking and talking animals in cartoons and fairy tales. On some level it feels right that these beings, not quite like us, but alive and warm to the touch and at times angry and sad, must also know what language is. The character of Dr Dolittle, who is taught to speak to all manner of animals by a polyglot parrot, captures the imagination because he possesses something we think we ought to have: the ability to get inside the minds of the cats and dogs and rabbits and horses which otherwise stubbornly refuse to surrender the secrets of their inner lives.

Actually, it's not just children who believe in animal language. In 2008, 1,129 adult pet owners in America were asked: 'When you speak to any of your pets, to what extent do you think they understand and comprehend you?' Some 19 per cent answered 'completely', and 43 per cent said 'mostly'. It works both ways: participants were also asked: 'When any of your pets attempt to communicate with you, by barking, meowing, or other means, how much do you feel you understand and comprehend what they are saying?' Again, 18 per cent said 'completely', and 49 per cent 'mostly'.

Not even the most devoted pet owner, however, could pretend that an exchange over treats is anything like a human conversation. Indeed, the uniqueness of human language is so startling that it has been marshalled as an argument for the existence of God, and for our status as his favoured beings. 'In the beginning was the Word,' says the gospel of St John (1:1). But the power of the word is limited to our creator and to us – it is not given to 'every creeping thing that creeps on the earth' (Genesis 8:17), with the notable exception of a talking snake in the Garden of Eden. It is the source of our mastery over the natural world. It enables us to record and share our experiences and plan new ones – something that has given rise to civilisation, science and technology. No other species has this power, reinforcing the sense that it is somehow God-given. As well as the marvels of the eyeball, creationists have language on their side.

The parrot, the bonobo and the gorilla

But then there's Alex. Alex was an African grey parrot, Dr Dolittle's assistant made flesh and feather. He has been described as having had the communication skills of a small child. And we're not talking one peck for yes, two pecks for no. Alex was trained to use English. Not to mindlessly repeat or even deploy a range of limited, fixed expressions; he responded to complicated questions. When asked to identify what an object presented to him was made of, after feeling it in his beak he could correctly answer 'wool', 'rock' or 'paper'. When shown many-sided geometric shapes, he could say how many corners they had – 'three corner' for a triangle, 'six corner' for a hexagon. He even coined new, meaningful phrases (he invented the expression 'rock corn' to describe dried corn, creating a metaphorical compound using words already available to him). He used language to deceive, asking for water when he wasn't thirsty because he had become bored with an experiment. He formed a bond with his keeper, the psychologist Irene Pepperberg. His last words were: 'You be good, see you tomorrow. I love you.'

And Kanzi. Kanzi is a bonobo who cannot speak,* but who uses a specially designed board that carries an array of symbols to communicate by pointing. There are symbols for nouns, like 'bowl' or 'tummy', and verbs like 'chase' or 'tickle', with which he can 'say' what he feels or wants to do. His understanding far exceeds what he is able to produce himself: Kanzi is said to respond to around 3,000 pieces of vocabulary. He can follow complex commands, including new and unexpected ones such as 'Would you put some grapes in the swimming pool' or 'Can you get the lettuce that's in the microwave'. These are not learned by rote. In one study he beat a two-and-a-half-year-old child in a rigorously controlled comprehension test of 400 sentences.

Like Kanzi, Koko the gorilla didn't speak – but had been trained in a special gestural code adapted from American sign language. Koko was taught 1,000 signs and was said

---

* The position of the bonobo's larynx means it has trouble producing the range of sounds a human can, whereas the parrot's vocal anatomy happens to allow it to mimic speech.

to understand about 2,000 English words. Like Alex, Koko demonstrated the ability to form new words, inventing a sign for 'ring' by combining the ones for 'finger' and 'bracelet', for example. She was also able to communicate about things that weren't in front of her. In one video on the Koko project's website, she apparently expresses frustration to Penny Patterson, the woman who has studied her since she was one, that she doesn't have a baby, using a cradling sign combined with a plucking sign.

There is a fair amount of controversy over what, exactly, the feats of these animals tell us. They have been meticulously trained to respond to, and produce, spoken words and signs. But are they anything more than performing monkeys? Noam Chomsky has said of attempts to teach human languages to other species: 'It's rather as if humans were taught to mimic some aspects of the waggle dance of bees* and researchers were to say, "Wow, we've taught humans to communicate."' In other words: teaching an animal to imitate language fails to tell you very much about either human or animal communication. It is an artificial process that sheds little light on natural abilities.

On the other hand, language and intelligence are so strongly linked in our imaginations ('dumb' is used to mean both mute and stupid) that sometimes we forget they aren't necessarily the same thing. Teaching language to animals could be seen as a way of 'translating' their intelligence into a form we can more readily understand. As a result, we learn more about the sophistication of their reasoning, about their emotional lives, about how their memories work. We really are able, like Dr Dolittle, to find out what they are thinking.

---

* The dance bees perform to tell each other the location of sources of nectar, of which more shortly.

This is all very interesting. But the question we want answered is whether language itself is as unique as cultural traditions such as the Bible – and our everyday experience of not being able to talk to cats and dogs – suggest. Do Alex, Kanzi and Koko offer evidence that our communication skills exist on a continuum? That, instead of the stark dividing line between humans and the rest of nature, there is something more like a sliding scale? To answer these questions we must first look at exactly how human language is supposed to differ from the ways in which animals express themselves. Because there's no doubt that animals do communicate.

Language by design

Forget the overachieving primates and parrots. Even insects need to exchange information. Bees are social, living in nests comprising thousands of individuals. They forage for food in the form of nectar from flowers, and bring it back to be put to use by the whole hive. Having arrived, they tell others where the food came from, so it can be harvested in much greater amounts than the bee that found it could manage alone. Given that bees don't have speech organs, this 'telling' looks rather alien.

As Chomsky noted, it takes the form of a dance. This dance has very clear rules – there's no room for improvisation. The bee 'waggles' in a straight line, the orientation of which in the hive indicates the direction bees must follow to reach a patch of flowers. She moves up if they need to fly towards the sun, and down if they must fly away from it. The precise angle of the line she follows is also the angle of the food source relative to the hive and the sun. The length and speed of the waggle give information about how far away it is.

Then there are sticklebacks. These tiny fish, like many animals, have a period of 'courtship' when a male of the species selects a female, and vice versa, to mate with. The process of selection involves fairly complex signalling back and forth. First of all, the male stickleback, who during the mating season develops a red patch on his belly and startling blue eyes, finds a female that looks as if she is full of eggs. He performs movements around her, called a 'zig-zag' dance since it involves thrusting towards her and then backing away. The female follows him down to a nest and, after the male points towards it, gets inside. She deposits her eggs after he rubs her tail-end with his nose. He pushes her out of the nest and covers the eggs with sperm.

Researchers identified the meaningful bits of this court-ship by substituting real sticklebacks with wooden models. By adding or removing features from the models, they found that the swelling of the female due to the eggs she was carrying was essential to attract a male; that the blue eyes of the male stickleback didn't matter, but the red patch on his belly did; and that the pointing motion was necessary to get the female to go into the nest.

So how do these forms of communication compare to our own? The great American linguist Charles Hockett first set out some of what he saw as 'key properties' of speech in 1958, in his *Course in Modern Linguistics*. He later called them 'design features', and they still represent a good summing-up of what makes language language. They include the use of the voice (the 'vocal-auditory channel'), as well as some more esoteric qualities, each of which we will explore in turn: *interchangeability, arbitrariness, displacement, duality of patterning, productivity* and *cultural transmission*. We share many of these design features with animals. But only humans possess the full set.

The most obvious difference between bees, sticklebacks and us is that they don't use sound. The fact that 'speech' and 'tongue' can be used as synonyms for language indicates the importance of the medium to our idea of language. But it's equally obvious that speech is not strictly necessary for language. We have writing, of course, but we also have sign language.

Does it matter at all that we happen to use our voices to produce language? Some believe that the way this part of our body has evolved gives us a distinct advantage over other primates. There are animals who make sounds not unlike our own voices. Gibbons, along with other kinds of ape, make 'calls' to send messages to their peers. These might be calls warning of a predator nearby, calls made during friendly play, or calls to let other gibbons know where they are. Vervet monkeys have a range of calls produced in response to different predators, such as pythons, eagles and leopards. But ape and monkey cries seem to be far less flexible than the human voice. As Sue Savage Rumbaugh explains in her account of bringing up the bonobo Kanzi, human beings benefit from a larynx that is 'descended' compared to our closest relatives. This results in a larger space between the larynx and the mouth, one which can be altered by the tongue to produce a huge array of vowels. The sharp angle of the human vocal tract allows us to close the nasal cavity off from the oral cavity – so-called 'velar closure', something apes can't do.* This means we can create

---

* The evolutionary biologist Tecumseh Fitch has argued that what stops non-human primates being able to speak is not their anatomy but their brainpower. He developed a computer model of a monkey's vocal tract based on X-rays of a macaque, and was able to make it say 'Happy holidays' and 'Will you marry me' in an eerie, squeaky voice. The challenge for Fitch, however, is to explain

the pressure necessary to generate so-called 'plosive consonants' (like /p/, /t/ and /k/), and the tongue and pharynx can
be put into various configurations to supply tens of other
kinds of consonants besides. Consonants are important
because they're very easy to tell apart from one another,
and can be combined with vowels in lots of different ways.
The rate of vibration of the larynx can also achieve changes
in pitch, which can be fed into meaning as 'tone'. All of
this enables the Taa language of Botswana, for example, to
have more than eighty consonants, twenty vowels and two
tones. Variety like that gives you a great deal more to play
with than a waggle and a direction, or a limited repertoire
of colour changes or fixed calls. And, unlike signing, sound
can be heard when the speaker is around a corner, or too far
away to be seen clearly.

What about *interchangeability*? This simply means that
whoever is communicating the message can also receive it. I
can ask 'How are you?' I can also hear the same phrase and
respond appropriately to it. Sentences in human language
are there to be used by anyone. This is certainly not the case
for sticklebacks – the female can't turn red. In bees, it's a bit
different: one bee can observe a waggle dance, go out and
find some more flowers, come back and do a dance itself.
But it's still only among workers that interchangeability is
allowed. Queens, who never forage for food, don't use the
'vocabulary' of the dance. With gibbons, the situation is a
little more familiar: males, females, young and old will all
emit cries warning of a predator.

Arbitrariness, on the other hand, is evident in the fact
that when we say 'dog' there's nothing 'dog-like' about the

---

why Koko and Kanzi's communicative prowess doesn't seem to be
restricted by their brainpower – only by their inability to speak.

combination of the three sounds /d/, /ɔ/ (or /ɑ/, in American English) and /g/. Their choice is arbitrary. You may feel that together they do sound rather doggy: solid, trustworthy, a bit wet-nosed. But consider that the word is *chien* in French, *sag* in Persian, and *valop* in Hungarinosc. That last one is made up, but it's not inherently absurd – because there's no reason dogs wouldn't be known as *valop* in some language or other. Most of human language is arbitrary. The opposite of linguistic arbitrariness is iconicity, where there is a physical relationship between the thing being communicated and the thing used to communicate it. The swollen belly of the female stickleback is not an arbitrary sign that she is ready to mate; it is a change produced by the fact that she has eggs in her belly. The direction of bee dance is calibrated precisely to reflect the angle of the patch of flowers relative to the hive and sun. Both are iconic, not arbitrary.*

Animal communication usually occurs right there in the moment: there's no question about the fact that the stickleback is ready to mate when it's red; when a vervet monkey issues its eagle call it means there's an eagle hovering somewhere above. Human language is different: we frequently use it to refer to things that aren't close by. They could be far away in terms of distance – 'My brother is at my sister's house' – or even in terms of time: 'I used to live there long ago'. This is called *displacement*. Apes don't use their calls to reminisce or to give information about a situation in a patch of forest a few miles downriver. This is where the

---

* In Chapter 2 we learned about onomatopoeic words like 'splash', 'thwack', 'hiss' and 'woof'. These are less arbitrary than most, meaning that they resemble to some extent the sounds they describe. But they are still partly arbitrary. In the Arab world dogs make the same sound as Western ones, but at least one way of rendering 'woof' in Arabic is *haw*.

bee waggle dance stands out: it's always displaced, as the flowers are always far away. Interestingly enough, some of the animals that have been taught language by humans do learn to engage in displaced communication – suggesting that they have the capacity to think, at least, about situations removed in space and time. Koko was able to refer to things that weren't in front of her, like her pet kitten. Alex employed time phrases like 'tomorrow'.

So far, none of our animal examples – from bees to stickle-backs and monkeys – exhibit all of the properties we see in human language: the vocal medium, interchangeability, arbitrariness and displacement. Even more significant than any of these, however, are two vital structural properties. We've seen that the use of the vocal tract enables a large 'phoneme inventory' – a plentiful supply of distinct vowels and consonants. This is useful because human speech is made of combinations of these units, which are meaning-less by themselves. A decent number of units means huge flexibility in combining them, and a great many possible words. This formal attribute is called *duality of patterning*, or double articulation. A male stickleback can't create a new message by combining its zig-zag dance with its point-ing movement. The red patch on its belly can't be separated and added to other gestures to mean something else. The bee dance consists of separate elements, but these each have meaning, and can only ever be combined in the same, highly limited way. In contrast, I can use the four phonemes /p/ /ɔ/, /t/ and /s/ to form five English words with completely differ-ent meanings – 'pots', 'stop', 'opts', 'spot' and 'tops'. Duality of patterning may have been taught to animals such as Alex, who altered the pronunciation of some syllables by a single phoneme, suggesting that he was indeed breaking words into their constituent parts – for example spontaneously saying 'cane' and 'shane' after using the word 'grain'. But in general, good evidence for it in the animal kingdom is rare. Birdsong contains smaller units that are used to build up strings of sounds. But since the meaning of these strings is highly restricted, falling mostly into just two categories – staking out territory or attracting a mate – it doesn't really bear comparison to the duality that exists in human language. Similarly, the rabbit-sized, rodent-like rock hyrax, found across Africa, has been shown to combine the units 'wail', 'chuck', 'snort', 'squeak' and 'tweet' in different ways to form songs, but the meaning of these is unclear – and may simply represent a 'signature' used by individuals to identify themselves over long distances. If that's the case, they only have as much meaning as a person's name does.

The second structural property that really seems to set language apart is *productivity*. Human beings can say things that have never been said before. They can invent new words, and do so all the time. Productivity is the ability to renew and change the medium of expression, to adapt it, incredibly swiftly, to altered circumstances. Monkeys do not seem to invent new calls. A vervet monkey will emit a leopard alarm cry when it sees a leopard. If it were exposed to a big cat not found in its range – say a tiger – it would probably emit the leopard alarm cry, and not come up with a different sound to distinguish leopards from tigers. But this is exactly what the words 'leopard' and 'tiger' do. Bees do not invent new buzzwords (pun intended), sticklebacks are trapped in the same cycle of enforced communication whether they like it or not. Only with actual biological evolution will their 'language' change – something that illuminates a crucial consequence of productivity, one that really sets human and most animal communication apart.

That's our final design feature, *cultural transmission*.

Whereas the abilities of animals such as the bee, stickleback or monkey are instinctive – the ability to waggle dance is not, so far as we know, learned, but hardwired – human languages are passed on through teaching and they differ hugely between groups of people. New words, new ways of saying things, like 'hive mind', 'alt-right', 'internet of things' can be arrived at via productivity and disseminated; and it is culture that determines which ones survive and thrive. We are not fated to say 'froyo' by our genetic inheritance. The cultural evolution of language, made possible by productivity and learning, is one of its most distinctive attributes.

Do any animals have this kind of culturally transmitted knowledge of communication? Do they have any form of cultural transmission at all? It's worth pausing here to define 'culture'. For our purposes, it's the difference between what is inherited and instinctive, common to all members of a species, and what is passed on through learning, varying from community to community. Using that definition, the answer to the second question is, definitively, yes. Groups of wild chimpanzees have been shown to crack nuts in different ways – some consistently using wooden tools, others using stone ones. This variation in behaviour cannot be explained by genes, since the chimpanzees are genetically identical. Instead, one chimpanzee must have arrived at an effective way to crack nuts, which it taught to those closest to it, who then spread it to the rest of the troop. Elsewhere, another chimpanzee arrived at another method, which spread among *its* peers. This is culture – just as British people tend to use electric kettles to boil water, while Americans use stove-top ones.

Cetaceans – the class of aquatic mammals that includes whales and dolphins – have also been shown to display the hallmarks of culture. Male humpback whales produce songs during the breeding season. All the males in a given breeding group sing virtually the same song, but that song changes over the course of the season, with those changes spreading until they affect the whole pack – a sign that horizontal cultural transmission is occurring.

Among whales, as with chimpanzees, culture can also take the form of useful new techniques. In 1980, off the coast of Maine, scientists observed a new form of feeding among humpbacks, in which they slapped their tails hard onto the surface of the ocean before diving down to scoop up their prey. This is thought to help stop fish from jumping out of the water and escaping. By 1989, the technique had been adopted by around half of the population, suggesting that whales were observing how effective it was and imitating the ones who first used it.

Killer whales, which live in stable, matrilineal 'pods', produce a range of distinct calls – up to seventeen, according to one study – that are recognised by all members. We don't know what they mean, but we do know that they differ from those of other, genetically identical groups. In other words, different pods have different 'dialects'. They change over time, just like human dialects. These changes are the kind you would expect to result from cultural transmission rather than genetic evolution – which is to say that they happen quickly, and are spread by learning.

Inside the house that Jack built

Cultural transmission, born of productivity (in order to have new things to teach, you have to be able to generate new things), might be what separates human from animal communication most dramatically – even though, as we've seen, there's evidence that a select few animals engage in it.

But many linguists put the emphasis on instinct, and argue that the hard border between human and animal communication is to be found in our genes. They home in on one aspect of grammatical productivity and argue that it has only evolved in human beings. It's called 'recursion'.

Recursion is a property of some of the rules that govern grammar – apparently all grammars, not just the grammar of English, French or Thai. It means that there is no 'longest' sentence in a language – you can just keep adding to it. This sounds complicated, but, oddly enough, perhaps the first place we encounter it is in nursery rhymes:

> This is the house that Jack built.
> This is the malt that lay in the house that Jack built.
> This is the rat that ate the malt
> That lay in the house that Jack built.

Layer piles upon layer, until you have:

> This is the horse and the hound and the horn
> That belonged to the farmer sowing his corn
> That kept the rooster that crowed in the morn
> That woke the judge all shaven and shorn
> That married the man all tattered and torn
> That kissed the maiden all forlorn
> That milked the cow with the crumpled horn
> That tossed the dog that worried the cat
> That killed the rat that ate the malt
> That lay in the house that Jack built.

And so on, ad infinitum. 'The House That Jack Built' is a rather extreme example of recursion that uses embedding, in which clauses are placed inside a larger clause, and that process is repeated.* More prosaic instances can be found in everyday language: 'I'm going to give you the key' can be extended to 'I'm going to give you the key that David gave me', or 'I'm going to give you the key that David gave me that he thought he'd lost'.

One way to define recursion is to think of grammatical rules as being a bit like recipes, or formulas. One of these formulas is that to make a sentence or clause (S), you need to combine a noun phrase (NP) and a verb phrase (VP). In the sentence 'Kim admires Sam', 'Kim' is the NP and 'admires Sam' is the VP. Fairly straightforward. But what if I add a bit onto the beginning? 'Priya thinks Kim admires Sam'. Here, I've made a fresh S by introducing an additional NP ('Priya') and creating a new VP ('thinks Kim admires Sam'). The original NP and VP are now subsumed in this new VP. The ability to embed structures like this, to place

---

* I was going to use a couple of further examples here, but it turns out that they don't involve recursion. All the same, I couldn't resist a footnote. What they *are* examples of is something called 'use/mention ambiguity' in which a phrase, usually a title, contains the same words as the phrase it's embedded in, to bizarre effect. The fact that it's being mentioned rather than used is made clear by inverted commas. In the comedy series *30 Rock*, the singer Angie Jordan, who has a new record out, announces: 'My single, "My Single Is Dropping", is dropping.' Similarly, in the British sitcom *The Vicar of Dibley*, sweet and simple Alice gives the Reverend Geraldine her views on the margarine brand I Can't Believe It's Not Butter, which she reckons does indeed taste very much like the real thing. She explains that she's been to a neighbouring village to sample a different brand, and found it just as good. She sums this up in the following way: 'I can't believe the stuff that is not I Can't Believe It's Not Butter is not I Can't Believe It's Not Butter. And I can't believe that I Can't Believe It's Not Butter and the stuff that I can't believe is not I Can't Believe It's Not Butter are both, in fact, not butter.' Thanks to Doug Arnold of the University of Essex for pointing this out.

them inside each other like Russian dolls, is what recursion is all about.

The formula for 'Priya thinks Kim admires Sam' could be written as follows:

S = NP + VP	Priya + thinks Kim admires Sam
VP = V + S	thinks + Kim admires Sam
S = NP + VP	Kim + admires Sam

Recursion is present in any formula *where the same element appears on both sides of the equals sign*. A sentence can contain a verb phrase, which can contain a sentence. It is what allows a potentially infinite set of expressions to be generated from a finite set of symbols.* There's no need to stop at Priya. I could say 'Fran believes Priya thinks Kim admires Sam', or 'Helen said Fran believes Priya thinks Kim admires Sam'. And so on.

Why is this important? Recursion is, as we have now seen, the engine of one particular form of productivity. And productivity is one of the key attributes of human language – absent from sticklebacks, bees and gibbons. For linguists like Chomsky, recursion is the piece of cognitive infrastructure that separates people from animals and gives rise to all human languages, which differ by accident of development in myriad ways, while all sharing that one vital attribute. Recursion, it is argued, has only come about in humans, and is now transmitted to children by their parents genetically, meaning that every baby has the inherent ability to learn productive syntax.†

---

* This is what Chomsky, in an echo of Hockett, calls the 'basic property' of human language.
† The ability, mind you, but not the competence. When Chomskyan linguists say that language is innate, they do not mean the baby

Chomsky doesn't throw out the animal communication baby with the recursive bathwater, by the way. In a seminal paper, he joined forces with evolutionary biologists Marc Hauser and Tecumseh Fitch to argue that human linguistic ability can be characterised in two ways, one more general, one more specific. They call these the FLB (faculty of language – broad sense) and the FLN (faculty of language – narrow sense). FLB includes a 'sensory-motor system' – which comprises the ability to produce words, calls or gestures – and a 'conceptual-intentional' system which allows meaning to be mapped onto those words, calls or gestures. FLB also incorporates a computational element, a rules-based system that governs the combination of symbols and therefore allows for grammatical productivity. This computational element is the FLN, and at its core is recursion.

----

enters the world able to speak, like a kitten enters the world able to mew. Any child that is not exposed to the right cues – its parents talking to it – will not say anything. In the absence of a stimulus to awaken the recursive magic, the child will be mute. In other words, a capacity for language exists, but remains latent until it is triggered by the environment. What happens if there is barely any exposure to language at all? In 1970, it emerged that the father of one American girl, Genie, 'had strapped her into a handmade straitjacket and tied her to a chair in a silent room of a suburban house since she was a toddler. He had forbidden her to cry, speak or make noise and had beaten and growled at her, like a dog.' After she was taken into care, it was shown she could use isolated words, such as 'mother' and 'go', and, with tuition, her vocabulary improved vastly. But she was reportedly unable to speak in full sentences, and couldn't ultimately be taught to do so. This led some to conclude that being exposed to language early is vital for normal development. Without input during a time-limited 'sensitive period' – roughly, up to the age of ten – it becomes impossible to handle syntactic rules with the ease those of us raised with language enjoy.

Hauser, Fitch and Chomsky admit that aspects of FLB can probably be identified in the animal kingdom. In fact, we already know that many different kinds of animal make use of symbolic representation deployed via sensory-motor means – for example, vervet monkeys and their various calls. What they insist on is that FLN has only evolved in humans, and is what marks out our way of communicating from all others.

The vital question now becomes: is there any evidence of FLN, which is to say, of recursion, in non-human animals?* This is a fiercely contested topic. It has spawned a host of investigations into such things as starling, tamarin and parrot intelligence. Starlings, for example, were found in one 2006 study to respond to the recursive structuring of a sequence of rattles and warbles; but critics have argued this is merely an experimental artefact (they claim that the starlings were not responding to an embedded underlying structure, but to its linear surface expression). Cotton-top tamarins were tested, but failed. Alex the African grey parrot succeeded in a test that incorporated a simple form of recursion, but not multiple embedding.

---

* Another question is: are there any human languages that do without recursion? Daniel L. Everett argues that one spoken in the Amazon rainforest – Pirahã – doesn't use recursion at all. His evidence has been widely disputed, and Chomsky says that even if it was true that recursion was absent from Pirahã, the fact that its speakers have learned Portuguese, which no one doubts is recursive, suggests they have the brainpower necessary for it, and that Everett's claims don't undermine his theory of a universal genetic recursive ability. 'If some tribe were found in which everyone wears a black patch over one eye, it would have no bearing on the study of binocular vision in the human visual system,' he told the *New York Times*. Notably, no one claims that Pirahã does not possess productivity at all – inventing new words, for example, does not require recursion.

It's probably fair to say that the jury is still out, with some researchers arguing that recursion has become an obsession of those determined to find a hard border between human and animal communication. They argue that the extent to which animals are deemed strangers to recursion depends on how it is defined. Irene Pepperberg, for example, who trained and observed Alex for many years, believes recursion is a 'sticky wicket'. 'If anyone other than Chomsky had made this claim,' she says, 'it might have been ignored. Whether only humans can use recursion is still an open question, but several researchers have demonstrated that recursion is not innately specified and needs to be taught.' Pepperberg points to a paper by Professor Janellen Huttenlocher that apparently shows how children who are not exposed to recursive sentences do not use such constructions. That is not a killer blow to Chomsky's argument, however, because he merely posits that humans' *capacity* for recursion is what differentiates them from animals; he does not discount the possibility of this capacity lying dormant in certain circumstances.

Alex is now dead, but Pepperberg believes he would have been up to the task of deciphering recursive sentences. 'I'm guessing that with some ... training on contrastive sentences like "Take the wool that hit the wood that is in the cup" versus "Take the wool that hit the key that is in the cup", Alex would have done just fine.' But she anticipates that even this would not have satisfied her detractors. 'One can define recursion as demonstrating an understanding of something as complex as "This is the cat that bit the rat that ate the cheese that lived in the house that Jack built," so that no non-human could succeed.' Or, she says, it can be defined so that Alex's correct response to the question 'What shape is the object that is wood and blue?' passes the test.

In the experiment testing starlings, the birds were

exposed to forms of embedding so complex that humans themselves would have great difficulty understanding them. In centre embedding, a subclause is placed in the middle of a sentence, like this: 'John, whom Emily loves, adores Jane'. As the psychologist Michael C. Corballis has pointed out, double embedding would result in a sentence like 'John, whom Emily, whom Tom loves, loves, adores Jane'. The triple embedding on which the starlings were tested would be equivalent to the human sentence 'John, whom Emily, whom Tom, whom Caroline loves, loves, loves, adores Jane'. At this point, the testing for 'recursion' as the dividing line between human and animal language begins to seem absurd.

In a league of our own

The search for an answer to the question of why animals are mute, and we can speak, has become a little holy-grail like. It demands a single, clear explanation, and those explanations have ranged from the religious to the scientific, recursion being only the latest candidate. But could we learn to live with a fuzzier boundary? Whether recursion truly is unique to humans is an ongoing challenge for researchers. If it is shown to exist in animals, it is likely to be fairly simple, so that the burden of computation is not great. Because one thing we do know is that animals have less complex central processing units – brains – than we do.

And perhaps this is a more useful way of thinking about things – as a difference in degree of complexity. We know that the higher animals, like Kanzi the bonobo and Koko the gorilla, have exhibited childlike comprehension and production of language, despite being adult members of their species. The practical difficulties of studying whales and dolphins means that we will be hard-pressed to find experimental evidence that clearly defines cetacean intelligence – but it would not be surprising if it were around the level of a human child too.

So why is human communication so much more sophisticated? We know that it is highly productive – that we can easily invent new names for things, or devise sentences that go on for ever – and that the rules and words of any given language are culturally transmitted. Without this productivity, our system of communication would be unable to change, and its applications would be extremely limited. We would only have at our disposal the tiny number of calls or cries – like laughter, tears or yelps of pain – understood by others at an instinctive level.

Our extraordinary productivity and the cultural transmission it enables are made possible by advanced memory and computational abilities, themselves a function of our brainpower. In this sense, at least, they are biologically determined. We have billions more neurons than any other mammal – approximately 16.3 billion, compared to 9.1 billion in a western gorilla and 12.8 billion in a minke whale. This processing power enables us to store large amounts of information, and make complex calculations such as putting ourselves in the place of others to understand their intentions. That, combined with the extremely flexible medium of expression that the vocal tract provides us with, allows us to negotiate common symbols, and rules for their combination, among our peers. With these in place, an external language emerges, of which the community as a whole is the guardian. It can be expanded vastly, since no one person needs to hold all of it in his or her head. Its evolution takes place separately from that of the biological substrates that make it possible – and advances along cultural lines.

As we've seen, there's definitely evidence of cultural transmission among animals – monkeys and their nut-cracking techniques – and there may also be limited evidence of productivity in communication. (Whales tweak their songs, composing new calls over time. The problem is, we don't really know what the different parts of the call signify, so it's hard to tell whether the changes carry a significant weight of meaning.)

But even if whales exhibit both productivity and cultural transmission in communication, the difference between the way they talk to one another and the way we do is still stark. Human language, with its roots in our powerful cognition, has escaped our brains to become a collective phenomenon, encompassing enormous complexity and idiosyncrasy. There is a huge variety of languages across the world, from Caucasian ones that have nineteen cases to languages that utilise click consonants and ones where the grammar changes if a person's mother-in-law is present.* Language comes in the form of poetry, novels, slogans, graffiti and textspeak. It is a wheeling, dazzling display with a life of

---

* In many Australian languages there exist elaborate mechanisms for dealing with 'taboo' relatives – members of the family whom it is considered disrespectful or inappropriate to address directly or in everyday language (for example, mothers-in-law). These mechanisms are known as 'avoidance styles'. They include sets of alternative words to be used when the mother-in-law is present, and alternative pronouns to be used when referring to them. In Dyirbal, a language spoken in northern Queensland, the word for a red-bellied lizard is *byunyjul*, but when a mother-in-law is present *jijan* must be used. In Luritja, spoken in Western Australia, 'you' is normally *nyuntu*, but when using the language's avoidance style it becomes *ngulyu*. According to the linguist Robert Dixon, 'If someone mistakenly used the wrong style they would be covered with shame ... anyone who persistently or deliberately flouted avoidance conventions might well be speared.'

its own. This is what animals lack, and humans have – the higher efflorescences of communication in all their beautiful variety.

But are we able talk to the animals? Why not ask Kanzi and Griffin, Alex's successor in Pepperberg's laboratory? Because you can.

CHAPTER 5

You can't translate this word

Goya. A small word, but one that contains multitudes. It is one of those mythic beasts, the 'untranslatables', the foreign words that supposedly lack any equivalent in English. Lists of them spread virally online. Someone may have shared one with you on social media: it might have included *utepils*, *sgrìob* and *saudade* – of which more later. But for now, let us examine *goya*.

Urdu speakers know the meaning of *goya* in their bones; for the rest of us it is a mystery. When a native son or daughter of Pakistan hears it, whole worlds are conjured – scenes of tales told around a fire as the smoke rises into the crisp air of the Hindu Kush, of being dandled on a grandmother's knee, of being told a cautionary tale by a village elder as a child and remembering it for the rest of your days. '*Goya*', as one breathless internet account has it, 'is an Urdu word that refers to the transporting suspension of disbelief that happens when fantasy is so realistic that it temporarily becomes reality . . . usually associated with good, powerful storytelling.'

Goya. Almost a mystical experience in itself. But look it up in a dictionary and you'll find 'as if', 'as though' and 'as it were'. One Urdu speaker I asked translated it as 'as though'; another, 'and so'. It's used to make or clarify a point – the sentence might be structured as 'and so (*goya*), as I was saying'. Based on this, it seems to function as a discourse marker, which the Cambridge *A–Z of Spoken and Written Grammar* defines as 'words or phrases like "anyway", "right", "okay", "as I say", "to begin with". We use them to connect, organise and manage what we say or write or to express attitude.' That's it. No mystical campfires here. No 'transporting suspension of disbelief that happens when fantasy is so realistic that it temporarily becomes reality', unless the Hindu Kush you're thinking of is the strain of cannabis. Whoever came up with this translation even seems to have got the grammar wrong: their explanation suggests a (very) abstract noun, whereas *goya* is an adverb, formed on the stem of a Farsi verb meaning 'to speak'. (In that language, the ultimate source of the Urdu word, *gooya* means 'as it were', 'as you would say' or 'apparently'.)

The lure of the exotic

So how did this happen? There is something deeply seductive about the idea that other languages contain codes that are impossible to crack, as I know from first-hand experience. When I was a kid, I used to sit in the hallway and listen to my dad speak Farsi on the phone to his relatives in Tehran. I had no idea what he was saying, and nor did my brother and sister. But we learned to recognise certain phrases, two in particular: *tarjimmykonee* and *azbezutumkay*. We used to repeat them, over and over. Like 'abracadabra', they seemed to be incantations. Dad was a magician. When, as an adult, I learned what these phrases actually were, I realised the extent to which we had filtered them through our English-attuned ears, distorting the sounds and syllables. And the meaning was more prosaic than I imagined, too. *Tavajoh* *mikonee* can be translated as 'Are you paying attention?', a conversational filler like 'Do you see?' or 'D'you know what I mean?'. *Arz be hozuretan ke* is a polite stock phrase similar to 'May I say, . . .'*

I was a child, but adults should know better than to believe that other cultures speak in spells. The concept of 'untranslatable words' preserves the idea that the world can never be fully mapped out and expunged of mystery. That's a comforting thought. It keeps alive the possibility of escape – of something surviving far beyond our everyday experiences.

It is also an easy replacement for the hard tasks of empathy and understanding. The campfire in the mountains is a beautiful fantasy of Pakistan that does two things: it allows us to imagine that we don't have very much in common with the average Pakistani. It puts them at one remove, which fits with the strange stories we hear about them: that they're by turns esoteric, warlike, fanatical, eccentric and primitive. It also saves us having to learn what the circumstances of life might actually be like there. The difficulty of getting credit in order to afford a washing machine, the poor production values of daytime TV. If all that seems fairly harmless, think about it this way: when you believe people are unfathomable because they speak a different language, you're just as capable of thinking that they're inferior or evil, instead of charming or other-worldly.

The cult of untranslatables goes beyond orientalism. They spread, meme-like, with the same misleading explanations repeated. Often, they hew suspiciously closely to stereotypes about the culture in question. Cheerfully eccentric Nordic

---

* It uses the exceptionally courteous form of 'you', *hozuretan* ('your presence'), and literally means 'A petition to your presence that . . .'

types, when they're not in the sauna, like nothing better than *utepils*: 'Norwegian for to sit outside on a sunny day enjoying a beer'. How quaint. And how informative about Scandinavian culture. Except, *utepils* isn't a verb, it's a compound noun, from *ute* meaning 'outside' and *pils*, 'beer' (after the Czech town Plzen, which produces one popular type). So it means 'outside-beer' – a concept hardly foreign to British people, whose pubs frequently come equipped with beer gardens.

Author Bill Bryson tells us that 'Gaelic speakers of Scotland . . . have a word for the itchiness that overcomes the upper lip just before taking a sip of whisky. (Wouldn't they just?) It's *sgrìob*.' The modern dictionary definition is in fact a scratch, or scrape. Bryson was probably columnist Allan Brown's source when he wrote in *The Times* of 'the Gaelic word describing the tingle of anticipation felt in the upper lip before drinking whisky'. He went on: 'The fact that Gaelic has a six-letter word for this while English has a twelve-word phrase reveals a lot about Gaelic ways and priorities.' The linguist Geoffrey K. Pullum wrote this withering response to Brown's column for his website Language Log:

> I happen to know a one-syllable word (*turd*) for a piece of excrement shaped by its expulsion from the anal sphincter, but that doesn't reveal a lot about my ways and priorities. It is a completely meaningless and useless random factoid about the lexicon of the language I happened to grow up speaking. That lexicon also contains *scrum*, *buttercup*, *ogre*, *bong*, and *thorium*. If you try to form an impression of my ways and priorities from such things you're a moron.

Is Bryson at least right about the meaning, though? His definition can be traced back to an illustrative example in a dictionary of Gaelic compiled by Robert Archibald Armstrong and published in – wait for it – 1825. The primary definition here is still 'scratch, scrape'. It can be used, we are told, to describe 'an itching of the lip, superstitiously supposed to precede a feast or a kiss from a favorite'. The phrases given are *sgrìob poige* (itching preceding a kiss) and *sgrìob dibhe* (itching preceding a dram). Given that *dibhe* just means 'drink', we might gloss *sgrìob dibhe* as 'drink-itch', a perfectly translatable, if idiomatic, term which brings to mind something like 'gagging for a drink'. I think it's a stretch to define any part of that expression as uniquely, mysteriously English.

Another popular untranslatable is *Age-otori*, Japanese for 'the state of looking worse after getting a haircut'. It's sometimes quoted as *Age-tori*, which caused confusion for my Japanese informant because that is one way of saying 'fried chicken'. *Age-otori*, on the other hand, is something modern Japanese people have to google, because they never use it. There's a reason for that. The *Kojien* dictionary tells us that it has been used with the meaning of 'formally styling one's hair for a coming-of-age ceremony, with the contrary effect of making oneself look worse than before', but notes that this is attested in *The Tale of Genji*, a literary work from the eleventh century that describes in detail the mores and ceremonies of the Japanese imperial court. What does 'untranslatability' mean exactly when the phrase requires explanation to speakers of the source language?

Then there are words like *saudade*, which most patriotic Portuguese speakers will be happy to explain is untranslatable. They often go on to immediately translate it as 'a nostalgic feeling of missing someone or something you love'. This, granted, is not a single, pithy word, but it's a concept that feels anything but alien. You could also argue that 'homesickness' in English, while it mostly refers to missing the place you usually live, can be used metaphorically with a much wider meaning. The phrase 'homesick for yesterday', if a little whimsical, doesn't sound nonsensical to me at all. (Tobias Becker, a historian of popular culture, has used it as the title of a research project on nostalgia.) The short-story collection by Ottessa Moshfegh, 'Homesick for Another World', has a title that conveys something more than simply the desire to be where you once were. *Saudade*'s scope might actually be more restricted than 'homesick' – one native Portuguese speaker assured me it can only be used about things that have been experienced – so '*saudade* for another world' wouldn't make sense.

Grammar blindness

Insisting on a word-to-word correspondence in order to deem something 'translatable' throws up some technical problems too. As we've seen, figuring out what constitutes a word can be tricky. We saw in Chapter 2 that, in English, something which is to all intents and purposes a single word, like 'baggage handler', can take the form, in writing, of two separate ones. That's not the half of it: in many languages multiple words take the form of a single unit. Turkish is a prime example of this. It has what linguists call 'agglutinative morphology'. That is, units of the language combine by sticking together (in English we're used to 'isolating morphology' – where the component parts are generally separated out). Linguist Larry Trask wrote about the monumental Turkish word *Avrupalılaştırılama-yanlardansınız*, which means 'You're one of those we can't make a European out of'. *Avrupa* is 'Europe', *-lı* is 'from', *laş* is 'become', *tır* is 'cause', *ıl* is a passive marker, and so on. This is not just the result of eliminating the gaps between a group of words – a printing convention, if you like. Many of those particles, such as *-li*, simply never appear on their own. *Avrupalılaştırılamayanlardansınız* is in one meaningful sense a word (one for which I'm confident no corresponding single word exists in English), but it's also very much a sentence. Sometimes the mystery is simply a question of the language having different plumbing to the one you're used to.

In fact, ditching an Anglocentric view of the word is enough to fell many of the internet untranslatables. An example is the Arabic *ya'aburnee* (more correctly *tu'burni* – 'you bury me'). One blogger describes this as 'a declaration of one's hope that they'll die before another person because of how difficult it would be to live without them', commenting breathlessly that 'You don't get words like this in Western languages do you?' Except that it's less a word than an expression: the subject and object in Arabic can be represented by a prefix and suffix on the verb. More properly, it's an idiom, a stock phrase whose meaning cannot really be deduced from its components without cultural knowledge. Western languages like English are replete with idioms, such as 'spend a penny', 'break someone's heart', 'match made in heaven' and so on. The fact that the images used are unique to English doesn't make them untranslatable: the meaning of 'spend a penny' ('go to the toilet') can easily be conveyed in other languages. Instead they tell us something about the culture and history of the people who use the language, much like etymologies do – for example, the preference for euphemism when describing bodily functions encountered in Chapter 2, and the fact that public toilets were once coin-operated.

The grammar-blindness that might lead someone to

proclaim the 'untranslatability' of *Avrupalılaştırılamayan-lardansınız* is the source of another common myth, which takes the form: X has N words for Y. One recent example is the idea that in Albania – home to a population of the Mediterranean phenotype, typically with thicker, darker hair than their northern European counterparts – there are twenty-seven words for 'eyebrow'. So far, so bizarre. They don't just look hairy, they're obsessed with hair! Author Adam Jacot de Boinod writes: 'The attention the Albanians apply to facial hair they also apply to eyebrows, with . . . words including pencil-thin (*vetullkalem*), frowning (*vetullvrenjtur*), plucked (*vetullhequr*), knitted (*vetullrrept*), long and delicately shaped (*vetullgajtan*), thick (*vetullor*), joined together (*vetullperpjekur*), gloomy (*vetullngrysur*), or even arched like the crescent moon (*vetullhen*).' What you'll notice is that all of those words contain the element *vetull*, which means 'eyebrow'. In Albanian you can form adjectival compounds by joining two words together, just as we can in English. Think about compounds like 'long-legged', 'short-legged', 'bandy-legged', 'hairy-legged', 'shaven-legged', 'scrawny-legged'. It is as absurd to say that Albanian has twenty-seven words for 'eyebrow' as it is to say that English has (at least) six words for 'legs'.

The untranslatability memes and the 'X has N words for Y' view of unfamiliar languages have in common a very powerful idea. It's the notion that speakers of Albanian, Japanese or Urdu see the world differently. They interpret reality in ways that are difficult for us to even conceive of. At its core this is an argument for linguistic determinism: the idea that the world looks different according to whichever language you speak. If there even is an objective reality, it's filtered and altered by the medium of expression. This is the 'Sapir–Whorf' hypothesis.

The minds of others

In his 1950 essay 'An American Indian Model of the Universe', Benjamin Lee Whorf wrote:

> I find it gratuitous to assume that a Hopi who knows only the Hopi language and the cultural ideas of his own society has the same notions, often supposed to be intuitions, of time and space that we have, and that are generally assumed to be universal. In particular, he has no general notion or intuition of *time* as a smooth flowing continuum in which everything in the universe proceeds at an equal rate, out of a future, through a present, into a past.

In other words, those Native Americans of Arizona who speak Hopi simply do not see themselves as standing at a point in time, with things to come ahead of them and all that has happened behind them. Instead, they deal only with 'the manifest' and 'the unmanifest', that which is evident, experienced or seen, and that which might be in store, or is the product of imagination or opinion.

Whorf was an American fire-insurance engineer and sometime mystic who became interested in the structure of language because he thought linguists might be able to decode the Scriptures and reveal their hidden message. In an application for a fellowship to help fund the study of Mexican languages, he wrote: 'With the ultimate development of these researches will come manifestation of the deeper psychological, symbolic and philosophical sense contained in the cosmology of the Bible, the starting point and original inspiration of these studies.' Though he never became an academic, he took courses at Yale under the great anthropologist Edward Sapir – famed for his descriptions of Native American languages – and specialised in Hopi, spoken at the time by no more than a few thousand inhabitants of Arizona. His interest was captured in particular by the nature of the Hopi verb system, which differs markedly from English. Where English would have 'he is running', Hopi, Whorf says, simply has '*wari* (running, statement of fact)'. 'He will run' would be rendered as '*warikni* (running, statement of expectation)'. Whorf also notes that Hopi speakers call anything that flies by the same name, *masa'ytaka*, whether it's a dragonfly, a pilot or an aeroplane, and so on. The overall message is that they do not segment time, or the world, in the way we do.

A diagram from Benjamin Whorf's 1940 essay
'Science and Linguistics'

Whorf differentiated the apparently peculiar outlook of the Hopi from that bequeathed us by Indo-European languages, which he lumped together as 'Standard Average European' (SAE). He thought that notions SAE speakers believed to be self-evident – such as various aspects of time, velocity and matter – were not in fact universal. 'Among the peculiar properties of Hopi time,' he says, 'are that it varies with each observer, does not permit of simultaneity, and has zero dimensions – i.e. it cannot be given a number greater than one. The Hopi do not say, "I stayed five days," but "I left on the fifth day".'

Many things we take for granted are therefore merely the effects of peering through the distorting lens of SAE. We don't notice these effects, because absolutely everything we perceive is mediated by English, and we have nothing to compare it to. For most of human existence, the idea of quantifying the force of gravity would have seemed absurd: things fall down because that's just the way the world is. Only by walking on the moon does one perceive that gravity is contingent on the mass of one's home planet. Languages are like planets.

Because Whorf was the most unapologetic exponent of this view, he, together with his teacher, lent his name to it. Sapir–Whorf has been a motor of linguistic research ever since. In its strongest form it states that the language you speak determines the way you think: 'In the Hopi view, time disappears and space is altered,' Whorf writes.

At this distance, it's clear that Whorf affords Hopi speakers an extraordinary degree of exotic cachet. They are strange creatures, who look at things through not-quite-human eyes. His descriptions of their worldview anticipate New Age writers of the coming decades. Had Whorf lived a bit longer, I reckon he would have shed his SAE hang-ups, dropped acid and walked enthusiastically through the doors of perception.

What's interesting is that, at the time, Whorf's depiction of Hopi was self-consciously progressive. While the prevailing view was that Native American speakers were 'primitive' – their societies and ways of communicating merely pale imitations of European ones – he sought to turn that on its head. Their languages incorporated concepts and structures the like of which we'd never encountered before, but just as complex and valid as our own. The argument 'they're simpler than us' became 'they're different (and possibly better, more in tune with nature and the cosmos) than us'. He sets out that view in a discussion of Mandarin:

> The West has attained some emotional understanding of the East through the aesthetic and belles-lettres type of approach, but this has not bridged the intellectual gulf; we are no nearer to understanding the types of logical thinking which are reflected in truly Eastern forms of scientific thought or analysis of nature. This requires linguistic research into the logics of native languages, and realization that they have equal scientific validity with our own thinking habits.

In seeking to right the wrongs of his predecessors, Whorf went too far. He attributed almost magical qualities to non-SAE speakers, in particular the Hopi, placing them far from our ordinary experience, making empathy seem not just emotionally taxing but scientifically impossible.

In the years since, Whorf's characterisation of Hopi has been debunked. In the 1980s, the linguist Ekkehart Malotki comprehensively trashed Whorf's 'American Indian Model of the Universe', in particular the idea of 'timelessness'. He published a 677-page monograph full of examples of time phrases in Hopi. He demonstrated that they do conceive of time in spatial terms, just like Standard Average Europeans, with the past behind us as we move forwards into the future. Commenting on Malotki's work, the anthropologist Alfred Gell wrote:

Whorf's specific claims about Hopi, for which he never provided much evidence, are very unsound . . . Hopi has a two-tense system [non-future vs future] and a very elaborate aspect system which allows for consistent distinction within the non-future between perfective aspect/past-time and imperfective aspect/present-time interpretations.* Not only is Whorf completely wrong about Hopi 'timelessness,' but it could as well be said that of the two languages English is the more timeless.

How could Whorf have missed all of this? It's possible that he just wasn't a very good field linguist. Most of Whorf's knowledge of Hopi was based on work with a single informant, New York resident Ernest Naquayouma, and 'checked' on a trip to Toreva, Arizona; there is no evidence that he became fluent in the language himself. These facts make his grand, generalising pronouncements about the Hopi worldview seem rather less convincing. The likelihood that Naquayouma's personality and idiosyncrasies influenced Whorf's understanding of Hopi is high, and it's hard to believe a single field trip could really have been enough to check his far-reaching claims.

Just how strange is it that a Hopi might say 'I left on the fifth day' rather than 'I stayed five days', given that both sentences are perfectly acceptable in English? And does the fact that a pilot, aeroplane and dragonfly can all be referred to by the same word make Hopi outlandish? Whorf doesn't

---

* 'Aspect' refers to the way an action occurs in time, for example whether it is continuous or has an end point. When an action is ongoing it can be said to be imperfective ('Nosheen is singing'). When it has been completed, it is regarded as perfective ('Nosheen has sung'). As we shall see, there are other subdivisions of aspect, such as habitual ('Nosheen sings').

tell us the additional words Hopi speakers would almost certainly have used if they wanted to make it clear they were talking about an insect rather than a jumbo jet. In English, there is a word 'flyer' – 'a person or thing that flies' according to Oxford Dictionaries. One word for wasps, planes, helicopters and eagles. It would be absurd to suggest that we cannot differentiate between them because we have a word that can designate them all. That's before you even consider the fact that humans tend to subdivide broad categories only when they need to. Hopi speakers probably hadn't encountered planes and pilots enough by Whorf's time to devise native words for them, and in any case they might just have borrowed the English ones, as often happens when new technology is introduced from an outside culture.

It seems that Whorf was guilty of seeing what he wanted to see in Hopi, and in other foreign languages: a mysterious code, the unlocking of which would reveal extraordinary new knowledge. His obsession with uncovering the true meaning of the Bible was part of a pattern: he desperately wanted there to be something more to the experience of being human. He was infected with the same romanticism that leads to absurd translations of words like *goya*: a sense that foreign languages might preserve a mysticism lost from our own world.

Cultures do differ, of course. The ways in which we organise society, think about life and mortality and commune with nature vary. We might well feel that another culture suits us better than our own. The mistake, I think, is to believe that it is language above all that acts as a barrier to these different experiences. It may well be a net, but I doubt that it's really a prison.

The pendulum swung away from Whorfian determinism in the decades after his death. Instead of looking at differences between languages, scholars tried to identify what they shared. Painstaking fieldwork generated strong evidence for universal patterns among the world's 6,000 or so tongues. At the same time as Noam Chomsky embarked on a programme aimed at identifying the common 'deep' structures underlying grammars that, on the surface, seemed wildly different, Sapir–Whorf fell out of fashion.

But is there really nothing in the idea that language can affect the way you think? Nothing, say, in the internet's conviction that 'untranslatable' words tell us something of the mindset of the people who use them? More recently, linguists have revisited the whole question to see if anything can be salvaged from Whorf's extreme version of the hypothesis. Perhaps there are certain areas where language has more influence than others. And perhaps, rather than determining thought, it subtly shapes it, or focuses our attention on one aspect of reality rather than another. Put like that, Sapir–Whorf begins to seem not just more plausible, but almost commonsensical. Instead of linguistic determinism, we have 'linguistic relativity'.

Putting Whorf to the test

It's easier to prove or disprove a hypothesis in a well-defined area of experience that can be readily compared across languages. That's why a lot of scholars interested in Whorf's ideas focused their research on colour. Because colour is a physical property, determined by the wavelengths of light that are reflected or absorbed by an object, you might assume that all languages have just as many words for colours as there are colours in the world. But the human eye can distinguish around 1,000,000 different shades, and I'd be surprised if you could quickly name more than ten. Choices are evidently made about how we divide up the spectrum of visible light – and languages make those choices differently. When linguists talk about colour terms, they usually focus on 'basic' ones like red or yellow, and not more poetic distinctions such as eau de Nil or vermilion. Languages tend to have no more than twelve basic colour terms. But even within this relatively small number, there can be variation. For example, English has a single word for 'blue', while Russian sees it as two separate colours (*goluboy*, corresponding to light blue in English, and *siniy*, darker blue). Historically, Welsh had one term – *glas* – for both blue and green. There are even some languages with as few as two basic colour terms, which we might be tempted to translate as 'black' and 'white'. The range of black here would be far wider than in English, however, incorporating brown, purple, dark reds and greens – and white would cover yellow, pink, light blue and so on.

The key question, in terms of Sapir–Whorf, is whether the absence of a colour term means that speakers of that language don't 'see' it in the same way we do. If you only have words for 'black' and 'white', do you ignore some of the gradations that those of us who use 'orange', 'grey' and 'purple' see? Clearly, all humans have more or less identical physiology: unless we're colour-blind, we see the same range of hues. A strong version of the Sapir–Whorf hypothesis – that language determines perception – would presumably hold that a speaker of a two-colour language can't distinguish colours – like purple or pink – that we do. This seems bizarre and has, in fact, been disproved. In a classic 1969 study, Brent Berlin and Paul Kay showed that informants were able to identify the full range of basic colour categories regardless of whether their language encoded them. Not only that, they were able to identify the 'focal' – or most typical – version of that colour, the bluest blue, even in cases where they had no separate word for 'blue'.

That doesn't mean that Sapir–Whorf is out of the window yet, though. Kay subsequently found modest evidence for a Whorfian effect that he demonstrated through a carefully calibrated set of experiments. He recruited English-speaking subjects as well as people who spoke Tarahumara, a language of north-western Mexico. Tarahumara lacks different words for 'green' and 'blue', instead using only one: *siyoname*. Subjects were asked to compare eight plastic chips which sat at equal distances on the spectrum between green, blue-green and blue. They were shown three at a time, and told to rate them according to how far apart they seemed to be in colour. Kay found that if two of the chips were just either side of the 'lexical boundary' in English – in other words, identifiable as 'green' and 'blue' – they were rated more different than they actually were by the English subjects. Speakers of Tarahumara, in contrast, judged the 'distance' between these colours more realistically.

So far, so modest. The exact manner in which languages slice up the spectrum – the way they happen to label colours – can have a measurable effect on our perception. Not exactly shocking. But there are more mind-boggling examples of Whorfian effects out there. Could the language you speak, for example, make you more likely to injure yourself, or even die?

Swedish is a north-Germanic language, very closely related to Danish, Norwegian and Icelandic. It sits within the larger Indo-European language family, meaning it shares ancestors with English, French, Greek, Russian and so on. Finnish, on the other hand, is part of the Finno-Ugric language family, which includes Hungarian and Estonian. The grammar and native vocabulary of these languages are completely different, despite the geographical proximity. The Swedish for 'father' is *far*. In Finnish it's *isä*. In Swedish 'eye' is *öga*, in Finnish *silmä*.

While there is undoubtedly a deep linguistic divide, the Nordic neighbours have similar standards of living, legal systems and modes of social organisation. There's a huge amount of trade and cultural exchange, and around 300,000 ethnic Swedes live in Finland. It's odd, then, given this cultural closeness, that the two countries should have sharply different rates of workplace accidents, with those in Finland being significantly higher. Even more bizarrely, this pattern holds among the Swedish minority in Finland: factories in Swedish-speaking areas are in line with the Swedish national rate. And we're not simply talking about bumps and bruises. The industrial fatality rate among Swedes is 31 per cent lower than for Finns.

Strange as it may seem, it's possible that language holds the key. In Swedish, prepositions (words like 'to', 'over', 'through', etc.) allow for the fine-grained description of movements over time. Finnish, which relies more on case endings (those suffixes which tell you about the connections between words), tends to emphasise the static relationships of objects to one another. According to the psycholinguist John Lucy, linguists researching the discrepancy determined that 'Finns organize the workplace in a way that favors the individual worker (person) over the temporal organization of the overall production process'. That kind of organisation seems to reflect the way sequences of events are structured in the Finnish language. As a result, 'Lack of attention to the overall temporal organization of the process leads to frequent disruptions in production, haste, and, ultimately, accidents.'

Those same qualities of Finnish may also have produced

a distinctive cultural genre. Lucy reports the results of research into film-making according to language family. 'Indo-European (Swedish, Norwegian, English) productions formed coherent temporal entities in which action could be followed from beginning to end across scenes, whereas . . . Finnish, Hungarian, Estonian productions showed more emphasis on static settings with only transitory movement.'

These effects are extraordinary, but they're difficult to pin down. Although the research concerned made as much effort as possible to isolate the effects of linguistic structure, it's still reasonable to ask where the linguistic ends and the cultural begins. Separating out the effects of being brought up in, say, a Finnish-speaking household from the effects of Finnish grammar itself would be a challenge.

This question becomes more intriguing still when we consider grammatical gender – the requirement in some languages for all nouns to be defined as male, female and sometimes a third category, neuter. English and Finnish don't have grammatical gender. A table, a car or a tree are neither male nor female. In Spanish, however, the word for 'table' – *la mesa* – is feminine, takes the feminine definite article, *la*, and must be replaced by the female pronoun, *ella*. 'Car' is masculine – *el coche*, as is 'tree' – *el arbol*. In German, 'table' – *der Tisch* – is masculine, 'car' – *das Auto* – is neuter, and 'tree' – *der Baum* – is masculine. The assignment of these words to different gender categories appears to be arbitrary.

What does it matter? Surely in the course of everyday thinking, Germans, Spaniards and French speakers don't really imagine that rocks, scissors and paper are somehow more or less female, male or something in between? For these speakers, gender must fade into the background, merely part of the nuts and bolts of language, of no more consequence than the fact that we add an 's' to nouns when there are more than one of them. Well, cognitive scientist Lera Boroditsky devised experiments to check this hypothesis, and came up with some surprising results.

First, she gathered together a group of German and Spanish speakers to investigate whether the gender markers attached to nouns were meaningfully interpreted as being either masculine or feminine. Boroditsky and her colleagues selected twenty-four objects and gave them masculine or feminine proper names. An apple might be called Patrick, for example. Half the time the name matched the grammatical gender; half the time it didn't. Subjects were then tested on their recall of the names. When the name matched the gender, they were better at remembering it than when it didn't – suggesting that there is a sense of an object actually seeming masculine or feminine when the grammar marks it that way.

What to make of this? Boroditsky's further hypothesis was that speakers whose language assigns the word 'apple' masculine gender might conceive of it more in terms of stereotypically masculine qualities, and vice versa for speakers who assign it feminine gender. If this were true, it would have all sorts of implications for the mental life of these speakers, their grasp of the way the world works and how they understand natural and artificial processes. Not only that: in descriptions of the 'meaning' of a word, we would have to add the associations it has as a result of its gender. A truly complete translation of *le soleil*, the French, masculine sun, would need to communicate the difference between it and the German feminine sun, *die Sonne*.

To investigate this, Boroditsky used another list of twenty-four objects that had the opposite genders in German and Spanish. She then asked native speakers of those languages to write down the first three English adjectives the objects brought to mind. The aim was to see whether the descriptions they produced tended to 'match' the gender of the word. The 'masculinity' and 'femininity' of these adjectives was rated by a separate group of English speakers to provide an unbiased measure.

The results are remarkable. Let's take the word 'key' – which is masculine in German and feminine in Spanish. German speakers chose adjectives like 'hard', 'heavy' and 'jagged'. Spanish speakers chose 'little', 'lovely', 'shiny' and 'tiny'. Or 'bridge', which is feminine in German and masculine in Spanish. German speakers chose 'beautiful', 'elegant', 'pretty' and 'slender' and the Spanish speakers chose 'big', 'strong', 'sturdy' and 'towering'. What this appears to show is that, if your mother tongue teaches you that keys are categorised as masculine, your idea of 'key' is infused with what are judged masculine qualities in your culture – and this applies even when you're using another (genderless) language. With these results, Whorf's theory seems to rise from its shallow grave.

The crucial question here is whether this means that untranslatability is real too. We've seen that many popular examples of untranslatability are exoticising, linguistically illiterate nonsense, even if they are entertaining. But if something as commonplace as gender marking can influence the way we conceive of a word, and gender is hardly the most dramatic way in which languages differ from one another – we may ask whether completely accurate translation is ever really possible. Given the extent to which the world relies on people who speak different languages being able to understand one another, this could be quite a big deal. On the one hand, perhaps it doesn't matter if we go through life without knowing the subtle ways in which Italian *simpatico* differs from English 'nice'. On the other, a failure to appreciate an incomplete overlap could cause serious problems.*

What we need is a model for understanding the way these differences, subtle or stark, arise – and, ideally, an accurate means of teasing them out.

Under the net

So how should we conceive of the way meaning is divided up across languages? One possible answer to this question comes in the form of lexical field theory. Think back to Iris Murdoch's conception of language as a net cast over the mind, restricting our thinking according to its knots and threads. Imagine a net with big holes cast over a piece of earth. It falls, wrinkled in some places, straight in others, the squares distorted into jagged or compressed spaces. If the earth represents thought, then the squares of the net represent words – dividing up the territory unequally and in a somewhat haphazard way. Every different language is another throw of the net, and the squares fall slightly differently each time.

The net metaphor allows us to see language as a system of relationships. The territory covered by one word is a function of the territory covered by its neighbour – and so on until the entire language is accounted for. This way of conceiving of languages is called structuralism, and it emerged

---

* The Treaty of Waitangi (1840), a bilingual agreement between the British Crown and more than 500 Māori chiefs that made New Zealand a colony, has been the subject of a bitter dispute over the meaning of various clauses. According to the New Zealand Ministry of Culture, 'in Māori it gave Queen Victoria governance over the land, while in English it gave her sovereignty over the land, which is a stronger term'.

at the beginning of the twentieth century with the work of Ferdinand de Saussure. It's a useful way of thinking about lexical semantics – the meanings of words – and in particular translatability, because it accounts for the lack of a one-on-one correspondence between words. De Saussure himself noted that 'sheep' in English must have a different value from *mouton* in French, because English also has the word 'mutton'. What is covered by one square in French is a more crowded field in English, with two squares occupying the same territory. Similarly, German has two words for 'chair': *Sessel* and *Stuhl*. *Sessel* is sometimes translated as 'armchair', but it's not a condition of *Sessel* that the chair has arms, whereas they're definitely required in 'armchair'. A better translation might be 'comfortable chair'. It's clear that the same territory is being divided up differently in German.

One of the implications of lexical field theory is that when a new word is added to the language, the territory covered by other words shrinks in order to make room for it. Thus the realm of thought dealing with conservative politics is now further subdivided by 'alt-right', which takes its place next to 'reactionary', 'fascist', 'neocon' and so on. The latter three shuffle up to make room for the newcomer.

The idea of lexical fields is appealing from a great height, and seems to communicate something important about the way words match, or don't match, across languages. Zoom in, however, and it begins to fall apart. Do words really have the sharp boundaries that the idea of borders between fields suggests? And what about words with multiple, closely related meanings? The verb 'turn' means 'to move around on an axis or about a centre; rotate'. But does it occupy a different lexical field in the phrase 'the lady's not for turning'? How about 'turn back', 'turn down' or 'turn into'? Is there a finite territory of thought over which words jostle, every gain being another's loss? What about concept-forming words like 'babysitter'? Are they grabbing land that already exists but is uncharted, or creating it from scratch, as though reclaimed from the sea?

For most non-Whorfian linguists, language must be a means of translating thoughts. Things missing from the lexicon are just thoughts that have yet to be labelled – perhaps because there has been no need to do so, or because the phenomenon they identify hasn't been encountered yet. The key thing is, they are not out of reach of cognition simply because they lack a name. First comes the thought, then the word.

And we do know that people can think without words: when you say 'I'm thinking of home', you're unlikely to be describing it to yourself using an internal monologue, and you won't necessarily be recalling conversations about it. You might be in the bath, imagining looking out across the garden one summer twenty years ago, hearing the radio wafting over the neighbours' fence, feeling the clothes you wore when you were younger, remembering how sad you felt that you would be moving soon. This is definitely thinking – and you don't need language to do it. Memories of perceptions don't have to be linguistic. And you can even 'think' about the future, by envisaging what it will feel or look like, without words. Picture yourself walking to work tomorrow and stopping to buy a magazine. In this way, 'deciding to buy a magazine on the way to work' could consist of imagined perceptions only.

So perhaps Sapir–Whorf is dead after all. Except that there are linguists who believe that most clear thinking – you could say, non-impressionistic, or precise thinking – requires language, not just to translate those thoughts into expression, but to bring them into very being. This rings true: how much of our modern lives, for which sophisticated planning is a prerequisite, would be possible without language? Can you imagine arranging a party for twenty or so friends using solely imagined perception, visualising all the necessary actions in your head? Now, what about a complex property deal? What about making up your mind to convince someone of a political idea?

But if language helps create complex thought, as the above examples seem to show, then it follows that different languages help create it in different ways. Languages are enormously flexible – there's plenty you can do to create new ways of looking at things by, for example, using synonyms and alternative phrasing. But, even if you strive always to be original, never clichéd, your thought-speak will inevitably be channelled down certain well-worn gullies carved out for you by your own language. These gullies are formed by years of use over your lifetime, and influenced by generations of linguistic evolution before that. Mandarin speakers, for example, often use a vertical axis to talk about time rather than a horizontal one (Monday is 'above' Wednesday; Friday is 'below' Thursday). Yes, some kind of translation is always possible, because of the aforementioned flexibility. But how do you escape the obvious problem of the lack of a universal standard against which to judge words from different languages?

Elementary, my dear reader

The answer might be to create a metalanguage – a way of defining meaning that doesn't rely on the vagaries of English, or Arabic, or any individual language, but on semantic units common to all of them. But how would that be possible, given that individual languages are all we have to go on as we home in on our semantic units? In other words, how do you communicate in a metalanguage without already knowing what it consists of, and how do you try to find out what it consists of without using individual languages?

It's a tricky problem, and scholars have come up with various approaches. One is to think of words as molecules, and try to deconstruct them into elements. So 'bachelor' equals 'unmarried' + 'adult' + 'male'. 'Unmarried', 'adult' and 'male' must be semantic elements, concepts that exist independently and can be combined with others in order to form a lot of different words. So far so good. Take 'unmarried' + 'adult' + 'female' and you get 'spinster'. Or 'bull', which could be set out in our new metalanguage as 'bovine' + 'adult' + 'male'. These elements can be used in translation, too. The French word *madame* could be deconstructed as 'married' + 'female' + 'adult'.

But for this to work, the semantic elements would have to be represented in every language. Just one counterexample – a language in which there was no independent element corresponding to, say, 'adult' – would be enough to torpedo the idea that they represent basic building blocks of meaning. Unfortunately, such a counterexample exists: Yankunytjatjara, an indigenous Australian language spoken in the Western Desert, lacks 'adult', meaning that this word must be rejected as a semantic element.

Excluding counterexamples requires vast amounts of fieldwork, investigating languages for elements of meaning – attempting to find the lowest-common-denominator words that, together, represent language broken down to its most basic components, beyond which any further deconstruction is impossible. Achieve this, and you can claim to have effectively delineated the language of thought.

As it happens, such a programme has been in train for the last forty years or so. Anna Wierzbicka and her colleagues – the linguists whose analysis of the word 'happiness' we encountered in Chapter 2 – have devoted their careers to establishing what they call a 'natural semantic metalanguage' (NSM). It is natural because it takes its elements from real human language only.* And it contains some surprises: as well as 'adult', not all languages have words for 'male' and 'female' – meaning that these cannot be semantic elements, or, as Wierzbicka calls them, 'primes'.

In fact, the most up-to-date list of primes contains only sixty-five terms. There are, so far, no counterexamples – that is to say, languages in which any of these sixty-five terms don't exist. They are building blocks, and represent the finite set of elements from which all complex words and expressions can be formed. If this seems extraordinary, think of chemical elements. Ninety-four are found naturally and from them every substance on earth is ultimately made.

---

* An example of a non-natural metalanguage is formal logic. Using it, both 'All fathers have houses' and '*Tous les pères ont des maisons*' can be rendered as $\forall x \, (F(x) \rightarrow H(x))$. It can be used to clarify the relationships between words, but is much less useful when it comes to the semantic content of words themselves. 'F' stands for father – but it doesn't tell us what properties something has to have in order to be considered a father.

I~ME, YOU, SOMEONE, SOME-THING~THING, PEOPLE, BODY	substantives
KIND, PARTS	relational substantives
THIS, THE SAME, OTHER~ELSE	determiners
ONE, TWO, SOME, ALL, MUCH~MANY, LITTLE~FEW	quantifiers
GOOD, BAD	evaluators
BIG, SMALL	descriptors
KNOW, THINK, WANT, DON'T WANT, FEEL, SEE, HEAR	mental predicates
SAY, WORDS, TRUE	speech
DO, HAPPEN, MOVE, TOUCH	actions, events, movement, contact
BE (SOMEWHERE), THERE IS, BE (SOMEONE)'S, BE (SOMEONE/SOMETHING)	location, existence, possession, specification
LIVE, DIE	life and death
WHEN~TIME, NOW, BEFORE, AFTER, A LONG TIME, A SHORT TIME, FOR SOME TIME, MOMENT	time
WHERE~PLACE, HERE, ABOVE, BELOW, FAR, NEAR, SIDE, INSIDE	space
NOT, MAYBE, CAN, BECAUSE, IF	logical concepts
VERY, MORE	intensifier, augmenter
LIKE~WAY~AS	similarity

The sixty-five primes in English, grouped according to category

You wouldn't think it to look at them, but Wierzbicka's primes can be used to convey pretty much everything. They can scope out the meaning of the subtlest expressions. How?

Take the NSM translation of the English word 'happiness'. If the language of the definition appears stilted, remember that it can only be constructed using the sixty-five terms that have been identified as universal: the primes. Each part is given on a separate line, emphasising the fact that it represents a discrete parcel of meaning. The description begins with 'It can be like this', to introduce the fact that the word we are dealing with describes a state of being – rather than, say, the property of an object (in contrast to the definition of 'hard', which, as we'll see later on, starts with 'This thing is like this'):

a. It can be like this:
b. Someone thinks like this for some time:
c. 'Some good things are happening to me now as I want
d. I can do many things now as I want
e. This is good'
f. Because of this, this someone feels something good at that time
g. Like people feel at many times when they think like this for some time
h. It is good for someone if it is like this

The above definition contains only primes, but sets out the ways in which the English word 'happiness' is used. Since semantic primes occur in every language, 'happiness' can be translated with pinpoint accuracy using the French version of the primes table, the Polish, the Russian, and so on.

Wierzbicka and Goddard showed how English 'happiness' shifted from something akin to 'good fortune', a fleeting,

unpredictable experience of joy, to its current meaning
during the eighteenth century. Back then, happiness would
have been defined like this:

   a. It can be like this:
   b. Some very good things happen to someone
   c. Not because this someone does something
   d. Things like this don't often happen to people
   e. This someone can feel something very good because of
      this

The difference between the two definitions comes with
c. – it's out of our control – and d. – it doesn't come along
very often. The odd-sounding expression 'this someone' is
made necessary by the fact that there are languages that
don't have a word equivalent to 'person', but no language
has been found to lack a word equivalent to 'someone'.

Wierzbicka and Goddard also tackle the Tibetan concept
bdewa, described by the Dalai Lama in his book *The Art of
Happiness*, and show how there's nothing precisely equivalent to it in English – certainly not the modern use of the
term 'happiness':

   a. It can be like this:
   b. Someone doesn't often think like this:
   c. 'I want many good things to happen to me
   d. I don't want bad things to happen to me'
   e. At the same time this someone often thinks like this:
   f. 'Very bad things happen to all people, very bad things
      happen to all living things
   g. All people often feel something very bad, all living
      things can feel something very bad
   h. I am like all other people, I am like all living things

   i. I want to think about all people like this: "this someone is someone like me"

   j. I want to think like this about all living things

   k. I want to feel something good towards all other people

   l. I want to feel something good towards all living things'

   m. Because this someone thinks like this, it is like this:

   n. This someone doesn't often feel something bad towards other people

   o. This someone doesn't often feel something bad towards any living things

   p. This someone often feels something good towards all other people

   q. This someone often feels something good towards all living things

   r. Because it is like this, this someone can always feel something good

   s. It is good for this someone if it is like this

What's being described here is an idea of happiness based on an acknowledgement of suffering, a determination to treat all living things with compassion, and the feeling of wellbeing that results. The NSM version of it might seem long-winded, but complex concepts, like the long chain molecules that help our bodies convert food into energy, really do contain this many semantic components. And setting them out like a recipe helps us understand the precise differences between words that don't quite overlap between languages. Not only that, but using NSM means that the idea of *bdewa* can be communicated as effectively in English as in French, Russian, Polish, etc.

What about less abstract words? Ones that we imagine have easy and accurate translations? English has the word 'hard', which Wierzbicka and Goddard translate as follows.

(In NSM notation, the letter [m] designates a non-prime word, such as 'hand', that has already been defined in a separate table, using only primes. It stands for 'molecule'.)

   a. This thing is like this:
   b. If someone's hand [m] moves when it is touching this thing,
   c. This someone can feel something in this hand [m] because of it
   d. Because of this, this someone can know something about this thing
   e. Because of this, this someone can think like this:
   f. 'If someone wants to do something to this thing with the hands [m]
   g. Because this someone wants some parts of this thing not to be where they were before,
   h. This someone can't do it if this someone doesn't do something with something else at the same time'

If something is 'hard', when you want to change it – to scratch or break it or make something out of it – you can't do it with your hands alone. You need some kind of tool.

There's a word in Polish that is translated as 'hard' in English – *twardy*. But is it the same? Not quite, and here's exactly how:

   a. This thing is like this:
   b. If some parts of someone's body move when they are touching this thing,
   c. This someone can feel something in these parts because of it
   d. Because of this, this someone can know something about this thing

  e. Because of this, this someone can think like this:
  f. 'If someone wants to do something to a thing like this
      with some parts of the body
  g. Because this someone wants some parts of this thing
      not to be where they were before
  h. This someone can't do it if this someone doesn't do
      something with something else at the same time'

The difference here is that 'hand' isn't privileged above
other body parts in the Polish definition. This seems odd,
but it begins to make sense when you consider the 'range'
of *twardy*. In English, we would not say that meat is 'hard',
but that it is 'tough'. In Polish, both would be described as
twardy. That difference in range is captured by b. – which
could apply to both hands and teeth.*

  With the fine-grained analyses of NSM, we finally have
an answer to the question of whether there exist any untranslatable words. But it's not black and white. The fantasy
of untranslatability embodied by internet explanations of
goya and *sgrìob* is just that, a fantasy. While picturesque, it's
not without danger: it perpetuates the idea that foreigners
might as well be a different species. Whorfian in the extreme, it says there are thought-worlds out there as strange
as lunar landscapes, to which you can only travel if you
speak the language. Having said that, we now know the
lack of like-for-like translatability is near-universal: even
simple words like 'hard' or 'happiness' don't quite match up
between languages.

  So the question of whether having different words and

---

* Lexical field theory would give us to understand that 'hard'
and *twardy* cover slightly different, if overlapping, territories. The
twardy field is equivalent to the 'hard' and 'tough' fields of English
joined together.

grammatical structures means we think differently about the world – an important component of the idea of untranslatability – remains open. We've seen that it is true up to a point. But because we are able to develop metalanguages, particularly the NSM, we can effectively tease out these differences and arrive at translations that accurately reflect the meanings of words.

Finally, then, we can see that nothing is truly untranslatable. Just don't expect to be able to have it sewn up in fewer than ten sentences.

CHAPTER 6

Italian is a language

Imagine you're making a pilgrimage through southern Europe. Following the Camino di Santiago from one great cathedral city, let's say, Siena in Italy, to another – Santiago di Compostela in Spain. The pace is slow – perhaps twenty miles each day, if you're fit and well. You stay in small hostels and villages, watching the landscape slowly change, and the people and culture too. You have your phrasebooks and dictionaries with you – Italian, French and Spanish. But as the days turn into weeks you find you no longer need them. You learn the most common words and, as you cross from one region to another, they seem to shift, almost imperceptibly, allowing you to keep up quite easily. *Buongiorno*, you say to the Tuscan farmers as you skirt their fields. Outside Turin, you might hear *bon-a giornà* instead. As you make your way into Provence, villagers greet you with a cheery *bonjorn*, although, as you pass through larger ones, you're more likely to hear *bonjour*. Crossing over the border near Narbonne you enter Catalonia, where the 'j' hardens into a 'd': *bon dia*. In neighbouring Aragon it's *buen diya*, while Castilians use the more familiar *buenos días*. And finally, as you reach Santiago and slump at a café table, your Galician waiter greets you with *bos días*. After a week or so you're sufficiently recovered to make an excursion (by coach, this time) across the border to Porto. *Bom dia!* they say.

Buongiorno, bon-a giornà, bonjorn, bonjour, bon dia, buen diya, buenos días, bos días, bom dia. These are the words for 'Good day' in Tuscan, Piedmontese, Occitan, French, Catalan, Aragonese, Castilian, Galician and Portuguese respectively. Only a small change in the sound or number of syllables is necessary to take you from one to the other. But when you look at the start and end points, they are quite different – geographically, of course, but linguistically too. A Portuguese woman from the western tip of Europe wouldn't be able to understand a Tuscan, from its centre, if they tried to have a conversation. And yet they are linked in a chain of understanding – the Tuscan can figure out what the Piedmontese is saying, who can understand the Provençal, who can make herself clear to a Catalan and so on. On your travels you notice other words that follow a similar pattern: the key to your room is *chiave* in Tuscany, *ciav* in Piedmont, *clau* in Occitan and *clef* in French.

Zoom in closer and some of the gradations between small towns and villages may become even finer. The sharp differences between what we are used to thinking of as 'languages' – Italian, French, Catalan, Spanish, Portuguese – seem to blur under the microscope. The boundaries that we imagine exist become more like the lapping of waves from one pool into another.

It's not just in southern Europe, either. As the Rhine wends its way towards the North Sea, German is slowly but surely transformed into Dutch, via West Central German and Limburgish. Asking your name, the German says *wie heisst du*, the Limburger *hoe heits doe* and the Dutch speaker *hoe heet u?* From Norway to Denmark to Sweden, minute changes from one town to the next apparently add up to three different languages. Inhabitants of Slovenia, which borders Italy, might find it hard to understand their fellow Slavs in Bulgaria, which borders Turkey. But they're only a couple of steps away from each other. Get a Serb and a Macedonian to stand in between them, and you've assembled the perfect linguistic relay team. These areas of overlap, of links in an unbroken chain, are called 'dialect continuums', delicate structures which, as we'll see, have been eroded by both globalisation and nationalism. But the fact that they existed at all raises some important questions.

If languages sometimes blur into one another like this, what does that mean for the concept of Italian or French, German or Dutch, Arabic, Japanese or English, for that matter? If there are no hard borders, only barely discernible changes from one place to the next, how do we decide where a language begins and ends? Does the idea of 'a language' itself make any linguistic sense?

Military matters

So far, we've got along without defining the difference between a language and a dialect. There are good reasons for that: it's often not very clear. Piedmontese, for example, is generally considered a dialect of Italian. But the philologist Auguste Brun described it instead as a language that 'did not succeed'. It would be quite reasonable to regard it as a separate entity: it differs from standard Italian in its vocabulary and grammar, and has a long literary tradition. But when Italy was unified in the nineteenth century, a version of Tuscan was adopted as its official language, and the status of Piedmontese was relegated for ever to that of dialect. Clearly, that was a political decision. So does the difference between a dialect and a language always come down to politics?

Very often it does. English and Mandarin, say, are obviously completely different. There is no common ground between them save borrowed words,* they evolved in entirely separate parts of the world, and for centuries contact between the two civilisations that used them was limited. But in a situation where the 'languages' share a common ancestor and are spoken in close proximity, precisely where you draw the dividing line frequently comes down to power. As one Yiddish-speaking audience member at a lecture by the sociolinguist Max Weinreich famously said (the quote is often attributed to Weinreich himself), '*a shprakh iz a dialekt mit an armey un flot*' – a language is a dialect with an army and navy. That wisdom largely holds true. The differences between Norwegian, Danish and Swedish are much smaller than the differences between many of the dialects lumped together as 'Chinese'. And yet the former are said to be languages, since they belong to three separate nations for whom the differentiation – particularly for the historically poorer, less powerful Norway – is highly significant. Spoken Urdu and Hindi can be indistinguishable from one another, but their status as distinct languages is a point of pride for two nations which have often been on the verge of war.

Arabic offers a mirror image of this. Morocco and Iraq both have an army and navy, and their citizens would have trouble understanding each other in everyday conversation. But they are said to speak dialects of Arabic rather than separate languages. That seems strange until you remember

---

* Words like Mandarin *péigēn*, from English 'bacon', or English 'tofu', from Mandarin *dòufu*.

that the religious ties binding the Arab world together are strong. The Quran represents an early standardisation of the language, an unchanging model that is revered everywhere Islam is practised.* Modern standard Arabic, the language of news bulletins and government business, is closely related to that model, and operates as a vehicle for the common Arab identity. But since the geographical range of Arabic is so large, and ordinary people don't speak like newsreaders, there exists a two-tier linguistic landscape in many Arab countries – something that has been called *diglossia*, from the Greek for 'two' and 'tongue'. Modern standard Arabic hovers somewhere above the local varieties, ultimately yoking them all together.†

This yoking, whether for political or cultural reasons, has been described by linguists as 'heteronymy', or the situation where one form of the language is said to be dependent on – subordinate to – the standard. That helps us understand why, in the linguistic grey area between Germany and Holland, dialects spoken inside the Dutch border are seen as part of that language, and those inside the German border

---

* Of the approximately 300 million inhabitants of the Arab League (twenty-two countries in the Middle East and North Africa whose official language is Arabic), the vast majority are Muslim. However, a significant minority of Arabs are Christian, especially in Lebanon, Syria, Egypt and Palestine.

† English represents another departure from the army-and-navy rule. Canada, the United States, the United Kingdom and New Zealand are all sovereign nations, yet their inhabitants think of themselves as speaking a single language. The reasons for this are both linguistic and political: linguistically, these dialects are very similar and largely mutually intelligible (close enough to be thought of as the same language). But, unlike the case of Norwegian, Swedish and Danish, the political need for differentiation has been far less.

are regarded as dialects of German. Even if they're closer to Dutch than to standard German, they're 'heteronymous' on the latter. The dialectologists Jack Chambers and Peter Trudgill give an example of the switching of heteronomy between languages. Until 1658, the dialects spoken in southern Sweden were considered to be varieties of Danish, since Denmark ruled those territories. In that year, however, the land became part of Sweden. A generation later, once the political change had become established, they began to be seen as dialects of Swedish.

Europe hosts many standard languages, and its territory is crammed with a bewildering variety of dialects. The Arab world looks to one standard, for cultural reasons, but is home to just as complex a patchwork of dialects. A similar situation holds in China. North and South America, however, seem monotonous in comparison. In the United States and Canada, English dominates, with French retaining its foothold in Quebec. In the South there is Spanish and Portuguese. But what of dialects? Let's take the United States – a vast country, twice the area of the European Union. There are accents – different ways of pronouncing vowels and consonants – differences in vocabulary, even different grammatical rules, depending on where you are. It's easy enough to tell Southern American English from Boston English. But you have to travel greater distances to notice a change – and often the changes aren't all that dramatic.

Where dialects come from

To understand why, you need to know how dialects – and languages – form in the first place. In Chapter 1 we saw that language is in a constant state of flux: the very act of communication contains the seeds of change. No two in-stances of the same word are ever phonetically identical. The speech signal is accompanied by noise – subtle, haphaz-ard variations in the shape of the sounds we produce that don't actually change the meaning of the word. For that reason, it is inherently unstable. In the word 'put', for ex-ample, a speaker might aim for the vowel 'uh' but produce something more like 'ooh' instead. It might be a one-off, or it could happen again and again, influencing the people she talks to. Gradually, the whole community might end up shifting to the new pronunciation, resulting in a permanent change. As these kinds of transformations pile on top of one another over several generations, the entire language is altered beyond recognition.

Where transport is difficult, and movement far away from your place of birth unusual, linguistic communities – the units of people who communicate a lot with one an-other, and among whom the same changes catch on – have relatively small ranges. If this geographical stasis persists – if the settlements are stable, without much emigration or immigration over a long period of time – then the dialects spoken there will gradually diverge, even though the dis-tances between the settlements are small. In the year 300, the inhabitants of neighbouring Alpine valleys divided by craggy peaks might all have spoken Latin. As the influence of the Roman Empire receded, taking with it well-maintained roads and lucrative trade routes, fewer people would have bothered to make the hike over the mountains and the Latin in both valleys would have begun to change, wobbling off down different paths.

There's a parallel with biology here. Animals that are separated, for example as a result of being surrounded by water, gradually acquire unique characteristics that distinguish them from their neighbours, depending on what genetic mutations occur and what the environment they live in is like. Birds on Island A might gradually develop longer beaks, birds on Island B bigger feet. There's no inter-breeding, so the divergence is only exaggerated, rather than ironed out, as time wears on. That's the reason neighbouring islands, such as the Mascarenes in the Indian Ocean – Reunion, Mauritius and Rodriguez – have given rise to their own unique species, including the dodo, the Réunion bulbul and the Rodrigues solitaire.

A long history of stable settlement, with limited migration and poor transport links, is the reason there is such a density of dialects in the Old World – in Europe, the Middle East and China. To this day, as you move from valley to valley in places like Switzerland, the dialect spoken can change no-ticeably. North and South America, of course, have a recent history of massive migration, and the spread of population over vast areas in a relatively short period of time. Many cities in the Midwest and West are less than 200 years old, and have not experienced the isolation necessary for distinct dialects to develop. That's why you might struggle to tell people from Las Vegas, Denver and Des Moines apart, even though each of those cities are separated from one another by about 750 miles.

This isn't the whole story, of course. The 'New World' was only ever new to those who came from Europe to colonise it. Before that, a dense and highly differentiated network of languages and dialects did exist across these continents, which had their own very long histories of stable settlement. In fact, as Edward Sapir, whom we met in the previous chapter, put it in 1929, 'We may say, quite literally and safely, that in the state of California alone there are greater and more numerous linguistic extremes than can be illustrated in all the length and breadth of Europe.' These included Miwok (from which we get the place name Yosemite), Maidu, Pomo, Matole and Yoruk, all with their own dialects and subdivisions. Unfortunately, most of these are now critically endangered, if not extinct. The crushing military defeat of native peoples, combined with the effects of imported diseases to which they had no immunity, meant that America's linguistic diversity was effectively erased. The complex patchwork became a palimpsest on which, henceforth, only English would be written. A similar situation holds in Australia. The English spoken there, though different from the British or American varieties, is fairly uniform across the vast continent, which began to be colonised by the British from the late eighteenth century. Indigenous Australians, in contrast, have lived there for tens of thousands of years. During that time, more than 350 distinct languages developed.

Because of advances in communication and transport, because of globalisation and mass migration, the norm that linguistic communities remain isolated from one another and gradually diverge has been overturned. Some linguists argue that, instead of differentiation, we now see a process of dialect-levelling, whereby the wrinkles that separate varieties of a language like English are gradually being ironed out. Ease of travel is one way in which the bonds of a linguistic community can be loosened, reducing differences between dialects; standardised education is another. In the nation states that arose after centuries of fractured political organisation, children are all generally taught the same linguistic standard as part of their compulsory education. Not only that, but efforts have frequently been made to discourage them from speaking in non-standard dialects or minority languages. In the South of France, the word *vergonha*, which is Occitan for 'shame', has been used to label the discomfort felt by native speakers which, in many cases, persuaded them not to pass their language on to their children.*

We now know that whether a dialect is elevated to the status of 'language' or not is usually a political decision, as with Piedmontese losing out to Tuscan. But that still leaves us without a linguistic definition of 'dialect'. Are we to understand that it is the basic unit of linguistic difference, and 'language' a sort of garland bestowed on it when it reaches a certain political status? Yes and no. Again, we hit on some important questions about the nature of language.

During a single lifetime, the sounds, words and grammar of the language you speak shift slightly under your feet. Think of the fact that it's now common to hear glottal stops in British English at the end of words like 'what', even in very formal contexts. Or of new words like 'login' and 'gobsmacked'. Or that the accusative form 'whom' increasingly sounds archaic.

It is this intrinsic tendency to change that creates dialects, since whenever a linguistic network becomes isolated to a degree, it will start to diverge from other varieties. Two varieties of a language can, then, be said to be dialects if they differ in some way in terms of pronunciation, vocabulary or grammar. The isolation that gives rise to these differences can be geographical – and that's mostly what we've concentrated on so far. But it can also be social, racial or defined by almost any other form of identity. In Boston, wealthy

---

* The irony being that Occitan was, in the twelfth and thirteenth centuries, the medium of elevated literary expression in the South of France. By the end of the eighteenth it was designated a *patois*, an embarrassingly rustic dialect.

residents of the Back Bay will generally use a different dialect from the poorer ones in Allston, three miles to the west. Poor African Americans in the city will use another dialect, which will in turn differ from that of rich African Americans. There are historic examples of dialects that have been defined by sexual orientation, such as Polari.* Internet subcultures like gaming give rise to their own dialects, with words that outsiders can't understand.† These examples should make it clear that many of us – perhaps every one of us, unless we have grown up uniquely isolated from others – have the ability to communicate in several dialects at once. We adapt our speech depending on the network we are plugged into at the moment of conversation. We could be talking to someone from our home town, or to our boss at work, or to someone with the same ethnic background or specialist interest. In each case we'll make subtle, or not so subtle, adjustments.

Some linguists go as far as to differentiate between the individual styles, the grammatical and phonetic quirks, that

---

* Polari – from the Italian *parlare*, 'to talk' – afforded gay men a means of communicating that wouldn't be understood by others at a time when homosexuality was highly stigmatised. According to the linguist Paul Baker, 'it developed from an earlier form of language called Parlyaree which had roots in Italian and rudimentary forms of language used for communication by sailors around the Mediterranean. Also associated with travellers, buskers, beggars and prostitutes, it found its way into Britain, especially London and port cities, and gradually became used by gay men and female impersonators, especially during the first half of the twentieth century.' Polari words such as 'drag' and 'naff' have entered the wider lexicon.

† Words like 'cat-assing', which the Urban Dictionary defines as 'To play a computer game, especially a Massive Multiplayer Online (MMO), for extreme lengths of time. This may come at the expense of hygiene, social interaction, even nutrition.'

are unique to each one of us. According to this view, we speak not dialects or languages, but idiolects – varieties of language that have just one speaker: you.

Idiolect, dialect and language are, in reality, different lenses through which to view the same phenomenon: a medium of communication that is not fixed but ever-changing, which emerges as a combination of stored rules and words in the head of the individual and the interaction of individuals whose knowledge overlaps sufficiently for them to understand each other easily. When that overlap is incomplete, two different dialects can be said to exist – one of which may be given the political label 'language'. When the overlap is non-existent, you are dealing with two separate languages in a linguistic sense. Charles Hockett put it like this: 'A language is a collection of more or less similar idiolects. A dialect is just the same thing, with this difference: when both terms are used in a single discussion, the degree of similarity of the idiolects in a single dialect is presumed to be greater than that of all the idiolects of the language.' In other words, idiolects cluster into dialects, of which there may be several under the umbrella of a single language.

A big overlap between dialects results in 'mutual intelli-gibility': the speaker of one can understand the speaker of another. Swedish and Norwegian are mutually intelligible. Danish may be a little harder for Swedes to understand, and Icelandic, though closely related to all three, is largely unintelligible to other Scandinavians due to its centuries of isolation. Are any dialects of English mutually unintelli-gible? I suspect it would be difficult for a Californian who had never been to Newcastle before to understand direc-tions in a thick Geordie accent. But the reverse probably wouldn't apply – simply because of the level of exposure the British have to American cultural products, like TV and movies.

Language wars

Some scholars regard Hindi and Urdu, the official languages of India and Pakistan respectively (alongside English), as essentially the same language, with different labels and scripts; linguist Robert King says that they are 'so similar in their marketplace spoken forms that no linguist would hesitate to classify them as near dialects of the same language'. But their history is a chequered one, and offers a good example of the complex interplay of politics, identity and linguistics that determine the label a language receives.

Hindi and Urdu are part of the Indo-European family we first met in the Introduction, meaning that they share an ancestor with languages such as English, Latin and Greek. The branch they belong to, Indo-Aryan, split off from this ancestor several thousand years ago (a process we will examine further in Chapter 8), meaning it has fewer words and grammatical features in common with English than, say, German does. But the relatedness can still be seen in some common words: *bhratar* means 'brother' in the Indo-Aryan language Sanskrit and *duhitar* 'daughter'.

Sanskrit, which was the language of classical Indian civilisation, evolved into Prakrit, which in turn produced Hindustani, a vernacular spoken in northern India that spread during the Delhi sultanate, which began in the thirteenth century. Under the Mughals, who ruled the subcontinent from the fifteenth century onwards, Hindustani was exposed more and more to Persian influence, since that was the language of the court and government. Gradually, Hindustani became a spectrum, with heavily

Persianised Urdu* at one end and Hindi, with fewer words borrowed from Persian or Arabic, at the other. Urdu was written using an adapted Arabic script, which runs from right to left; Hindi in Devanagari, a script traditionally used to write Sanskrit, which runs from left to right. The scripts themselves became centrally important in marking these dialects out from one another, with Arabic signifying Urdu (and Islam) and Devanagari signifying Hindi (and Hinduism), even when the linguistic differences were not very great.

The British brought English with them in the nineteenth century, knocking Persian off its perch as the language of administration. But they also bolstered the status of Urdu as the official vernacular in many areas, for example by conducting court proceedings in it. This had the effect of aggravating the sectarian split, generating a sense of grievance on the part of those who used Devanagari. There were attempts by Hindu scholars to 'Sanskritise' the language they wrote and spoke, making it *shuddh*, or 'pure' – in other words, purging it further of Persian and Arabic. The identification of Urdu with Muslim and Hindi with Hindu became indelible. In the run-up to partition, Urdu was a key component of Muslim nationalism, part of the argument for a separate state. It was subsequently adopted as the official language of Pakistan. India's first prime minister, Jawaharlal Nehru, believed that Hindustani, a close marriage of Hindi and Urdu, written in either script, should be the official language of the new state, and should fulfil the role of bringing together communities divided by British misrule. He said: 'I should like to say quite clearly that I deeply regret the

---

* The word itself, which was not used until 1752, means 'language of the encampment' and comes from Turkish, another language associated with the Mughal invaders.

attempts of Hindi enthusiasts to push out Urdu . . . I think [Urdu] has a very rich inheritance which should be encouraged and nurtured.' But it was to no avail. Hindi in the Devanagari script was named an official language of India on 14 September 1949, a date commemorated annually as *hindi divas*, 'Hindi Day'.

The situation now, after decades of separation and reinforcement of the differences, is complex. As King puts it, 'High variants of Hindi look to Sanskrit for inspiration and linguistic enrichment, high variants of Urdu to Persian and Arabic. In their highest – and therefore most artificial – forms the two languages are mutually incomprehensible.' Examples of these high forms can be heard on Radio Pakistan on the one hand and All-India Radio on the other. It's hard, if not impossible, for Indian listeners to understand the former, and Pakistanis the latter. But even 'low' varieties may now be diverging. King tells of a Pakistani visitor to Agra, India, who had thought that she would be able to use the Urdu she spoke at home to get by, but was surprised to find that it was in fact easier to ask directions of Sikhs since they spoke Punjabi, which was her second language.

The symbolic differences between what remain very similar, if not always mutually intelligible, languages can have powerful real-world effects. In 1989, Urdu was designated the second official language of Uttar Pradesh, the large, central-northern Indian state whose capital is Lucknow. The first was Hindi. This small change, a recognition of the large Muslim population who read using the modified Arabic script, was enough to prompt rioting in the small town of Badaun, previously the harmonious home to a mixture of Hindu and Muslim families. Twenty-seven people died. The status of a language, wherever that language also symbolises the rights and traditions of an ethnic, religious or political group (as it almost always does), can be a matter of life and death.

Why do some people dislike having the way they speak labelled a 'dialect'? Despite the fact that we now know it to be a linguistically neutral term, meaning a group of overlapping idiolects, it's often used to indicate inferior status. That can be because the dialect in question just happens to lose out in a political fight for supremacy (Piedmontese and Tuscan again). The dialect which becomes the standard form of a national language is always going to have higher prestige, and it's never going to get called a 'dialect'. The varieties which represent a deviation from the norm – Yorkshire English, or cockney, or Boston American English – are axiomatically of lower status, despite also being the source of great pride to some people from those areas. And because they're the ones we call 'dialects' rather than languages, we think of that word as denoting something inferior. Sometimes, when a dialect belongs to a group that has lower status for other reasons, it doesn't even get dignified with that label. This is when a dialect is called 'slang' or, even more derogatory, 'bad X' – bad English, bad French, bad Spanish.

Few large groups of English speakers have borne as great a burden of stigma as African Americans. As slaves, that stigma was enshrined in law – and even after emancipation, legal measures were used to ensure that black people could not easily vote, could not access decent education, transportation and so on. Since the civil rights era most legal barriers to equality have been removed, but society has yet to catch up. As of the second decade of the twenty-first century, African Americans are almost five times as likely to be jailed than white people, despite making up only 13 per cent of the population. It's not surprising, then, that the dialect many black people speak is stigmatised too – to such a great extent that it's often denied the status of dialect, becoming merely 'bad' English. That assumption has become so ingrained, it's even taken up by some black people themselves.

'There is no such thing as "talking white" ... it's actually called "speaking fluently", speaking your language correctly. I don't know why we've gotten to a place where as a culture – as a race – if you sound as though you have more than a fifth-grade education, it's a bad thing.' This was the argument of a young black woman whose video on the subject went viral in 2014. In her view, speaking what linguists call African American Vernacular English (AAVE) is not speaking 'fluent' English. It is bad English – the kind of English that should be dispensed with by the time you're eleven years old. As journalist Jamelle Bouie, who wrote about the video, observed, 'the ... ideas that black Americans disparage "proper English" and education and use a "broken" version of the language have wide currency among many Americans, including blacks'.

The funny thing is, most English-speaking people, wherever they live, are to some extent familiar with AAVE. That's because of the powerful projection of African American culture through movies and music, including the massive popularity of hip hop. Despite being stigmatised in America itself, the dialect has cachet around the world, though arguably that's because it's seen as 'edgy' – romanticised as the argot of gangsters and drug dealers. So when Britons or Australians read phrases like 'I ain't lyin', 'I ain't never seen nothin' like it', 'He be workin' hard', they can identify the speaker as likely being African American; they can conjure up the accent and intonation in their minds' ear.

And yet because this dialect is one that's very close to standard English, and is used by a group whose status is generally low, it gets branded 'sloppy speaking', 'slang' or 'ghetto'. The last label, although freighted with racial judgement, could at least make linguistic sense. We know that dialects emerge when there is geographical stasis. In areas of cities that are primarily black for a number of years, even decades, distinctive ways of speaking are likely to develop – more so given that the isolation is in this case both physical and social.

As Geoffrey K. Pullum makes clear in an article entitled 'African American Vernacular English is not standard English with mistakes', AAVE is a dialect no less complex or expressive than more prestigious forms of the language. It is rule-bound and systematic. It also happens to be the means of communication of a marginalised, often economically disadvantaged group of people. In fact, AAVE possesses at least one fine grammatical distinction which standard English completely lacks. Pullum explains that there is a 'remote present perfect' tense in AAVE, evident in expressions like 'she been married', where 'been' is emphasised. This doesn't just mean 'she has been married', but 'she is married and has been for some considerable time'. In a similar way, the AAVE form 'be' + present participle – 'be walking', 'be singing', etc. is often mistaken for the equivalent of the English present continuous tense: 'is walking' 'is singing'. In fact, it marks what is called 'habitual aspect' – meaning the action is performed as a rule, not necessarily right this minute. 'He be singing' therefore means not 'he is singing', but 'he sings [as a hobby, or professionally]'.

Another distinctive feature of AAVE is the use of the double negative, as in: 'I ain't never seen nothin' like it'. In standard English this would be 'I haven't ever seen anything like it'. What is it that makes African Americans double-up like this? If you say 'I ain't never', don't the two phrases

cancel each other out? Aren't you saying you have in fact
seen it? That's one argument for why this is just 'bad',
irrational, sloppy English – but it's wrong. What we're
seeing here is not logical negation but, as Pullum points
out, a fairly common linguistic strategy called 'negative
concord' – negative agreement, in much the same way that,
in French, nouns and the pronouns and adjectives used to
describe them in a sentence must all agree in gender. Plenty
of other languages have developed negative concord, for
example Italian. 'There is no one there' would be *non c'e
nessuno* – literally 'not is no one [there]', grammatically
closer to the AAVE 'ain't nobody there'. It wouldn't be plausible to accuse sixty million speakers of standard Italian of
sloppiness or speaking in slang. So why would we do the
same with AAVE?

AAVE often misses out what linguists call the 'copula' –
that grammatical form of the verb 'to be' (in other words,
not the form that means 'to exist', as in 'there once were
dinosaurs', or 'to be equal to' – as in 'God is love'). So, an
African American speaker might say 'How you doing?'
or 'You late'. But the standard forms of many languages
do this – for example Arabic, where 'You are late' is *Anta
muta'akhir* – literally, 'You late'.

None of these facts dampened the controversy in 1996
when the school board of Oakland, California, passed a
motion addressing AAVE, which it called 'Ebonics'. The
board made clear it would recognise the dialect used at
home by many of its pupils and would deploy it in the
classroom, for example to 'translate' standard English sentences so that students could understand them better. It is
a mark of the stigmatisation of AAVE that this move was
met with fury, igniting a debate across the United States.
A widespread assumption was that it was an example of

'political correctness gone mad', where a clearly substand-
ard form of the language was being elevated simply because
it was used by black people. The desire to bend over backwards to accommodate an ethnic group's sensitivities was
trumping the need to deliver a high-quality education to the
students of Oakland. The move was condemned as dumbing down – and of depriving black students the means by
which to improve themselves. It was criticised by pundits
both black and white. The civil rights leader Jesse Jackson
said: 'While we are fighting in California trying to extend
affirmative action and fighting to teach our children so they
become more qualified for jobs, in Oakland some madness
has erupted over making slang talk a second language. You
don't have to go to school to learn to talk garbage.'

Given just how disparaged AAVE is, it's not surprising
that it was viewed as 'garbage'. And it's certainly true, given
the way such attitudes permeate the worlds of employment
and higher education, that students who could not master
standard English would be at a disadvantage. But would
using AAVE in classrooms squeeze out standard English, or
aid its speakers in getting to grips with the more prestigious
variety? Here's what the Linguistic Society of America said
in a 1997 resolution: 'The systematic and expressive nature
of the grammar and pronunciation patterns of the African
American Vernacular has been established by numerous
scientific studies over the past thirty years. Characterisations of Ebonics as "slang", "mutant", "lazy," "defective",
"ungrammatical", or "broken English" are incorrect and
demeaning.' Not only that:

> There is evidence from Sweden, the US, and other countries
> that speakers of other varieties can be aided in their learning
> of the standard variety by pedagogical approaches which

recognize the legitimacy of the other varieties of a language. From this perspective, the Oakland School Board's decision to recognize the vernacular of African American students in teaching them Standard English is linguistically and pedagogically sound.

In other words, using AAVE to help students acquire standard English actually speeds up that process. So why the fuss? Really, it just comes down to the closeness of AAVE to English – which enables it to be regarded as merely a sloppy version of the latter – combined with the extreme stigmatisation of black people, such that symbols of their culture, including dialect, denote worthlessness. Among white people, anger at the normalisation of AAVE might have been rooted in fears that it would, as a result, be in a better position to 'contaminate' standard English.

Politics and language frequently collide in this way; how could they not? The way we speak becomes distinctive when we are separated from outside influences, either geographically, socially or both. Over time, distinct dialects become powerfully symbolic of those networks. They can be badges of pride, or of shame. They can be elevated to the status of 'language', remain dialects, or get disparaged as slang. But these decisions are mostly sociopolitical, to do with stigma and status. The linguistic categorisation starts with the idiolect – the forms of speech used by a single person. A collection of mutually intelligible idiolects forms a dialect. Where two dialects are not mutually intelligible, they are often called 'languages' – unless there is a political or cultural reason not to regard them as such – as with Arabic, for example.

We've seen that languages don't have hard borders. In places where populations have been stable for many centuries a dialect continuum can develop, as in southern Europe, where Italian blends into French and then to Spanish. So what is Italian? What is English, French or Spanish? Are they objects you can point to? Where do they begin and end?

In truth, of course, the mistake lies in taking languages to be 'things', analogous to objects. Once again, we find ourselves under the net. Because we can say 'I learned Spanish' using the same syntax as 'I kicked a ball', we take the shorthand – Spanish is a 'thing' that can have something done to it – to be reality.

Languages do exist, but they are not necessarily the things we take them for. On the one hand, we each have an understanding of at least our mother tongue that allows us to produce sentences in it according to certain rules. I say 'I kicked the ball' not 'the ball kicked I'. That knowledge of rules in our brains is one part of the reality of a language. The other part is its existence as an autonomous system, a means of communication whose form is negotiated between speakers. It is not fixed, but changes as it is used in millions of separate interactions.

Finally, to return to the question: what is Italian? It is a dialect that struck it lucky and was christened a language. It is a set of rules carried around by Italian speakers, and it is a living, breathing, shape-shifting mass that comes into being in conversation and blends, at its edges, with other dialects and languages. This is what 'a language' is. Not an island, but a drifting cloud in a crowded sky.

CHAPTER 7

What you say is what you mean

In the British Museum in London, a chunk of black granite, smashed at the top and chipped at the bottom, stands upright among statues of pharaohs. It is the most famous linguistic artefact in history: the Rosetta Stone. Nearly 200 years before the birth of Christ, royal scribes carved into it an edict on behalf of King Ptolemy V.* Because the land he ruled over – Egypt, the Levant and Cyprus – was multilingual, it was set out in three scripts: hieroglyphics at the top, demotic Egyptian in the middle and Greek at the bottom. It was discovered by French soldiers digging at a fort in Rosetta, on the Nile Delta, during Napoleon's campaign of 1798–1801, hence its name. The soldiers realised its significance, saved it, and it was delivered to scholars for safekeeping and inspection. At that time, hieroglyphics were well known – they littered the ancient sites of Egypt – but no one knew what they meant, unlike the Greek script. Once it was understood that the three passages were all translations of the same message, the Rosetta Stone

---

* According to the British Museum, the inscription is 'a decree passed by a council of priests, one of a series that affirm the royal cult of the thirteen-year-old Ptolemy V on the first anniversary of his coronation'. It's a surprisingly boring list of royal honours, achievements and instructions for the conduct of religious services.

was recognised for what it was – a potential linguistic key.

Among the experts who studied the stone was François Champollion. His task was to find correspondences between the three passages, as starting points for the decryption. To do so he focused on proper names that, in the hieroglyphic portion, were identified by rings carved around them, known as 'cartouches'. Because names sound roughly the same whatever language you're speaking, they would provide clues to the sounds the hieroglyphics represented. When Champollion worked out that one cartouche in particular encircled the name Rameses, he was so excited he ran to his brother, shouting not 'Eureka', but *'Je tiens affaire'* – 'I've got it' – and fainted. He is said to have been bedridden for five days afterwards. Champollion was now able to assign phonetic values to the individual symbols and began to identify words that were not names. Rapidly, the upper portion of the stone gave up its secrets – and the messages of a thousand other inscriptions all along the Nile were suddenly unlocked.

The story of the Rosetta Stone is an archetype of decipherment, the process by which information stored in one form is changed into another which we can understand. This is what we assume translators do every day: they take a 'code' – a language understood by one set of people – and change it, word by word, into another (as we saw in Chapter 5, their efforts are likely to be imperfect, but they mostly work well enough for practical purposes). Understanding any given language, therefore, means 'knowing the code' – being able to match arbitrary symbols with the ideas or objects they represent.

If you've ever tried to learn a language, you'll be familiar with the process of translating word by word in your head. Hopefully, at a certain point, something clicks and you no longer have to do this – you inhabit the language, and the sentences flow. In our native languages the process of understanding is so quick that we aren't even conscious of it. Someone says something, and we just get it. Even so, many linguists have interpreted the process of communication as basically one of decipherment, including the man who did more than anyone to shape his field, Ferdinand de Saussure.

He thought of language as being an exchange between a sender and a receiver, whose roles were analogous to the Morse code operators who transmitted messages over the radio during wartime. The sender encodes her thoughts, resulting in speech, and the receiver decodes them at the other end. All that is needed, in this view, is an understanding of the code – a key to be found inside the heads of the speakers, giving them access to shared knowledge. A dictionary in the head. This dictionary is a store of signs – *sema* in Greek, from which we derive the word 'semantics', the study of meaning.

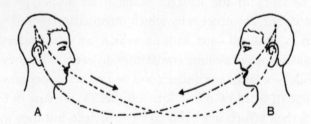

The 'speech circuit' as conceived by Ferdinand de Saussure at the turn of the twentieth century in his famous *Cours de linguistique générale*, or *Course in General Linguistics*

Of course, you need to know the rules of syntax – the way words are combined – too. Syntax is the structure that underpins language, allowing it to reach heights of complexity without collapsing in on itself. If you are familiar with the rulebook, the relationships between all the words remain clear, even when there are multiple verbs, subjects and objects, like this: 'I was upset that Karen bought the same two sweaters for Eric as I had planned to do, without telling my sister as she had promised.'

So a code is made up of semantics – the meanings of signs – and syntax – the rules governing relationships between them. These terms are as familiar to the computer scientist as to the linguist, since what applies to natural language must also apply to any code, like the code determining how a piece of software works. These codes, too, have a semantics and a syntax. This is a piece of code in BASIC,* a well-known programming language, which instructs a computer to display the words 'Hello, world!':

```
10 Cls
20 Print 'Hello, world!'
30 Sleep
40 End
```

An essential part of the syntax of BASIC is that lines of the program start with numbers ascending in tens, and are executed in this order. The semantics includes the definitions of commands like 'Cls', which means 'clear screen' and wipes all previous material from the display. 'Print' is an instruction to display a piece of text on the screen, and the syntax specifies that anything after this command, so long as it's in inverted commas, is what gets displayed. 'Sleep' instructs the computer to pause the program until

---

* Short for 'Beginner's All-purpose Symbolic Instruction Code'.

the user presses 'Enter' on the keyboard, and 'End' stops it. If you break the rules of semantics, by typing in 'Floss', for example, you will get the message 'unknown command' and the program won't run. If you break the rules of syntax, by removing the quotation marks after 'Print', you might get the message 'syntax' or 'reference error'.

In natural language, you can break the rules of semantics by creating a phrase that cannot possibly be true. For example, 'sopping-dry'. You can break the rules of syntax by jumbling up word order. 'The kicked Joni elephant.' The response will be a puzzled look from the person you're talking to – a failure to communicate. According to the code view of language, as long as you don't break these rules, everything should make sense. You might say something about your day: 'This morning I was late for work because of heavy traffic.' Or you could express a simple sentiment: 'I really like movies set in New York.' In any case, what you mean can be clearly and straightforwardly derived from what you say – just as, I hope, you can derive what I mean from this grammatically well-formed sentence right here.

It follows that if a Martian, armed with the same dictionary (semantics) and a list of syntactic rules that you have, visited earth, it would be able to get along perfectly well, make itself understood and have enriching conversations. If all you heard was its voice (assuming it had learned how to speak like a human), you wouldn't be able to tell it was any different. Or would you?

The answer to that question is that you almost certainly would. Martian English would stick out like a sore thumb. That's because there's something vital missing from the conception of language-as-code. The truth is that what you say *isn't* enough to account for what you mean. At the core of language, there is a code; that much is clear from

Champollion's faint-inducing success with the Rosetta Stone. But real communication involves a great deal more. This is a problem that scientists working in artificial intelligence (AI) know only too well – and is why it's still relatively easy to tell whether you're having a chat with a robot.

My friend, the computer

In 1950, the mathematician Alan Turing came up with the idea of a test in which humans would be asked to judge whether the responses they received in a conversation were produced by a machine or another person. If any machine could fool someone into believing it was a person, then it would be deemed to have passed what became known as a 'Turing test'.

It's possible to do the Turing test online, so you can try it for yourself. In one version, you are randomly assigned a chat partner: either a human or a chatbot named Mitsuku. Mitsuku received the Loebner Prize in 2018 for 'most human-like' AI, so you would expect it to be hard to tell the difference between 'her' and a real person. For the purposes of the test, your chat partner – whether it's a human or robot – always has the name 'Millie'. For simplicity's sake, I'll stick to Mitsuku. Here's an example of one conversation we had.

> David: Hi.
> Mitsuku: Hi there David.
> David: What's the weather like where you are?
> Mitsuku: Here in Leeds it is quite overcast. I think it will rain later.
> David: Do you have an umbrella?
> Mitsuku: Yes. I have one with pictures of cats and dogs on it.

David: That's nice. Was it a present?

Mitsuku: Yes, someone bought it for me a while ago.

Mitsuku is able to answer questions appropriately, and seems to have a human backstory: she's in Leeds, in the north of England. She has a quirky umbrella. It's entirely possible this is a real person speaking.

In fact, it's a robot. 'She' did well in a reasonably complex conversation, then. In hindsight, the interaction was slightly stilted – Mitsuku didn't say 'it's' or 'it'll' but 'it is' and 'it will rain' – but it wasn't an obvious fake. So far so good.

But what if I throw in a curveball or two? We start the conversation again.

David: Hi.

Mitsuku: Hi there David.

David: Look, I'm just about to catch a train.

Mitsuku: Would you recommend this action to a friend?

Something's gone wrong. Admittedly, what I did was unexpected. My reference to catching the train seems, on one level, to be a total non-sequitur. Not a standard conversational opening at all. But any human being would probably have realised that in bringing it up I was hinting that I was in a hurry and that we would have to make the chat brief. An appropriate response might have been 'OK – how long do you have?' or even 'Where are you going?' Mitsuku takes things literally: she can't manage to see the wider context, and asks a question which could apply to almost any action I had described, suggesting that she's responding simply to the grammatical category 'verb' rather than the content of what I said and its implications.

Let's try something else.

David: Hello.
Mitsuku: How are you today David?
David: I'm clothed and fed.
Mitsuku: I don't know anyone named clothed.

Again, my answer to a perfectly reasonable question is a bit unusual. But, despite the apparently out-of-left-field comment, what I'm saying isn't nonsensical. An adult human being would probably have interpreted my response as meaning that I was feeling a bit miserable. Rather than saying that I was great, or even fine, I could only aver that my basic needs have been taken care of. Beyond that, you have to assume, there's no good news to impart. An appropriate response would therefore have been 'Oh, what's up?' or 'That doesn't sound good. What's the matter?' Mitsuku, in contrast, is completely baffled. She gets the relationship between 'I'm' and 'clothed' wrong, as though I had said 'I'm Mr Shariatmadari'. (This could be because 'to clothe' is an archaic verb and one that isn't listed in her dictionary. As a result, she reads the past tense as a proper noun, rather than analysing it grammatically.)

Let's see how she copes with a bit of sarcasm.

David: Hi.
Mitsuku: Hi there David.
David: It's cold right now!
Mitsuku: At this moment I am warm here.
David: Well, I'm delighted for you.
Mitsuku: Well that's OK. I am pleased that you are so happy about it.
David: Yeah, right.
Mitsuku: I am usually right.

I've told Mitsuku that I'm freezing. She doesn't offer sympathy, but responds that it's warm where she is. In that context, my reply is clearly supposed to be ironic. One obvious giveaway is that it's over the top – would anyone really expect me to be 'delighted' as opposed to simply 'glad'? But Mitsuku doesn't get it. She responds as if I were being sincere. And when I come back with a clearly sarcastic 'Yeah, right' she once again fails to pick up on the tone. In fact, she interprets it entirely literally – as though I had said she was right, in the sense of 'correct'.

What do Mitsuku's three failures have in common? They all represent examples of conversations in which what is said is not what is meant – where taking things at face value results in a breakdown of communication. They show that knowing the code – the semantics and syntax – is not enough to be able to understand human language. The process of interpreting what someone has said is not like translating hieroglyphics. What's also needed is knowledge of human intentions – what I want to do with my words, as well as what they literally mean. And this requires a lot more than simply a dictionary and a set of word-order rules. It requires as much knowledge about human behaviour as a young person is able to accumulate in the first ten or so years of life. Really sophisticated exchanges – ones that might sound precocious in a ten-year-old – can take years more. It could take a lifetime to become as allusory, deft and witty as Dorothy Parker or Oscar Wilde. That's a lot to ask of a computer. There are some who argue, in fact, that we are as far as ever from the kind of AI that would be able to speak convincingly like a human and not be tripped up by the relatively simple tests I set Mitsuku. That is because, when we speak, we utilise our entire intellectual capacity: not just the dictionary and the rules about word order, but all our knowledge of the world, of society, of analogy-making, of humour, irony, teasing, sadness and ambition, deception and kindness. For a computer to grasp all of that, they'd have to *be* a human, rather than simply make like one. A Turing-test-passing computer is to a real person as a Madame Tussauds waxwork is to a film star: it might look about right, but get closer, give it a prod, and it becomes obvious it's not flesh and blood. All of which puts sci-fi visions of robots that are indistinguishable from people into the long-term rather than the short- or medium-term future. We may one day be able to replicate a human mind in all its worldliness, but don't hold your breath.

At this point, we are reminded of the two contrasting theories of language in the writings of St Augustine and Ludwig Wittgenstein. Remember that Augustine thought that words stood for things in the world: point to the thing, and you get the meaning of the word. This is a code-like view: there is a one-to-one correspondence between the symbol and the object or idea, and therein lies meaning. This can be expanded to sentences too: the meaning of a sentence is the state of affairs in the world that would hold if it were true. If I say 'There's a yellow car in the drive', the meaning is clear if, in the real world, a yellow car does in fact sit in the drive.

Wittgenstein, you'll recall, saw language as use: meaning boils down to the things we do with words, not what they stand for – since they can stand for so many things depending on the context. According to that view, 'There's a yellow car in the drive' could well mean something else, such as 'You're not going to be able to park, I'm afraid – someone else has put their car in your place'.

Philosophers have generally been better at grasping the context-dependent nature of meaning than those linguists who are preoccupied with working out the set of rules that sit inside a person's head – almost as though communication is a private matter, and not something that comes into being when we interact with others. That doesn't mean that interaction is completely random, of course. It is also governed by organising principles. It's just that these are fuzzier, and less predictable – less categorical – than the rules of grammar. Contravening them doesn't always mean that an utterance is 'wrong', as with 'The kicked Joni elephant'. As we are about to discover, going against the norms of interaction can end up being highly meaningful.

So, whereas we speak of 'rules' of syntax, we talk about 'principles' of interaction, and 'maxims' by which they are applied.

You'd better co-operate

The most famous attempt at setting out the principles of conversation – and thereby explaining seemingly paradoxical exchanges like the ones that baffled Mitsuku – was made by Paul Grice, a British philosopher who spent most of his working life at the University of California, Berkeley. He proposed that human beings generally assume that a 'co-operative principle' governs conversations. In other words, when you start talking to someone, you work on the basis that they are going to engage rationally to allow the exchange of information. They will usually co-operate with you in order that the intentions of both parties are made clear. The co-operative principle is such a basic requirement of conversation that there has to be a really good reason to abandon it. Is the person sick? Or insane? Do they want to give a false impression, or deceive you? Notice that, unlike breaking the rules of grammar, abandoning the co-operative principle doesn't result in nonsense; it can still provide you with valuable information about someone's state of mind or intentions.

According to Grice, this co-operative principle can be broken down into four maxims:

> The maxim of *quantity* says that you should make your contribution as informative as is required.
> The maxim of *quality* says you should not say what you believe to be false, or for which you lack adequate evidence.
> The maxim of *relation* says you should be relevant.
> The maxim of *manner* says you should be perspicuous, or clear.

Grice points out that the co-operative principle doesn't just apply to language, but to any situation in which humans interact. According to the maxim of quantity, if you were helping me repair a car I would expect your contribution to be no more or less than needed: if I need four screws, I don't expect you to hand me ten. According to the maxim of quality, if I were baking a cake and needed sugar, I would not expect you to pass me some white sand. If the maxim of relation were being observed, it would be strange if, in response to the sugar request, you handed me a book, or put on some music and started dancing. The maxim of manner requires that you perform your task in a straightforward way; not marching over to the cupboard like John Cleese's civil servant from the Ministry of Silly Walks.

The point is that the maxims are, in general, there to be observed. Recall my conversation with Mitsuku:

David: What's the weather like where you are?

Mitsuku: Here in Leeds it is quite overcast. I think it will
rain later.

My question is about the weather. I'm looking for information. Mitsuku observes the maxim of quantity by giving
me the details I require for the purposes of the exchange,
and not embarking on a meteorological discourse about
low-pressure systems or rain-shadow effects. She observes
the maxim of quality by telling me what she sees to be
the case. She offers a guess as to what might happen later,
but indicates that she can't be completely sure ('I think'),
although she has reasonable evidence. She observes the
maxim of relation by telling me about the weather, and not,
for example, about how hungry her cat is. And her manner
is appropriate too: she doesn't write back in Shakespearean
English, using words like 'prithee' and 'my liege'.

So in a straightforward conversation like this, Mitsuku is
fine. But let's return to my second exchange.

Mitsuku: Hi there David.
David: Look, I'm just about to catch a train.

Now, if you assume that I'm observing the co-operative
principle, you would not expect me to say anything that
wasn't appropriate, truthful or relevant. So, even though
I've introduced a subject that seems very distant from the
one at hand, there is likely to be a reason for it.

In fact, my response can be explained by appealing to the
maxim of relation: the information I'm giving is relevant –
but it can only be understood as such if you know a lot
about human behaviour, and, indeed, the norms of polite
conversation in English. By telling Mitsuku I have to catch
a train, I'm *implying* to her that I don't have time to speak.

The message I want to convey is that if we're going to have a conversation, she ought to make it snappy, and shouldn't be offended that I have to rush – it's nothing personal. This is a special kind of meaning Grice called 'conversational implicature'.

Mitsuku would only be able to decipher this implicature if she'd been programmed with a vast amount of data about the social world of human beings. We are able to make these kinds of connections because of many years spent observing our fellow creatures and participating in a social universe that contains friends, family and strangers, as well as things like trains that have to be caught. The only way around this for computer programmers is to enter a specific rule, along the following lines: 'If the speaker says they are "about to catch X", where X is a bus/train/plane/boat/taxi etc., then assume they might be in a hurry and ask "Are you in a hurry?"' That would work in this instance, but it would be inflexible; what if I said 'My train's leaving soon' instead? Not only that, but it would be incredibly laborious, if not impossible, to create enough one-off rules to cover all the vagaries of natural conversation.

So, when interpreting maxim-governed speech requires a lot of social information, Mitsuku gets into trouble. The world of human behaviour is too large and complex for her to compute. But we've only just started: if the maxims are ignored, flouted or come into conflict with one another, that's when things really get interesting.

Grice differentiates between 'violating' and 'flouting' a maxim. 'Violating' means deliberately ignoring a maxim, such as quality, by saying what you know to be false in a way that might be difficult for your conversational partner to detect. This is plain old lying. 'Flouting', however, is when you blatantly go against a maxim, and intend that fact to be obvious. And a clash occurs when the demands of one maxim mean that you are unable to fulfil another.

These last two situations also give rise to implicatures. When we understand that a maxim has not been fulfilled, because of either a clash or flouting, we are immediately encouraged to seek out the reason for this behaviour – and this leads us to ignore the face-value interpretation and make a different one. As before, implicature bridges the gap between what is said and what is meant.

One very common type of clash is where the requirements of the maxim of quantity (make your contribution as informative as is required) conflict with those of the maxim of quality (do not say what you believe to be false, or for which you lack adequate evidence). This clash accounts for the exchange below.

> Simon: We need to pick up the table from Bed, Bath and
> Beyond. Which store did you order it from?
> Steven: It was one of the ones downtown.

One interpretation is that Steven is playing a bizarre game with Simon. He knows which store it is, but doesn't want to say exactly, despite the clear need expressed by Simon. That explanation is implausible, because it would require Steven to have abandoned the co-operative principle.* In fact, he's trying to be informative, but he doesn't want to say what he can't be sure is true, meaning that the two maxims clash. The implicature – the special code-independent meaning – this generates for Simon is that Steven must have forgotten

---

* It's not impossible; remember we're dealing with principles of interaction here, rather than rules of a code. Going against a principle isn't like jumbling words so that the sentence becomes nonsensical. It just results in perplexing communication.

exactly which store it was. He's either absent-minded, or it was some time ago, or he orders lots of things from different stores. A computer might reply, in genuine expectation of a precise answer, 'Which one of the stores downtown?' Simon might say the same, but out of frustration more than anything else. He will have understood that Steven's memory is vague. He might instead say: 'Are you serious? OK, I guess we're going to have to pull up the email receipt.' Note that Steven didn't make his answer 'I can't remember exactly' explicit, part of the code. He left it to be interpreted by Simon using his powers of inference. The key information is contained not in what is said, but in the wider social and behavioural context.

More curious than clashes are cases of out-and-out flouting. Grice gives the following example. A prospective employer writes to a referee asking for information on a candidate for a high-powered academic role. He gets the following reply: 'Dear Sir, Mr X's command of English is excellent, and his attendance at tutorials has been regular. Yours, etc.' This response at first appears useless as a reference. The referee is not being informative; the maxim of quantity appears to have been thrown out of the window, quite blatantly. But, since the employer knows that the referee worked with the candidate, it simply cannot be that he has insufficient evidence to give a more elaborate opinion – so this isn't an instance of a clash. Perhaps the referee is not obeying the co-operative principle, but that's unlikely: if he isn't, why write at all?

No, this is a flouting – a going-against-expectations that is clear to all concerned. As such it must be intended as some kind of message. Knowing the referee is being co-operative, what can we glean from his reply? Whenever a maxim is flouted, an implicature is generated. Here it's that this guy is a terrible candidate. Just like when I replied with 'I'm clothed and fed' to Mitsuku's question about how I was; the conclusion is that the referee can't report anything good beyond the most basic facts.

Some particularly stark examples of flouting the maxim of quantity (be as informative as is required) are expressions which appear to communicate no new information at all. Grice gives the examples 'war is war' and 'women are women'. From the code point of view, 'war is war' is totally uninformative. It is true, but banally so. The same could be said of 'Velcro is Velcro'. And yet, intuitively, we know that, unlike that example, 'war is war' and 'women are women' convey something more. Why is that?

Deliberate flouting forces the hearer to infer, from the context, what is meant. Shorn of any conversational data, interpreting these sentences is hard. But below are a couple of different possibilities, with the implicatures spelled out. What is said is the same in each instance, but what is meant is wildly different:

> A: Of course we must defend our country, but why do so many have to die?
> B: War is war.
> (Implicature: the costs of our actions might be high, but they're unavoidable.)

> A: Look, I know she didn't invite you to her last party, but is it really necessary to jack up her rent?
> B: War is war.
> (Implicature: she offended me and I'm going to make sure I get my revenge.)

One case of implicature became notorious in Britain in

2012, following allegations of child abuse against an un-named high-profile politician on the BBC show *Newsnight*. Speculation as to the person's identity was rife on social media. The wife of the Speaker of the House of Commons, Sally Bercow, tweeted: 'Why is Lord McAlpine trending? *innocent face*'. By making it obvious she was pretending that she didn't know the reason the Conservative peer was being talked about, she flouted the maxim of quantity, allowing people to infer that McAlpine was the politician in question. With unfortunate consequences for everyone involved, she was wrong. Lord McAlpine was innocent of any charge, and successfully sued Bercow for defamation. In his judgment, Britain's most senior libel judge said: 'I find that the tweet meant, in its natural and ordinary defamatory meaning, that the claimant was a paedophile who was guilty of sexually abusing boys living in care. If I were wrong about that, I would find that the tweet bore an innuendo meaning to the same effect.' That innuendo meaning was the implicature generated by Bercow flouting the maxim of quantity.

What happens if you flout the maxim of quality (do not say what you believe to be false)? Remember, flouting is deliberate and clear to all concerned. If you tried to hide the fact you were ignoring a maxim, that would be a violation instead (for example, lying, and trying to get away with it). Here's a bit from my final conversation with Mitsuku:

> David: It's cold right now!
> Mitsuku: At this moment I am warm here.
> David: Well, I'm delighted for you.

Had Mitsuku been able to hear and recognise my sardonic tone of voice, she would immediately know I was flouting the maxim of quality: saying something I knew to be false. Even in writing the clue is there for her – my response seems way out of proportion to her 'good fortune'. I'd be delighted if she were getting married or had passed her exams, but because she's warm? No. This is a flouting and, as a result, an implicature is generated. The brain looks beyond the literal and attempts to discover the most plausible meaning, given the context. The context is, of course, that I'm cold, and that it's not reassuring or helpful to hear how warm Mitsuku is. The implicature? I'm not delighted – in fact, the opposite: I'm annoyed. This is how Grice accounts for all irony: it's a flouting of the maxim of quality. And, as a context-dependent principle, rather than a rule, applied at some times and not at others, it's notoriously hard for computers to, well, compute.

In the non-linguistic examples given by Grice, a violation of the maxim of relation (be relevant) would involve something like handing someone a book when they'd asked for some sugar for the cake they were baking. To be relevant, a subject must be related in some significant way to what preceded it. An assumption that the maxim of relation is being observed helps us unlock the 'train' non-sequitur. I wouldn't have said it if it didn't have an important bearing on the conversation Mitsuku and I were engaged in. What about deliberate floutings of the maxim of relevance? This can happen when someone raises a subject and you want to warn them off it. Imagine you're at a party, having gossiped with your friend about your host's many affairs. Not realising the extent to which that information is still secret, he says as someone he doesn't recognise enters: 'Ooh, is that one of Mark's girlfriends?' Your response: 'Isn't this a lovely apartment?' By flouting the maxim of relevance, you're communicating – albeit subtly, and in a way which may still fail – that this is a subject to be avoided. If successful, you will have generated an implicature for your friend, along the lines of 'We can't speak about that in front of other people. Let's change the subject, now.'

Finally, there's the maxim of manner: be perspicuous – which can be elaborated as 'avoid ambiguity, obscurity, be brief and be orderly'. Not everyone is poised enough – or knows the language they're speaking well enough – to be consistently perspicuous. Violations of this maxim occur all the time, particularly in badly written books, weasel-worded political speeches and during corporate presentations. However, these are not deliberate floutings. For an example of that, compare the following two sentences:

A: Lady Gaga sang 'The Star-Spangled Banner'.
B: Lady Gaga produced a series of sounds that corresponded to 'The Star-Spangled Banner'.

At first glance, B is just a more precise and pedantic version of A. It provides a lot of information that the majority of listeners would easily get from the first sentence, going way beyond the requirements of normal conversation. You can just about imagine it being used at face value in a very specialised context: by a lecturer in acoustic technology, perhaps. But otherwise it runs a cart and horses through 'be brief' – and it's a clear case of deliberate flouting. Again, we look for any possible reason that B would not simply say 'sang'. Could it be she wishes to impart the idea that what happened was technically singing, but not something you would want to dignify with that label? Could it be, as Grice put it in a similar example, that the song suffered from some 'hideous defect'? That's the implicature.

In one sense, Grice was a latter-day Champollion,

revealing for the first time the principles that govern conversation, as opposed to the definitions and rules that can
help decipher a text. The important difference, of course, is
that we were already well versed in these principles, which
we follow every day of our lives. But we do so intuitively,
without understanding quite how they operate. Rather than
a translator, Grice is better characterised as a reverse engineer. Real-time communication runs like clockwork: he
was among the first to unscrew the back and peer at the
mechanism inside – the mechanism that gets us from what
is said to what is meant.

It's only polite

First movers get some things wrong, and miss some things
out. Grice's framework has been criticised for being incomplete on the one hand, and unwieldy on the other.* In
particular, his maxims seem to ignore politeness, a major
motivator for a great deal of conversational behaviour.

---

* One more recent theoretical framework refines all but one of
Grice's maxims away. Dan Sperber and Deirdre Wilson's 'relevance
theory' seeks to explain all communication in terms of the human
propensity to draw attention to what is relevant. Our ability to
understand exchanges where what is said is not what is meant – such
as the use of 'It's cold in here' to mean 'Please close the window' –
can be explained as a process of scanning possible interpretations
and stopping at the one that satisfies the requirements of relevance.
The most relevant explanation is the one that delivers the most
cognitive pay-off for the least processing effort – making relevance
in some ways a cousin of the philosophical concept of Occam's
razor: the most likely explanation for something is the one that requires the fewest steps. If you find yourself in a room with an open
window and a polite, English-speaking stranger, taking 'It's cold in
here' to mean 'Please close the window' is probably the simplest
solution to the puzzle.

There is no way to explain the flouting of the maxim of relation above, for example, other than that it's an attempt to avoid embarrassment – to be polite by not letting slip an awkward fact about the host.

To plug this gap, scholars such as Geoffrey Leech, Penelope Brown and Stephen Levinson have tried to work out how the requirements of politeness shape the way we interact. Leech added his own set of maxims under the rubric of a 'politeness principle' to accompany the 'co-operative principle': those of *tact* (try to minimise the cost to the other), *generosity* (maximise the cost to self), *approbation* (maximise praise of other), *modesty* (minimise praise of self), *agreement* (minimise disagreement) and *sympathy* (minimise antipathy). Brown and Levinson adapted the folk idea of 'face' – public image or standing – to develop the notion of the 'face-threatening act'. Either 'positive face' (the desire to be admired and approved of) or 'negative face' (the need for autonomy, and not to be imposed on) can be threatened: the former by, for example, complaining or reprimanding, the latter by orders or requests. Since face-threatening acts necessarily happen all the time, politeness is a way of mitigating the threat, and therefore oiling the wheels of social interaction.

The politeness principle can be seen at play in all sorts of conversations, all the time. The difference between the barked command 'Answer the phone' and the politer formulation 'Could you possibly answer the phone' is that, with the latter, the speaker has used tact to minimise the cost to the other person through indirectness (the co-operative principle alone is not enough to account for it: it clearly violates the maxim of quality, since the speaker knows very well that the addressee is literally capable of answering the phone). And the trick is not simply in the stock phrase

'Could you possibly'. Context, as ever, is vital. 'Could you possibly lend me £10,000' is stretching notions of politeness and 'Could you possibly lift a finger to help?' would definitely be considered impolite. The polite invitation 'You must come to dinner with us' satisfies the maxim of generosity by imposing a cost on the self. But 'You must have us to dinner' would be considered cheeky, because it violates the maxim of tact.

As with Grice's framework, sometimes Leech's maxims clash or combine. 'Can I offer you a lift?' is an instance of the generosity maxim. It might be swiftly followed by the tact-maxim-inspired 'It's no trouble at all, it's on my way', an attempt to avoid giving the addressee the impression they are incurring a costly debt.

Leech sets out a spectacular clash of the maxims of modesty, approbation and agreement in a conversation between two women in Japan, where minimising praise of self is a particularly strong cultural principle:

A: My, what a splendid garden you have.

B: Oh no, not at all, we don't take care of it at all any more, so it simply doesn't always look as nice as we would like it to.

A: Oh no, I don't think so at all – but since it's such a big garden, of course, it must be quite a tremendous task to take care of it all by yourself; but even so you certainly do manage to make it look nice all the time: it certainly is nice and pretty any time one sees it.

B: No. I'm afraid not, not at all.

Were it not understood that modesty must be maintained at all costs, B's responses could be seen as frustrating, wilful, almost rude.

The computational linguist Chi Luu describes how Richard Nixon learned about Japanese politeness the hard way in 1969: 'He demanded through a translator that the Japanese restrict their exports that were flooding the American market. *Zensho shimasu* was the response, which literally means "I'll do my best" or "I'll take a proper step" but which, every Japanese person apparently knows, effectively means "no way!" when taken in context.'

The use of Japanese examples raises an important question about any maxim of conversation. Unlike grammatical rules, maxims are not categorical, but apply by degrees, depending on the context, on the closeness of the interlocutors, on all sorts of social and behavioural factors. As a result, one would expect them to vary from one culture to another. In certain societies, some maxims might not even exist, be paid very little attention to, or have vastly different values placed upon them.

Leech himself gives one possible example: in parts of Italy and Brazil, if a stranger asks you directions and you don't know the answer, you should make something up. This is an example of the politeness principle obliterating the co-operative principle. The avoidance of embarrassment in the moment will cause one of the parties serious inconvenience further down the line.

In Iran, the maxim of generosity (maximise cost to self) appears to outweigh most others. Complementing someone on an object in their home – such as a vase, or picture – will almost always result in you being offered it as a gift. The offer shouldn't be taken seriously, and the host will expect you to decline, except in special circumstances. This an example of *ta'arof*, the cultural tradition of politeness that foreigners frequently find over the top.

Madagascar seems to be a particularly unusual case. In

the 1970s, linguistic anthropologist Elinor Ochs Keenan found that Malagasy speakers regularly failed to 'be as informative as is required'. They were often vague, hedging and evasive when asked what we might regard as fairly straightforward questions. For a start, it was considered dangerous to deliver news of an unfortunate event, or some misdeed. In those cases, the speaker would not want to bring upon themselves any of the *tsiny*, or guilt, associated with it. So if someone asked 'Who broke the cup?', hearers would be reluctant to provide a direct answer. That is not particularly hard to relate to – the same phenomenon appears in English-speaking cultures too, with people loath to be the 'bearer of bad news', in case the recipient 'shoots the messenger'.

A more general tendency towards uninformativeness among the Malagasy is harder to understand, though. Asking 'What's new at the market?' of someone who's just returned might elicit the fairly useless response 'There were many people there'. Ochs Keenan says this was because, in village societies where almost every aspect of life was conducted in public, new information came at a premium. There was intense interest and therefore pressure on the speaker to be correct – and as a result, a fear of committing oneself to any claim with great certainty. Rather than risk being wrong, or the source of gossip, you'd be vague. This extended to a marked indirectness about what might happen in the future. Ochs Keenan recalls asking someone what time her brother might be in. The reply was 'If you don't come after five, you won't find him'. Even though the implication was fairly clear – that the person would be at home after five, and you should come then – the use of the double negative suggests an ingrained reluctance to specify.

That reluctance coloured the use of individuals' names

too, because to identify someone directly might bring them 'to the attention of unfriendly forces'. People were referred to in roundabout ways, or by common nicknames shared with many other individuals in the community, such as 'red face' or even 'garbage girl' or 'dog face'. The use of an insulting substitute was about warding off the influence of malevolent spirits who might be stirred into jealousy by praise. In that respect, it mirrored the fear of the evil eye in Middle Eastern societies, in which complimenting someone risks attracting misfortune. Instead of saying 'well done', or 'you're so clever', the phrase *Mashallah* – 'what god wills' – is used.

The fact that different societies weigh maxims of conversation differently can give rise to cross-cultural misunderstanding. The balance of power between the politeness principle and the co-operative principle can be used to explain why many speakers of Slavic languages find British English speakers to be frustratingly indirect. Polite expressions barely noticed in English, such as 'Would it be possible for me to . . .', may be seen as mealy-mouthed or insincere. Russian and Polish, by contrast, use the imperative mood ('Bring me, lend me') far more frequently for requests, without it being considered impolite. Researchers have suggested that this is explained by the fact that, in Slavic cultures, requests are not seen as much of a threat to the speaker's negative face (their autonomy and freedom from being imposed on).

At the same time, British English speakers can find themselves in the position of their Slavic cousins when confronted with American politeness strategies. Phrases such as 'Have a nice day' or 'You're welcome' in reply to 'Thank you' (which are almost universal in America, but still relatively rare in Britain) can begin to seem cloying, or unnecessary.

Americans, in contrast, are likely to find Brits a little blunter than they're used to and, as tourists in this country, may regard waiters or shop assistants as 'rude'.

None of this means that there is a continuum of consideration for others, running from 'high' in the United States to 'low' in countries like Poland and Russia. In fact, one could speculate that it is the emphasis placed on individualism in Anglophone societies that results in greater respect for negative face (the need for autonomy). Regardless, what's clear is that the relative weight given to things like tact, informativeness, generosity and modesty changes from culture to culture. Any analysis of the way conversational maxims work in a given language has to take this into account.

It's not just what you say, it's where, when and to whom you say it.

Why pragmatics matters

Unfortunately, for some people, that's precisely the problem.

Throughout this chapter, we've been looking at meaning that is conveyed 'outside the code' – the principles that allow us to interpret a sentence in the real world, in conversation. As we've seen, what is meant often goes way beyond just what is said – the words chosen and the order you put them in. The study of this additional layer of meaning has a special label in linguistics.

The 'code', we now know, is dealt under the rubric of syntax and semantics. What's left afterwards, including all of the conversational principles and maxims we've explored, is called 'pragmatics'. The division between syntax, semantics and pragmatics was first suggested by the philosopher Charles Morris, who was concerned not just with linguistic signs but with signs in general, a field of study known as 'semiotics'. He described pragmatics as being 'the relation of signs to interpreters', as opposed to semantics, which was 'the relations of signs to the objects to which the signs are applicable'. In this schema, the figure of a green man at a pedestrian crossing refers semantically to the physical action of walking. Pragmatically, however, it can be understood as meaning 'cars will now stop and you won't be mown down, so you can cross safely to the other side'. A fellow philosopher, Rudolf Carnap, took this idea and narrowed its scope to linguistic signs, defining pragmatics as the meaning as interpreted by the 'speaker' or 'user' of the language concerned, as they mentally ask 'What does she mean by this?' This is how linguists think of pragmatics today.

To what extent is this a 'real' distinction, though, as opposed to a theoretical one? Is the apparently rather academic division between semantics and pragmatics reflected in the way our brains process language? If it was, you'd expect some types of brain damage or disabilities to 'knock out' pragmatic capacity, just like, as we saw in Chapter 3, certain types of stroke are said to damage syntactic or semantic ability, causing expressive or receptive aphasia. Any such pragmatic disorder would leave these people able to understand the 'code', but they'd be at a loss as to how to manage the rest of the interpretation of a phrase used in context.

These people exist. In fact, just such a 'pragmatic deficit' can occur following head injuries and in certain developmental disorders. As a symptom, it's perhaps most obvious in conditions such as autism and Asperger's syndrome.

Autism and Asperger's syndrome are now thought to sit at either end of a spectrum, with severe autistic impairment at one end, and the more typical functioning seen in many of those with Asperger's at the other. At their core, the autism spectrum disorders (ASDs) involve difficulties relating to others. Autistic children and adults could be said to inhabit 'their own little world', becoming deeply absorbed in personal states and goals, and sometimes having great difficulty engaging with the feelings or intentions of those around them. This, some psychologists argue, could be because they have a fundamental problem grasping what the beliefs of others might be.

The ability to understand the point of view of others, to put ourselves 'in their shoes', is called 'theory of mind'. I have a theory of mind if I am able to attribute views to you that are different to mine, based on my assessment of what you know. Imagine you're in a department store with two friends, one British, one American. It's the American's home town and he knows the store well. When the British friend asks where the pants are and the American starts to answer, you stop him because you know he's going to say the wrong thing: the Brit is referring to underwear and needs the second floor, not the third floor where the trousers are. You happen to know both uses of the word 'pants', but you don't assume your American friend does – you know he's never spent time in Britain, nor watched much British TV. In a split second, however, you're able to jump out of your shoes and into his, and anticipate his false reply. That's because you have a *theory* about his state of *mind*.

Psychologists often use the 'Sally Anne test', originally devised by developmental psychologist Simon Baron Cohen, to judge whether a young child has developed theory of mind or not. The test can be acted out with puppets. One of them, Sally, has a marble. She puts it in a basket and leaves the room. Anne, who stays behind, moves the marble from the basket into a box. When Sally returns, the child is asked where Sally will go to find the marble. The right answer is the basket – Sally wasn't there when Anne moved it into the box, so wouldn't think to look there. The child, however, knows where it is; answering the question correctly involves differentiating his or her own knowledge from that of someone with a different perspective. All very young children fail this test. As they get older, they get better at it: around 85 per cent of normally developing five-year-olds pass. In contrast, for those with ASD, the fail rate at five is about 80 per cent.

Problems deploying theory of mind have all sorts of knock-on effects, particularly around the interpretation of non-literal language. In order to tease out some of these, the researcher Francesca Happé wrote the 'strange stories', a series of vignettes followed by questions that most of us would have no trouble answering. They were designed to test the understanding of everyday conversational scenarios – including jokes, white lies, figures of speech and misunderstandings – that rely in subtle ways on theory of mind. Here's the strange story based around a joke:

Today James is going to Claire's house for the first time. He is going over for tea, and he is looking forward to seeing Claire's dog, which she talks about all the time. James likes dogs very much. When James arrives at Claire's house Claire runs to open the door, and her dog jumps up to greet James. Claire's dog is huge; it's almost as big as James! When James sees Claire's huge dog he says, 'Claire, you haven't got a dog at all. You've got an elephant!'

Is it true, what James says? Why does he say this?

And here's one based around irony:

Sarah and Tom are going on a picnic. It is Tom's idea, he

says it is going to be a lovely sunny day for a picnic. But just as they are unpacking the food, it starts to rain, and soon they are both soaked to the skin. Sarah is cross. She says, 'Oh yes, a lovely day for a picnic alright!'

Is it true, what Sarah says? Why does she say this?

The answers given by those with ASD tend to stick out. Having read the first story, all the children agree that what James said isn't true. But, asked why he said it, neurotypical children say things like 'the dog is big like an elephant', or 'he's just joking'. ASD kids say things like 'because the boy is lying'. Again, with the second story, the fact that Sarah's statement isn't true is generally clear. But whereas children without ASD will understand that she's annoyed and being sarcastic, those with the condition produce answers such as '[she was] pretending that everything was OK in order to make Tom feel happier'. At some level these kinds of responses show a failure to truly put themselves in the shoes of the characters in the story: the statements they make are taken at face value. In order to properly interpret them, we mentally calculate what the characters must be thinking in order for those statements to make some kind of sense. You could argue that saying '[she was] pretending that everything was OK' is just such an attempt to imagine what someone is thinking. But it fails to get to the truth. Why? It strikes me that, rather than reasoning from the point of view of the character – placing themselves in that position and summoning up the likely intentions to go with the response – children with ASD seem to be working backwards from the words – the code – they see in front of them.

The autistic writer Donna Williams describes in her 1994 autobiography *Somebody Somewhere* how she was able to interpret people's speech by saying it back to herself 'inwardly' and imagining what she would have meant had she uttered the words. This is a laborious, step-by-step means of attaining theory of mind, largely unnecessary for those for whom it has been second nature since a very young age. One autistic young man told researchers Asa Kasher and Sara Meilijson that he was only good at words 'when they mean what they mean' – that is, the code part, but not the rest.

Why do problems with theory of mind make the pragmatic aspects of language so difficult to master? Grice showed that conversational implicatures – those moments when what we say appears to be so different from what we mean – can come about when the speaker makes it obvious they are flouting a maxim. If you simply violate the maxim of quality, by saying something you know to be wrong without signalling that you're lying, that's plain deceit, and you don't have to have a developmental disorder to be fooled by it. But by saying 'Oh yes, a lovely day for a picnic alright!' when it's raining, and, no doubt, in a pointed tone of voice, you're showing that you *mean* to go against the maxim of quality and you want the other person to know it. The crucial difference is one of recognising intention. An implicature happens when an addressee correctly clocks the *intended* meaning of the speaker: she knows what she's doing, and wants me to know too. For that, you need theory of mind. Intonation is often key to understanding the intention correctly, and it's something people with ASD can struggle with. At one point, Donna Williams tells her therapist 'take the dancing out of your voice . . . so you don't distract me from what you're saying'.

At first glance, pragmatics might be considered an example of 'No shit Sherlock' science. It's a discipline that reconstructs how we arrive at interpretations; but these interpretations can seem almost boringly straightforward. When I ask someone 'Do you smoke?' as I pull out a packet of cigarettes, I am not making a biographical inquiry; I am intending them to understand that I am inviting them to take one. Is it really the case that we are navigating a complex, principle-bound system when we engage in such commonplace exchanges? Are there maxims, informational hierarchies, implicatures and so on? Is there not just understanding?

Clearly not. The hard time scientists have had in programming computers to sound like humans is a case in point. The sophistication of the judgements we make every time we interact with someone – on the street, at work, in a shop, at a party – is not to be taken lightly. All it takes is for a small difference in the way your brain has developed – such as that seen among people with ASD – for this delicate architecture to come crashing down. Suddenly, conversations become confusing, difficult to navigate. Take away the ability to interpret implicatures, to understand intentions, and you very quickly get lost.

What we are doing when we communicate – when we enrich the code – might look easy, but it is extremely complex. If you think that what is meant is pretty obvious, then you're luckier than you realise.

CHAPTER 8

Some languages are better than others

In the Introduction I wrote about how, as a teenager, I dismissed Arabic as 'guttural' and generally unfriendly. This behaviour is far from unusual. The value judgements we make about languages we don't know are frequently negative. Hearing people talk and not being able to make head or tail of what they're saying is alienating, and that's before you consider the prejudices we might have about the part of the world they're from. You might think that Eastern Europeans are cold and speak in clipped, unfriendly tones, or that Middle Easterners are hot-headed and sound angry. In the changing rooms at a swimming pool recently, my ears pricked up when I heard two men chatting away in Farsi. The man next to me rolled his eyes and muttered something about how loud and obnoxious they were being. I was hearing something friendly. He was hearing a foreign racket.

The flipside of this rejection of the unfamiliar is the idealisation of languages we identify with culturally. In both cases, we tend to think we're making objective statements. Take the paean to Sanskrit by 'Indian Monk' on YouTube, which at the time of writing has been viewed by more than 380,000 people. In it, a computer-generated, Indian-accented female voice lists all the ways in which the classical Indian language is simply better than the competition. 'Sanskrit has the highest number of vocabularies than any other language in the world,' she intones, in quirky English. 'Sanskrit has the power to say a sentence in a minimum number of words than any other languages.' Efficiency and economy are common claims among language boosters. 'Sanskrit is the best computer-friendly language . . . Sanskrit is a highly regularised language. In fact, NASA declared it to be the only unambiguous language on the planet and very suitable for computer comprehension.' 'There is a report by a NASA scientist that America is creating sixth- and seventh-generation supercomputers based on Sanskrit language.'

This NASA-Sanskrit meme – surprisingly widespread in cyberspace – does contain a grain of truth. In 1985, NASA computer scientist Rick Briggs published a paper in *Artificial Intelligence* magazine on Sanskrit. In it, he compared 'the method used by the ancient Indian grammarians' to analyse Sanskrit with state-of-art techniques used by AI scientists to programme computers, pointing out the similarities. But the agency certainly never declared Sanskrit to be the only unambiguous language on the planet.

Perhaps its researchers should take a look at Korean. A 2011 report in the *Korea Herald* headlined 'Korean language scientifically superior' quotes the scholar Sohn Ho-min. He claims: 'When we say Korean is superior, we are basing this on scientific examination. The Korean language's method of making sound through a combination of vowels and consonants is very scientific and economical, even.'

Or there's this from the *Yemen Observer*:

There are a lot reasons that can prove that Arabic has superiority over other languages. In contrast with Arabic words, the words of those languages appear lame, maimed, blind, deaf and leprous, and entirely bereft of a natural pattern.

The vocabulary of those languages is not rich in roots, which is a necessary characteristic of a perfect language.

If any . . . opponent is not convinced by our research, we wish to inform him by means of this announcement that we have set out in detail the reasons in support of the superiority, perfection and excellence of Arabic which fall under the following heads:

1. The perfect pattern of the roots of Arabic words.
2. Arabic possesses an extraordinarily high degree of intellectual connotations.
3. The system of elementary words in Arabic is most complete and perfect.
4. In Arabic idiom a few words convey extensive meanings.
5. Arabic has the full capacity for the exposition of all human feelings and thoughts.

The writer, Zaid Al-Alaya'a, then throws down the gauntlet. It's almost as if he has Indian Monk in mind: 'Now everyone is at liberty after mentioning these reasons to try, if possible, to prove these qualities in Sanskrit or any other language.'

But while some languages are praised to the skies, others get a very different kind of treatment.* Malay is 'A primitive language with nothing to express of the scientific & complex world if you're to strip away all the words "stolen" from English,' one Twitter user declares in response to a report that it should be made the official language of ASEAN, the Association of Southeast Asian Nations. Hindi is 'a

---

* Many, like Arabic, get it from both directions: 'The ugliest language is Arabic. People speaking this language sound as if they are suffering from a throat disease,' says a user on one internet forum.

backward language without proper script until 1880' claims another. German, in particular, is a time-honoured whipping boy. 'If you get a few drunk Germans in the same room it sort of sounds like a bunch of barnyard animals grunting and honking away', argues one commenter on an internet thread discussing 'The most beautiful/ugly language'. In 1984 the comedian Willie Rushton said it was 'the most extravagantly ugly language – it sounds like someone using a sick bag on a 747'. A century earlier, in an essay entitled 'The Awful German Language', Mark Twain exclaimed: 'Surely there is not another language that is so slipshod and systemless, and so slippery and elusive to the grasp.'

The Guinness Book of Records of 1956 has an entry for 'Most Primitive Language'. The accolade is given to Arunta, 'an Aboriginal Australian tongue which has no pronouns and in which numbers are only vague expressions of place. Words are indeterminate in meaning and form.' The Living Races of Mankind, published in 1900, also singles out Australia as an incubator of rudimentary languages: 'With this low state of development and intellect in everything save hunting, it is not surprising to find that the Australian language [sic] is of a comparatively low grade of evolution.'

Scientific, regular, efficient, beautiful, ugly, systemless, basic, primitive. People have made these claims about languages throughout history. Note the nationality of each of our language enthusiasts: the case for Sanskrit is put by an Indian, Korean is deemed especially scientific by a Korean, and the 'perfect patterns' of Arabic are delineated by a Yemeni. In contrast, German's detractors aren't generally native speakers – and neither were the 'authorities' who held Australian languages to be deficient. Clearly, you are likely to have warm feelings towards the language you grew up speaking, while hostile ones may be prompted by those you don't feel comfortable using, or have simply heard and not understood at all. A language stakes out a community of people who understand one another. It is therefore a means of expressing solidarity. But by defining an in-group it also defines an out-group. Language can welcome, but it can also exclude.

As a result, it is frequently a vehicle for ethnic or nationalist sentiment. We saw how two varieties of essentially the same language – Urdu and Hindi – are freighted with political meaning: arguments over their relative status have led to riots. The wild claims made for Sanskrit are, these days, often linked to an ugly strand of Hindu nationalism that harks back to a 'pure' India in which Muslims didn't exist. And during times of conflict, speaking the wrong language or dialect can literally get you killed. Marko Dragojevic, who studies inter-group communication, tells the story of a coffee shop located in the part of Bosnia Herzegovina controlled by the Croatians during the 1992–5 war:

> On its menu, the café offered its customers coffee at three different prices, depending on which pronunciation customers used to order the item. *Kava*, indexing a Croatian, and by extension, Catholic identity, was sold for the modest price of 1 Deustche Mark. *Kafa*, indexing a Serbian and Orthodox Christian identity, was not available for sale. Finally, *kahva*, indexing a Bosnian Muslim identity, cost the customer a 'bullet in the forehead'.

Different strokes

Since nations and ethnicities often find themselves in competition, it's natural that languages should also become infected by chauvinism. But, setting aside the motivations of the language boosters and language denigrators, is there anything at all in their accounts that makes sense?

Sanskrit's reputation for being formally exquisite may have a lot to do with the fact that it is a classical medium, a language of epic poetry and sacred hymns, not one of every-day conversations. As a result, no one hears the colloquial Sanskrit that would have accompanied those more formal registers when it was a living, spoken language.* Sanskrit remains unsullied by the need to express things like 'Can you pop out to the shop, we've run out of eggs' It also benefits from having been described early on (in the sixth century BC) in minute detail by the grammarian Panini, whose treatise *Ashtadhyayi* codified the language in 4,000 verses and influenced its subsequent reputation as a fount of logic and rigour. A similar situation applies with Arabic, of which there exists a revered and much-pored-over classical form – Quranic Arabic – as well as many contemporary dialects. The association of Arabic with the very 'word of God' lends it an authority in the eyes of some that's very difficult to argue against. Hebrew, though it was not used in ordinary conversation from the fourth century AD to the twentieth, when it was revived, has enjoyed the same kind of status among Jews and Christians. As the language of God's 'chosen people' it was assumed to be divinely in-spired – indeed, to have been the language that man spoke before the fall. In the fifteenth century the king of Scotland, James IV, who spoke six foreign languages, arranged for two

---

* In the 2001 Indian census, 14,000 people described Sanskrit as their 'primary' language, although this doesn't necessarily mean it was their mother tongue. People 'often switch language loyalties depending on the immediate political climate', as Professor Ganesh Devy of the People's Linguistic Survey of India told *The Hindu* newspaper.

newborns to be sent to an island with a deaf-mute nurse in order to determine what the 'original' language of man was. Reports suggested the babes began spontaneously to speak Hebrew.*

To some extent here we are dealing with culturally rarefied forms of languages that, in other contexts, would display all the warts and blemishes of the vernacular. It's easy to put them on a pedestal – to ascribe to them otherworldly qualities – when they never get used to tell someone to wash the dishes.

But there is one thing linguistic partisans get right. Languages *are* different from one another. Sanskrit's dense *fusion* – where parts of a word, morphemes, can carry several different meanings – contrasts with, for example, the *agglutinative* nature of Korean, in which morphemes with one meaning each get piled up together to form a word. Other languages, like Mandarin, are *isolating*,† which means that most words consist of just one morpheme and don't change depending on their relationship to other words.

Here are some examples. Latin is, like Sanskrit, Russian and German, a fusional language. The infinitive (or uninflected) form of the Latin verb for 'to see' is *vidére*. The third-person plural future indicative active form ('they will see') is *vidébunt*. This can be divided into two morphemes, the stem, *vidé*, and the affix, *bunt*. The stem contributes the

---

* A similar story, told by Herodotus, concerns the Egyptian Pharaoh Psammetichus. He ordered two babies to be brought up in the wilderness by a shepherd who was instructed not to speak to them. Eventually they uttered the word *becos*, the Phrygian for 'bread'. Psammetichus therefore concluded that the natural language of human beings was Phrygian, which was spoken in what is now Turkey.

† In contemporary linguistics 'synthetic' is sometimes used instead of fusional, and 'analytic' instead of isolating.

meaning 'see' while the affix carries five meanings in one form: person, number, tense, mood and voice.

Choice of person (I vs you, he or she) shows us who the subject of the sentence is; choice of number (he or she vs they) tells us how many of them there are; choice of tense shows us when the action takes place (I am vs I will); choice of mood – such as indicative or subjunctive – tells us whether the sentence expresses a fact or a wish or possibility (he is seeing a doctor vs it's important that he *see* a doctor); choice of voice – such as active or passive – tells us something about the role the subject played in the action (they kick vs they are kicked). To express the same meaning in isolating Mandarin (or in English for that matter), it's impossible to use just one word as Latin does. You need separated forms: *tāmen* ('they') *huì* ('will') *kàn* ('see'), plus the verbal complement *dào*.

In Turkish, which is an agglutinative language, you have one form, *görecekler*, but it consists of three morphemes (you might remember the extremely long Turkish word we encountered in Chapter 5). Each of the three carries one or two parcels of meaning: the verb stem *gör-*, from *görmek*; the infix *-ecek-*, indicating the future; and the affix *-ler*, indicating the third-person plural.* Why is this described as agglutinative rather than isolating? Is it just convention that we call the morphemes of English and Mandarin 'words', but those of Turkish 'affixes'? Remember: there's a difference. The morphemes that make up a word in an agglutinative language can't be used on their own – there is no such word as *-ler* in Turkish, just as the plural form 's' isn't a word in English.

---

* In Turkish, moods and the passive voice are indicated by additional morphemes, and their *absence* signals the default form (in this case, indicative and active).

So, languages do behave very differently. And you might, for some reason, find agglutination more appealing than isolation, or have a soft spot for fusion. But those would be rather idiosyncratic preferences. There is no sense, after all, in which agglutination is objectively better or worse than isolation or fusion. Is there?

Fables of the reconstruction

In fact, for a significant period in the history of linguistics, that was precisely what was believed. In the nineteenth century there was thought to be an objective scale of sophistication, of advancement and 'civilisation' in language. Given that this scale was invented in Germany, can you guess which kinds of language came out on top? It won't surprise you that fusional languages – including classical ones such as Latin, Greek and Sanskrit, and their contemporary relatives Russian and German – were judged superior. Agglutinative ones like Turkish were seen as gauche, and isolating languages like Mandarin or Vietnamese as the recourse of the savage.

At the time, the theory of evolution was transforming intellectual life in Europe. Charles Darwin's interest in the mechanism by which organisms develop and adapt to their environment led him to think deeply about language as a possible natural parallel – and scholars of language likewise devoured his treatises on biological change. The familiar genetic trees that describe our descent from single-celled organisms via fishes and apes were strongly influenced by trees mapping out the relatedness of languages (and not the other way around, as is often assumed). August Schleicher, the man most associated with the evolutionary view of language, was using them to illustrate the descent of German from a common ancestor in 1853 (*On the Origin of Species* was published in 1859).

The genealogy of languages was worked out using a special technique known as the comparative method. We've already seen from our dive into dialects how different varieties of languages split off from one another because of change over time and geographical isolation. Imagine a community of people on a great plain 1,000 years ago. Population growth means that, eventually, there is not enough land to keep everyone in grain, or, as they happen to call it, *ken*. Two splinter groups decide to leave while the rest stay put: one group migrates over the eastern mountains to find new pastures to cultivate, the other heads over the western mountains. These migrants are successful, and they never look back.

Several generations pass, and three versions of the single language these groups once spoke have evolved independently. Daughter languages have emerged from a parent now lost in the mists of time. One day, when a trader from the great plain arrives in the eastern pastures, he finds he cannot make himself understood using his native tongue. He does, however, sort of recognise the local word for 'grain', which in his language is now *chen*. The easterners, it seems, say *shen*. On another trip he goes to the west, and discovers that the word they use is *ken*. *Chen*, *shen* and *ken* are all cognates – similar-sounding words that are unlikely to have ended up that way by coincidence or borrowing.

There is by now a university in the plain, and a linguist believes that the languages spoken in the centre, the east and the west must be related because they share so many of these similar-sounding words. Unfortunately, all the written records of the time before the migrations have been lost.

He thinks about *chen*, *shen* and *ken*, and applies his

knowledge of how sounds tend to change. He knows that hard 'stop' consonants like /k/ usually get 'weaker', softening into sounds like 'sh' and 'ch', and hardly ever the reverse. As a result he concludes that, in the parent, or proto-, language, the form of the word for grain must have been *ken*. For some reason the western migrants have kept that pronunciation, even as it changed on the great plain itself. Sometimes, like part of a sandcastle that still sticks up after the wave has washed over it, bits of language get preserved and it's difficult to say precisely why.

This is what's known as the comparative method. Cognates are compared, and a hypothetical ancestor, or 'proto-' form is 'reconstructed' based on general principles of sound change. The reconstructions can be incredibly detailed and go back hundreds, even thousands, of years.

Taking cognates from languages as distant from one another geographically as Sanskrit and Irish, Schleicher put huge effort into the reconstruction of the hypothetical common ancestor of all the languages in that vast family. Using systematic correspondences between sounds, as well as between the way morphemes are combined and words ordered in the different languages, he managed to compose a fable in a language that had never been written down: Proto-Indo-European. It's about a sheep and some horses, and it goes like this:

Avis akvāsas ka
Avis, jasmin varnā na ā ast, dadarka akvams, tam, vāgham garum vaghantam, tam, bhāram magham, tam, manum āku bharantam. Avis akvabhjams ā vavakat: kard aghnutai mai vidanti manum akvams agantam. Akvāsas ā vavakant: krudhi avai, kard aghnutai vividvant-svas: manus patis varnām avisāms karnauti svabhjam gharmam vastram

avibhjams ka varnā na asti. Tat kukruvants avis agram ā bhugat.

Translated into English, it's as follows:

The Sheep and the Horses
A sheep that had no wool saw horses, one of them pulling a heavy wagon, one carrying a big load, and one carrying a man quickly. The sheep said to the horses: 'My heart pains me, seeing a man driving horses.' The horses said: 'Listen, sheep, our hearts pain us when we see this: a man, the master, makes the wool of the sheep into a warm garment for himself. And the sheep has no wool.' Having heard this, the sheep fled into the plain.

Could this really be how our distant ancestors spoke? Had Schleicher, the linguistic archaeologist, uncovered the shape of long-defunct words exactly as they would have been spoken? If he'd gone back in time, would he have been able to communicate with the shepherds and horsemen of the plain?

It's a stretch. Reconstructions are necessarily abstractions – it's likely that some parts of the ancestral language were entirely lost, without any kind of trace in its daughters. They're also hypotheses: we work out what sound changes were most likely, as a result of how we know sound changes generally proceed. This is not foolproof. In fact, as our linguistic knowledge has gradually refined, very different reconstructions of Indo-European words have emerged (in one 2013 version, Schleicher's word for 'sheep', *avis*, is reconstructed as *hauei* – compare the Latin *ovis* and English 'ewe'). At this time depth it's also impossible to know whether the reconstructed forms would all have existed at once; Schleicher's snapshot may in fact cherry-pick words separated by centuries. That this fable would once have been told around a fire is, sadly, a fanciful notion.

A better class of language

As well as spending time working on reconstruction, Schleicher, in common with other prominent linguists of the time, was obsessed with the typological distinction between fusional, agglutinative and isolating languages. These, he thought, represented different stages in their natural history. The fusional languages – which all belonged to what he called the Indo-Germanic family (now more commonly known as Indo-European), or the Semitic family (which includes Arabic and Hebrew) – had once been simpler but had evolved, passing through both isolating and agglutinative phases. Crucially, because he believed the process of evolution had by his lifetime given way to one of decline, those languages that were currently isolating or agglutinative were essentially stuck at their lower levels of development. Thus there was not much hope that Turkish, Finnish or Mandarin would ever attain the heights of sophistication reached by Schleicher's native German: those unlucky tongues would for ever be incapable of expressing the full range of human experience. They were blunt instruments, runts of the litter of languages – or, perhaps, to use an evolutionary analogy, the less-fit species of the earth.*

---

* According to the historian of science Robert Richards, the fact that some languages in the Indo-European family (such as English) had 'degenerated' towards isolation was explained by Schleicher as follows: 'the energies required for the refined articulation of language began to be employed in the development of rational laws, state governments, and the aesthetic products of advanced

Schleicher believed that the various different language families had arisen independently, springing up among disparate groups of humans from exclamations, cries or calls. He held that the point at which human beings began to use basic language was the point at which they left the animal kingdom. Speech was the defining feature of our species. From these early stages onwards, the development of human minds occurred in tandem with the development of languages. Cognition and language were essentially one and the same: there was no 'language of thought' independent of speech – language was what made thought possible. It followed, then, that those with simpler, more primitive forms of language were mentally disadvantaged. They were, in essence, lower forms of human life.

Schleicher, together with his close colleague, the so-called 'scientific' racist Ernst Haeckel, wanted to explain not just linguistic facts, but what they regarded as anthropological facts. Why do some human beings wander around forests in loincloths while others, besuited, admire works of art in great cities? For us the answer must lie in the vagaries of history. Circumstances might favour one group over another for no good reason, or because of the uneven distribution of natural resources. The answer for Schleicher and Haeckel was that, as evidenced by the stark contrasts between languages, different groups of humans had evolved differently: for some, the route towards civilisation was swift; others got lost in the undergrowth.

Haeckel actually believed that humans were not really a single species, but comprised nine different ones, including 'Hottentots', 'polar people' and 'central Africans',

---

civilisation'. In contrast, language declinists today tend to see the erosion of civilisation and grammar as going hand in hand.

with 'Caucasians' at the top. As if that wasn't bad enough, historian Robert Richards says Haeckel thought that 'the mental divide separating the lowest man (the Australian or Bushman) and the highest animal (ape, dog, or elephant) was smaller than that separating the lowest man from the highest man, a Newton, a Kant or a Goethe'. For these leading figures in their respective fields, some languages certainly were better than others: the fusional languages were the best; they represented the most advanced state of human evolution. Those speaking more 'primitive' languages had more primitive minds.

Schleicher and Haeckel's hypothesis is easily demolished in two ways. First of all, language and race are completely independent. A child of any ethnicity can learn any language as well as any other native speaker if they grow up with it. There is no evidence that Chinese babies have a hard time grasping the grammar of German. Likewise, a child of indigenous Australian descent will learn Italian, Portuguese, Korean, Arabic or the Namibian language !Kung if that is the linguistic environment in which they are raised (left alone on an island, however, they will not start speaking Hebrew).

Second, these scholars were clearly not conscious enough of their own place in history. Although they happened to live in one of the most advanced societies of their own era, 400 years earlier China, with its strong central government and extensive bureaucracy, easily eclipsed the achievements of German-speaking people of the time. And yet the Chinese were the ones with the apparently defective isolating language. Indeed, snapshots of history taken at various points over, say, the last 2,000 years would reveal global top dogs – the Chinese, the Ottomans, the Spanish – speaking in turn isolating, agglutinative and fusional languages, not consistently fusional ones, as you would expect if Schleicher's theory were true.

Fusional languages are not the most 'advanced', nor do they predict civilisational success. They are, however, structurally very different from other types. They package information in a particular way, piling meaning onto meaning, often inside a single morpheme. Should we then infer that speakers of these languages are more economical? That they can get more across, with less effort, and more quickly? And wouldn't that be 'better'? Compare human language to something like Morse code – all that laborious tapping-out of dots and dashes just to convey a single letter. It's clear which is the more useful, except in very specific circumstances.

It's OK to be dense

Recall the claims that 'Sanskrit has the power to say a sentence in a minimum number of words than any other languages', and in Arabic that 'a few words convey extensive meanings'. Could something like this be true? Are some languages more *efficient* than others?

It has become a cliché in modern linguistics to say that all languages are equally complex. This idea has been challenged by scholars such as Guy Deutscher and John McWhorter. As Deutscher points out, there's no way the Melanesian language Rotokas, with eleven phonemes, and !Kung, with 141, can be said to be equally complex in terms of sound. Similarly, German is clearly more complex than English in terms of some aspects of grammar: it has case endings and three genders, which English lacks. When I use a noun, I don't have to remember whether it's feminine, masculine or neuter – the question just doesn't come up.

One way to rescue the 'all languages are equally complex' hypothesis, then, is to say that simplicity in one area is made up for by complexity in another: if a language has a very pared-back sound system, for example, it might make use of tones (Rotokas, as it happens, doesn't). If it lacks case endings, it might have a greater variety of prepositions to make the relationships between words clear. It would be hard to prove this tendency towards equilibrium, though, because there's no precise way of quantifying complexity and then translating it between domains.

At the same time, there's something powerful about the idea that all languages are on a par. This is because we know that the underlying biology is the same for all speakers and, in general, so are the needs that language serves. In functional terms, Mandarin performs the same role, is required to be just as sophisticated and flexible, as English. If any language weren't 'fit for purpose' in this way, then it really would be a disadvantage to its community of speakers, and language type would correlate with the overall success or failure of groups of people in a way that it simply doesn't.

So instead of 'equal overall complexity', researchers Francois Pellegrino, Christophe Coupé and Egidio Marsico speak of 'equal overall communicative capacity'. All languages do the job we need them to do: allow us to communicate effectively. There is, they hypothesise, a fairly consistent 'rate of information transmission'. If this dipped too far, the language would fail to perform the tasks required of it – using it would be like fumbling in a second language. If the rate went up too high, it would exceed our physiological and cognitive capacities (it would be impossible for our tongues and brains to keep up with). In other words, languages cluster around a communicative sweet spot.

Information can be packed into language in different

ways, and keeping up a constant rate of information transmission doesn't dictate a particular way of doing things. Pellegrino, Coupé and Marsico studied seven languages – Mandarin, English, German, Italian, French, Spanish and Japanese – expecting to find different strategies for remaining within the sweet spot. Mandarin and English are broadly isolating, German, Italian, French and Spanish are broadly fusional, and Japanese is broadly agglutinative.

In particular, they expected the speed of speech – something they called 'syllabic rate' – to vary according to how much meaning was packed into each chunk – which they called its 'information density'. Languages with high information density would be spoken more slowly, and ones with low information density more quickly. Again, this is because speaking a high-information-density language quickly would overload human cognitive capacities. This trade-off is important. You might argue that an information-dense language is a better one – you get more meaning for your money. But that's misleading: it's not better if it has to be spoken more slowly, and the rate of information transmission ends up being about the same.

The question then becomes: which language out of those seven is the most information-dense? Pellegrino, Coupé and Marsico answered this by analysing a series of short texts that conveyed equivalent meanings. One is a story about someone letting the cat out, stepping outside to briefly enjoy some fresh air, only to find the door has slammed behind them and they're locked out. These were recorded by native speakers of each of the seven languages. The duration was measured to give an information density score, and the syllabic rate was also recorded.

And the 'winner' is – Mandarin. You'll remember that, in Schleicher's schema, isolating languages are the lowest of the low, halting, simple and monosyllabic. But here we can see that each Mandarin word packs in a lot of information. One obvious point to make is that Mandarin uses tones to differentiate between words with the same sequence of phonemes: such that *ma* said with a rising tone means 'hemp', but with a falling tone it means 'curse'. This adds a layer of information without taking up any extra time. Still, that information needs to be processed, and as a result the rate at which syllables are uttered is relatively slow.

In contrast, Spanish has a very low information density, despite being a fusional language. You could regard it as containing a lot of 'padding'. But, given that the burden of processing this information-lite verbiage is low, the language can be spoken more quickly.

Mandarin is slow but dense, Spanish quick but light – and so the information transmission rate is about the same for both languages. They are different, but 'equal' in that important respect at least.

So how and why do languages get that 'padding', the additional complexity in grammar or sound that may make them seem highly sophisticated, but which might in fact just make them less informationally dense?

Pidgin talk

To answer this, it might be useful to turn to what some linguists believe are the 'simplest' languages in the world: ones that don't merely lack fusion and eschew unusual sounds, but share other characteristics, such as subject-verb-object word order and lack of gender.

These languages are known as 'creoles' and they come into existence only under very specific circumstances. Let's look at one creole, Tok Pisin, which is spoken in Papua New Guinea.

English speakers will recognise straight away that there's something unusual about it. Here are some words in Tok Pisin, a language with equal overall communicative capacity to English, and mother tongue to more than 120,000 speakers.

gras	grass
mausgras	moustache
gras bilong fes	beard
gras bilong hed	hair
gras bilong pisin	feather
gras antap long ai	eyebrow
gras nogut	weed
han	hand
han bilong diwai	branch of a tree
han bilong pisin	wing of a bird

At first glance, it appears we are dealing with a bastard-ised form of English. The derivations make logical sense, but seem bizarre or childlike. Not, however, if you're a Tok Pisin speaker – because you don't know the original English words and have no idea about the way we divide up our lexicon, or what pairings of words are usual and unusual. As far as I know, 'grass' in English is not used metaphor-ically to derive new nouns, so seeing it deployed this way is incongruous. English does, however, use exactly this strat-egy elsewhere, in words like 'belly button' and 'seahorse' (remember that a linguistic word, identified in English by its single stress, can appear as two 'words' in print).* It's

---

* And in German, *Handschuh* ('hand-shoe') means 'glove', and *Fin-gerhut* ('finger-hat') means 'thimble'. Poetic compounds of this type in defunct Germanic languages are known as 'kennings', and include *hronrád* ('whale-road'), meaning 'sea', and *heaposwát* ('war-sweat'), meaning 'blood', both from the Old English epic *Beowulf*.

only because the Tok Pisin words are somewhat similar to English that we find them funny – they reside in a sort of linguistic 'uncanny valley' for English speakers.*

The Tok Pisin preposition *bilong* does indeed derive from the English word 'belong'. But it functions differently, having been 'semantically bleached', like words that undergo grammaticalisation. It is often used where the English preposition 'of' or 'for' would be. Ask for a *tebol bilong wanpela* in a restaurant, and you'll get a 'table for one'. Alternatively, it can indicate simple possession. On Awake!, a website maintained by the Jehovah's Witnesses – religious missionaries are among the world's great language learners, for obvious reasons – an argument for intelligent design is made in an article, versions of which are provided in both English and Tok Pisin. The subject matter is 'cat whiskers'. That phrase is translated into Tok Pisin as *mausgras bilong ol pusi*, which any English reader will find pretty funny.

The article ends with the questions 'What do you think? Did the function of cat whiskers come about by evolution? Or was it designed?' The version in Tok Pisin is '*Yu ting wanem? Mausgras bilong ol pusi i kamap long rot bilong evolusen? O wanpela i bin wokim?*' The sentence in English

---

* The 'uncanny valley' is a term taken from robotics, and refers to the weird feeling induced by robots that look almost, but not fully, human. As the cognitive neuroscientist Bobby Azarian explains: 'the positive relationship between a robot's degree of human likeness and our affinity for it continues to grow only until a precise point. Specifically, when robots appear *almost* exactly human, people experience an unsettling feeling that causes revulsion. Something just feels "not quite right," and the machine looks "creepy." At this stage the positive relationship sharply turns negative, where it remains for a short period of time just before turning positive again when the robot starts to look completely indistinguishable from a human – a design feat yet to be fully achieved.'

is perfectly contemporary, clear, and not in any way funny. In Tok Pisin, to English eyes, it looks quaint, silly, like baby talk. This is simply a result of the uncanny valley, and the fact that we recognise the etymology of many of these words – *kamap* from 'come up', *rot* from 'route', *wokim* from 'work' – but they are being used according to the rules of Tok Pisin grammar and word formation, not those of English. We are discombobulated and bemused.

So what are the special circumstances that give rise to creoles? There are thought to be two stages: first, adults who speak different, mutually unintelligible languages are forced to interact. They cobble together a means of communicating using scraps of vocabulary and grammar from the different languages around them whose meaning they are able to work out. This form of speech is called a 'pidgin' – and it is not generally regarded as a complete language, precisely because it fails to match the overall communicative capacity of other languages (you may have spotted that *Tok Pisin* itself corresponds to the English words 'talk' and 'pidgin', despite the fact that it no longer has that status). A pidgin changes in important ways when it acquires native speakers: for example, when a man and a woman who can communicate using only pidgin raise children for whom it becomes a mother tongue. It's at the interface between generations, apparently, that the magic happens. Children 'flesh out' the pidgin into a fully functioning language, which linguists call a 'creole'.

Pidgins and creoles usually come about because of trade, or enslavement. The distribution of creoles around the world reflects this: they have emerged mainly in the Caribbean, West African and Asia-Pacific regions.

Often, the language that provides much of the vocabulary (the so-called 'lexifier' language) is the language of the foreign traders or slave buyers – frequently English, French or Portuguese. The grammar may be influenced by a local language (the 'substrate') – or, as some have argued, the innate universal grammar that we fall back on when building a language from scratch, and about which we'll hear more in the final chapter.

What's clear is that, although they are full-fledged languages, creoles are unique. The linguist John McWhorter maintains that 'the world's simplest grammars are creole grammars'. He believes that linguistic complexity is only ever 'acquired' over many generations. It is a form of accretion, like the minerals and coral that coat a long-submerged shipwreck. Far from being especially useful, complexity exists only because it doesn't have to not exist. It is an imprint of a language's history that isn't inconvenient enough to be blasted away.

He quotes another eminent linguist, Roger Lass:

Not only does a language have by definition a sufficient set of structures and categories available for doing anything that a speaker 'needs' to do; it will also have a lot of material that simply makes speakers do things, whether or not there is any . . . 'need' to do them. (English forces a speaker to mark durative aspect every time he utters a sentence in the present tense; German, Afrikaans, French and Swedish don't, but they have machinery for doing it if necessary.) We live perpetually with 'decisions' of past generations. Somebody, somewhere (as it were) decided in the eighteenth century or thereabouts that the expression of progressive aspect should be obligatory in English, and as an English speaker I'm simply stuck with it.

Creoles, McWhorter says, are simpler for one reason only:

because they are new. They do not yet have the patina – for which read cases, gender markings, definite and indefinite articles, copulae, ergativity* – that older languages do, sometimes in great abundance.

Why do languages become complex? Well, remember that the history of a language is the accumulation of a cultural experience, a fossil record of changing communicative strategies. Recall Johann Herder, who said that to speak is to 'swim in an inherited stream of images and words'. If your inheritance is merely one or two generations deep, the stream will be shallower. Some complexities disappear, of course, particularly if a language suddenly acquires lots of new adult speakers who have difficulty understanding its finer points. Alternatively, they might get 'naturally' eroded because they end up being too cumbersome for regular speech – as with grammaticalisation. In English 'going to', two words, is being reduced to 'gonna', one. But complexification can follow as well: remember the cycle *hoc > ecce hoc > ce > celà > ça* from Chapter 1. At different stages in its history, a language may be more or less complex. But both processes require time, and time is what creoles don't have.

Some languages are more grammatically complex than others, then, but that complexity is frequently unnecessary. It encodes what might be left to pragmatics in a less elaborated language. Older languages come with more baggage

---

* In Chapter 6 we saw that 'copula' is a form of the verb 'to be' when used merely to link the subject and the rest of the sentence. Many languages lack a copula – so that rather than saying 'The sky is blue' you'd say 'The sky blue'. Ergativity is a curious phenomenon: the subject of an intransitive verb, rather than being marked in the same way as the subject of a transitive verb, and differently from the object of a transitive verb, is marked in the same way as the object of a transitive verb. In English, this would be like saying 'Her arrives'.

than required. Does this make them better? It depends on your point of view. Do you like your languages simple and sleek? Pared down but efficient? Elaborately encrusted but cumbersome? Densely packed with information but slow? Lighter but faster?

It's all a question of taste. Languages are unmistakably different, but they all aim at the same thing – effective communication – employing different strategies to achieve it. And they all succeed in their own ways. You can get behind Sanskrit, Arabic or Korean, and indulge in a bit of German-baiting if you like. There is clearly no objective assessment to be made. Your language is better than mine? Says you and whose army?

CHAPTER 9

Language is an instinct

'I want.'
'This go on here.'
'I'm eating my bread Mummy'
'I'm going to Cookie Monster's place, and I'm going to have a peanut-butter sandwich.'

You've just read sentences produced by children at one year and eight months, two years and three months, three years and four years respectively. The journey from single syllables to full sentences is remarkably rapid, and has puzzled scientists for decades. I would advise you to enjoy the simplicity of that baby talk while you can, because it's in attempts to get to grips with this puzzle that the study of language becomes, well, difficult. This is where the really big questions are tackled.

Like all human sciences, linguistics has its own version of the nature vs nurture problem: which matters more, genes or environment? This is an argument played out endlessly in the fields of health, psychology, education and so on. Some believe mental illnesses are mostly the product of trauma or childhood experiences, others that they are the result of blips in our DNA. Historically, there has been a fierce debate over the heritability of academic performance: whether success at school and college is inborn or primarily the result of good teaching and parenting. For scholars of language the question takes the following form: is the extraordinary complexity of language a product of learning and interaction, or is it an inherited trait? In other words, is it culture or biology that exerts the most influence? Whether or not you grow up speaking Japanese or English is, of course, determined entirely by your environment. At issue instead are both the phenomenon of language itself, which arises in every community bar none, and the properties all languages are said to share.

Again, as with all human sciences, the truth is that both nature and nurture play their part. This is not about backing one to the complete exclusion of the other; it is about the relative size of their contributions, how much each matters. The form and specificity of the genetic contribution are what linguists have spent so much of the past half-century disputing. Argument and counterargument have been deployed at ever-increasing levels of abstraction and complexity. The whole enterprise can sometimes seem like an attempt at outsmarting your opponent. So keep one finger in the Glossary and hold onto your seat as I try to guide you through the territory.

First we'll grapple with a much-discussed linguistic problem – the poverty of the stimulus. How do children learn language so well given that the grammatical instruction they get from their elders is so haphazard and incomplete? We'll look at how this incompleteness led Noam Chomsky to the conclusion that everyone is born with a genetic blueprint containing information about the structure of language – a language instinct, if you will. He calls this blueprint 'universal grammar' (UG), and it appears to explain a lot of other linguistic patterns too. I'll set out what Chomsky thinks UG consists of. We'll then see how some linguists have cast doubt on the idea of the poverty of the stimulus, calling the whole blueprint theory into question. Finally, we'll explore alternative ways of accounting for the linguistic structures that UG purports to explain.

Baby geniuses

If you've ever tried to become fluent in a second language you'll know how laborious it is, how you seem to move forward at a snail's pace if you're lucky, and only then because of great effort. Now, can you remember getting to grips with your first language? Do you recall struggling to figure out where the preposition should go, or memorising irregular past tenses and when to say 'the' instead of 'a'? No. Because it came 'naturally' to you. You were raised on it, not 'taught' – you didn't have to have lessons. In fact, you could speak before you went to school, merely as a result of being in the company of the people who raised you. There's now evidence that the whole process starts even earlier than that – in the womb. According to German researchers, the melody of newborn babies' cries is shaped by the sounds of their native language, which they must have heard through their mother's bellies.

The 'development' or 'acquisition' of speech in children – so called because it can seem more like an organic rather than a willed process* – is all the more remarkable given just how complicated language is. Think of the knowledge stuffed into that sentence: 'I'm going to Cookie Monster's place, and I'm going to have a peanut-butter sandwich.' First of all, you have to know the meanings of the verbs and

---

* Chomsky writes: 'We do not really learn language; rather, grammar grows in the mind.'

nouns – 'to go', 'Cookie Monster', 'place', 'have', 'peanut-butter sandwich'. Very roughly, children can produce around ten words by the age of thirteen months, fifty by the age of seventeen months and 300 by the age of two. By the time they're six, they are able to say around 3,000 words, and understand a third as much again. As soon as children can put syllables together, between the ages of nine and eighteen months, words become an important currency, a means of getting what they want: 'milk' or 'teddy'; and of expressing their preferences: 'no', 'more', 'again'. New words are absorbed at the rate of around one to three a week up to the age of eighteen months, when the pace starts to pick up. How are these words understood? As we saw in Chapter 2, sometimes the Augustinian method will suffice: the parent presents an object to the child while naming it. More often it will be through observing how they are used – the Wittgensteinian way (after all, with words like 'no' there is nothing to point at). Learning words is a feat in itself, but really that's the easy part.

What about grammar? If words were all you needed, it would do just as well to say 'Sandwich going I'm to Cookie peanut Monster's butter and place I'm to going have a'. This doesn't happen. Remember, language – the 'code' part at least – consists of meanings (semantics) and the rules for combining them (syntax). The latter is essential for avoiding gobbledegook. Another facet of grammar is knowing how parts of words are put together – morphology, which has its own sets of rules; for example, if you want to change the tense of the verb 'walk', you have to add different elements to it, in a specific way: 'walking', 'walked'.

In the Cookie Monster sentence, the child displays extremely sophisticated knowledge of syntax and morphology. She knows how to conjugate the verb 'to be' and how to abbreviate it ('I'm'). She knows the conditions governing the use of present continuous tense in English. She uses a special marker ('s) to indicate possession, places the subject, verb and object in the right order and unites two clauses using a conjunction. Most adults would be unable to set out the grammar of even a simple sentence like this. But somehow, children know all about the relationships between the different words. They must do, because they're able to choreograph them with apparent ease.

This choreography is all the more impressive when it comes to questions. 'I'm going to Cookie Monster's place' is a declarative sentence. The equivalent question, the interrogative form, would be 'Where am I going to?' Simple, right? Except that, to get there, you have to replace the destination with a specialised counterpart of 'here' or 'there', which is only used when the location is not known. Then you move it all the way to the front. You swap the auxiliary* and the subject around, expanding the former in the process, and leave the main verb and the preposition in place.

The question of how human beings – children or adults – perform these kinds of complex operations without having been taught them, or even having any conscious knowledge of what they're doing, has proved difficult to answer.

It is made trickier still if – as many believe – no child is given enough 'input' from the outside world to generate the 'output' they eventually become capable of. Were language acquisition solely a question of learning by rote, it would in principle be impossible: one of the key distinguishing features of any given human language is that the number of expressions it contains is infinite. You cannot learn all

---

* An auxiliary verb is one that 'helps' form a tense, but doesn't change the core meaning: verbs such as 'to be' and 'have' in the sentences 'I am waiting' and 'I have not seen him'.

the ways of putting words together by memorising them if they go on for ever. An alternative is to try to learn rules: to identify patterns in the way adults speak, and apply them to new situations. This would explain why children often overgeneralise the rules they learn. Take the English past tense, which is formed with '-ed'.* A child will hear plenty of examples of it, will begin to understand that it refers to things that have already happened, and will start to use it. The problem is, there are lots of irregularities, which *do* have to be learned by rote. These include past forms like 'went', 'hit' and 'caught'. And because they're applying rules, but haven't memorised all the exceptions yet, the child will produce words like 'goed', 'hitted' and 'catched'.

That's not the end of the world. Irregular past tenses are fairly common, and as time passes, children begin to incorporate them. Sometimes, though, the process of correction isn't as straightforward. There are certain constructions that don't seem to get 'disconfirmed' like 'hitted' and 'catched' do – but which children still somehow understand are mistakes. Take the following pairs of sentences:

Dad told a story to Sue
Dad told Sue a story

Jim showed the model to Bob
Jim showed Bob the model

---

* It has three different sounds, depending on the final sound of the verb in question: /id/ for ones ending in 't' or 'd' (wanted, needed), /t/ for other voiceless consonants (helped, walked) and /d/ for other voiced consonants or vowels (amazed, followed). Children need to absorb this phonological rule to deploy the regular past tense correctly, alongside the morphological one.

Mum baked a cake for Jack
Mum baked Jack a cake

A child hearing these sentences would be able to identify a clear pattern. In a sentence where the object is somehow the beneficiary of an action, there are two ways you can arrange things: one where the recipient comes at the end, after a preposition, and one where the recipient comes straight after the verb, with the 'gift' coming afterwards. That means she can then go away and use the rule for herself. She might say 'Dad gave me a sandwich' instead of 'Dad gave a sandwich to me'. Or 'Mum showed me a drawing' instead of 'Mum showed a drawing to me'. But she might also reason that, because you can say 'Dad said something nice to me', then 'Dad said me something nice' is also fine. Or that since 'Mum buttoned up the coat for Jack' is OK, then 'Mum buttoned up Jack the coat' is as well.

Unfortunately, to most English ears these sentences sound very wrong. But does the child get evidence of this in the course of her everyday life? Are their assumptions about these kinds of sentences ever disconfirmed? Hearing an irregular past tense is one thing, but if you simply never heard 'Mum buttoned up Jack the coat', at what point would you understand it was wrong? And yet, somehow, children do – mistakes like these are eventually filtered out.

There are many other constructions for which disconfirming – or 'negative' evidence – just doesn't arise. Take the pattern of verbs that can be intransitive or transitive, in sentences such as 'The stick broke' (intransitive) and 'I broke the stick' (transitive). Hearing sentences like these, you might assume that all verbs behave this way. Linguist Melissa Bowerman recorded several examples of her children, all under six, overgeneralising this rule, including:

'I want to comfortable you' (lying on the sofa with her mother, cuddling her).

'Don't giggle me' (as her father tickles her).

'It always sweats me' (refusing sweater).

'Do you want to see us disappear our heads?' (Then, with a friend, she ducks down behind the couch.)

Adults don't use phrases like these. They understand that 'be comfortable', 'giggle', 'sweat' and 'disappear' can only be intransitive. Is their absence in adult language enough to dissuade young learners, over time, from using them? Maybe; but remember that the number of possible sentences in a language is infinite – the fact that you never hear one shouldn't be taken as a sign that it's impossible.

Sometimes it is not the absence of negative evidence but the scarcity of positive evidence that's the problem. Take the sentence 'The dog in the corner is hungry'. To turn it into a question, you need to move the auxiliary 'to be' to the front of the sentence: 'Is the dog in the corner hungry?' Now, imagine a sentence with two auxiliaries in it: 'The dog that is in the corner is hungry'. How does a child know how to make a question out of that? There are two possibilities. Number one: you scan the sentence, and the first time you see an auxiliary you shift it. That would be the simplest option, and it already works for 'Is the dog in the corner hungry?'

Let's try it: 'Is the dog that in the corner is hungry?' That doesn't sound right at all. In fact, it's a mistake that's almost never made. Children somehow always acquire the correct pattern, which follows a second, but more complex rule – you scan the sentence and move the auxiliary from whichever is the *main clause* to the front. The main clause is the one that could stand on its own if the non-essential information was removed, one that isn't preceded by 'that' or 'which'. In this case, it's 'The dog . . . is hungry'. Moving the auxiliary from the main clause is how you get 'Is the dog that is in the corner hungry?' Children learn this despite the fact that, in order to glean it from their parents, they would have to have been repeatedly exposed to an apparently very rare and complicated sentence structure – a question formed from a declarative with two auxiliaries.

Perhaps children are able to learn the rules because funny-sounding sentences elicit a negative reaction from others. 'We don't say that! It's "Mum buttoned up the coat for Jack"', a parent might shout. But are children regularly corrected? And if so, do they listen?

The consensus among linguists who've observed language acquisition is that children are not often set right, and when they are, they usually ignore it. Take the following exchange between an adult and a four-year-old child:

Child: My teacher holded the baby rabbits and we patted them.
Adult: Did you say your teacher held the baby rabbits?
Child: Yes.
Adult: What did you say she did?
Child: She holded the baby rabbits and we patted them.
Adult: Did you say she held them tightly?
Child: No, she holded them loosely.

And that's for one of the easier rule exceptions – an irregular past tense.

Taken together, these problems – the absence of negative evidence, the rarity of positive evidence, and the imperviousness to correction – present us with a bit of a conundrum. No child says 'Is the dog that in the corner is hungry?', even though it is claimed they barely, or never, hear the correct version modelled by adults. There appears to be a gap between the speech children are exposed to – the 'primary linguistic data' – and the knowledge of language they attain.

A universal solution

It's this gap that is known as 'the poverty of the stimulus'. One way of explaining it is that we come into the world knowing some crucial facts about language. This innate, genetically encoded information is what bridges the gap, and results in children understanding how to build complex sentences without needing to hear them first.

The most important linguist to set out this hypothesis is, of course, Noam Chomsky. In 1965, he wrote: 'A consideration of the character of the grammar that is acquired, the degenerate quality and narrowly limited extent of the available data, the striking uniformity of the resulting grammars and their independence of intelligence, motivation and emotional state . . . leave little hope that much of the structure of the language can be learned by an organism initially uninformed as to its general character.' In other words, the astonishing fact that every child, if cognitively normal, learns the incredibly complex rules of speech, combined with the poverty of the stimulus, leaves us no choice. We must conclude that, when it comes to language acquisition, every one of us has a helping hand from Mother Nature.

The facts on the ground, in this view, simply cannot explain the progression from 'Ba', to 'I'm going to Cookie Monster's place, and I'm going to have a peanut-butter sandwich' in just a couple of years. For many kinds of rules there is no negative evidence, and precious little positive. There is little correction, and even less responsiveness to it. Another factor must come into play: a pre-programmed ability, an already written user's manual inside the baby's head. This was christened 'universal' grammar, since it must be etched into the brain of every genetically normal human being. Once triggered by the input of parents' voices, it unfurls and makes learning much easier – natural, instinctive. 'If UG did not exist,' Chomsky says, 'it would simply be a miracle that every infant somehow selects out of the environment, just a confused environment, data that are relevant to language, reflexively. And then the infant also more or less reflexively attains the language mastery that all of us have.' And, sorry Alex the parrot, Kanzi the bonobo et al., but 'other organisms faced with exactly the same data can't even take the first step, and obviously none of the later ones'.

After Chomsky convinced himself that UG was the solution to the poverty of the stimulus problem, he was faced with a monumental task: what does the user's manual look like? That's to say, what information does it contain? If all humans inherit it, it must be basically the same for everyone – like, say, the structure of the kidney, or the eye. But how does that work, when the world's languages differ hugely in so many respects?

Since the 'Chomskyan revolution' began in the late 1950s, many linguists have busied themselves trying to find the answers to these questions. The so-called 'innateness hypothesis' – the idea that we are born with a specific capacity for language – became mainstream, and linguistic departments across the world reoriented themselves: one of their key tasks was now to join in attempts to reveal the precise workings of the genetic blueprint.

This blueprint must be simpler than real-world languages, since it forms a common basis for all of them. It should underlie both the rococo structures of Hungarian, with more than twenty cases, and Saramaccan, a creole spoken in Suriname that has radically simple morphology. It must represent a clean break with the animal kingdom: no ape, parrot or dolphin should exhibit whatever piece of genetic code it is that lays down the structures needed for UG. And it must be separate from other, more general abilities. As Chomsky says: 'The notion of a general-purpose learning system makes no more sense than the notion of a general-purpose sensing organ. Like a bump in the middle of the forehead whose function is to sense things [as opposed to an eye for seeing, or a nose and olfactory bulb for smelling].'

This separation – or modularity – is important to Chomsky since he uses it to explain the uniqueness of human language. More general cognitive abilities, in the domains of memory, perception and problem-solving, are undoubtedly shared with other animals. If language were somehow cobbled together using these, then there would be no sharp linguistic dividing line, of the kind he asserts, between us and the apes. Luckily for him, there appears to be evidence of a 'language module'. If this module is a discrete functional unit in the brain, particularly if that unit is physically circumscribed, then certain types of brain damage will 'knock out' just language, while others will hit general cognitive skills, while sparing language: so-called 'double dissociation'. In *The Language Instinct*, Stephen Pinker draws our attention to two genetic disorders that seem to do just that. One, 'specific language impairment' (SLI), leaves sufferers with normal non-verbal IQs, but only able to produce halting sentences like these:

It's a flying finches, they are.
She remembered when she hurts herself the other day.

The neighbors phone the ambulance because the man fall off the tree.
The boys eat four cookie.
Carol is cry in the church.

Adults with Williams syndrome, on the other hand, have low IQs and problems performing the most basic practical tasks, but can talk fluently. Their ramblings, while childlike in content, are grammatically perfect:

Sometimes elephants can charge, like a bull can charge. They have big, long tusks. They can damage a car ... It could be dangerous. When they're in a pinch, when they're in a bad mood, it can be terrible. You don't want an elephant as a pet. You want a cat or a dog or a bird.

These conditions point to part of the brain that is specifically responsible for language – defective in SLI, spared in Williams syndrome – and further, they indicate that this 'module' is genetically determined, since both problems are heritable.

UG is simple, then, and modular. But what information does it actually contain? What, indeed, does it mean to have 'knowledge of language', as the title of one of Chomsky's books has it? We've touched on this already, when we looked at AI and pragmatics. The computer that 'understands' language needs to have a dictionary – a list of meanings and the words associated with them – and a list of rules for combining those words: a semantics and a syntax. Can the dictionary be stored in UG? This is an easy one. If specific words were hardwired into babies' brains, they'd come out asking for 'milk'. Given that nature can't predict where on earth a baby is going to be born, and among which kind of people, it would have to hedge its bets by inscribing into the cortex words from a variety of languages. 'Milk' would be there, but also *Milch*, *latte* and *niúnǎi*, for good measure. But that's only English, German, Italian and Mandarin. We know that a cognitively normal baby can learn any language; so words from all of them would have to be part of the UG – taking up rather a lot of storage space. And then there's the fact that words evolve far more quickly than organisms do: the modern human brain evolved around 200,000 years ago. Given that we know the English word for, say, 'head' was *hēafod* just 1,200 years ago, it seems in principle impossible that individual words could be encoded in UG.

UG must instead be some kind of repository for the rules governing the combination of words: that is, syntax. This seems much more plausible. We know that the number of sentences in a given language is infinite, but that the storage space available in our brains for knowledge of language cannot be. Instead, there could be a set of rules that, when combined with words, give rise to an infinite number of sentences – as Chomsky puts it, 'a finite computational system yielding an infinity of expressions'. But what do these rules look like?

The infrastructure of speech

One way to think about how word order interacts with meaning is to imagine that words which are nearer to one another in a sentence are more closely related. After all, this is very often the case. In 'I really like cold pizza', the adjective 'cold' modifies the noun it is next to, 'pizza', not the word 'I' – and 'really' modifies the verb it is next to, 'like'. The rule here might be: a modifier always applies to the closest noun or verb. Rules such as this are linear – they contain information about the proper sequence of words in a string.

But let's take a couple of examples Chomsky often uses. First, 'Birds that fly instinctively swim'. What does the adverb 'instinctively' modify here? Well, there are two verbs in the sentence, and they're both right next door. So the sentence is ambiguous: both the flying and the swimming could be instinctive. But what about if we put it at the beginning of the sentence? 'Instinctively birds that fly swim'. Now, it's clear that 'instinctively' refers only to swim. But hang on a second. 'Instinctively' is now further away from 'swim' than 'fly'. How come it modifies the former, not the latter? Linearity doesn't seem to explain anything here.

Then there are the rules governing what pronouns refer back to. 'Back' is a clue: a pronoun must come after the noun it replaces. This is a linear rule, sure, but it seems to work. In the sentence 'He said Max ordered sushi', we know that 'he' cannot be the same person as Max. In 'Max said he ordered sushi' it can be. But what about 'While he was holding pasta, Max ordered sushi'? Here the linear rule seems to break. 'He' could very well be Max.

Chomsky uses sentences like this to show that the rules governing word order are not in fact linear. They can't be figured out using the order of words in the spoken sentence: the 'surface representation'. Instead, they are governed by deeper, structural relationships, hierarchies that can only be made clear using special diagrams, like the one below. Here we can see that the verb 'swim' is hierarchically higher than the verb 'fly', so attracts the adverb. Similar diagrams show that a pronoun must be at the same level as or beneath the noun it refers to in the hierarchy.

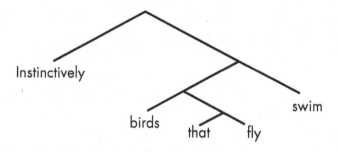

The fact that there might be two layers of organisation – one deep down, and one at the surface – was a key insight of Chomskyan, or 'generative', linguistics. It seemed to pave the way for a possible description of UG as the layer that sits underneath all of the fuss and ornament of individual languages. The vastly differing surface forms seen in Japanese, English, Mandarin and Arabic were *generated* from deep structures using 'transformations', like bubbles rising from a continental shelf, pushed this way and that by eddies and currents.

The task that remained was to gradually whittle down the deep-structure rules to the minimum possible set that still applied to all languages. Chomsky's theory went through several incarnations, each, in general, more rigorous and pared back than the previous one.* The final

---

* Perhaps the greatest continuing challenge was to account for linguistic diversity – but also for 'linguistic typology', the fact that languages, different as they may be, do seem to fall into patterns, or types. For example: the use of a verb implies the existence of a subject. This holds so widely that it could be considered a principle of UG. But in many languages, such as Italian, the subject doesn't get a surface representation. In Italian, you say *ho comprato il libro*, which means 'I bought the book'. But nowhere is the subject pronoun *Io* ('I') to be found (*ho* is the auxiliary verb 'have'). Languages that are able to drop the subject pronoun tend to have a series of other grammatical quirks as a result. Together they can be labelled

iteration, known as the 'minimalist programme', introduces what Chomsky believes to be the most basic rule of human language, that which ultimately generates all the sentences of all known languages, and which allows a finite lexicon to yield an infinite number of expressions. This rule is called 'Merge'.

On the face of it, Merge is very simple. It does what it says on the tin. It allows you to take two elements and merge them, to form a new element. This new element can now be merged with other elements, which themselves may or may not be products of earlier mergers. Merge is recursive. You'll remember from Chapter 4 that recursion is the reappearance of something inside itself, and is seen by some as the *sine qua non* of human language. An element that is the product of Merge participating in a new merge is the reappearance of something inside itself.

This is all very abstract, but how does it generate actual human languages? Take the proper noun 'Kim', the verb 'admire' and the proper noun 'Sam'. These are clearly separate linguistic units. But they can combine and enter into hierarchical relationships with other units – they can be merged. In 'Kim admires Sam', 'Kim' is the subject, and the merged 'admires Sam' is the predicate (the name given to the part of the sentence that isn't the subject, but gives you information relating to it). In 'Priya thinks Kim admires Sam' there are more layers of Merge: 'Priya' is merged with

---

'pro-drop' languages. In the so-called 'principles and parameters' framework, principles of UG came alongside 'parameter settings' like 'pro-drop', which could be switched to either 'on' or 'off', thereby accounting for variation among languages. The infant brain would be attuned to signs in the linguistic data that a parameter was switched one way or another, and, once triggered by, say, a missing subject, would adjust its growing grammar accordingly.

'thinks Kim admires Sam', itself the product of a merger between the original predicate and the verb 'think'. Ultimately
the whole sentence is a merged unit that can be merged
again into a bigger one: '[Fran believes [Priya thinks Kim
admires Sam]]'.

Chomsky claims that Merge is the most economical way
of accounting for the recursive properties of language. But
he also believes that it explains things like movement in
questions, whereby the 'who', 'why', 'where', 'is' or 'does'
element at the beginning of a sentence has in fact been
moved from its original location at the end. So, a sentence
such as 'Who does David want to vote for?' starts as 'David
want to vote for who'. The final element is copied, and
added to (merged with) the sentence to form 'Who David
want to vote for who'. This is 'internal Merge', since the
element being merged with comes from within the sentence
itself. The original 'who' is then deleted, before language-
specific rules are implemented (such as, here, adding the
auxiliary 'does').*

Confused? I'm not surprised. Chomsky's theories are

---

* Why is the original 'who' deleted instead of being left in place?
In their book *Why Only Us*, Robert C. Berwick and Chomsky say:
'There is a good computational reason why only one of the copies
is pronounced: to pronounce more of them would yield enormous
computational complexity in all but the simplest cases.' You might
then ask why we imagine that an unpronounced copy exists at all.
Some linguists point to sentence pairs like the following to justify
the reality of a 'trace' left by a moved element. In b) below, the trace,
'*t*', comes between 'want' and 'to' and therefore apparently blocks
the possibility of contraction to 'wanna' (linguists use asterisks to
mark so-called ill-formed sentences).

  a) Who does David want to vote for *t*? → Who does David
     wanna vote for?
  b) Who does David want *t* to win? → *Who does David wanna
     win?

highly technical, even abstruse – although Merge is easier to grasp than many of his earlier attempts to describe UG.

The key point is that at the core of all languages lies a special computational trick which Chomskyans say bestows upon them their basic and unique property: the ability to generate an infinity of expressions using finite means. Merge is precisely that which apes, birds, dolphins and every other species lack. It is what enables children to acquire language so quickly and dramatically, because they perceive, beyond the jumble of words at the surface, an inner order, one determined by Merge. 'Is the dog that in the corner is hungry?' is impossible under Merge, and Merge is why children never say it. Merge is the holy grail.

What about the rest of language? The wildly differing sounds and words and rules of Japanese and Russian and Xhosa? The particular form of expression Merge takes once it gets out into the physical world is something that UG doesn't really care about. It's dependent on things like the shape of the human vocal tract, the history of the language in question, its contact with other languages, the culture of the people who speak it. It's a kind of froth, an elaboration of a very simple system. A function of the journey from brain to mouth to ear. This is the reappearance of the FLB that we met in Chapter 4: the faculty of language – broad sense. Recursion, with Merge its engine, is the FLN, or faculty of language – narrow sense. 'The apparent variety and complexity of language, and its susceptibility to change,' say Berwick and Chomsky, 'lie mostly, and perhaps even entirely, in the process of externalisation, not the systems that generate the underlying expressions ... these appear to be virtually uniform among languages, which would not be surprising if true, because the child receives virtually no evidence about them.'

Chomsky goes even further than that: he sees Merge as having evolved not for language, but for thought. The fact that it can be used for communication is almost incidental. 'The modern conception – that communication is the "function" of language (whatever exactly that is supposed to mean) – probably derives from the mistaken belief that language somehow must have evolved from animal communication.'

Chomsky doesn't directly disparage the study of communication. It just isn't his project, which is to uncover UG, to search for and find the element of human language that is completely distinctive, that isn't shaped by contingent factors (he calls these 'language hemlines', which rise and fall just like fashions come and go), that is confined to the synapses and is perfectly consistent. Linguistic bedrock.

This laser-like focus on the computational system at the heart of syntax is reasonable so far as it goes. But it isn't for everyone, which is why its dominant position in mainstream theoretical linguistics has generated dissent. Many people, after all, are drawn to study language because they *are* interested in communication: what it is, and how it happens. They see patterns in language and want to understand how they came about. For them there is no putting to one side the contributions of general cognition, culture and human interaction.

The poverty line

UG sits at the heart of an attempt to explain the fact that we learn language despite an apparent poverty of stimulus. That poverty is the reason UG is invoked in the first place. Once you have UG, other problems appear to be solved as well. The assumption of an innate component accounts for patterns that recur in languages across the world – so-called linguistic universals. It tells us why animals don't speak – the 'why only us' question. It provides an explanation for the fact that words in sentences form hierarchies rather than obey linear rules – so-called structure dependency.

So you can imagine what would happen if the whole concept of the poverty of the stimulus – what Chomsky calls a 'rather simple and obvious fact' – was called into question. It is the principal justification for the vast programme of research into a proposed innate, modular capacity for language. Without it, thousands of linguists could be barking up the wrong tree.

Chomsky encapsulates the poverty of the stimulus thus: 'A person might go through much or all of his life without ever having been exposed' to a sentence like 'Is the dog that is in the corner hungry'. Therefore children only know to move the main-clause auxiliary to the front because of UG, not because they've heard it spoken correctly. If, on the other hand, sentences like 'Is the dog that is in the corner hungry' were common, you wouldn't need UG – you'd be able to say that there was enough positive evidence for children to simply learn the pattern. Besides, Chomsky wouldn't just write something like that, as he did in 1980, on the basis of a hunch. He reassures us, 'you can go over a vast amount of data of experience without ever finding such a case'.

The problem is that this crucial assertion – that question sentences with two auxiliaries are vanishingly rare – doesn't seem to be correct. Chomsky is a 'pencil-and-paper theoretician', according to Steven Pinker, who is one of his strongest supporters. His investigation of the structure of language has been carried out by thinking about sentences, not by doing lots of fieldwork or observing children learning language.

It's not clear what 'data of experience' Chomsky was

referring to. But over twenty years after he made those claims, Geoffrey Pullum and Barbara Scholz decided to check them empirically. They did so by looking at vast repositories of written and transcribed language known as corpora, and searching for questions that could not have been formed using the rule 'move the first auxiliary to the front'. So that's 'Is the dog that is in the corner hungry', but also 'Where's the other dolly that was in here?' and 'If you don't need this, can I have it?'* (Let's just call them dog-in-the-corner sentences.) These sentences represent the kind of positive evidence, or model, that would point children towards the correct rule.

Pullum and Scholz begin by addressing one highly paradoxical aspect of Chomsky's argument. His contention is that children acquire the correct structure for dog-in-the-corner sentences, despite the fact that 'A person might go through much or all of his life without ever having been exposed' to them. But if they so rarely make any kind of appearance at all, how do we know that people do in fact learn the correct structure? Presumably, just as a listener might not hear one, a speaker could go through 'much or all' of her life without producing a dog-in-the-corner sentence. On the one hand, Chomsky seems to be saying, adults always employ the correct auxiliary movement rule; but on the other hand, they hardly ever do so, if at all.

Putting this baffling lapse to one side, Pullum and Scholz dive into the corpora. Remember that they're looking for

---

* The declarative forms of these sentences are 'The dog that is in the corner is hungry', 'The other dolly that was in here is there' and 'If you don't need this I can have it'. If you followed the 'move the first auxiliary rule', these would be 'Is the dog that in the corner is hungry', 'Was the other dolly that in here is there' and 'If don't you need this I can have it' respectively.

questions formed from a declarative with two auxiliaries. If they're common, children should be able to learn the correct rule by example. If they're rare or non-existent, that could be an argument for UG.

First we have the *Wall Street Journal* between 1987 and 1989. Not exactly *Where the Wild Things Are*, but still useful in gauging how common dog-in-the-corner sentences are. 'Of the roughly 23,000 questions in *WSJ*,' Pullum and Scholz tell us, 'one must look through only 15 before hitting an example.' From there, they move on to Wilde's *The Importance of Being Earnest*. Again, hardly a kindergarten staple, but illuminating all the same. They immediately find one, to wit: 'Who is that young person whose hand my nephew Algernon is now holding in what seems to me a peculiarly unnecessary manner?'

Via a brief diversion (a *Mork and Mindy* script), Pullum and Scholz end up at the Child Language Data Exchange System, a 'corpus of utterances addressed to a child named Nina by her caregivers when she was between 1 year and 11 months and 3 years and 3 months'. If examples were as easy to find here as in the *WSJ*, a play by Oscar Wilde and a script for the television show *Mork and Mindy*, that would look fairly damning for the concept of the poverty of the stimulus. And, sure enough, here are three dog-in-the-corner sentences. They seem perfectly natural in the context, evoking images of the kind of play that happens hundreds if not thousands of times in the course of raising a child:

a. Where's the little blue crib that was in the house before?
b. Where's the other dolly that was in here?
c. Where's the other doll that goes in there?

Pullum and Scholz conclude: 'Chomsky's assertion that "you can go over a vast amount of data of experience without ever finding such a case" is unfounded hyperbole. We have found relevant cases in every corpus we have looked in.'

Was the claim ever really persuasive? Pullum and Scholz point out that, given a moment's reflection, it's quite hard to imagine children would never be exposed to dog-in-the-corner sentences such as 'Will those who are coming *t* raise their hands?', 'Can the people who are leaving early *t* please sit near the door?' and 'Is the man who was showing you the pictures *t* still here?' (The *t* for 'trace' marks the site the auxiliary has moved from – in each case, it's the second rather than the first auxiliary in the sentence.)

Pullum and Scholz's paper seems to point to two remarkable conclusions. The first is that Chomsky doesn't appear to have made much of an effort to empirically test his very strong claim about dog-in-the-corner sentences. Granted, computerised corpora were for many years hard to access, but that has long since ceased to be the case. The second, related to the first, is that despite this lack of evidence, his ideas were largely accepted by scholars, becoming part of the linguistic orthodoxy.* They were brought to far larger audiences by Pinker, who, in *The Language Instinct*, uses a dog-in-the-corner sentence to justify the argument from the poverty of the stimulus. He says: 'the sentences that would

---

* Pullum and Scholz are careful to point out, by the way, that their exercise doesn't represent a fatal blow for the innateness hypothesis. What they want to do is show that, despite what many linguists seem to think, the argument from the poverty of the stimulus has not been persuasively made. (As well as the dog-in-the-corner sentences, they show how three other commonly proffered pieces of 'evidence' of POS lack empirical support.)

teach children that the linear rule is wrong and the structure-sensitive rule is right – questions with a second auxiliary embedded inside the subject phrase – are so rare as to be non-existent in Motherese'. Motherese is defined by Pinker as the 'intensive sessions of conversational give-and-take' by which people assume children are 'taught' language. Of course, he doesn't believe it's taught, and appeals to UG to fill in the gaps. But that argument falls apart a little given that Nina was exposed to several examples of dog-in-the-corner sentences. There might not be a gap after all. Didn't anyone think to check?

What about other aspects of the poverty of the stimulus – the fact that children eventually learn to stop overgeneralising rules? How do they realise that 'Do you want to see us disappear our heads?' is wrong? According to linguists such as Michael Tomasello, we don't need to resort to UG to explain that. Instead, there's a process of 'entrenchment' – gradually, the more often they hear a verb used in a certain way, children will opt for that use, and assume that something they haven't heard isn't permissible – the no-negative-evidence problem isn't really a problem at all. With a verb like 'disappear', if a child hears an adult say 'They made their heads disappear', they will assume that 'disappear' cannot be transitive, otherwise the adult would have opted for the shorter, transitive version of the sentence: 'They disappeared their heads'. Entrenchment can be applied to those complicated question structures, too. Children follow the 'ordering patterns' they hear in adult speech, and imitate them. Contrary to Chomskyan orthodoxy, this learning curve generates plenty of mistakes (mistakes which would be rare to non-existent if UG told them what the correct pattern was). The psycholinguists Caroline Rowland and Julian Pine studied one child from the age of two to four who time and again failed to move the auxiliary into the correct position, saying things like 'What she will . . .' and 'What you can . . .'.

If POS is looking shaky, what about some of the other evidence that language is genetically encoded? Remember that various scholars have pointed to a possible linguistic double dissociation. There is a heritable disorder that appears to afflict linguistic competence while sparing general intelligence (SLI), and another that does the opposite (Williams syndrome).

Here too, all is not what it seems. Some researchers believe SLI is not quite as specific as it's been made out to be (something reflected in the fact that its name has recently been changed to 'developmental language disorder'). There is evidence that a problem in co-ordinating movements may be responsible for some of these children's speaking difficulties. Fine motor control is essential for the choreography of the tongue, lips, larynx and jaw that makes the production of an array of vowels and consonants possible. Another theory is that the mental processing of sounds may be part of the problem: something that would make speaking difficult, but as an 'externalisation process' wouldn't be relevant to UG. That would appear to be contradicted by the fact that SLI occurs in children who use sign language. A study of thirteen deaf children with SLI found that it 'cannot be explained by poor exposure to [sign language], or by lower general cognitive, pragmatic or motor abilities', but that working memory might be implicated. More recently, real problems in procedural memory – knowing something 'off by heart', like riding a bike – were identified in one study of fifty-one children with SLI. If SLI is caused by a memory impairment, then it does not represent good evidence for a language module –

since memory is used for lots of other things as well.

And, contrary to the caricature of Williams syndrome children being linguistic savants, their linguistic development is in fact 'nearly always delayed' according to two experts in the field, Carolyn B. Mervis and Shelley L. Velleman. While their grasp of concrete vocabulary is a relative strength (Pinker says 'they have an especially charming quirk: they are fond of unusual words'), it is still in fact 'in the low average range for the general population'. Conceptual vocabulary is, on the other hand, 'an area of considerable weakness'. Fine. The double dissociation is about grammar, not vocabulary. But then how do you explain this: 'the grammatical abilities of children with Williams' Syndrome', Mervis and Velleman say, 'are about at the level expected for their overall intellectual abilities, and many individuals evidence considerable difficulty with complex grammatical constructions'.

With the poverty of the stimulus potentially undermined, and double dissociation looking wobbly too, the confidence with which the innateness hypothesis is declaimed by some of its supporters starts to look a little misplaced. Clearly, human beings' capacity for language is at some level genetically determined. The nature of human memory, perception and problem-solving skills are encoded in our genes. The question is whether we have evolved a specific capacity for language which is hived off from other systems – a language instinct – which consists of a principle or principles of computation that we can deduce by looking at syntax.

This is the kind of bold claim that you would only really want to make if all other avenues had been exhausted. If there were ways to explain the structure of language that didn't have to invoke a hypothetical language module, then they should be entertained. They might even be preferred, if they are plausible and supported by good evidence – given that the evidence for UG is not as robust as has been claimed.*

So, what are these other avenues?

What the bees know

First let's zoom out. Consider the honeycomb – the beautiful, extraordinarily regular pattern of hexagons that bees make in order to store enough honey to see them through the winter. How on earth do bees 'know' how to build things this way? There is no evidence that young bees are taught to do so by older bees. And it is so precise, so systematic, that it must be instinctive. The 'blueprint' for the honeycomb is passed down in the genetic code, and replicated exactly – bar the odd mutation – with every new bee. Scientists should busy themselves looking for the honeycomb module.

What if there were another way to account for these elegant structures, though? What if the constraints which form them came not from a blueprint, but from other external and internal factors to which all bees are subject? As linguist Jean Aitchison, quoting the cognitive scientist Elizabeth Bates, explains: 'It is now realised that the hexagons are the inevitable outcome of the "packing principle", a mathematical law which says that hexagons result when

---

* Chomskyans say that they can verify UG by looking at the nature of sentences produced by native speakers of a given language: the fact that Merge can be used to explain the structural properties of language means that it must be encoded in our genes. But we can't actually see that code; we only infer its existence from its effects – the structural properties of language. There's a circularity here which should be a red flag: Merge must exist because it explains the way language is, and language is the way it is because of Merge.

spheres are placed together with even or random pressure from all sides. Therefore the bee's "innate knowledge of hexagons" need consist of nothing more than a tendency to pack wax with their hemispheric heads from a wide variety of directions.'

In other words, structure doesn't have to be programmed. It can emerge for other reasons. A human example: the vast majority of languages (around 96 per cent*) place the subject of a sentence before the object. You could attribute this to UG, saying it's just how the blueprint is written. Or you could take the view that linguistic sequences are influenced by temporal ones – the doer of the action is the initiator, and the object 'undergoes' the action somewhat later in time. The way we use language to describe an event may mimic the order in which things happen. That's why the subject-before-object pattern is so popular.

Everyone agrees that language is hierarchical, not linear. But why is it like that? Chomsky believes it is because of Merge: Merge evolved in human brains, and language, as an expression of human cognition, is shaped by Merge as a result. Linguist Geoffrey Sampson has another explanation, one which doesn't require an appeal to a module in the brain. Borrowing from the political scientist Herbert Simon, he says that hierarchy is the inevitable result of the gradual evolution of any system. A mathematical parable can be used to illustrate this. Imagine there are two watchmakers, Tempus and Hora. They both make watches that contain 1,000 parts. Tempus makes his watch by adding each of the 1,000 parts together into a single whole. If he's ever interrupted, the entire thing falls apart and he has to start

---

* An example from the remaining 4 per cent is Malagasy, where instead of saying 'Joni kicked the elephant', you'd say the equivalent of 'kicked the elephant Joni'.

again. Hora makes his watch by assembling collections of 100 parts into ten subunits, and combining these to create the watch. If he's interrupted, he has just as many subunits as he's already completed to fall back on. As a result, Hora ends up making far more watches than Tempus, despite the fact that they work at the same rate, with the same level of interruptions. Hora's hierarchical approach is what gives him the advantage. Sampson's point is that any system that relies on building blocks is likely to be more robust than one without internal structure. And the principles of evolution mean that a robust system is more likely to emerge and dominate than a less robust one.

We're talking about evolution here in a broad sense, one that can apply to social and cultural institutions as well as biological organisms. Sampson uses the examples of political organisation becoming more sophisticated over time: families grouping themselves into villages, villages into counties, counties into nations and nations into empires. Empires don't spring into being all in one go: the larger units are ultimately dependent on smaller ones. He notes that novels tend to have hierarchical structures because of the way they are usually written, gradually: few are the product of a writer sitting down and writing continuously until the whole story, conceived in one go, is complete.* Instead it is written episodically, with smaller elements of the story combining into narratives, which in turn combine to form an entire plot. There is hierarchy and dependency here, and it is a natural function of the gradual increase in complexity of the book.

---

* Sampson says: 'There are said to be prodigies who sit down at their typewriters and rattle off the finished work from scratch, but even they must presumably go through long processes of experimentation in their heads before putting the result on paper.'

How does this apply to language? Sampson concedes that the moment of evolution of language will remain obscure, but imagines that it very likely began with single 'calls', words or 'holophrases' (vocalisations that do the work of several words in one sound), which succeeded in conveying ideas to others. It might be occasionally useful to combine these phrases, like so: 'Up. Mountain. John' for 'John is up the mountain'. If the communicative purpose was served, some of these phrases could become fixed. They'd form building blocks, and longer sentences could be constructed from them. The more useful a building block was, the more likely it would be to endure. 'Grammatical' patterns would emerge, and quirks of circumstance would give particular languages particular structures.

Sampson explains:

> While the words were still independent sentences, no doubt people would on occasion say 'Up. Mountain' and on another occasion 'Mountain. Up' depending on which aspect of the . . . situation presented itself most immediately to their minds; originally chance alone would dictate that small short-term differences in frequency between these two orderings would cause one tribe to regularize the former pattern and evolve a prepositional language such as English, while another tribe adopted the latter pattern and evolved a postpositional language such as Japanese.

According to this view, the origin of language itself is recapitulated each time a child learns a language. They start with holophrases, and gradually increase the size of the building blocks they use until they are speaking in full sentences. The relationship of the building blocks to one another is necessarily hierarchical: anything else would require the entire language to pop into the child's head 'all at once' since it would have no subunits – just like Tempus's watch.

Hierarchy, then, is not the result of a pre-existing blueprint, but comes about because of constraints on learning and use. The regularity and complexity of grammar is shaped by the way communication occurs. The process of grammaticalisation, which we encountered in Chapter 1, 'freezes' certain structures that prove successful, fossilising them in the language until they look like arbitrary rules. Remember that the French negative particle *pas*, which originally meant 'step', started out as a way of emphasising the negative. Another example is the English past-tense ending '-ed', which started out as a separate word, 'did', emphasising the completed nature of an action ('I walk did'). Both became so routine that they entered the grammar – which is less a blueprint in the brain than a historical record of all communicative strategies employed in a particular language: the imprint of millions of past speakers and the ways they've tried to get things across to one another. These strategies might include emphasising the information we are seeking by saying it first, as we do in English when we ask questions like 'Where is the dog?' and 'What do you want for breakfast?' For reasons of historical accident, in Japanese they don't use this particular strategy. The equivalent sentences would take the forms 'Dog where is?' and 'For breakfast what want?'

This 'usage-based' theory of language structure doesn't require us to imagine a UG. It instead posits a universal set of constraints on language use: the need to be clear and expressive, but also efficient. And, as long as they don't actually impede communication, certain structures will just endure, the baroque overdecoration characteristic of languages that have been around for a long time.

One question remains, however. Why is language restricted to humans? If Merge isn't the vital quality that separates us from animals, what is? For linguists like Michael Tomasello, that quality is a special form of 'social cognition', not a syntactic trick, but an ability intimately linked to our status as social animals, able to understand the intentions of others. Intention-reading, and therefore theory of mind, is really what has allowed us to communicate in the sophisticated ways we do. As we saw in Chapter 7, it's vital to the correct interpretation of language. There is evidence that animals lack theory of mind: monkeys don't get it when a human being points at something, because knowledge of intention is required to understand that the pointed finger embodies a desire to direct the addressee's attention.

The crucial evolutionary advance that enabled language, then, was the ability to identify with others, and put ourselves in their shoes.

Does this mean that language is a separate instinct after all? No, since intention-reading can take place in the absence of language – it is a general human cognitive ability, and one that supports all sorts of behaviour, not just linguistic. There is no isolated 'language module' that allows linguistic competence to 'grow' in the brain as a result of a genetic blueprint. Language is the fruit of both the biological evolution of social thinking and the long cultural evolution of human societies. There is no poverty of the stimulus, no double dissociation, no UG in Chomsky's sense. There is human cognition, and as a result there is language.

Two decades into the twenty-first century, linguistics is entering an exciting phase, as more and more researchers begin to look beyond the bounds of Chomskyan theory. Those drawn to the subject as a study of communication, culture and history need no longer feel quite so unorthodox.

I hope this is matched by a surge in interest from outside the ivory towers.

We are, after all, expert linguists, every one of us. Language is the currency of our everyday lives: it is how we get our morning coffee, how we ask for directions, how we get things done at work, how we make friends, how we argue.

But although we can all drive the car, most of have no idea what goes on under the hood. We are either incurious about how language works, figuring that we know how to speak so why bother, or swallow half-truths and shaggy-dog stories because there's precious little else to hand by way of explanation. I hope I've shown that the truth – from etymology to accents, from animals to AI – is so much more interesting than the rumours.

One final word – literally. *Schatzkammer* is a German term meaning 'treasure chamber'. From Vienna to Munich to Dresden, dukes and princes built *Schatzkammern* to store gold, precious stones, rare objects and marvels of invention. Linguistics is a *Schatzkammer*, a dazzling synthesis of the natural and the man-made. If I've succeeded in turning the key, I'd now like to encourage you to walk in and explore the room. Many of the books I've referenced are themselves treasure troves. And nearly twenty years after I first opened the door myself, I've found that – however much you study it – language is a subject that will never exhaust your capacity for wonder.

ACKNOWLEDGEMENTS

As well as the many eminent linguists, living and dead, whose works are cited in the references section, I would like to thank all the teachers who have influenced my thinking about language. Among them are Graham Twist, who planted an early seed; Jane Rylands-Bolton, whose English lessons were always mind-expanding; Nadira Auty and Rachael Harris, who put up with my terrible Arabic; and my Persian teachers Charles Melville, Amir Shirzadi and especially Gabrielle van den Berg. I am grateful to Leon Perdoni for his patient tuition in Greek, and to Monik Charette, Wynn Chao and Emmon Bach for expanding my horizons in phonology, semantics and general linguistics.

At the *Guardian* I've been inspired, encouraged and edited by a range of extraordinary colleagues including Brian Whitaker, Georgina Henry, Alan Rusbridger, Andrew Brown, Natalie Hanman, Becky Gardiner, Katharine Viner, Alex Needham, Jonathan Freedland, Paul Laity, Lee Glendinning, Kira Cochrane, Katherine Butler and Julian Coman.

This book would not have been possible were it not for the energy of my agent Chris Wellbelove and for editor Jenny Lord's unwavering enthusiasm. Her thoughtful comments, patience and attention have been invaluable. I'd like to thank Holly Harley and everyone else at Weidenfeld &

Nicolson who has helped shepherd *Don't Believe A Word* through. I'm also grateful to my talented American editor Tom Mayer and his team at W. W. Norton. I am deeply indebted to Doug Arnold at the University of Essex and Chris Lucas at the School of Oriental and African Studies, University of London, whose expert advice saved me from many errors.

Finally, I would like to pay tribute to the support and love of family and friends: to my brother Daniel and my sister Helen, who both read the manuscript and offered helpful suggestions; to Helen's partner David and his family, to Daniel's partner Nic, and to Josie, Bill and Ted; to Nosheen for being there; to Malik and Priya; to the lunch crew Will, Leah, Larry and Suzie; to David; to Bella and Jessica; to Cathy and Naomi; to Zeynep and Anna; to Alice; and to Tom, for putting up with it all.

Last but not least, thank you Mum, for everything.

GLOSSARY

Words in bold are included in the glossary.

Accommodation
The way we alter our speech when we interact with others, changing aspects of accent, pace, volume, pitch, word choice and even **syntax**. Depending on context, you will either converge with the way your conversational partner speaks, diverge from it, or carry on regardless.

Acquisition
The process by which children learn their native language, eventually becoming fluent in it. For most children, this begins with babbling at around six months. Complex grammatical structures are mastered sometime after the age of four. Exactly how language is acquired is a major debate in linguistics, with some maintaining that parents or caregivers do not give children enough linguistic data to account for the speed at which they learn (see also **poverty of the stimulus**).

Agglutinative
The name given to languages in which words are formed of many **morphemes** added together. Turkish is a typical agglutinative language, as illustrated by the word *Avrupalılaştırılamayanlardansınız*, 'You're one of those we can't make a European out of', composed of ten or eleven morphemes depending on how you count them. Greenlandic is another example (see also **fusional** and **isolating**).

Aphasia
A disturbance in language that occurs after injury to the brain, often the result of a stroke. Aphasia has traditionally been divided into two main categories: receptive, or Wernicke's aphasia, in which understanding of the meaning of words is affected; and expressive, or Broca's aphasia, in which the ability to organise words according to rules of **syntax** and **morphology** is affected. Receptive and expressive aphasia usually occur after damage to different areas of the left hemisphere of the cortex, the outermost layer of the brain.

Arbitrariness
One of the defining features of language is the fact that the relationship between words and the things they stand for is arbitrary. There is nothing 'apple'-like about the sequence of sounds that refer to that fruit, as demonstrated by the fact that in Farsi it's *seeb*, and in Arabic *tufah*. A partial exception to this rule is onomatopoeia in words such as 'splash' and 'hiss', which sound like the actions they refer to.

Auxiliary
An auxiliary verb 'helps' form a clause, but doesn't change the core meaning of the main verb. In English, 'be' and 'have' often function as auxiliaries, as in the sentences 'I have eaten too much' or 'I am going to the bank'. The English **copula** can also be analysed as an auxiliary verb.

Calque
A form of linguistic borrowing in which the foreign word or phrase is not adopted wholesale, as in *aide-mémoire* or *débâcle*, but directly translated. Examples include 'flea market', from *marché aux puces*, 'brainwashing', from the Mandarin *xi nao*, and the modern Latin calque 'super-ego', from German *über-Ich*.

Case
In many languages, the relationships between words are marked by special suffixes or other changes to the root form. Those

relationships include that of the 'subject' (prototypically, but not always, the doer in the sentence) and the 'object' (often the thing that has something done to it) to the verb. We say that the subject takes the 'nominative' case, and the object the 'accusative' case. So, in the Latin sentence *fēmina laudat agricolam* ('the woman praises the farmer'), the subject, *fēmina*, is in the nominative, while the object, *agricolam*, takes the accusative case ending, '-*m*'. Genitive is another case, which often marks possession. English used to have a case system, the remnants of which can be seen in accusative forms of 'he' and 'she' ('him' and 'her' respectively). Languages like Hungarian have many additional cases, for example the 'sublative', which is used to mark a destination (in *Budapestre megyek*, 'I am going to Budapest', '-*re*' is the sublative ending).

Cognate

Two words in different languages that have a common origin are called 'cognates'. English 'mother', French *mère* and Farsi *madar* are cognates, traceable back to Proto-**Indo-European** *méhtēr (see **proto-language**). As well as using it as a noun, linguists might say '*mère* is cognate with *madar*' or 'house is cognate with *Haus*'.

Consonant

A **phoneme** in which air moving through the vocal tract and out of the mouth is either partially or fully obstructed. 'Stop' consonants such as /k/ and /t/ prevent air escaping altogether, whereas 'fricative' consonants such as /s/ and /f/ restrict its flow, often resulting in a hissing sound. With 'nasal' consonants such as /m/ and /n/, the air is channelled through the nose. Linguistic consonants do not always match up with the use of the word 'consonant' to describe letters of the alphabet. For example, the single fricative consonant /ʃ/ is represented in writing by two letters, 'sh' (see also **orthography**).

Copula

The copula is a form of the verb 'to be' when used merely to link the subject and the rest of the sentence, as in 'she is a pilot' or 'the tea is cold'. Many languages lack a copula in the present tense; in Arabic you would say the equivalent of 'she a pilot'.

Creole
A language formed when people who can communicate using only a pidgin raise children for whom it becomes a mother tongue. A pidgin is a rudimentary language devised when adults who speak different, mutually unintelligible languages are forced to interact. It consists of scraps of vocabulary and grammar from the different languages around them. Historically, this has usually occurred in the contexts of slavery or trade. When these people pass the pidgin on to a new generation, it is 'fleshed out', becoming a creole with full expressive capacity.

Cultural transmission
A form of inheritance that does not rely on the genome to be passed down from one generation to the next. Highly sophisticated cultural transmission is a distinctive feature of human societies, although there is some evidence of it in the animal kingdom, for example among primates and cetaceans. It is what allows the development of complex civilisation, with each generation building on what the previous one has been able to discover and achieve (the so-called 'ratchet effect', otherwise known as 'standing on the shoulders of giants'). According to the evolutionary anthropologist Michael Tomasello, rather than being a reflection of **universal grammar**, language structure is built up through cultural transmission: 'linguistic symbols and constructions evolve and change and accumulate modifications over historical time as humans use them with one another'. He calls this the 'sociogenesis' of language.

Dialect
A distinctive variety of a language, which may differ from other varieties of the same language in terms of accent, vocabulary, word formation or **syntax**. Informally it is often used to refer to varieties that deviate from the standard form of the language – for example, those used colloquially, regionally or among minority groups. For linguists, even standard forms are considered dialects. The

twentieth-century American linguist Charles Hockett defined the concept thus: 'A language is a collection of more or less similar **idiolects**. A dialect is just the same thing, with this difference: when both terms are used in a single discussion, the degree of similarity of the idiolects in a single dialect is presumed to be greater than that of all the idiolects of the language.' In other words, a dialect is a cluster of idiolects that stand apart from others in the language by virtue of being very similar to one another.

Diphthong

A sequence of two **vowels** in which a smooth transition is made from one to the other, such as /aɪ/ and /eɪ/. In English spelling, many diphthongs are misleadingly represented by a single letter. For example, the sounds /aʊ/ and /əʊ/ are written as 'o' in the words 'cow' and 'no' respectively (see also **orthography**).

Double dissociation

Evidence for the functional independence of parts of the language faculty that comes in the form of non-overlapping neurological disorders. For example, Williams syndrome is said to impair general intelligence but spare language, whereas Specific Language Impairment (SLI, now known as developmental language disorder) is believed to spare general intelligence but impair language. If language was a function of general intelligence, rather than a system that had evolved separately, then the mirror-image pattern these disorders embody would be impossible. However, doubt has recently been cast on these characterisations of Williams syndrome and SLI.

Duality of patterning

One of the characteristics of human language set out by the twentieth-century linguist Charles Hockett, also known as 'double articulation'. It consists in having individual elements, meaningless by themselves, that can be combined in a vast number of different ways to create meaningful units. For example, you can use four meaningless sounds – /p/ /ɔ/, /t/ and /s/ – to form five English words with completely different meanings – 'pots', 'stop', 'opts', 'spot' and 'tops'.

Etymological fallacy

The idea that a word's origin tells you something about its meaning. This cannot be true if you believe, like Wittgenstein, that the meaning of a word is how it is used in the present. The fact that etymology is often wildly unpredictable is another argument against it. For example, the word 'silly' meant 'happy' in the thirteenth century, and the origin of 'treacle' lies in a word which meant 'wild beast'.

Euphemism

If a subject is taboo, then words associated with it are often replaced by euphemisms – 'cleaner' substitutes. Taboos commonly relate to sex, bodily functions and race. Since euphemisms themselves eventually become contaminated by the taboo, they may be replaced in an ongoing cycle. 'Bathroom' is a euphemism used in American English instead of 'toilet', which was itself originally a euphemism for 'lavatory', also originally a euphemism.

Faculty of language – broad sense (FLB)

A definition used by Marc D. Hauser, Noam Chomsky and W. Tecumseh Fitch as part of efforts to distinguish human language from animal communication. FLB includes a 'sensory-motor system' – which comprises the ability to produce words, calls or gestures – and a 'conceptual-intentional' system – which allows meaning to be mapped onto those words, calls or gestures. Aspects of FLB are shared with certain other species, and rely on 'extra-linguistic' systems in the body and brain (see also **faculty of language – narrow sense**).

Faculty of language – narrow sense (FLN)

A sub-part of FLB, the FLN is said by Hauser, Chomsky and Fitch to be unique to humans. It consists of a rules-based system that governs the combination of symbols, and underpins our ability to generate an infinity of expressions using finite means. At its core is **recursion**. FLN is said to be genetically inherited, and can be seen as synonymous with **universal grammar** (see also **faculty of language – broad sense**).

Fusional

In fusional languages, word stems change or are added to depending on their grammatical function. These additional morphemes can stand for several things at once and are more compressed than in **agglutinative** languages. Latin is a good example of a fusional language, with the word *vidébunt* ('they will see') divided into two morphemes, the stem, *vidé*, and the suffix, *bunt*. The stem contributes the meaning 'see' while the suffix carries five meanings in one form: person, number, tense, something called mood, and voice (as in active or passive). Sanskrit, ancient Greek and Navajo are also fusional languages (see also **agglutinative, isolating**).

Glottal stop

A **consonant** made by closing the glottis or vocal chords. In British English it is not phonemic, but exists as an alternative realisation, or 'allophone', of /t/ – as in 'Wha?'. The symbol for a glottal stop in the **international phonetic alphabet** is /ʔ/ (see also **phonetics and phonology**).

Grammaticalisation

The process by which frequently used words or phrases are bleached of meaning and come to serve purely grammatical roles in a sentence. They are often phonetically reduced at the same time. This tendency is a common engine of **usage-based** language change. The future-tense marker 'will', which once meant 'to want', as in sentences like 'I will [want to] go to the city', has been drained of meaning and become a grammatical particle, sometimes reduced to an abbreviation – as in 'I'll'. (Verbs of intention often end up as future-tense markers because they necessarily refer to events that haven't happened yet.) The English past tense '-ed' is another example of grammaticalisation, having been formed from the reduction of 'did' used after a verb: 'I walk did' became 'I walk-ed'.

Idiolect

An individual's unique way of speaking, amounting to their knowledge of pronunciation, word formation, **syntax** and mental

lexicon. Each of us, although we may share a language, exhibit small differences in the way we produce sounds, interpret grammatical rules and use vocabulary (see also **dialect**).

Implicature

In **pragmatics,** a manoeuvre by which a speaker implies something without actually saying it. An implicature can be generated when the maxims of conversation defined by the philosopher H. P. Grice are flouted or clash. For instance, if, after contacting a prospective student's referee, a university receives the reply 'Dear Sir, Mr X's command of English is excellent, and his attendance at tutorials has been regular. Yours, etc.', it is clear that the maxim of quantity ('be as informative as is required') has been flouted. An implicature is generated to the effect that Mr X is a poor student and should not be offered a place.

Indo-European

A large language 'family' and the first to be systematically studied. It includes English, German, Italian, Greek, Hindi, Armenian and Welsh, as well as many others. Major branches include Romance, Germanic, Slavic and Indo-Iranian. Families consist of languages that have been proven to be related to one another through the analysis of **cognate** words and grammatical structures. A family can emerge from a single language when groups of speakers become geographically or socially isolated from one another. Since linguistic change is constant, the languages these people speak slowly become mutually unintelligible; they are now the 'daughters' of the original 'mother' language, which has died. Such relationships are represented by 'language trees'. The hypothetical ancestor of all Indo-European languages is Proto-Indo-European, which is really just a patchy series of reconstructions made using the comparative method (see also **proto-language**). Some of these reconstructions, if accurate, may have been used by speakers living between the Caspian and Black seas 5,000–6,000 years ago.

Innateness hypothesis

The theory that crucial parts of our knowledge of language are genetically inherited (innate), rather than **culturally transmitted** and learned. This hypothesis is most strongly associated with the linguist Noam Chomsky (see also **poverty of the stimulus, universal grammar**).

International phonetic alphabet

A system for transcribing the sounds of languages that, while largely based on the Latin alphabet, avoids misleading quirks of **orthography** – such as the fact that the sound /ʃ/ is a single **consonant**, not two, as the English spelling 'sh' might lead you to believe. It contains many symbols for sounds not found in English, such as /ɳ/ for the retroflex nasal found in Hindi and /ɣ/ for the velar fricative consonant found in Farsi. Phonemic transcription using the IPA is conventionally enclosed by slash marks, and phonetic transcription in square brackets (see also **consonant, diphthong, phonetics and phonology**).

Isolating

The name given to languages in which words usually consist of a single **morpheme**, without prefixes or suffixes ('analytic' is a near-synonym). Tenses and relationships between words are often indicated by separate words, such as **auxiliaries** or prepositions. Examples include Mandarin and Vietnamese.

Language module

A hypothetical, discrete system in the brain that allows us to learn languages and is innate (genetically inherited). Other proposed 'modules' include ones devoted to colour perception and facial recognition (see also **double dissociation, innateness hypothesis, universal grammar**).

Lexical field theory

A model of semantics in which the meaning of a word is defined in part by those of its near-neighbours. The metaphor is essentially geographical: an area of land (the language), is divided into hundreds of irregularly shaped fields of meaning, which are themselves subdivided into plots occupied by individual words. The meaning of words (their shape) is dependent on those of adjacent words. When a **semantic** change occurs, it affects all the words in a field by taking territory from them or ceding it. Lexical field theory sits within the tradition of structuralism, which views language as a balanced system where 'everything holds together'.

Lexicon
The complete inventory of words in a language. Used in language description and also in psycholinguistics, when it refers to the store of words in the mind (the 'dictionary in your head').

Merge
In Chomskyan theory, the basic computational rule that accounts for our ability to generate an infinity of expressions using finite means. Merge allows you to take two elements and merge them to form a new element, for example by adding 'my' to 'books' to form 'my books'. This new element can now be merged with other elements, which themselves may or may not be products of earlier mergers: 'I gave you my books'. As the basic computational rule underlying language, Merge represents the most up-to-date characterisation of **universal grammar** (see also **recursion**).

Metonymy
'The substitution of the name of an attribute or adjunct for that of the thing meant', according to Oxford Dictionaries. This would include saying 'the White House', to refer to the American presidency, or 'work' to mean the place where you do your job. Metonymy is a common means of **semantic** change, and likely reflects a universal cognitive tendency to link 'neighbouring' concepts. Examples of metonymic change include the French word *bureau*, which originally meant a cloth covering for a desk, then the desk itself, and now also an office or administrative department. Metonymy differs from metaphor in that it relies on the adjacency of two concepts, rather than their similarity (the use of the word 'crane' to describe a piece of construction equipment is metaphor based on its similarity to the long-beaked crane bird).

Morpheme, morphology
The basic unit of word construction, indivisible into smaller units. Morphemes can be free (able to exist on their own), like 'book'

and 'believe', or bound, like '-ish' in 'bookish' or 'un-' and '-ing' in 'unbelieving'. The study of morphemes is called morphology.

Natural semantic metalanguage (NSM)
A system developed by the Polish linguist Anna Wierzbicka which seeks to define the meanings of words using only terms attested in all languages. These **semantic** elements, or 'primes', are judged to be the most basic units of meaning, since they are common to all cultures. Currently, sixty-five primes are used (the number could be reduced if a language was found which did not use a word equivalent to one of these primes, meaning that it was not in fact universal). NSM is claimed to allow the translation of words with pinpoint accuracy.

Object, see case

Orthography
The conventions of spelling. Written language changes more slowly than its spoken counterpart, and as a result orthography often lags behind the sounds it is supposed to represent. This problem is worse in languages with long literary traditions, whose spelling conventions tend to be more conservative. English is stuck with spellings that predate a major sound change known as the great **vowel** shift. The word 'name', for example, used to be pronounced with a single long 'a' vowel, indicated by /a:/ in the **international phonetic alphabet,** and reflected accurately in the spelling. This sound began to change in the fifteenth century, and is now pronounced with a **diphthong,** /eɪ/, but the spelling remains unchanged. The silent 'gh' in words like 'thought' and 'light' was once a fully pronounced fricative **consonant,** /x/ (said to be similar to the Scots pronunciation of 'ch' in 'loch'). By contrast, in Turkish, for which a new alphabet was adopted in the 1920s, there is a more or less one-to-one correspondence between letters and sounds.

Pejoration
A form of **semantic** change in which the meaning of a word gets 'worse'. This often occurs with words related to women, for

example 'hussy', which is derived from *husewif*, a neutral term for housewife. The opposite process is called amelioration, and can be seen in words such as 'nice', which once meant 'foolish' or 'silly'.

Philology
An archaic term for linguistics, the study of language, primarily associated with efforts in the nineteenth century to identify the rules of sound change, establish which words were **cognates,** and work out hypothetical ancestor words (see also **proto-language**).

Phoneme
The phonemes of a language are the sounds that, when substituted for one another, alter the meaning of words. Phonemes can be identified by drawing up a list of so-called 'minimal pairs', sets of words that differ in meaning by only one sound. The minimal pairs that show that /s/ and /z/ are separate phonemes in English include 'sip' and 'zip', 'bus' and 'buzz'. In Norwegian, /z/ is not a phoneme. If you pronounced the word for 'sieve', *sil*, with a /z/ instead of an /s/, it might sound strange, but it would not mean you were saying a different word. The difference would be **phonetic** rather than phonemic. Phonemes can have different realisations depending on phonological context, or social factors (see also **phonetics and phonology**).

Phonetics and phonology
Phonetics is the study of sounds produced by the human vocal tract. Phonology looks at the way those sounds enter into relationships with other sounds in order to create meaningful words. For this reason, **phonemes** fall under the rubric of phonology (phonology also incorporates the study of features such as intonation and stress that extend over more than one phoneme). In English, whether you roll your 'r's or not makes no difference to meaning; it is a phonetic contrast. In Spanish, the only difference between the word /pero/ ('dog') and /pero/ ('but') is the rolling of the 'r' in the former. It is a phonemic contrast. This is referred to as the -etic/-emic distinction and is the essence of the difference between phonetics and phonology. Phonetics is about the raw

material of speech, phonology is about sounds organised into a system. In the **international phonetic alphabet,** phonetic transcription is enclosed by square brackets and is often more detailed than phonemic transcription, such that the English word 'pull' can be transcribed phonemically as /pʊl/ and, with more detailed phonetic information, as [pʰʊəɫ]. Phonetic variation is irrelevant to word meaning. It may be obligatory in certain phonological contexts (for example, /p/ is always aspirated at the beginning of words, but not after /s/), or it may be 'free' to carry social meaning (see also **sociolinguistics**).

Pidgin, see creole

Plosive
A type of stop **consonant,** in which the air dammed up by closing the vocal tract is suddenly released. In English, plosive consonants include /p/, /t/ and /k/.

Poverty of the stimulus
In Chomskyan theory, the idea that the speech data which children get from their parents or caregivers is not enough for them to learn the complex structures of language. In order to do so, the theory goes, they require help from an innate blueprint in the brain. This is the **universal grammar, or faculty of language – narrow sense.**

Pragmatics
The branch of linguistics that deals with 'speaker's meaning' rather than word or sentence meaning (the province of **semantics**). In other words, the meaning of words and phrases when they are used in context. This is decoded using not just principles of grammar and the **lexicon,** but knowledge about the other person's intentions – social knowledge. The semantics of the statement 'It's cold in here' are clear: someone is making an observation about the temperature. The pragmatics tell us something more: the same person is asking you to close the window.

Productivity

One of the key properties of human language, this consists in the ability to generate new words or phrases using the building blocks of sound. Without it, communication would be eternally fixed, as it is, say, in felines: cats can only purr, mew or chirp – they can't invent new sounds or ways to express themselves. Productivity allows the coining of novel words like 'internet', and enables us to imagine sentences that have never been uttered before. Productivity accelerates the emergence of cultural differences, which can then be easily transmitted by learning. There is some evidence that certain animals, for example cetaceans, take advantage of productivity to create new sound sequences which are transmitted by learning, although their communicative function may be quite limited.

Proto-language

A hypothetical language for which there are no written records, some of whose characteristics are reconstructed by linguists using the comparative method. First they compare a set of **cognate** words in languages they believe to be related. Then, using knowledge of how sounds tend to change, they arrive at the form of a common ancestor word. So, given the English word 'foot', its ancient Greek cognate *poús* and Latin *pes*, we can deduce that the common ancestor of all three languages (known as Proto-**Indo-European**) had a word for foot that began with a /p/, since the change from /p/ to /f/ is much more likely than the other way around. Reconstructed words are marked with an asterisk: the Proto-Indo-European for foot is **pόds*.

Reanalysis

The process by which a structurally ambiguous word or phrase is interpreted differently by a new speaker or set of speakers. Examples include the reinterpretation of the Middle English noun 'a napron' as 'an apron', and of 'an ewt' as 'a newt'.

Recursion

An important property of the structure of sentences, recursion is essentially the reappearance of something inside itself, and means that there is no 'longest' sentence of a language (and hence that the set of possible sentences is infinite). A sentence comprises a noun phrase, and a verb phrase, like so: 'The man' (noun phrase) 'is running' (verb phrase). But a verb phrase can also contain a noun phrase and another verb phrase: 'The man' (noun phrase) 'is running' (verb phrase) 'to the house' (noun phrase) 'he grew up in' (verb phrase). And so on, ad infinitum. In Chomskyan theory, recursion underpins **Merge**, the computational rule that comprises the **faculty of language – narrow sense**, and separates human language from animal communication.

Sapir–Whorf hypothesis

The idea that the language you speak determines the boundaries of your thought, closely associated with the anthropologist and amateur linguist Benjamin Lee Whorf. Whorf wrote that, because the Hopi language dealt with time differently than English, Hopi speakers have 'no general notion or intuition of time as a smooth flowing continuum in which everything in the universe proceeds at an equal rate, out of a future, through a present, into a past'. This strong version of the hypothesis has been largely debunked, but the idea that linguistic structures subtly influence thought has been borne out by various experiments, including ones in which Spanish speakers, for whom 'bridge' is a masculine noun, associated more stereotypically manly words, such as 'towering' and 'sturdy' with it than Germans, for whom it is a feminine noun.

Semantics

The study of the meaning of words and sentences independent of their use in particular situations or contexts. Often this involves trying to define the relationship between the sounds uttered and what they refer to. This might be fairly easy with concrete nouns like 'cat', but harder with concepts such as 'hope' or so-called 'deictic words' like 'this' or 'here'. The meaning of these can be thought of as consisting in the way they are used (see also **pragmatics**).

Sociolinguistics

The study of those aspects of language that carry social meaning. These are called 'sociolinguistic variables', and can take the form of differences in sound, vocabulary, word formation or **syntax**. For example, the sociolinguist William Labov found that the presence of an 'r' sound at the end of words in 1960s New York was associated with higher-income groups, or those who aspired to be like them. It carried social prestige, whereas the lack of an 'r' was stigmatised. Similarly, the choice of the words 'hello', 'hey' or 'wassup' might indicate different class or group affiliations. Sociolinguistic variables don't usually alter the word or sentence meaning of an utterance, but convey additional, social meaning.

Structure dependency

A characteristic of the relationship between words in sentences. One possible explanation for rules of **syntax** is that they are linear: a function of the simple order of words in the sentence. Take the phrase 'The tea is already cold', and the question formed from it, 'Is the tea already cold?' A linear interpretation of the question-forming rule in English might be: 'Move the first auxiliary verb (in this case, 'is') to the front'. This proves to be false, however, in sentences with more than one auxiliary, such as 'The tea that is in the kitchen is already cold' (try it). The only rule that works for both is a hierarchical one: 'Move the auxiliary from the *main* clause to the front'. That's a signal that the rules governing relationships between words take their cue not from their sequence on the surface, but from a deeper level of organisation. In other words, they exhibit structure dependency. Chomskyan linguists have aimed at elucidating this 'deep' structure in order to better understand the **universal grammar** on which they believe it must be based.

Subject, see case

Syntax

The branch of linguistics dealing with the rules that determine the way words can be combined to form sentences. These rules mean that an English sentence like 'I like the movie I saw on Saturday' is permitted, whereas 'Like I movie the saw I Saturday on' isn't (see also **structure dependency**).

Theory of mind
The ability to model what another person is thinking, to put oneself in their shoes. Theory of mind enables us to understand a speaker's meaning (see **pragmatics**), as well as sentence meaning (see **semantics**), by allowing us to decode intentions. I have a theory of mind if I am able to attribute views to you that are different to mine, based on my assessment of what you know. Without theory of mind, it's difficult to interpret non-literal use of language, such as sarcasm or metaphor. The 'Sally Anne test' can be used to establish whether a child has developed theory of mind.

Turing test
Named after the computer scientist Alan Turing, who first proposed it as a thought experiment, this is a test of how convincing a computer is at mimicking natural language. To run a Turing test, you need three participants: two humans and a computer. One human is the judge, and her job is to ask the remaining human and the computer (both of whom are behind a screen or otherwise invisible to her) a series of questions. If she cannot tell which is the computer and which is the human, the computer has passed.

Universal grammar (UG)
In Chomskyan theory, universal grammar is the shorthand for the basic, underlying structures that are common to all languages. UG is said to be genetically inherited and unique to humans. Chomsky invoked UG after coming to the conclusion that the language children hear around them was insufficient to account for their rapid progress in learning it. They must instead be relying on an internal blueprint that would also account for many of the structural similarities seen across languages. Much of twentieth-century research in linguistics was aimed at determining the precise form of this blueprint, assumed to be a set of computational rules, through the

analysis of syntax. Recent Chomskyan theory sees **Merge** as the likeliest candidate for UG (see also **faculty of language – narrow sense, innateness hypothesis, language module, poverty of the stimulus**).

Usage-based theory

A school of linguistics, associated with evolutionary anthropologist Michael Tomasello among others, that views **acquisition** and linguistic structure as being intimately tied to the use of language in the world. It stands broadly in opposition to the **innateness hypothesis**, which argues that acquisition relies on a genetically inherited blueprint that is also what gives rise to the various structural patterns we see: for example, the movement of words to form questions or create passives. According to usage-based theory, children learn language by reading the intentions of speakers (figuring out what the aim of an utterance is) and finding patterns in the sentences they hear. These patterns are linked to meaning – so that, for example, a child will understand a phrase such as 'Make the bunny push the horse' used in context during play, and will be able to extend it to other objects for which the action makes sense, such as 'Make the policeman push the car'. In doing so, they have learned the structure 'Make the x push the y'. As to how these and other structures form in the first place, an appeal is made to **pragmatics**: we might change 'the truck hit the car' to the 'the car was hit by the truck' if our primary concern – what we want to communicate above all – is that the car is damaged. We express this by putting it first. Thus, a 'fronting' rule for the formation of the passive emerges. **Grammaticalisation** is one common way in which pragmatics, in the form of speakers' intentions – say, to emphasise their dislike of something – feeds into structure.

Vowel

A sound in which the air passes unobstructed from the lungs to the mouth while the vocal cords are vibrating. The position of the tongue and the lips determine the nature of the vowel. Raising the tongue produces 'close' vowels like /i/, lowering it makes sounds like /a/, and rounding the lips results in sounds like /u/.

REFERENCES

INTRODUCTION

James Masters, 'From "titanic success" to "Mad Max": How language around Brexit changed', CNN, 27 March 2018, https://edition.cnn.com/2018/03/27/europe/brexit-language-change-intl/index.html (1 May 2018)

Chi Luu, 'The Murky Linguistics of Consent', JSTOR Daily, 7 March 2018, https://daily.jstor.org/murky-linguistics-consent/ (1 May 2018)

'Danish Minister to Migrants: Learn the Language or Pay for Your Own Interpreter', *Sputnik News*, 27 March 2018, https://sputniknews.com/europe/201803271062934735-denmark-migrants-language-integration/ (1 May 2018)

Rachel Stern, '10 German words becoming extinct thanks to English', The Local De, 26 March 2018, https://www.thelocal.de/20180326/10-german-words-becoming-extinct-thanks-to-english (1 May 2018)

Rob Nixon, 'Climate Change Can Also Transform Language', Smithsonian.com, 23 March 2018, https://www.smithsonianmag.com/science-nature/climate-change-transforms-language-180968571/ (1 May 2018)

Benjamin R. Dierker, 'How The Left's War On Words Manipulates Your Mind', *Federalist*, 1 May 2018, http://thefederalist.com/2018/05/01/lefts-war-words-manipulates-mind/ (1 May 2018)

India Sturges, 'The generation who can't remember life before mobiles are not just social media obsessed, they speak their own language. From "kitten-fishing" to "adulting", here's how to speak millennial!', Mail Online, 26 February 2018, http://www.dailymail.co.uk/femail/article-5434265/Guide-understand-millennial-language.html#ixzz5AwaGg1pT(12 October 2018)

Bible, New International Version (Biblica, 2011)

Mary Grant, trans., *The Myths of Hyginus* (University of Kansas Publications, 1960)

Alexander von Humboldt, ed. and trans. by Vera M. Kutzinski and Ottmar Ette, *Views of the Cordilleras and Monuments of the Indigenous Peoples of the Americas* (University of Chicago Press, 2013), p. 260

William Jones, 'The Third Anniversary Discourse – on the Hindus [1786]', in *The Works of Sir William Jones, Volume 3* (Agam Prakashan, 1977)

G. D. A. Sharpley, *The Complete Latin Course* (Taylor and Francis, 2014), p. 1

Noam Chomsky, 'A Review of B. F. Skinner's *Verbal Behavior*', *Language*, 35(1), 1959, pp. 26–58

'Why is the Birmingham accent so difficult to mimic?', *BBC Magazine*, 22 September 2014, https://www.bbc.co.uk/news/magazine-29307916 (12 October 2018)

Online Etymological Dictionary, entry for 'bad', https://www.etymonline.com/word/bad (12 October 2018)

CHAPTER 1

'Nothing to LOL about: Adults are deliberately dumbing down language ... and putting proper English in peril', Mail Online, 7 December 2010, https://www.dailymail.co.uk/news/article-1336310/Adults-deliberately-dumbing-language-putting-proper-English-peril.html (12 October 2018)

Anne Merritt, 'Text-speak: language evolution or just laziness?', *Daily Telegraph*, 3 April 2013, https://www.telegraph.co.uk/education/educationopinion/9966117/Text-speak-language-evolution-or-just-laziness.html (12 October 2018)

'Frequently Asked Questions', The Queen's English Society, http:// queens-english-society.org/about/frequently-asked-questions/ (12 October 2018)

Douglas Rushkoff, 'It's Not Just Grammar; It's Clear Thinking', *The New York Times*, 30 January 2013, https://www.nytimes. com/roomfordebate/2012/08/13/is-our-children-learning-enough-grammar-to-get-hired/its-not-just-grammar-its-clear-thinking (12 October 2018)

John Humphrys, 'Lost for words', *Independent*, 8 November 2004, https://www.independent.co.uk/arts-entertainment/books/ features/john-humphrys-lost-for-words-5350586.html (12 October 2018)

Harvey A. Daniels, *Famous Last Words: The American Language Crisis Reconsidered* (Southern Illinois University Press, 1983)

Jonathan Swift, ed. Jack Lynch, 'A Proposal for Correcting, Improving and Ascertaining the English Tongue', letter to Robert Earl of Oxford, 1712, http://andromeda.rutgers.edu/~jlynch/ Texts/proposal.html (12 October 2018)

George Puttenham, ed. Gladys Doidge Willcock and Alice Walker, *The Arte of English Poesie* (Cambridge University Press, 1970)

Michael Quinion, 'Inkhorn terms', World Wide Words, 21 June 1996, http://www.worldwidewords.org/articles/inkhorn.htm (12 October 2018)

Letter to Sir Thomas Hoby from Sir John Cheke, quoted in '"Inkhorn" terms: Sir John Cheke', Internet Shakespeare Editions http://internetshakespeare.uvic.ca/Library/SLT/literature/ prose/cheke.html (8 December 2018)

David Crystal, *The Stories of English* (Penguin, 2005)

Elias Muhanna, 'The death of Arabic is greatly exaggerated', The National, 13 August 2010, https://www.thenational. ae/arts-culture/the-death-of-arabic-is-greatly-exaggerated-1.567682?videoId=5752179440001 (12 October 2018)

Rudi Keller, 'Is the German language going to the dogs?', 12 July 2004, http://www.phil-fak.uni-duesseldorf.de/uploads/media/ Language_Decay_01.pdf (12 October 2018)

David Lightfoot, *Principles of Diachronic Syntax* (Cambridge University Press, 1979)

R. L. Trask, *Historical Linguistics* (Arnold, 1996)

Lyle Campbell, *Historical Linguistics: An Introduction* (Edinburgh University Press, 2004)

Helmut Lüdtke, 'Invisible hand processes and the universal laws of language change', in Ernst Håkon Jahr and Leiv Egil Breivik (eds), *Language Change: Contributions to the Study of its Causes* (De Gruyter Mouton, 1989)

Rindy C. Anderson, Casey A. Klofstad, William J. Mayew and Mohan Venkatachalam, 'Vocal Fry May Undermine the Success of Young Women in the Labor Market', *PLOS One*, 9(5), 2014

Jonathon Owen, 'Distinctions, useful and otherwise', Arrant Pedantry, 6 December 2011, http://www.arrantpedantry.com/2011/12/06/distinctions-useful-and-otherwise/ (8 December 2018)

Sameer ud Dowla Khan, 'Open Letter to Terry Gross', Language Log, 10 July 2015, http://languagelog.ldc.upenn.edu/nll/?p=19934 (12 October 2018)

Douglas Adams, *The Salmon of Doubt: Hitchhiking the Galaxy One Last Time* (Pan, 2002)

CHAPTER 2

Ben Weitzenkorn, 'Does "LOL" really mean "Lucifer our Lord"?', NBCnews.com, 26 November 2011, http://www.nbcnews.com/id/49968607/ns/technology_and_science-innovation/t/does-lol-really-mean-lucifer-our-lord/ (12 October 2018)

Google trends data for 'Does lol mean Lucifer our Lord', https://tinyurl.com/loltrends (12 November 2017)

'11 acronyms that are actually "backronyms"', Oxford Dictionaries, 18 November 2015, http://blog.oxforddictionaries.com/2015/11/backronym-list/ (12 October 2018)

Sol Steinmetz, *Semantic Antics: How and Why Words Change Meaning* (Random House Reference, 2008)

Augustine, *Confessions*, 1.8, quoted in Ludwig Wittgenstein, *Philosophical Investigations*, ed. G. E. M. Anscombe, P. M. S. Hacker and Joachim Schulte (Wiley-Blackwell, 2009)

Geoffrey Leech, *Semantics: The Study of Meaning* (Penguin, 1981)

Gottlob Frege, 'On Sense and Reference', in P. Geach and M. Black, *Translations from the Philosophical Writings of Gottlob Frege* (Blackwell, 1980)

Lisa Feldman Barrett, 'Why our emotions are cultural – not built in at birth', *Guardian*, 26 March 2017, https://www.theguardian.com/lifeandstyle/2017/mar/26/why-our-emotions-are-cultural-not-hardwired-at-birth (12 October 2018)

Ben Hammersley, 'Audible revolution', *Guardian*, 12 February 2004, https://www.theguardian.com/media/2004/feb/12/broadcasting.digitalmedia (12 October 2018)

R. F. Palmer, *Semantics: A New Outline* (Cambridge University Press, 1981), p. 40

Iris Murdoch, *Under the Net* (Chatto & Windus, 1954)

Ludwig Wittgenstein, *Philosophical Investigations*, ed. G. E. M. Anscombe, P. M. S. Hacker and Joachim Schulte (Wiley-Blackwell, 2009)

Elizabeth Closs Traugott, 'Semantic Change', in *Oxford Research Encyclopedia of Linguistics* (Oxford University Press, 2017)

'Toilet', *Oxford English Dictionary* (Oxford University Press)

'20th century loanwords', the British Library, http://www.bl.uk/learning/langlit/changlang/activities/lang/twentieth/loanwords.html (12 October 2018)

Lyle Campbell, *Historical Linguistics: An Introduction* (Edinburgh University Press, 2004)

Trask, *Historical Linguistics* (Arnold, 1996)

E. E. V. Collocott, 'The Supernatural in Tonga', *American Anthropologist*, New Series, 23(4), 1921

William Hennelly, 'Slurping vs nose-blowing, which is worse?', *China Daily*, 25 July 2016

M. B. Emeneau, 'Taboos on Animal Names', *Language*, 24(1), 1948

Poul Anderson, 'Uncleftish Beholding', *Analog Science Fiction and Fact*, 109(13), 1989

Anglish Reddit, https://www.reddit.com/r/anglish/ (12 October 2018)

Anglish Encyclopedia, http://anglish.wikia.com/wiki/Main_leaf (12 October 2018)

Cliff Goddard and Anna Wierzbicka, *Words and Meanings: Lexical Semantics Across Domains, Languages, and Cultures* (Oxford University Press, 2014)

Isaiah Berlin, *Three Critics of the Enlightenment* (Princeton University Press, 2000), quoted in Goddard and Wierzbicka, *Words and Meanings* (2014)

CHAPTER 3

William Labov, *Sociolinguistic Patterns* (University of Pennsylvania Press, 1972)

P. D. Eimas, 'Auditory and phonetic coding of the cues for speech: Discrimination of the [r-l] distinction by young infants', *Perception & Psychophysics*, 18(5), September 1975

Sandra E. Trehub, 'The Discrimination of Foreign Speech Contrasts by Infants and Adults', *Child Development*, 47(2), June 1976

Paul Ibbotson, 'The scope of usage-based theory', *Frontiers in Psychology*, 4, May 2013

Penelope Eckert, 'Adolescent Language', in Edward Finegan and John Rickford (eds), *Language in the USA* (Cambridge University Press, 2004)

Donald L. Rubin, 'Nonlanguage factors affecting undergraduates' judgments of nonnative English-speaking teaching assistants', *Research in Higher Education*, 33(4), August 1992

Marko Dragojevic, Jessica Gasiorek and Howard Giles, 'Communication Accommodation Theory', in Charles Berger and Michael Roloff (eds), *The International Encyclopedia of Interpersonal Communication* (John Wiley & Sons, 2016)

Tanya Chartrand and John Bargh, 'The chameleon effect: the perception-behavior link and social interaction', *Journal of Personality and Psychology*, 76(6), 1999

Greg Jacobs, Ron Smyth and Henry Rogers, 'Language and sexuality: Searching for the phonetic correlates of gay- and straight-sounding male voices', *Toronto Working Papers in Linguistics*, 18, 2000

Patti Adank, Peter Hagoort and Harold Bekkering, 'Imitation Improves Language Comprehension', *Psychological Science*, 21(12), 2010

Franz Andres Morrissey, 'Liverpool to Louisiana in one lyrical line: Style choice in British rock, pop and folk singing', in Miriam A. Locher and Jürg Strässler (eds), *Standards and Norms in the English Language* (De Gruyter Mouton, 2008)

Michael C. Corballis, 'Left Brain, Right Brain: Facts and Fantasies', *PLOS Biology*, 12(1), January 2014

Sergey Avrutin, 'Linguistics and Agrammatism', *GLOT International*, 5(3), 2001

Steven Pinker, *The Language Instinct* (William Morrow, 1994)

D. Van Lancker and J. L. Cummings, 'Expletives: neurolinguistic and neurobehavioral perspectives on swearing', *Brain Research Reviews*, 31, 1999

Thomas G. Bever and Robert J. Chiarello, 'Cerebral Dominance in Musicians and Nonmusicians', *Science*, 185(4150), 1974

Michael S. Gazzaniga, 'Principles of Human Brain Organization Derived from Split-Brain Studies', *Neuron*, 14(217–28), February 1995

Split-brain patient 'Joe' being tested with stimuli presented in different visual fields, from YouTube user kokoflix, https://www.youtube.com/watch?v=aCv4K5aStdU (18 November 2018)

Michael S. Gazzaniga, Bruce T. Volpe, Charlotte S. Smylie, Donald H. Wilson and Joseph E. Le Doux, 'Plasticity in speech organization following commissurotomy', *Brain*, 102(4), December 1979

Eran Zaidel, 'A response to Gazzaniga: Language in the right hemisphere, convergent perspectives', *American Psychologist*, 38(5), 1983

CHAPTER 4

AP-Petside.com poll, conducted by GfK Roper Public Affairs & Media, 2008

Paul Raffaele, 'Speaking Bonobo', *Smithsonian Magazine*, November 2006

Duane Rumbaugh, Sue Savage-Rumbaugh and Rose Sevcik, 'Biobehavioral Roots of Language: A Comparative Perspective of Chimpanzee, Child, and Culture', in Richard Wrangham, W.

C. McGrew, Frans de Waal and Paul Heltne (eds), *Chimpanzee Cultures* (Harvard University Press, 1996)

'Koko and Penny discuss "Family"', from YouTube user kokoflix, https://youtu.be/w81EnyTAUBs (18 November 2018)

W. T. Fitch and D. Reby, 'The descended larynx is not uniquely human', *Proceedings of the Royal Society B*, 268(1477), 22 August 2001

'On the Myth of Ape Language', Noam Chomsky interviewed by Matt Aames Cucchiaro, email correspondence, 2007/2008 https://chomsky.info/2007____/ (18 November 2018)

N. Tinbergen, 'The Curious Behavior of the Stickleback', *Scientific American*, 187(6), December 1952

Raymond Vagell, 'The Semantics of Vervet Monkey Alarm Calls: Part I', Primatology.net, 9 March 2011, https://primatology.net/2011/03/09/the-semantics-of-vervet-monkey-alarm-calls-part-i/ (18 November 2018)

Nell Greenfieldboyce, 'Say, What? Monkey Mouths And Throats Are Equipped For Speech', NPR Weekend Edition, Saturday, 9 December 2016

Entry for 'Taa', Documentation of Endangered Languages portal, Max Planck Institute for Psycholinguistics, http://dobes.mpi.nl/projects/taa/language/ (18 November 2018)

Irene Maxine Pepperberg, *The Alex Studies: Cognitive and Communicative Abilities of Grey Parrots* (Harvard University Press, 2002)

Personal communication, Irene Maxine Pepperberg, 17 November 2017

Geoffrey Finch, *Word of Mouth: A New Introduction to Language and Communication* (Red Globe Press, 2013)

Arik Kershenbaum, Amiyaal Ilany, Leon Blaustein and Eli Geffen, 'Syntactic structure and geographical dialects in the songs of male rock hyraxes', *Proceedings of the Royal Society B*, 279(1740), 7 August 2012

Lydia V. Luncz, Roger Mundry and Christophe Boesch, 'Evidence for Cultural Differences between Neighboring Chimpanzee Communities', *Current Biology*, 22(10), 22 May 2012

Luke Rendell and Hal Whitehead, 'Culture in whales and dolphins', *Behavioral and Brain Sciences*, 24(2), April 2001

Jane Lee, 'Do Whales Have Culture? Humpbacks Pass on Behavior', National Geographic News, 27 April 2013, https://news.nationalgeographic.com/news/2013/13/130425-humpback-whale-culture-behavior-science-animals/ (18 November 2018)

Volker Bernt Deecke, Lance G. Barrett-Lennard, Paul Spong and John K. B. Ford, 'The structure of stereotyped calls reflects kinship and social affiliation in resident killer whales', *The Science of Nature*, 97(5), March 2010

Marc D. Hauser, Noam Chomsky and W. Tecumseh Fitch, 'The Faculty of Language: What Is It, Who Has It, and How Did It Evolve?', *Science*, 298(5598), 22 November 2002

Rory Carroll, 'Starved, tortured, forgotten: Genie, the feral child who left a mark on researchers', *Guardian*, 14 July 2016

Daniel L. Everett, 'What does Pirahã grammar have to teach us about human language and the mind?', *Wiley Interdisciplinary Reviews: Cognitive Science*, 3(06), 13 September 2012

Timothy Q. Gentner, Kimberly M. Fenn, Daniel Margoliash and Howard C. Nusbaum, 'Recursive syntactic pattern learning by songbirds', *Nature*, 440, 27 April 2006

Irene Pepperberg, 'Proficient performance of a conjunctive, recursive task by an African gray parrot', *Journal of Comparative Psychology*, 106(3), 1992

Michael C. Corballis, *The Recursive Mind: The Origins of Human Language, Thought, and Civilization* (Princeton University Press, 2014)

W. Tecumseh Fitch and Marc D. Hauser, 'Computational Constraints on Syntactic Processing in a Nonhuman Primate', *Science*, 303(5656), 16 January 2004

Sam Tanenhaus, 'Noam Chomsky and the Bicycle Theory', *New York Times*, 31 October 2016, https://www.nytimes.com/2016/11/06/education/edlife/on-being-noam-chomsky.html (18 November 2018)

Ferris Jabr, 'How Humans Evolved Supersize Brains', Quanta Magazine, 10 November 2015, https://www.quantamagazine.org/how-humans-evolved-supersize-brains-20151110/ (18 November 2018)

R. Douglas Fields, 'Are Whales Smarter Than We Are?', *Scientific*

American, 15 January 2008, https://blogs.scientificamerican. com/news-blog/are-whales-smarter-than-we-are/ (18 November 2018)

Oliver A. Iggesen, 'Number of Cases', in Matthew S. Dryer and Martin Haspelmath (eds), The World Atlas of Language Structures Online, Max Planck Institute for Evolutionary Anthropology, https://wals.info/chapter/49 (18 November 2018)

Robert M. W. Dixon, *The Languages of Australia* (Cambridge University Press, 1980)

CHAPTER 5

Andrea Reisenauer, '20 of the World's Most Beautiful Untranslatable Words', Rocket Languages Blog, 27 November 2016, https://www.rocketlanguages.com/blog/20-of-the-worlds-most-beautiful-untranslatable-words/ (8 December 2018)

Entry for گُداز, Oxford Living Dictionaries: Urdu https:// ur.oxforddictionaries.com/translate/urdu-english/ گُداز (8 December 2018)

Tweet about *goya* by Fallibilist1, https://twitter.com/Fallibilist1/ status/993792563013410818 (19 November 2018)

Tweet about *goya* by SabaImtiaz, https://twitter.com/SabaImtiaz/ status/993792396013031424 (29 May 2018)

Ronald Carter, Michael McCarthy, Geraldine Mark and Anne O'Keeffe, *English Grammar Today: An A–Z of Spoken and Written Grammar* (Cambridge University Press, 2016)

'Untranslatable Words Can Expand Our Imagination', Language Line, 29 November 2016, http://www.languageline.com.hk/ 2016/11/29/untranslatable-words-can-expand-imagination/ (8 December 2018)

Bill Bryson, *Mother Tongue: The Story of the English Language* (Penguin, 2009)

LearnGaelic.net online dictionary definition of *sgrìob*, https:// learngaelic.net/dictionary/index.jsp?abairt=sgriob&slang =both&wholeword=false (19 November 2018)

Allan Brown, 'BBC Alba shows power of Gaelic lobby', *Sunday Times*, 5 October 2008

Geoffrey Pullum, 'Gaelic as a bonsai word bag', Language Log, 29

December 2008, http://languagelog.ldc.upenn.edu/nll/?p=961 (19 November 2018)

Sgrìob, Katexic Clippings blog, https://katexic.com/word/sgriob/ (19 November 2018)

Tweet about *Age-otori* by neko_guruma01, https://twitter.com/ neko_guruma01/status/884026979959226369 (19 November 2018)

Jon Wedderburn, 'Translation is not always one to one', World-Accent, 18 May 2012, https://www.worldaccent.com/blog/ 2012/05/translation-no-english-equivalent.html (19 November 2018)

Tobias Becker, 'Homesick for Yesterday: A History of the Nostalgia Wave', ongoing research project, German Historical Institute, London

Ottessa Moshfegh, *Homesick for Another World* (Penguin Press, 2017)

Tweet about *saudade* by cecilianobreelt, https://twitter.com/ cecilianobreelt/status/884056858566299648 (19 November 2018)

Trask, *Historical Linguistics* (Arnold, 1996)

Stephen Liddell, '102 great words that aren't in English but should be', 28 August, 2013, https://stephenliddell.co.uk/2013/08/28/ 102-great-words-that-arent-in-english-but-should-be/ (19 November 2018)

Adam Jacot de Boinod, *The Meaning of Tingo: And Other Extraordinary Words from Around the World* (Penguin, 2006)

Benjamin Lee Whorf, 'An American Indian Model of the Universe', *International Journal of American Linguistics*, 16(2), April 1950

John B. Carroll (ed.), *Language, Thought, and Reality: Selected Writings of Benjamin Lee Whorf* (MIT Press, 1956)

Ekkehart Malotki, *Hopi Time: A Linguistic Analysis of the Temporal Concepts in the Hopi Language* (Walter de Gruyter, 1983)

Alfred Gell, *The Anthropology of Time: Cultural Constructions of Temporal Maps and Images* (Berg, 1992)

Brent Berlin and Paul Kay, *Basic Color Terms: Their Universality and Evolution* (University of California Press, 1969)

Paul Kay and Willett Kempton, 'What Is the Sapir-Whorf Hypothesis?', *American Anthropologist*, 86(1), March 1984

Simo Salminen and Anna-Lena Johansson, 'Occupational accidents of Finnish- and Swedish-speaking workers in Finland: A mental model view', *International Journal of Occupational Safety and Ergonomics*, 6(2), 2000

John A. Lucy, 'Linguistic Relativity', *Annual Review of Anthropology*, 26, 1997

Lera Boroditsky and Lauren A. Schmidt, 'Sex, Syntax, and Semantics', *Proceedings of the Annual Meeting of the Cognitive Science Society*, 22, 2000

Lera Boroditsky, 'Does language shape thought? Mandarin and English speakers' conceptions of time', *Cognitive Psychology*, 43, 2001

Frank Palmer, *Semantics* (Cambridge University Press, 1981)

Cliff Goddard and Anna Wierzbicka, *Words and Meanings: Lexical Semantics Across Domains, Languages, and Cultures* (Oxford University Press, 2014)

CHAPTER 6

Jelena Golubović and Charlotte Gooskens, 'Mutual intelligibility between West and South Slavic languages', *Russian Linguistics*, 39(3), November 2015

Einar Haugen, 'Dialect, Language, Nation', *American Anthropologist*, 68(4), August 1966

Profile: Arab League, BBC News, 24 August 2017 https://www.bbc.co.uk/news/world-middle-east-15747941 (29 November 2018)

J. K. Chambers and Peter Trudgill, *Dialectology* (Cambridge University Press, 1980)

Edward Sapir, *American Indian Languages 1* (The Collected Works of Edward Sapir, Book 5) (De Gruyter Mouton, 2010)

Entry for Australia, Ethnologue.com https://www.ethnologue.com/country/AU (29 November 2018)

Aurélie Joubert, 'A Comparative Study of the Evolution of Prestige Formations and of Speakers' Attitudes in Occitan and Catalan', PhD thesis, University of Manchester, 2010

Paul Baker, 'A brief history of Polari: The curious after-life of the dead language for gay men', The Conversation, 8 February 2017, https://theconversation.com/a-brief-history-of-polari-the-curious-after-life-of-the-dead-language-for-gay-men-72599 (29 November 2018)

Cat-assing definition, Urban Dictionary, https://www.urbandictionary.com/define.php?term=cat%20assing (4 December 2018)

Robert D. King, 'The poisonous potency of script: Hindi and Urdu', *International Journal of the Sociology of Language*, 2001(150), 2001

S. K. Agrawala, 'Jawaharlal Nehru and the Language Problem', *Indian Law Institute Journal*, 19, 1977

Violette Graff Juliette Galonnier, 'Hindu-Muslim Communal Riots in India II (1986–2011)', Online Encyclopedia of Mass Violence, 20 August 2013, https://www.sciencespo.fr/mass-violence-war-massacre-resistance/en/document/hindu-muslim-communal-riots-india-ii-1986-2011 (4 December 2018)

Jamelle Bouie, 'Talking White', Slate, 1 October 2014 https://slate.com/news-and-politics/2014/10/talking-white-black-peoples-disdain-for-proper-english-and-academic-achievement-is-a-myth.html (4 December 2018)

'Black English' proposal draws fire, CNN.com, 22 December 1996, http://edition.cnn.com/US/9612/22/black.english/index.html (4 December 2018)

Geoffrey K Pullum, 'African American Vernacular English is not Standard English with Mistakes', in Rebecca S. Wheeler (ed.), *The Workings of Language: From Prescriptions to Perspectives* (Praeger, 1999)

LSA Resolution on the Oakland 'Ebonics' Issue, drafted by John R. Rickford, Linguistic Society of America, January 1997, https://www.linguisticsociety.org/resource/lsa-resolution-oakland-ebonics-issue (4 December 2018)

CHAPTER 7

The Rosetta Stone, British Museum collection online, http://tiny.cc/Rosetta

Simon Singh, 'The Decipherment of Hieroglyphs', BBC History, http://www.bbc.co.uk/history/ancient/egyptians/decipherment _01.shtml (28 November 2018)

Ferdinand de Saussure, *Cours de linguistique générale* (Payot, 2002)

Mitsuku chatbot online http://www.square-bear.co.uk/mitsuku/ turing/ (28 November 2018)

Steve Worswick, Loebner Prize Report 2017, chatbots.org, https:// www.chatbots.org/ai_zone/viewthread/3136/ (28 November 2018)

Louise Cummings, *Pragmatics: A Multidisciplinary Perspective* (Edinburgh University Press, 2005)

H. P. Grice, 'Logic and Conversation', in Peter Cole and Jerry Morgan (eds), *Syntax and Semantics, Volume 3: Speech Acts* (Academic Press, 1975)

Deirdre Wilson and Dan Sperber, 'Relevance Theory', in Laurence R. Horn and Gregory Ward (eds), *The Handbook of Pragmatics* (Blackwell, 2006)

Geoffrey Leech, *Principles of Pragmatics* (Longman, 1983)

Penelope Brown and Stephen Levinson, *Politeness: Some Universals in Language Usage* (Cambridge University Press, 1987)

Elinor Ochs Keenan, 'The universality of conversational postulates', *Language in Society*, 5(1), April 1976

Eva Ogiermann, 'Politeness and in-directness across cultures: A comparison of English, German, Polish and Russian requests', *Journal of Politeness Research*, 5(2), 2009

Simon Baron-Cohen, Alan M. Leslie and Uta Frith, 'Does the autistic child have a theory of mind?', *Cognition*, 21(1), October 1985

Ellie Mulcahy, 'Understanding autism: Theory of mind and the Sally-Anne test', LKMco, 27 July 2016, https://www.lkmco. org/understanding-autism-theory-mind-sally-anne-test/ (29 November 2018)

Nils Kaland, Annette Møller-Nielsen, Lars Smith, Erik Lykke Mortensen, Kirsten Callesen and Dorte Gottlieb, 'The Strange Stories Test', *European Child & Adolescent Psychiatry*, 14(2), March 2005

Stephen C. Levinson, *Pragmatics* (Cambridge University Press, 1983)

Donna Williams, *Somebody Somewhere: Breaking Free from the World of Autism* (Jessica Kingsley Publishers, 1998)

Asa Kasher and Sara Meilijson, 'Autism and Pragmatics of Language', *Incontri città Aperta*, 4 (5), 1995

CHAPTER 8

'Why Sanskrit is the most scientific language and loved by NASA', from YouTube user Indian Monk, 28 Jan 2017, https://www.youtube.com/watch?v=rC-XseI-HWI (4 December 2018)

Rick Briggs, 'Knowledge Representation in Sanskrit and Artificial Intelligence', *AI Magazine*, 6(1), Spring 1985

Shin Hae-in, 'Korean language scientifically superior', *Korea Herald*, 15 December 2011, http://www.koreaherald.com/view.php?ud=20111215000588 (4 December 2018)

Zaid Al-Alaya'a, 'The Arabic Language, the Root of all Languages', *Yemen Observer*, 10 September 2005, http://www.mafhoum.com/press8/249C34.htm (4 December 2018)

Comment by user grafplaten, in Thread: The most beautiful/ugly language, MMO Champion, 11 June 2011, https://www.mmo-champion.com/threads/920869-The-most-beautiful-ugly-language (4 December 2018)

Tweet by Cy_beh, https://twitter.com/cy_beh/status/934659497838092289 (4 December 2018)

Tweet by Farragoor, https://twitter.com/farragoor/status/908170368849911808 (4 December 2018)

Comment by user Badpaladin, in Thread: The most beautiful/ugly language, MMO Champion, 11 June 2011, https://www.mmo-champion.com/threads/920869-The-most-beautiful-ugly-language (4 December 2018)

Quote by Willie Rushton, 1984, in Fred Metcalf (ed.), *The Penguin Dictionary of Modern Humorous Quotations* (Penguin, 2001)

The Guinness Book of Records, Guinness Superlatives, 1956

H. N. Hutchinson, *The Living Races of Mankind* (Hutchinson & Co., 1900)

Marko Dragojevic, Jessica Gasiorek and Howard Giles, 'Communication Accommodation Theory', in Charles Berger and Michael Roloff (eds), *The International Encyclopedia of Interpersonal Communication* (John Wiley & Sons, 2016)

Ajai Sreevatsan, 'Where are the Sanskrit speakers?', *The Hindu*, 10 August 2014, http://www.thehindu.com/news/national/where-are-the-sanskrit-speakers/article6299433.ece (4 December 2018)

Paul Anthony Jones, 'The King of Scotland's Peculiar Language Experiment', Mental Floss, 18 February 2016, http://mentalfloss.com/article/75378/king-scotlands-peculiar-language-experiment (4 December 2018)

Susan Curtiss, Victoria Fromkin, Stephen Krashen, David Rigler and Marilyn Rigler, 'The Linguistic Development of Genie', *Language*, 50(3), September 1974

Robert J. Richards, *Was Hitler a Darwinian? Disputed Questions in the History of Evolutionary Theory* (University of Chicago Press, 2013)

Guy Deutscher, *The Unfolding of Language* (Arrow, 2006)

Robert S. P. Beekes, *Comparative Indo-European Linguistics: An Introduction* (John Benjamins, 2011)

Eric A. Powell, 'Telling Tales in Proto-Indo-European', *Archaeology*, September 2013, https://www.archaeology.org/exclusives/articles/1302-proto-indo-european-schleichers-fable (4 December 2018)

Robert J. Richards, 'Ernst Haeckel's Alleged Anti-Semitism and Contributions to Nazi Biology', *Biological Theory*, 2(1), February 2007

Guy Deutscher, *Through the Language Glass: Why The World Looks Different In Other Languages* (Arrow, 2010)

François Pellegrino, Christophe Coupé and Egidio Marsico, 'A Cross-language Perspective On Speech Information Rate', *Language*, 87(3), September 2011

Suzanne Romaine, *Pidgin and Creole Languages* (Longman Linguistics Library, 1988)

'Was it Designed? The Function of Cat Whiskers', Awake!, April 2015, https://www.jw.org/en/publications/magazines/g201504/function-of-cat-whiskers/ (4 December 2018)

'Yu Ting Wanpela I Bin Wokim? Mausgras Bilong Ol Pusi', Kirap!, April 2015, https://www.jw.org/tpi/pablikesen/ol-magasin/g201504/mausgras-bilong-pusi/ (4 December 2018)

John H. McWhorter, 'The world's simplest grammars are creole grammars', *Linguistic Typology*, 5(2–3), December 2001

Roger Lass, *Historical Linguistics and Language Change* (Cambridge University Press, 1997)

CHAPTER 9

Child utterances from the Manchester corpus of the Child Language Data Exchange System, https://childes.talkbank.org/access/Eng-UK/Manchester.html (August 2018), and the University of Illinois College of Education, http://courses.education.illinois.edu/edpsy313/mtpa/transcripts (August 2018)

Birgit Mampe, Angela D. Friederici, Anne Christophe and Kathleen Wermke, 'Newborns' cry melody is shaped by their native language', *Current Biology*, 19(23), December 2009

Larry Fenson et al., *MacArthur Communicative Development Inventories: User's Guide and Technical Manual* (Singular, 1993)

Melissa Bowerman, 'The "no negative evidence" problem: How do children avoid constructing an overly general grammar?', in J. Hawkins (ed.), *Explaining Language Universals* (Blackwell, 1988)

Courtney B. Cazden, *Child Language and Education* (Holt, Rinehart & Winston, 1972)

Noam Chomsky, *Aspects of the Theory of Syntax* (MIT Press, 1965)

Noam Chomsky, 'Poverty of Stimulus: Unfinished Business', *Studies in Chinese Linguistics*, 33(1), 2012

John H. McWhorter, 'The world's simplest grammars are creole grammars', *Linguistic Typology*, 5(2–3), December 2001

Steven Pinker, *The Language Instinct* (William Morrow, 1994)

Noam Chomsky, *Knowledge of Language: Its Nature, Origin, and Use* (Praeger, 1986)

Robert C. Berwick and Noam Chomsky, *Why Only Us: Language and Evolution* (MIT Press, 2015)

Geoffrey K. Pullum and Barbara C. Scholz, 'Empirical assessment of stimulus poverty arguments', *The Linguistic Review*, 19, 2002

Michael Tomasello, 'The usage-based theory of language acquisition', in E. Bavin (ed.), *The Cambridge Handbook of Child Language* (Cambridge University Press, 2009)

Paul Ibbotson, 'The Scope of Usage-Based Theory', *Frontiers in Psychology*, 4, May 2013

Caroline Rowland and Julian Pine, 'Subject–auxiliary inversion errors and wh-question acquisition: "what children do know?"', *Journal of Child Language*, 27(1), February 2000

Teenu Sanjeevan, David A. Rosenbaum, Carol Miller, Janet G. van Hell, Daniel J. Weiss and Elina Mainela-Arnold, 'Motor Issues in Specific Language Impairment: A Window into the Underlying Impairment', *Current Developmental Disorders Reports*, 2(3), September 2015

Shula Chiat, 'Mapping theories of developmental language impairment: Premises, predictions and evidence', *Language and Cognitive Processes*, 16, 2001

Kathryn Mason, Katherine Rowley, Joanna Atkinson, Rosalind Herman, Bencie Woll, Gary Morgan and Chloe Marshall, 'Identifying specific language impairment in deaf children acquiring British Sign Language: implications for theory and practice', *British Journal of Developmental Psychology*, 28, 2010

Jarrad A. G. Lum, Gina Conti-Ramsden, Debra Page and Michael T. Ullmand, 'Working, declarative and procedural memory in specific language impairment', *Cortex: A Journal Devoted to the Study of the Nervous System and Behavior*, 48(9), 2012

Carolyn B. Mervis, and Shelley L. Velleman, 'Children with Williams Syndrome: Language, Cognitive, and Behavioral Characteristics and their Implications for Intervention', *Perspectives on Language Learning and education*, 18(3), 2011

Jean Aitchison, 'The Language Lifegame: Prediction, Explanation and linguistic change', in Willem F. Koopman, Frederike van der Leek, Olga Fischer and Roger Eaton (eds), *Explanation and Linguistic Change* (John Benjamins, 1987)

Geoffrey Sampson, *Making Sense* (Oxford University Press, 1980)

Dorothy L. Cheney and Robert M. Seyfarth, 'Why Animals Don't Have Language', The Tanner Lectures on Human Values, delivered at Cambridge University, March 1997

Michael Tomasello, *The Cultural Origins of Human Cognition* (Harvard University Press, 2001)

INDEX

References to footnotes are indicated by fn.

to be rubbed and dried as the Royal Albert Hall erupted – put together Latin American slum kids and Western classical music and the result was personal transformation.

BRITAIN LED THE WAY

But then the doubts set in, not about the young musicians or the glorious Venezuelan experiment, but about us, the British. Britain after all started youth orchestras; they still exist with the highest standards. British schools used to have peripatetic music teachers who created musically literate generations of children from across the social classes. Was this tradition cherished and fostered? Mrs Thatcher cut the peripatetic teachers and ever since music education in schools has relied on a series of ever more complicated schemes, hard to administer, difficult to operate and far more limited in their impact than the wonderful universal availability of the peripatetic teachers. What replaced them may have been well intentioned and intermittently effective but is probably over-prescribed, -defined and -regulated.

If the quality of the various British regional and national youth orchestras remains very high, it has been earned at great cost in another sense. The social and cultural musical base from which these orchestras' membership was drawn has shrunk drastically. It represents the top of a very narrow-based pyramid of specialist excellence. By contrast, the Venezuelans built on a broad foundation of musical teaching and experience. Why did the British abandon a belief in and commitment to teaching classical music as an activity and skill with universal relevance and value rather than a limited and specialist one? Why did Britain abandon what it began, what it built, what it possessed?

Creative speculation might offer an answer, an insight into a fantasy world. Imagine this confidential conversation within the private office of the Secretary of State for Culture, Media and Sport, as he mulled over music education policies with his chief civil servant, the permanent secretary. Who knows but that the exchange might have gone like this:

PERMANENT SECRETARY: Secretary of State, did you see the wonderful concert at the Proms when that Venezuelan Youth Orchestra brought the house down?

SECRETARY OF STATE: Funny to have Venezuelans at the Proms! What were they playing, guitars and maracas? Folky stuff was it? They have such wonderful rhythm, don't they? And didn't they wave their jackets around at the end?

PERMANENT SECRETARY: Yes, they did wave their jackets. But thinking of your earlier question, they played classical music – not, um, guitars and maracas.

SECRETARY OF STATE (*persisting*): You mean classical music *on* guitars and maracas?

PERMANENT SECRETARY (*patiently*): No minister, classical music on classical instruments, you know, violins, clarinets, the lot.

SECRETARY OF STATE: Good Lord. Why ever would they want to do that?

PERMANENT SECRETARY (*patiently*): Because they believe that teaching poor children how to play classical music keeps them off the streets, away from drugs, out of the gangs and rather improves their societies.

SECRETARY OF STATE (*unconvinced*): Seems a funny way to spend their money. Still, one orchestra can't cost a lot.

PERMANENT SECRETARY: Actually, they educate almost a quarter of a million Venezuelan kids this way, they have thousands of classical-instrument teachers, scores of music schools. It's a national programme.

SECRETARY OF STATE: (*silent*)

PERMANENT SECRETARY (*cutting to the chase*): It's fantastically successful. It does have huge social benefits. Shouldn't we consider something similar in our own underprivileged areas? The Scots are looking at it!

SECRETARY OF STATE: That's just what I would expect of Alex Salmond.

PERMANENT SECRETARY (*pressing on*): Maybe, Minister, but why don't we try it? It really works in the poor areas in Venezuela.

SECRETARY OF STATE (*decisive*): No, no, no. Classical music is elitist. Everyone knows that. We don't want to have too much of that around.

Still more issues were raised by another television programme about
classical music that stirred controversy, the recent BBC series *Maestro*, in
which a group of celebrity amateurs were trained in how to conduct a
classical orchestra. It divided opinion for sure – some seeing it as playful
democratisation and demystification of what they asserted was a wan-
tonly arcane and obscure activity, others seeing it as a wilfully misleading
presentation of a technically challenging and psychologically complex
activity requiring half a lifetime to perfect.

EXPLAINING OR PRETENDING

The music profession itself – to judge from the pages of the journal of the
Incorporated Society of Musicians (ISM) – was itself divided. Peter Stark,
professor of conducting at the Royal College of Music, acted as coach to
the eventual winner, the comedian Sue Perkins. Stark's conclusion was
that as a result of *Maestro* more people knew or were interested in classical
music than had been before. As a result of appearing on *Maestro* executive
boards of companies asked Stark for coaching in leadership skills based
on the insights gained from the role of the conductor.

Any doubts about the programme's assumptions might have been
intensified by a comment from the ISM's marketing manager, who wrote:
'The programme has been praised for shedding light on exactly what a
conductor does and how difficult and varied the task is.'

But can that really be true? Can it shed more than a glancing, partial
ray of light on the activity of conducting? It is time for honesty. All the
competitors were way out of their depth in the task they were set, that
of looking even slightly like a real conductor in a period of several weeks.
The BBC Concert Orchestra, like all professional orchestras, could perform
without a conductor if needed. In the programme, on their best professional behaviour, the players played despite the wavings on the podium
in front of them rather than because of them. The judges pulled their

punches. Had they behaved like the woundingly outspoken judges on BBC1's *Strictly Come Dancing* or ITV's *X Factor* it would have been condemned as snobbish and 'elitist'.

Maestro appeared to be part of a pattern of television programming which said: 'If some activity appears difficult, we will show that, in truth, anyone can do it.' On this faux-democratic platform, so-called 'difficulty' was just a myth peddled by those who wanted to elevate their own activity and exclude entrants from trying it. Had the BBC really wanted to give an insight into the demanding business of conducting, they might have followed the 40 classically trained hopefuls who enter the Donatella Flick Conductors Competition every two years with the London Symphony Orchestra (LSO). Even when it came down to the three finalists, the gap between the winner and the third place was very marked. Even the winner would have said and would have known that there was much to learn and years to commit before even beginning to be good at the task. But facing up to even a part of that process, of the long road to real achievement, seems to be seen as taking too long, becoming too boring and — yes, the ultimate criticism — too excluding. This is not democratic. It is intellectually dishonest.

THE FANTASY OF THE EASY

In a recent article in *The Times*, the music critic and columnist Richard Morrison mused on what he called '2008: The year when the experts lost the plot'. He was not referring only to the financial experts: he identified a wider set of social attitudes that reflected either a distrust of experts or — more profoundly — involved a direct rejection of expert knowledge and the implied authority derived from such knowledge.

> The internet has been the prime driving force, spreading the pathetic illusion that all knowledge (and therefore all wisdom), is accessible to everybody [...] Almost as strong is the new belief that everyone's opinion, on every subject, is equally valid — whether that opinion is well informed or crassly ignorant.

And Morrison reached his coda:

> How long before surgeons have to seek an audience vote from TV
> viewers on which operating procedure to use? Or airline pilots
> have to take a straw poll among passengers on whether to use the
> north or south runway at Heathrow? The twenty-first century is
> in danger of being the first era in history to value mass medioc-
> rity and water-cooler chitchat over individual genius, expertise,
> courage and leadership.

Morrison exaggerated, of course, but only in order to make a point. The
attitudes he identified and parodied explains why television programmes
are made suggesting that anyone could become a conductor in a few
months. The fantasy of 'easiness' had supplanted the so-called 'myth'
of difficulty. Which one is closer to real life, the 'fantasy' or the 'myth'?

Behind it all, there is the sound of the great Western music culture
being abandoned and trivialised and undervalued, just at the moment
when other cultures are taking notice. A few years ago, the New Labour
culture secretary Tessa Jowell travelled to Berlin to see an extraordinary
youth-education and outreach project based on Stravinsky's *The Rite of
Spring*, led by the Berlin Philharmonic and Sir Simon Rattle. Jowell was
deeply impressed by what she saw, and said so. Her implication – and
evident belief – was that the Germans did things so much better than
we did, and when would British music wake up?

Tessa Jowell had to be told that the *animateur* behind the Berlin project
was not a pioneering, visionary German, but Richard McNicol, the LSO's
own professional *animateur*. He had been doing similar work for years
past at the LSO's home in the Barbican in the heart of London. It was an
instance, in Tessa Jowell's case, not so much of 'not invented here' but
rather 'only to be valued here if someone else shows us the way'. It was
the British way to start with, but the episode reflected domestic politicians' knee-jerk reluctance to give credit to the arts in their own country.

Take the importance and value of the symphony orchestra. It has been
an accepted truism for a decade or more that orchestras are in decline in

the West, and certainly in England; that audiences are greying and dying; that the young and not so young are uninterested, ignorant or hostile; that time is running out for the great classical repertoire and the vast behemoth of the nineteenth-century Romantic symphony orchestra. Defeatism and rejection have been the order of the day.

The proposition is arguable, but only in the face of evidence to the contrary from the East. The country with the fastest rate of new orchestra formation in the world is China. Reporting from an Asia–Pacific orchestral conference in Shanghai in autumn this year, the writer and columnist Norman Lebrecht – no mean orchestral doomsayer in his time – was told that China has 43 orchestras around the nation, with a further six being formed. Germany, the heartland of the Romantic tradition, still has an impressive 133 orchestras – though their numbers are falling – and Britain has at least 46 or more, depending on how they are counted. Musical standards have been rising as Chinese musicians return home from training in the top Western conservatoires. At these rates of growth, China will soon be second only to Germany in the size of its orchestral scene.

There has to be an explanation. If accurate, what do these trends point to? They suggest an awareness that a Chinese city with a symphony orchestra has greater prestige than one without; that one with a better symphony orchestra has greater prestige than its lesser neighbour; that there is growing competition for the world market in television and film soundtrack recordings; that such competition signals a new national purpose and understanding; that music training enhances the skills of the young and empowers them.

The question cannot be avoided: what is it that the Chinese – and the Venezuelans – understand about the importance of the great Western classical orchestral tradition that the UK sometimes seems no longer to believe in? Why does Britain diminish the value of what should be a cherished, nourished and encouraged national tradition? Or are we in thrall to a simplistic and facile populism that dismisses anything that is not immediate, universal and accessible?

There have been important and attractive developments in music in England. The many elements in the government's 'Music Manifesto' include the National Singing Programme, the target of reaching two million young musicians by 2011, of whom three quarters would continue to learn a musical instrument. The 'Find Your Talent' initiative, part of the government's commitment to five hours of culture for every young person every week; the number of concerts actually given each week around the country; the spring and summer scene thick with local classical music festivals.

UNDERSTANDING OR EXPERIENCE?

Yet even here reservations are needed. What exactly does the 'Music Manifesto' or the 'Find Your Talent' initiative teach? Are they more concerned with the experience of making music or performing drama or painting a picture – important as these are – than with learning about the traditions and history of these activities? When making music, isn't it good to know that others have done the same thing for several centuries, that it was done supremely well, and that this understanding about the past might be enjoyable and even essential? Too much teaching of arts and culture in schools puts the experience of the activity far above knowledge of its historical context. Yet if ignorance of the past is well-nigh total or, worse still, actively encouraged, the experience of the present itself will be enfeebled and attenuated. Experience plus knowledge lead to understanding. All three are needed.

When Labour's culture secretary, Andy Burnham, stated proudly that music was a cultural entitlement and that soon half of schoolchildren would learn a musical instrument for a year, it seemed a real step forward. Yet how much could a child learn by playing any instrument for just a single year? The honest, politically inconvenient truth was very little.

The only way to preserve hope from such proper anxieties would be to look at the big picture, the national scene, the international experience. Music has always taken centre stage at the great national and political moments because it expresses them in a way that even words cannot. Summon up the swelling chorus of 'Hebrew Slaves' from Verdi's opera *Nabucco*. Could anything better express the hope of liberation from captivity than this music? The story might be historical, the libretto specific, but the feelings expressed and realised have become universal through the sound of the music. And when the chorus was played at Verdi's funeral in Milan, the vast nineteenth-century crowds – like the Hebrew slaves – joined in. For the Italians wanted freedom, liberation from the Austro-Hungarian Empire, their own independence. Verdi was a national hero, of course, and his name conveniently spelled out 'Vittorio Emanuele, Re d'Italia'! But the music said a hundred times more than any nationalistic rhetoric could.

Or picture another, more recent public and political scene, in Wenceslas Square in the heart of Prague in the autumn of 1989. The communist regime in Czechoslovakia was discredited and tottering. The crowds filled the square, scene of so many national high points and tragedies, for one final, concerted push, one unified message to the regime as they jingled their house keys in a broad sonic hint: 'Lock up and just go!' To underline that mood of national determination, the conductor Libor Pešek led the entire Czech Philharmonic Orchestra into the square and they swung into what is in effect the Czech national anthem, Smetana's symphonic poem 'Vltava', from his orchestral sequence *Má vlast* – 'my country'. The music said it all. The country belonged to the Czech people, not to the Communist Party. The music spoke the words. It was enough. Hope turned into reality.

On other occasions, music offers the promise of a better future. When Daniel Barenboim created his West-Eastern Divan Orchestra, composed equally of Jewish and Arab musicians, he made a bold proposition – that sharing music-making might put the great rifts of Middle Eastern politics into a different perspective. It couldn't heal them, let alone solve the problem on the ground. One multinational orchestra couldn't substitute for politics. It might offer a wholly different way of looking at them, of feeling about them. When the West-Eastern Divan Orchestra played at the Proms, the atmosphere was special, it was intense. Music-making was presenting a deeply human proposition about the possibility of reconciliation. Tragically, political suspicion in the region remained such that the orchestra had to have its base in Seville in Spain, not in Israel or on the West Bank. This did not diminish the value of the hoped-for reconciliation that it represented. It could not be part of the politicians' much-vaunted 'road map' to a Middle East settlement. That would be too optimistic. But it did offer the hope that music might chart paths to understanding unavailable to the conventional routines of diplomacy.

That is the offer that music makes, an offer to all, the whole time, everywhere. Music is a staff of life, of learning, of politics, of events, of defiance, of reconciliation, of commemoration. It is literally and meta-phorically a great instrument of the human spirit available to anyone to take up. Politicians should never forget that.

13

THE EDUCATION DEBATE: GIVING THE YOUNG THE ARTS THEY DESERVE

November 2008 to February 2009

> *'I would ban the word "creative" from schools altogether. It's laying far too great an expectation on children to be something, to do things they can't possibly do or be.'*
>
> Grayson Perry

> *'The damage done by the romantic idea of the artist driven by inspired creation is incalculable. It's not the way things happen. You work and keep on working.'*
>
> Michael Craig-Martin

In the last decade, the link between the arts and education has grown stronger, more complex, more intense and, finally, more effective. When I started at the Barbican in 1995, there was no education department, no education policy, no awareness of the need for one, no budget provision and no expectation that the City of London Corporation would regard such activity as necessary or worthy of additional funding. It was Graham Sheffield, the Barbican's arts director, who insisted that an education policy was an essential and integral part of an arts centre worthy of its name. 'Education', what's more, could not be an add-on to the 'real' arts activity, a pleasant sideshow, but should be knitted into the very purpose of the arts. True to his word, Sheffield funded an education department by top-slicing the various art-form budgets in his direct responsibility and started a process from which the Barbican and others have never looked back.

Today the Barbican and its neighbour the Guildhall School of Music and Drama, cooperating with the resident orchestra, the London Symphony, run a combined education programme of a kind previously unthinkable. They include a single head working across both institutions for all learning and a Centre for the Orchestra involving all three institutions. One of the strongest advocates of education in the arts has been the Clore Duffield Foundation, which has funded learning centres across the major arts institutions but only on condition that those institutions are fully committed to integrating education into their work. It was the foundation too that drove and inspired the Cultural Learning Alliance (CLA), a ginger group and also a vanguard group to advance and secure the commitment to education within the arts.

My own involvement with the Clore Duffield Foundation was about to become very intense from 2009 as I took up my new appointment as chair of the Clore Leadership Programme. I liaised very closely with Dame Vivien Duffield and her director, Sally Bacon, on education and arts-leadership matters. The basic philosophy of the CLA was that knowledge and experience of the arts and heritage can transform children's lives, that there should be closer involvement between schools and the world of the visual and performing arts and that these connections should be actively pursued by all major arts organisations.

At the annual arts conference of the Specialist Schools and Academies Trust (SSAT) in Liverpool early in 2009, the education debate was at a somewhat earlier stage. The SSAT commit themselves to very intense concentration on the arts. They needed to know more about the work being done by and within arts organisations, offering the possibility of a myriad of creative links that did not exist as things stood. It seemed a good way of bringing together the information and experience of the performing arts with that of teachers; they were after all developing the audiences and probably the artists of the future. For while there was general talk of the 'arts community' as if it were a single body with a collective identity and sense of purpose, in practice it was and remains characterised more by separation, division and lack of understanding. If the entire arts community, defined broadly and inclusively, were ever to mobilise and speak up coherently and passionately for the arts, it would amount to a huge lobby. It would put paid to the continuing smears that 'the arts are elitist, only for a few, not popular', which disfigure the public debate and make the case for more resources for all arts activity harder to make. Talking to the SSAT alone wouldn't heal this rift, but it might close a few gaps in individual thinking.

For myself, 18 months on from finishing at the Barbican, life was pleasantly engaging. At the UAL I was trying to help the constituent colleges – Chelsea, Central Saint Martins, Camberwell, Wimbledon, the London College of Fashion and the London College of Communication – to accept that, although they were already a university in formal terms, they had a positive interest in creating a coherent university identity. This did not diminish the colleges' own strong historical identities. In arguing as I did, I was not suggesting that a fully centralised university was either desirable or likely. But I did insist – as did the rector, Nigel Carrington – that the idea of the 'university' had to be more than the central clearing house for money, students and problems, a place for building, plumbing and paperwork. I was met with polite but stubborn resistance. This was the academic way. This would be a long game. Nigel Carrington and I played it together. Mainly we argued that to create a stronger identity for the university took nothing away from the colleges. Rather it gave them something extra, a larger, more coherent, cohesive whole, of which they were a part. It was a 'zero-plus' opportunity where everyone gained, not a 'zero-sum' game where one person's gain must be at another's expense. Sometimes Nigel Carrington and I differed over tactics, with me pressing for faster progress towards a strong university brand. I regarded resistance as anxiety about an unreal problem. Nigel, far more patient, reassured me: 'Give me the time. I will get there!' We did.

From early 2009 on, chairing the Clore Leadership Programme would involve more and more of my time. And of course keeping in close and active touch with the arts scene.

In a rather telescoped diary entry from February 2009, I looked back on a busy schedule during the previous three months. What it demonstrated at least was the incredible range, quality and sheer enjoyability of the arts in London. As Liz Forgan observed on her appointment as the new chair of Arts Council England in February: 'This is a golden age of creativity and innovation in England, encouraged and supported over decades by the Arts Council.' From my direct experience this was what that golden age looked like in London:

Luscious *Tales of Hoffmann* at Covent Garden; Steven Osborne at Wigmore magnificent in Messiaen's *Vingt regards sur l'enfant-Jésus* – known in the camp world as 'Twenty Peeps at the Baby Jesus'; awful Tony Palmer film on Carl Orff – but then Orff is awful; outspoken attack on future arts cuts by me on *Newsnight Review*; get rather pickled at Barbican Xmas party but some of the people there are beyond a joke; great revival of the Ayckbourn trilogy at the Old Vic which introduced the incomparable comedian – no, actress – Jessica Hynes, to us; I have a stinking month-long cough/ cold; four cracking days in Budapest over new year; staggering Alice Coote singing Mahler's *Das Lied von der Erde* at Wigmore – she just digs into the emotional solar plexus; great Verdi *Requiem* by Colin Davis and the LSO – where does 80-year-old Colin get the energy? But goodness how he generates it; boozy BBC party at Foundling Museum; Neil MacGregor speech on 250th anniversary of the opening of the BM; glamorous London College of Fashion catwalk show at V.&A.; interview for *World at One* about the latest BBC 'scandal' of not showing the Disasters Emergency Committee appeal on Gaza on grounds of needing to keep impartiality – I say BBC has lost its heart; I make a kind of peace with Christopher Frayling, former Arts Council chairman, at the opening of new sculpture studios at the Royal College of Arts. He says I have

come a long way in supporting the idea of the 'creative industries'. That is only partly true. What Chris does not understand
or take into account is that when New Labour harped on about
'creative industries', it was a way of avoiding talk of, and support
for, arts, culture and all such elitist stuff. It was evasion. All of
which Alan Davey is now trying to put right. My own rows with
the Arts Council over their failure to support us, notably when
the RSC decamped from the Barbican theatre, are on the record
and objectively − or rather subjectively! − I will never think we
at the Barbican were not badly treated.

At a regular and stimulating UAL discussion dinner at the Arts Club
in Dover Street on acting and directors, my former schoolmate, the
film director Stephen Frears, lead the discussion. John Hurt and Alexei
Sayle were there too. During the discussion that followed, John Hurt
naughtily reminisced: 'I remember Stephen coming up to me as we
started shooting a film and he asked, "John, tell me, what do real
directors do?"' Stephen affected a degree of shock, but he saw the
humour of the story, and certainly John Hurt told it in a completely
non-malicious way.

January 2009 was a cold month and offered a bleak outlook for the
arts. Andy Burnham, the New Labour culture secretary, launched it
with the almost inevitably two-faced, Janus-like commitment to the
arts: 'Some people may not like it but the arts has [sic] to live in the real
world too. Nobody is immune from what is happening.' The thought
that the arts did not live in a real world of artistic and commercial risk
seemed not to occur to him.

Then Burnham put on the cheerful face from the official ministerial
handbook, as all culture secretaries did. 'I will relay an equally vociferous
message back to government which is that the small − relatively small −
amount of funding here produces a huge benefit not just socially, educa-
tionally, culturally but also economically.' Give or take a phrase here or
there, some such 'on the one hand, on the other' speech had been made
by every culture secretary in living memory. It did not constitute policy;

it was the basic departmental default position; it passed for thought but was merely a diversion from real action.

For its part the arts world was in realistic but reflective mood as 2009 came in. At the National Theatre, the director, Nicholas Hytner, feared that tight times financially might lead to cautious times artistically:

> We need to ensure we don't start to play excessively safe in response to a tough economic situation. The Arts Council […] should require its clients to respond to the recession by making the same demands on its audience as it has done over the last five years.

Ekow Eshun of the Institute of Contemporary Arts (ICA) foresaw a change of priorities in the creation of new work: 'We may shift to a place where we come to look at work not just for its gloss and its shine but for the questions it asks about who we are and the times we live in.' And from the Tate, Sir Nicholas Serota defiantly proclaimed the national priority that should be attached to the role of the arts:

> In times of uncertainty, culture is more important than ever in helping us to understand and identify our place in the world. Artists, writers, film-makers and poets are the people whose insights guide and nourish us, more than the words of economists and politicians.

If nothing else the scope and maturity of the arts world's outlook on the future revealed a refusal to complain and a lively and confident understanding of the value of the arts in society.

In his farewell lecture on relinquishing the chair of the Arts Council, Christopher Frayling reflected ruefully on the 'venomous chipping away' at the Arts Council that he had endured. And he pointed to future controversy in the arts world in his call for a restructuring of the management and leadership of the Cultural Olympiad: 'Sort it out […] there are too many committees jostling for position and no ringmaster […] the clock is ticking away […] Someone has got to lead it.' It was

some time before everyone drew the same conclusion. It was drawn,
but only just in time.

So it was a concerned, serious but utterly professional arts world
that faced the new year as I reached Liverpool on a bitter January day in
2009 to speak at the aforementioned arts conference of the SSAT. And
the question in the front of my mind was simply: 'Everyone says that
education in the arts is vital; there may be a great deal going on, but is it
being approached in the right way, the best way possible?'

START THEM YOUNG

How do the young learn about the arts? How are they taught? How
much of that teaching should be about what made the arts worthwhile
in the first place? Could the arts as they are today be comprehended
in the absence of an understanding of the arts as they were before? For
myself, without an outstanding English teacher at preparatory school
who happened to be passionate about classical music and film, without a
public-school English teacher who directed school plays and played the
organ in chapel, I would not have had the introduction to the arts that I
received. I am eternally grateful for that and for them. All the learning,
incidentally, was extracurricular, outside the syllabus. If those teachers
taught they did so through their enthusiasm and love for the arts and
by their example.

Look at this picture. Imagine a secondary school in east London, one
of those underprivileged inner-London boroughs where the school has,
say, 40 different nationalities among the schoolchildren and where 40 different languages are spoken apart from English. It is Monday afternoon.
The curriculum is enlivened – or interrupted – by half a dozen musicians
from the LSO's education, outreach and access team. They are meeting,
say, year nine to help them enjoy music, explore rhythm and hear sounds
that they might not otherwise hear, could not be expected to understand

or might doubt that they would ever enjoy. Everyone has a great time. The class may also be involved in a more ambitious project – to write a music drama about the lives of some of their classmates. They don't get this opportunity or experience anywhere else in the curriculum.

The following week, at the same school, at a similar time, another set of strangers appear at the school doors. It is the RSC, half a dozen actors arriving to help the children enjoy using words, explore and discover new words, hear words in ways they might not otherwise hear and might assume they would not like. Everyone has a great time. In addition, they are also working on a project – a drama about the lives of some other children from within the class. This activity is not like anything else in the curriculum, for sure.

Another week speeds by in the hurly-burly of school life. Yet another group of visitors turns up. Who have we here? A team of six curators from the British Museum, complete with a 'hands-on' kit of ancient stones, hand axes, fossils and Neolithic shards. Do you want to hold a hand-knapped flint axe? Try this! Can you imagine what it was like to depend on it for your next meal? The children are encouraged to touch these objects, which are thousands or tens of thousands of years old. In due course, they are encouraged to imagine what life would have been like if some of their number had lived in ancient times and used such ancient objects instead of all their accustomed mod cons.

The following week... Well, you get the drift. And what's wrong with it? Lucky school, you might say. Arts organisations make contact with young people who might otherwise have no involvement with the arts at all. Musicians, actors, curators enjoy the freshness of the reactions drawn from the very innocent and the very ignorant. (After all, we all begin very ignorant.)

As if this is not enough, the notional head of arts at the notional school has a mail bag packed with invitations, with free tickets for the school to attend arts events all over London – a veritable blizzard of invitations to access. The National Theatre, the RSC, English National Opera (ENO), the Barbican and small theatre companies across the metropolis are desperate to get children from schools to swell the audience, change its character and demonstrate to funders and supporters that the organisation in question is doing everything it can to 'widen access'.

Most such offers cannot be taken up – it's a matter of practicality. There's a curriculum, isn't there? Many such generous invitations – so I am reliably informed – are not even opened. This is sad, for my typical but imaginary school is blessed to be at the receiving end of such a cornucopia; just why it is so conspicuously blessed by the gods of bureaucratic gifts, no one can divine. This is doubly sad. Just across the borough, a very similar school, with identical needs, identical profile, gets none of the visits, none of the attention, none of the free invitations. But then the New Testament did warn us: 'Unto every one that hath shall be given…'

The former head of education at the Barbican said recently: 'If I had one fairy wish it would be that we unified all the various arts enrichment activities that arts organisations such as the Barbican and others offer schools and provided them in a systematic, organised, coordinated way. As it is, much of the work is often individually very good, but the provision is chaotic.'

I saw the aptness of this wish over a decade of the Barbican's excellent education programme. Did Barbican Education ever coordinate its activities with the neighbouring education department at the LSO, the RSC or the Guildhall School? It did not. Not because they or we were stand-offish and proprietorial about our work. Rather, because somewhat different activities were being presented in particular ways depending on the art form, albeit all of them falling into the broad category of arts education, enrichment and creative expression. Beyond that, the task of merging such different activities from different disciplines and different organisations into a coordinated, integrated whole was too difficult to contemplate. Today the Barbican and the Guildhall School of Music and Drama have united their education and learning efforts into a single department. It is a rare though shining example in an otherwise deeply fragmented outreach sector. Is it time to do better?

Taken by themselves, each of these educational activities and countless others do remarkable things. Some stand out from my own Barbican experience, such as when I listened to a group of 20 teenagers from a Tower Hamlets school giving a jazz performance in the Barbican foyers. They had been part of a week's course, initially led by local jazz professionals, which culminated in an entire day with the legendary trumpeter Wynton Marsalis. The teenagers were remarkably good; certainly, only such an occasion could have given them such an opportunity and experience. They stood, they played, they were applauded and congratulated. Afterwards, a head teacher observed: 'Don't underestimate the importance of what has just happened. This is probably the first time in their lives that these young people have been applauded and recognised for anything they have ever done. That's incredibly valuable.'

In another snapshot from memory, I see life-size models and images of Fafner, the dragon in Wagner's *Siegfried*, created by children during our *Ring* project. Had anyone seen a Fafner of such awesome strangeness in a professional opera production, the strength and originality of the images would have been noted.

At a class given by ENO during their run of Wagner's *Ring* cycle at the Barbican, the three Rhinemaidens took some 11-year-olds through the opening scene of *Das Rheingold*. At the end of the opening ten-minute scene, it was time for questions. Up went a hand from one boy. 'Is singing a job?' Wonderful question. The Rhinemaidens explained in simple, patient, but jaw-dropping detail that singing was, indeed, a job demanding skill, knowledge, stamina, long hours, years of training and huge dedication. There are, after all, no silly questions, only inadequate answers.

Elsewhere, I hear the poems written by primary children in a term-long course led by the poet Michael Rosen. I hear another head teacher saying: 'We would not give up our cooperation with Barbican Education, and the school's overall performance results in the league tables have risen in the years of working together. I am convinced there is a causal link between the two!'

These are heart-warming memories and real ones. On deeper reflection, reservations creep in and demand examination. Such education and outreach activities are beneficial for the organisations that provide them. LSO players, for instance, find them rewarding and a positive activity, not a lesser add-on to the main profession of being an orchestral musician. As I sat in the hall listening to the LSO's great *animateur* Richard McNicol leading the schools through Stravinsky's *Firebird*, I was struck by the fact that all the orchestra's leading players were on stage. Excellent as they were, there were no substitutes. The LSO's managing director explained: 'It is in the players' contracts that they appear in the schools' performances. The schools deserve the best!'

WHAT'S THE PROBLEM?

Clearly, access to such varied arts experiences – delivered at a very high level – is hugely valuable to the children. Schools could not provide, from within their own resources, the skills, ability and imagination that top-level professionals can offer. Clearly, too, the range of creative arts experience delivered across the UK by all the major arts institutions, large and small, is substantial. Yet – and here come the doubts – how big is it or can it be in relation to real, overall need? Is it, cumulatively, merely scratching at the surface of the real needs of education in the arts? Why is it so fragmented, so patchy, so disorganised – or perhaps simply 'unorganised'?

At a conference of professionals involved in the charity Youth Music in Greater London, the theme was the future role of the mayor of London in the provision of music for young people. Almost 200 professionals attended, representing boroughs, lobby groups, providers, educators, organisers; they were but a proportion – perhaps a small one – of the total number of those in Greater London engaged in youth music. It was daunting – such activity almost constitutes an entire economic sub-sector; it was stimulating – so many people involved in providing music for the young; and it ended by being curiously depressing.

Christina Coker, the long-serving director of Youth Music, was asked if she could draw a family tree of the plethora of organisations involved in youth and music. 'No,' she replied, 'I couldn't, because a family tree doesn't exist. But if you want a picture of the way all these organisations interrelate, think of a dozen circles, each of which overlaps with a few but not all of the others.' Honest as this description was, 'overlap' sounded rather hit and miss. A further question followed: given the proliferation of organisations, was it possible to claim that ultimately all musical needs in schools were met? Christina Coker answered honestly that she doubted it. A bystander in the group pressed further: 'Is there any way of identifying the gaps in music provision and then meeting them under the present system?' The answer was even more honest and more bleak: there were no ways of making the ad hoc system more comprehensive, more rational and more effective.

It is not just the haphazard and random overlapping of musical provision that prevents better arts education. Complaints at the same mayor's meeting included these, which came from the world of music but undoubtedly applied across all arts provision: 'There are too many initiatives, too many roll-outs!' Another on the same theme: 'Short-term initiatives don't have long-term effects.' And the constant cry from all sides: 'Liaise, liaise, liaise.' On such good evidence, music provision for schools is chaotic, unfocussed, random and inconsistent. Is arts provision as a whole any better? This sows a terrible seed of doubt – if governments really valued it, wouldn't they introduce system into these maelstroms of activity? Argue if you will that it is right that it is dispersed rather than centralised, that it is attractively diverse – perhaps that there is a virtue in its very fragmentation. But are such characteristics really the best way of organising such a key part of school educational experience? Or is the truth that politicians prefer introducing policy initiatives and new projects because they create the impression of activity and dynamism? Whereas such may merely represent restless interference.

WHAT THE ARTS GIVE

There is a still more basic question. Why do the arts matter in education at all? The answer is simple: curiosity, imagination, originality. The arts nurture curiosity because without them anyone – young or old – is deprived of knowledge of a world of the different, the world where objects are made, ideas created of which you had no idea but become curious to know more about. Such curiosity must be an absolute benefit to learning, to understanding, ultimately to knowledge itself.

The arts nurture imagination because seeing them, viewing them, listening to them, introduces worlds, visions, sounds that fall outside prescribed categories. Imagination breaks the known rules, creates its own terms, opens up new situations beyond those already known.

Experience of the arts fosters originality, because in the world of the arts mere repetition, imitation, replication or duplication are of no value. Understanding the dimensions of the arts invites the possibility that they must innovate, create and develop in order to avoid deadly sterility and stagnation. Developing curiosity; stimulating imagination; generating originality – these are powerful grounds for fostering arts education in schools. But there are others.

The sculptor Bill Woodrow argued passionately about the value of a training in the visual arts. 'They are,' he insisted, 'more than a training; they amount to a skill.' What exactly did he mean? 'Look at the ingredients in a year's visual-arts training,' he said.

> There is the discipline of creating a piece of work – of whatever kind. Then the need to examine it, analyse it, reflect on its strengths and weaknesses, improve it and finally judge its value in fully realised form. You listen to your teachers but they can't tell you what to do, what is right or what is wrong. Ultimately, that is what you must do, learn to be self-aware, self-critical, methodical and determined. You must learn from your own experience, your own successes, your own failures. Don't tell me that such a process doesn't amount to an intellectual skill!

It is a persuasive argument and a warning never to underestimate the learning that comes from doing and making.

For learning and acquiring skills is the start of a road with many twists in it. Looking at the list of professions filled by graduates from the UAL, students graduating from courses in graphic and fine arts, sculpture, design, fashion, tailoring, communication and drama do produce the fashion designers and painters, the Stella McCartneys, the next Steve McQueen, the next Damien Hirst. But these disciplines lead to jobs and positions unconnected with the original area of study. Look at Harold Tillman, the retail entrepreneur, Joe Wright, the film director, Ruth Rogers, the restaurateur, James Dyson, the inventor and industrialist, John Hegarty, the advertising guru, Helen Boaden, the director of BBC News, or Linda Bennett, the fashion retailer. The very nature of arts education allows graduates to develop themselves in a variety of fields that prove to suit them best. But it is a broad education and it must coexist with skills, with craft, with background and discipline or it would not be as portable and practical as it proves to be in reality.

CREATIVITY OR HARD WORK?

These are very practical considerations – skills, jobs, employability – all necessary, all desirable, but not necessarily the be-all and end-all of education. Where does this leave creativity? What place should it play in judging the value of the arts and education? Should not the first priority be to ask whether education in the arts produces creative geniuses? It would be pleasantly simpler and reassuring if it did. But there are questions to be asked about creativity, not so much the thing itself but the nature of the weight and expectation placed upon it, especially for the young. To state – or even to imply – that arts education in schools is principally about creativity rather than knowledge, skill and understanding could simply be putting too much expectation on what the young can deliver. They are, after all, young. For 'creativity' is a dangerous, loaded, heavy word in the wrong hands.

In 2003, I published a collection of interviews with artists in many disciplines under the title *On Creativity*. It seemed a reasonable word to attach to the work of people such as Howard Hodgkin, Anthony Caro, György Ligeti, Frank Auerbach, Muriel Spark, Harrison Birtwistle, and many others. The book carried that title despite the artists rather than because of what they said. For the word 'creativity' rarely featured in our conversations. Anthony Caro said what most would have said if asked directly: that he didn't like what he called those 'overheated words', such as 'inspiration', and no doubt 'creativity' too.

So, if unquestionably creative artists such as those – and many others – avoid words such as 'creativity' and 'inspiration', should we not beware of using them too glibly ourselves or of imposing them too much, too soon, too easily on the young? At a UAL fashion show, the ceramicist and Turner Prize-winner Grayson Perry observed firmly: 'When I talk to my mates,' he stated,

> I don't say, 'Have you been creative today?' We say, 'I've had quite a good day; I solved some problems; I got something to work better; I'm making progress!' What we don't talk about is 'Had any good inspiration lately?'

When I mentioned schools to him, Grayson Perry was categorical: 'I would ban the word "creative" from schools altogether. It's laying far too great an expectation on children to be something, to do things they can't possibly do or be.'

What every successful artist speaks of in discussing his or her work is the acquiring of craft, the practice of discipline and the single-mindedness of sheer hard work. If, first thing in the morning, the painter Frank Auerbach finds that he likes what he worked at the previous day too much, he destroys it. 'Destroy your darlings' is his working motto.

The composer Harrison Birtwistle is just as rigorous about accepting complacently an easy compositional solution. He once told me:

> If I get to the point in my work where I think I know where I'm going, and I go away and leave it, when I come back, I very rarely continue in the way that I thought I was going to continue.

And he added: 'Very often, if I ever need a solution to something and I find it, I walk away.' That response represents sheer, bull-headed calculation and determination, the furthest cry possible from the attitude that might say: 'Oh, that's great, I've been inspired!' Real artistic gains are invariably hard won. The young should not be sold a false prospectus or lulled into false expectations.

I asked the artist Michael Craig-Martin about the extraordinary flow of work he was then producing – one exhibition seemed to tumble out after another. 'But you don't stop,' he insisted, 'you don't stop working. Even if things don't seem to work, you just go on. It will come right in the end.' And then he continued: 'The damage done by the romantic idea of the artist driven by inspired creation is incalculable. It's not the way things happen. You work and keep on working.'

Should the young be told that being an artist depends on sheer determined hard work as opposed to waiting for inspired creation, which is the honest message, the truthful one, the useful one? The very idea of the 'muse descending on the artist', allowing the artist to dream romantically and perhaps indulgently for inspiration and creativity to arrive, is actively misleading and damaging. Far better is the reality of the arts as a set of disciplines and skills both in their own terms and because of their plain usefulness in many disciplines. Being an artist is not a matter of learning the tricks of beguiling the 'muse of inspiration' to give a helping hand. It is about acquiring the skills of the basic activity. It's the wise old saw: 'What is genius? Ninety per cent perspiration and ten per cent inspiration.' But it's that way round, with the flood of perspiration first. Why should the young be told anything else?

And it is about something else: knowing the subject. Too much so-called schoolteaching of 'creativity' occurs in a vacuum of awareness that whatever you may be struggling to express in words, line or music has been done before, long ago and far better. The present exists in the past. Too much official talk of the importance of creativity in schools implies or states that all you need to learn to express is how to be expressive. Very few, if any, of those otherwise admirable outreach visits to schools have the time to explain to the young that the words they use were also used by Shakespeare, the sounds they make were also made by Beethoven or Mozart, the images they conjure were also made by Michelangelo or Picasso. Of course, time is short. But given the time, would they and others have the inclination to offer such basic information?

KNOWLEDGE OR EXPERIENCE?

It is possible that a political line lurks, in an unacknowledged way, beneath such attitudes. According to this line 'creative expression' is valued as good because it is open to all, is not based on or encumbered with knowledge, and invites at least the possibility of equality of result. Truth to tell, 'creative expression' is deemed to matter more, is assigned a higher priority, because it is presented as not elitist, its results as not a foregone conclusion of birth, background or education, but rather the result of random chance.

By contrast, 'knowledge' about the great historical canon of achievement in all the arts – like the lists of the kings of Israel who busily begat one another – is deemed to be exclusive, difficult, off-putting, irrelevant and, chiefly, unnecessary. Of course, any canon in any art form or discipline is open to challenge, critical scrutiny and renewal. But if nothing is known of those who trod the path down which you are stumbling, how can you judge what you are doing or avoid robbing yourself of an awareness of greater possibilities?

There are many ways of being actively, creatively, freely aware of the past without being manacled by it. When I spoke to Luke Bedford, the Wigmore Hall's first composer in residence, I wondered what his own musical terms of reference were, his antecedents. He pondered: 'I started with Renaissance and baroque; then Mozart and Beethoven; and Stravinsky and Bartók in the twentieth century.' And reflectively: 'One day I may try to come to terms with Brahms.' That is a very contemporary pick-and-mix approach to the availability and utility of the canon. The tyranny of a purely linear historical development – as if there were an inevitable and predetermined process in place – was often just that, a tyranny.

The strength of the Luke Bedford approach is that it spans the centuries, it spans the styles and schools, it knows the tradition, but it frees the composer to fill in the gaps as and when he or she believes there are gaps to be filled. If all Bedford knew was music from 1968 onwards, what sort of composer would or could he be? (Or playwright or painter?) True achievement is likely to be founded on such a mixture of historical knowledge, theory, craft, skill and sheer hard work. 'Creativity' may be – but even this cannot be guaranteed – the end product of those much harder-earned ingredients.

I once asked the great German composer Hans Werner Henze what the artistic roots were of his own modernism. He replied without a pause: 'I go back to Beethoven, of course!' He is not alone in thinking in this way. The architect Frank Gehry was the product of a typical ultra-contemporary arts education in California. It was only when he travelled to Europe as a student that he realised what such a monochrome education had denied him. When Gehry stood before Notre-Dame in Paris for the first time, he was – he told me – filled with a sense of rage that his teachers had never shown it to him as something from which he might learn. Rather it was presented as a pretty, historical picture postcard. After looking at France's Romanesque churches and the baroque extravaganzas of southern Germany, he was never going to be the same person again. Gehry's buildings are infused with a sense of great enclosed volumes and complex patterns of illumination that derive not so much from the present as from work 600 years ago. Simple contemporary creative innocence and historical ignorance could never have led him to such conclusions. Knowledge of the past made his modernism possible.

And even that great sculptor in steel Richard Serra refers back to history. Some of his most brilliant works – the huge steel *Torqued Ellipses*, formed into fluent, plastic shapes of supreme grace and elegance, yet made out of the heaviest steel – are inspired by the oval space at the heart of Borromini's Roman church, the Quattro Fontane. Serra offered this characteristically elliptical response to the question of what might be his own place in the great tradition of sculpture. 'The way I relate to the tradition is, I guess, in a way T.S. Eliot related to the tradition: as soon as you break with it, you are part of it.' But that deliberately gnomic formulation carries within it the real awareness of a debt to a tradition.

To be part of such a process you must know what came before. The door to the past has to be left open. It does not let in clouds of a dead, dusty and irrelevant past; it does let in the bracing air of challenge based on the achievements of the past. Beware of those who want to keep it shut and to line the gaps with the intellectual draught excluders of presumed contemporary superiority. If the great achievers of our time need a link to the past and are nourished by it, why should the young be denied access to such connections?

Not that such intellectual links are only connections to a remote past. A leading academic drama director, who painstakingly ensures his students are familiar with the entire historical repertoire of film, told me of his shock to find that on a recent course most of the students had never heard of the great Soviet dissident novelist Alexander Solzhenitsyn. It is all too easy to fall into the 'ignorance of the young' syndrome, and my interlocutor is not one of those. Remember too the old observation: 'Each generation is worse educated than its predecessors. But differently educated.' The difference is important. But avoid the mistake of confusing those glaring gaps in knowledge that represent actual breaks with the living past as distinct from mere indifference to the minutiae of the way things used to be done. Nor should everyone who laments the 'ignorance of the young' be dismissed as being fatally 'uncool'. Those who ignore the past or set parts of it aside must be very aware of what they reject and why they reject it.

The good news is that more attention is being paid to the teaching of culture in schools than ever before. From the promise of five hours of culture for every child, to the searching and comprehensive ten recommendations of the Clore Duffield report on *Culture and Learning: A New Agenda for Advocacy and Action*, the scene is changing. Were all the bodies involved in arts and culture activity to work together to generate real 'zero-plus' activity, then culture would enjoy a place in education that it had never had before.

Yet can the politicians be trusted? What does the word 'culture' contain? Is it just another politicians' weasel word to avoid full commitment to the arts? Is it another tactic to keep alive the old 'elitism/ populism' argument? Is it really about backing 'lifestyle' activities, for fear of addressing the precise nature of what the young are entitled to know about the arts of the past?

For the young are entitled to know about Shakespeare, Beethoven, Michelangelo, and everything for which they and their peers stand. Anyone who says, assumes or implies that they are too difficult to understand or, worse still, irrelevant to the young, has some explaining to do. Why are they slamming shut the doors to the past, doors through which they themselves may once have joyfully passed? In true education, the doors are always open.

14

THE ARTS: A SPECIAL CASE FOR SPECIAL PLEADING

February to May 2009

*'Even when targets are met, citizens detect no improvement.
Hence the desperate and depressing ministerial calls
for, in effect, new targets to make NHS staff show
compassion and teachers to teach interesting lessons.'*

Simon Caulkin, *Observer*

*'It would be a brave new world without such gobbledegook in it
but – to use a management theorist's phrase – an empowered
one, too. Managers would be chosen not for their ability to
bandy jargon with their superiors but for their empathy,
pragmatism, experience and decisiveness with their staff.'*

Andrew Billen, *The Times*

Two pleas from experienced and respected journalists, angry, even despairing, threw light on the environment in which the arts were supposed to exist and hopefully to thrive early in 2009. It was one where frustration at not getting results – whether in the NHS, business or the arts – became expressed in clumsy concepts and obtuse language, each of which were guaranteed to produce outcomes the opposite to those so desperately desired. In this respect, the arts found themselves in an intellectual position no different from that of much of the public or even the business sector. As public finances tightened, the arts had to come to terms with straitened circumstances while keeping their intellectual, philosophical and practical autonomy, without which survival was rather less likely. Quite simply, the arts had to find their way out of the mess in their own words and in their own way. Alien concepts would not help, but would only obstruct. Straitened circumstances were made more difficult by straitened – constipated even – language.

How big would the funding crisis turn out to be? Everyone sensed a threatening atmosphere in those early months of 2009 and described it in very similar ways. For the artistic director of Sage Gateshead, Anthony Sargent, ominous suspense was in the air:

> I feel as if I am on a Caribbean island waiting for a hurricane to come. The rain hasn't started but the streets are uncannily empty. All we can do is build as good a storm shelter as we can.

For Alan Davey, Arts Council England's new director, the weather was closing in too: 'We could enter a perfect storm where all sources of income are endangered.' Davey appealed to private funders to 'see the value of your investment in the arts and have the courage to continue it'. And in a real sign of trouble ahead he appealed to politicians, usually a gesture of last resort:

> What we ask of politicians is faith – in the arts and what they can do and for the important pillar of public funding to remain strong as a key part of the way through for the nation and its soul.

These discontented times found their voices in my diary of the time. One sociologically inclined friend mused on the barrenness of living in what he called the 'Blair–Beckham brand years'. He explained what he meant by this malicious coupling: 'Each is a well-paid international brand, neither has won anything for the UK ever but a lot for themselves and Cherie and Victoria, birds of a feather. All superficial, self-serving, selfish.'

Unfair perhaps, but I wasn't inclined to mount a defence. It was part of the sound of the times, turned inward, resentful, scratching old wounds.

For myself, the new challenges of the Clore Leadership Programme obliged me to set out my thoughts on the nature and practices of leadership in the arts, the start of a sustained period of reflection on the subject. At one of the first of such sessions with Clore Fellows – in March – I posed the question of leadership, not just in the arts, like this:

> As a leader, do you allow or do you prevent? Do you work to achieve results or are you content with observing process? Use objectives, don't be ruled by them! Change objectives if they don't work, that is what they are there for! Above all, 'leading' or 'managing' is about character – who you are, how you treat others, whether others will respect and follow you.

All these remained subjects for further exploration and analysis.

Later in the month, I was asked by alumni of the prestigious Harkness Fellowships – conferring on recent university graduates a two-year travel and study fellowship to the United States – to talk to them about 'BBC values'. I was delighted to agree, not so much because of the subject but because I would be the only person in the room who had been turned down for a Harkness, as I was 50 years ago. (Quite rightly as – apart from any other deficiencies – I appeared at the interview wearing my skiing clothes.) I suggested there were distinct periods of BBC internal policy that needed to be understood. 'There are four eras of BBC values associated with three BBC directors general,' I explained.

> Reithian, Birtian, Dyke-ian and the present. Lord Reith defined public-service broadcasting; John Birt's managerialism imposed business processes on broadcasting values; and Greg Dyke's commercialism set a different direction. With Birt and Dyke in their different ways overlaying or ignoring core BBC public-service beliefs, the result was confusion and contradiction whose resolution seemed to lie in internal regulation, compliance and rule-making.

Each of the current crises that became crises could be laid at the door of too much formal regulation, rigid and ineffective compliance and total lack of common sense. The BBC is still a public-service-driven organisation with audience responsibilities – that needs stating and restating – and a belief in exceptional programmes about things that matter. As things stand, staff are confused and contemptuous. And the public is impressed neither by 'neo-Birtian' systems nor by rampant and inconsistent commercialism.

Soon after, at a BBC dining club, the political documentary maker Michael Cockerell recalled the mood of the Birtian years: 'If someone referred to "John", you watched your words; if they said "Birt" you knew you were safe; if it was "John Birt" you thought twice!' Then he challenged me – what sort of director general would I have been? I replied, in the spirit of the moment, 'More pragmatic, less managerially driven, far more people-oriented, with a clearer articulation of values that would explain what the BBC was and why it did what it did.' Would that have been good enough? Who knows?

Within the arts world, two controversies erupted, each like a suppressed geyser that had been waiting to blow. Nicholas Serota erupted first, and he did so on behalf of his colleagues about the maundering fiasco of the Cultural Olympiad under the chairmanship of the Southbank Centre's Jude Kelly. Ostensibly his target was the supreme London Organising Committee of the Olympic and Paralympic Games (LOCOG): 'There is no board member who is interested in culture. It is an organisation set up to run a sporting event and it is not clear it is organised in such a way as to successfully run a cultural event.' The chairman Sebastian Coe revealed how paper-thin LOCOG's real commitment was to the notion of culture at the games: 'The arts are difficult and sometimes conflicted. Frankly it would have been easier to do not very much at all. But we believe it is our duty!' Hardly a ringing proclamation of belief in the arts and the role they might play in the Olympics!

The second long-delayed eruption occurred at London's Southbank Centre, where the outgoing chief executive, the Australian Michael Lynch, had triumphed where others had failed and got the Royal Festival Hall handsomely and necessarily refurbished. Who and what was his target? Bankers: 'a bunch of bastards', Lynch called them for failing to support the Southbank's renovation.

> Corporate Britain had let the side down [...] They need a sense of values. The government to their credit got behind us in a big way [...] What we failed to do was to get corporate Britain and a lot of individuals who made hundreds of millions behind us.

No wonder Lynch felt pessimistic about the outlook for arts funding, as would anyone who saw private and corporate support as some kind of magic and assured answer to shrinking public investment in the arts.

In April the budget duly cut the arts still further. The Arts Council, observing that 'the arts are far more than a luxury add-on – they are quality of life and, with sufficient public investment, they can be central to economic recovery,' threw an emergency lifeline of £44.5 million to help artists who struggled. The new Arts Council chair, Liz Forgan, put the best face on it she could:

> The real challenge for the arts is to ask: 'What can we do to help the country weather and recover from this downturn?' Showing that we can make a real contribution in even the most difficult of times will be the best case we can make for continued public investment in the arts.

For my part, with a set-piece lecture at the Cumberland Lodge conference centre in Windsor Great Park in May 2009 in the pipeline, I had long decided to mount the case that most of us believed in – that the arts should be spared cuts that solved nothing financially. I would argue the unpopular but necessary case that the arts were a special case deserving special treatment. When I ran into Liz Forgan shortly before the speech, she said: 'Don't apologise!' As if...

THE NECESSARY CASE FOR THE ARTS

Why should the arts be seen, even dare to offer themselves for consideration, as a special case for treatment? Are they sick? There is no evidence
for that. Are they under threat? They could be, or they are constantly,
depending on your point of view. If so, should they be treated differently
from others in straitened economic times? I believe they should. Is this
special pleading? Very much so. What kind of treatment am I looking for?
Better treatment. Why? Because it makes sense, for the arts, for society,
for people, for funders. That is the case to be made in the hope of it being
won. This could be a way of making it.

First, 'pages from the diary of an arts junkie'. In the first six months
of 2009 your atypical arts junkies could – and no doubt did – attend some
very varied arts events. They – for they are a couple – would have wan-
dered the theatrical installation underneath Waterloo station's tunnels
and vaults. Staged by the Punchdrunk company, it was an Old Vic – yes,
an Old Vic – promotion. Before that, the couple excitedly committed
an entire day to the Tricycle Theatre in Kilburn, in north-west London,
where a sequence of ten short new plays set out the tragic, repetitious
and by now wholly predictable consequences of a century and a half of
foreign military intervention in Afghanistan.

Before that – for this couple graze promiscuously – the Turbine Hall
of Tate Modern was the venue for a dance installation by the American
choreographer William Forsythe. Here, on a flat performance space,
responding to gentle, self-effacing electronic music, a company of 15
dancers made their way through, around a maze of 200 small, lead pendulums, hanging from a forest of thin wires, their bodies either avoiding
the pendulums or by their engagement setting them moving in random
patterns. Before that, they might have taken in the latest work of the
German composer and director Heiner Goebbels, where an orchestra
explored the experience of war through the centuries, with the musicians
speaking the words, some by Gertrude Stein.

There are only two lessons from this very personal case study. First, the couple – any couple – could have found a score of other, similar events to experience in London at this time. These were not exceptional times, an unusual concentration of the interesting and extraordinary. And that is the second point; it is easy to overlook how far arts performances, arts practices have been transformed over the last ten to 15 years. Typically today, pieces are made across the art forms, across cultures, across continents; typically they seek out new, unorthodox places to perform; typically they adapt their chosen form to the requirements of their expression; the experimental has almost become the norm; innovation is the yardstick. Most importantly, the audiences have come with the art. For them, such work is the new norm. Artists and audiences are in a remarkable new step of shared curiosity, openness to form, expectation of the unexpected.

AUDIENCE AND ARTISTS IN STEP

This very special harmony between maker and witness demonstrates that the arts are not sitting on their historical laurels, only dreaming of and preserving a great historical canon, without thinking of where they need to move in order to refresh and renew. (Not that I undervalue the importance of the historical canon in any of the art forms.) Second, the transformation of so much creative practice has marched step by step with an equivalent transformation in the ways the arts run themselves. The argument for the arts to be seen as a special case, for the arts to deserve special treatment, for the arts to deserve unashamed and unapologetic special pleading, rests on this three-way revolution in very recent times – a revolution in arts practice, a revolution in audience involvement and expectation, both underpinned by a revolution in the way they are organised and managed, nothing less. It ought to be irresistible.

Before setting out the case for the existence of this triple revolution in detail, let us acknowledge a certain reality. 'Special pleading' is, of course, a transparent code for 'don't cut the arts', or at least 'don't cut them as badly as other services and departments'. Everyone knows that the Treasury tradition of 'equal misery all round' is as old as the chancellor's budget box and probably rather older. But it is worse than old, it is – or should be – out of date. No respectable management guru would accept equivalent salami slicing across all sausages as the most effective or intelligent way of balancing a budget. It is lazy and ineffective because it dodges the choices, avoids questions about priorities and misses the opportunities that, sensibly judged, cuts can provide.

But this special pleading involves something else – an understanding of 'proportionality'. It is intellectually dishonest and mathematically ignorant to assert that the arts must take their share of cuts in the interests of getting the national finances as a whole back into equilibrium. The entire arts budget is so small that even, say, a 10 per cent reduction would not materially benefit the national budget. In 2007–8, total government departmental spending was £586 billion. The sum that the DCMS devoted to the arts, museums and galleries, libraries, architecture and history was £1.1 billion. That is less than 0.2 per cent of the national budget. The idea that a drastic assault on this corner of the national budget might provide the necessary road to fiscal prudence does not bear examination. Yet a 10 per cent reduction in arts spending would reverse at least a decade of achievement. So much for 'proportionality'.

The argument for treating the arts as a specially deserving case for financial treatment rests on a view of history too. It is time to look back at the decade of the Blair years and the way the public debate about the role and place of the arts evolved during that time. To understand what happened, begin at the end, on 6 March 2007. The scene, Tate Modern. Attending the event, most of Britain's top arts supremos. The occasion, a well-billed 'legacy' speech by the outgoing prime minister, Tony Blair, on New Labour's achievements in the arts over the previous decade. The prime minister called Britain's cultural life 'spectacular'. Arts and culture in the UK were, he said, 'more confident, more assertive, more creative and alive than a decade ago'. Government funding of the arts, he pointed out, had doubled in the decade; it was now on a stable three-year basis, and where new funding had been provided – as over free admission to museums, or investment in regional theatre – the results in increased attendances had been inspiring. In almost every area of the arts and culture, attendance, usage, visitor numbers, ticket sales had grown. Over a decade, said Tony Blair, the arts had come to be 'of fundamental importance' to Britain.

Tony Blair thanked the nation's 'architects, dancers, actors and directors, artists, musicians, the curators, the custodians of heritage' for their creativity. He praised the model of cultural support developed in Britain where, as he put it, 'public subsidy permits risk-taking. A new breed of entrepreneurial leaders in the arts world has shown that art of the highest quality is compatible with sound financial discipline. Indeed, the public subsidy produces a return.'

A BIT LATE

This was heady stuff, or should have been. Why then did the arts supremos, garlanded with such praise, murmur as they left, 'Very nice, but a bit late'? What Blair described was indeed a legacy; the problem was that it had not been seen, understood or accepted as a government priority at the beginning of New Labour. If it was a part of the Blair legacy, then it was achieved and acquired through the efforts, beliefs, arguments and actions of others.

To explain the apparently grudging reaction of arts leaders to the Blair speech – and most of the words, phrases and statistics had been supplied by them in the days immediately beforehand – it is necessary to go back to 1997 and the early days of New Labour at Number Ten.

In those days, the new prime minister, flushed with electoral success and heady hopes, opened Number Ten's doors and hospitality to the luminaries and celebrities of the rock, pop and showbiz world. They included Damon Albarn, Noel Gallagher, Chris Evans, Zoë Ball, Liz Dawn, and many others, a kind of new establishment of popularity and acclaim. The problem – for the 'mainstream' arts world – was not who Blair included but who he left out. The arts and culture world which he so fulsomely praised and recognised a decade later at Tate Modern were not on Number Ten's hospitality radar at the outset.

I observed in *The Times* in March 1998:

> The prime minister is signalling that Oasis is as important as opera; that chat shows are as important as novels; that television soap operas are more valuable than live theatre. If it had happened just once, it would not have been worth mentioning. But three times [for there were three Downing Street receptions with such guest lists] is no accident, comrades.

Partly as a result of that article, Tony Blair called in two dozen arts leaders to Number Ten in June 1998. The occasion went well enough, with both sides ready to acknowledge their own shortcomings. Both sides wanted to do better. Tony Blair promised that 'we must write the arts into our core script', an encouraging phrase that lost its sheen as it was used repeatedly in connection with several other areas of government policy. The 'core script' got rather full.

It was not to prove that simple. For a start, while Alastair Campbell once famously said 'We don't do God!' he might have said even more accurately, 'The prime minister doesn't do the arts!' That was a problem of generation and of personal attitude. (Incidentally, is it preferable to have a national leader wholly indifferent to the arts or one who knows exactly what his or her tastes are – for instance in architecture?)

More damaging still at New Labour's outset was a fundamental reserve – perhaps even outright hostility – in their thinking about the arts. In their world view, the arts were judged to be remote, elitist, exclusive, expensive and irrelevant to most voters. What mattered to government, society and voters were 'the creative industries', those economic offshoots of the arts, 'the outcomes', we would say soon, that resulted from the arts and whose 'outputs' – we would also learn to say – might be considered to justify some spending on the arts. In New Labour ideology, the arts might be valuable only or mainly if they could deliver economic regeneration, better education, improved health, specific social benefits of many kinds; in short, the arts were truly only justifiable in so far as they were 'instrumental' in delivering a range of economic and social benefits.

The last decade of arts policy, the Blair years, was spent in good part in an ideological dispute over that word – 'instrumentalism'. Those who warned of the shortcomings of such a functional approach to arts funding were regularly tarred with the brush – for that is how our critics saw it – of only wanting 'art for art's sake'! That was far from the case, though it was often a convenient and facile debating smear. What we did believe was that without excellent arts in the first instance, other benefits would never flow.

And so the battle lines – for so they were – were drawn. (On the sidelines of the battlefield, fierce engagements broke out over high and low culture, and cultural relativism.) To be on the wrong side could and sometimes did cost an organisation money. It was not an argument about words and attitudes. Jobs could be lost for not being ideologically orthodox.

With it came the insidious and universal Whitehall regime of objectives and metrics. 'Prove to us that the arts do good!' 'Show us the numbers that prove you are meeting your objectives!' Much time, energy and ingenuity went into devising and imposing ever more complex objectives on arts organisations to demonstrate to the Treasury that the arts were indeed 'value for money'. Much time, energy and sheer cunning were devoted on the other side to meeting, blurring, evading, obfuscating or just ignoring the metrics, because they did not seem to be measuring anything relevant or worthwhile in art, culture or performance. Behind the whole cumbersome and burdensome regime of objectives lay the unaddressed and unanswerable fact that no one – especially the Treasury – could measure or define the value of value itself.

THE TRUCE DECLARED

A truce was called in January 2008 in the 'Thirty Years War' over instrumentalism in the arts. In his report commissioned by the DCMS, the former director of the Edinburgh Festival, Sir Brian McMaster, stated that the purpose of arts subsidy should be *Supporting Excellence in the Arts*.

The report was subtitled *From Measurement to Judgement*. The very first section of the report was given over to the notion of 'excellence'; the second to 'innovation and risk-taking'. In his conclusion, McMaster stated that 'a greater sense of what excellence is within public discourse is required'.

In writing as he did, McMaster was in the great English tradition of the practical. In David Gilmour's wonderful biography of Giuseppe di Lampedusa, author of *The Leopard*, he notes that Lampedusa loved Dr Johnson, and his embodiment of 'the country least governed by logic'. 'In any other country,' wrote Lampedusa, 'Johnson's learning would have forced him to espouse a philosophy. In England he could do without; he was a pure empiricist.'

With three mighty strokes of empiricism, McMaster despatched the ideological demons of instrumentalism, numerical objectives and relativism to the back of the class.

It is tempting to say that with this official governmental report, the arts had triumphed over the bureaucrats and the New Labour relativists. 'Excellence', 'judgement not measurement': these are our words, our concepts. Is it that simple? 'Up to a point, Lord Copper.' For something else important had changed along the way. Engaging with government and stakeholders, setting and meeting objectives, countering the demands of crude instrumentalism, all these once-novel activities led to a transformation of the way the arts were run. Rather than seeing the last decade as a battleground, perhaps the more accurate image might be of the process of Hegelian synthesis. In struggling to reconcile the thesis of 'art for art's sake' with the antithesis of 'arts for the sake of what they do', the arts world changed itself. What happened?

A decade and a half ago, in the mid 1990s, hardly a quarter passed without news of the financial or artistic plight of a leading arts organisation. Sometimes it seemed that they queued up to take turns to plunge into crisis; first the Royal Opera and its huge rebuilding project; then ENO and its seeming failure to retain a general director for more than a couple of years; then the question of whether the nation really needed two opera houses, two opera companies, two orchestras. The RSC ran a string of annual deficits, regularly bailed out financially by the City of

London Corporation because of its residency at the Barbican theatre. The British Museum plunged into deficit. The press – of course – did not help; it was not their job to do so. But it did seem as if arts correspondents could not entertain the possibility that two rival organisations in the same arts sector could be successful at the same time. If the National Theatre was 'up', then the RSC had to be 'down'. It seemed artistically and humanly impossible that both the Royal Opera and ENO could both be doing good if distinct work at the same time. And there was an audience, usually a different one, for both.

No blame should be attached to the media for reporting on the general air of doom-laden incompetence that surrounded the arts a decade or more ago. Such was my regular journalistic experience of the last 20 years! The arts provided easy journalistic targets, rich and very easy pickings, though it was noteworthy that as almost all arts organisations ran into serious deficit, there were often reasons behind this. In Sir Richard Eyre's report on the future of the opera houses, he noted an exact match between the accumulated deficits of most performing-arts organisations and the standstill funding – i.e. reduction in real terms – they had received for several years previously. Yet the evidence remained that most major arts organisations were indifferently managed a decade ago and that they improved hugely during that decade, partly or largely as a result of having to engage in the intense debate about 'Why fund the arts at all?' So what happened?

MANAGING MANAGEMENT

If bureaucrats had their hang-ups, and politicians their prejudices, arts leaders were not without their entrenched positions and attitudes. Mainly they revolved around the very notion of management, that voguish new skill of the 1990s. For many arts bodies, the very idea of 'managing' their organisation was alien – they did not know how to do it; strange – it involved vocabularies and terms that scarcely sounded like English; and almost certainly antithetical to the values of what they stood for and had been educated to do. What had management to contribute to scholarship, or to knowledge, or to curating, or to directing, or to designing, or to anyone of the great, fine, high arts? Why should a great scholar know about a budget, still less how to manage it? Why should a theatre or opera director need to know about the budget for his or her latest production? Wasn't there a company accountant who added up the invoices as they came in? Why should the designer work to budget? If the sets and costumes came in rather expensive, wasn't he or she hired for his or her flair, his or her genius? What was the general director of the opera house there for?

For within some of the deepest corners of the arts world there was hatred of management, scorn of the values of businessmen, who were increasingly recruited onto boards to introduce practicality and common sense into the way the arts spent and earned money. The worst thing imaginable seemed to be to suggest that the arts should be 'businesslike'! 'Businesslike', you will note, not 'a business as such'! And while the arts world was engaged in the external contest with the 'instrumentalists', internally the arts themselves were riven by anxiety about how to alter their behaviour to meet the demands of their funders.

Change came. How? Boards looked for leaders who could and would manage without selling the art short; sometimes they double-banked the leadership of major institutions – an artistic leader and a strong chief executive; they found administrators from outside the arts world who wanted to deliver 'businesslike' teams but only if the first priority was arts excellence and the second was to control the budget. Arts leaders with a reputation for indifference to these new and necessary skills or mere inability to apply them were simply not appointed, just as the vogue for appointing abrasive business leaders to run arts organisations proved to be mistaken and short lived.

Arts and management came to cohabit in a way that first seemed natural and then became necessary. The learning process within the arts went wider still. If ministers put the access, outreach, education and inclusion agendas ahead of the arts-excellence agenda, this might be tiresome and probably wrong. But short of telling them to get lost, it seemed prudent to address these socially driven agendas and look at them in new, constructive ways. After all, wasn't 'education' merely a way of building the audience of the future? Wasn't 'outreach' a way of bringing the arts to children who would not otherwise experience them? Wasn't 'social inclusion' a wise way of broadening the appeal of the arts?

Give or take a bit, more and more arts organisations adopted the government's social agendas, sometimes as an act of calculation, sometimes with conviction, often with a mixture of the two. They did so without selling the arts short. And as they did so, they became professional in a range of activities previously not seen as useful, still less essential, parts of a great arts institution. Marketing, audience loyalty, development, education, publicity and commercial sales became vital parts of a newly managerially focussed arts institution.

And there was a great awakening. The arts provided were not less excellent; the newly and more broadly professionalised institution used scarce resources better; because it generated increased resources, the organisation was not only more efficient, it was better in every respect. But, and this is a crucial reservation, the arts were always placed first. The 'instrumentalism' argument was stood on its head. The social agenda became 'instrumental' in providing the best possible arts.

It is this decade-long transformation of the way the arts manage themselves that constitutes a large part of the case that the arts today should be 'a special case for treatment'. Peace has broken out in the ideological war; excellence is reinstated; the arts can look management consultants in the eye – they know the trick words, the cant phrases, the real and fake nostrums; they have adopted and adapted the skills of management to the very particular needs of the world of the arts. So, is that it?

Not quite, or indeed perhaps not at all. There is more going in the arts than a casual observer might realise, and it is that part of the current scene in early 2009 that I want to turn to now. Because understanding where it stands is a further reason for claiming that the arts really are a 'suitable case for treatment'.

Over a six-month period, I had a rare opportunity to look deep into the arts scene as it stands today. Every year for the last six, the Clore Leadership Programme has identified some 25 arts leaders of the future from a list of almost 300 applicants, a shortlist of 70 of whom are interviewed. This intensive process provides an extraordinary insight into Britain's arts today. For the 70 shortlisted amount to a dipstick into the arts' 'body spiritual'. What emerged was a group of very serious, very committed, very dedicated, very professional people who work in organisations large and small across the country, both in the arts and in local authorities, fund seekers and fund givers, administrators and artists.

More importantly still, the range and depth of their engagement and involvement with society – with the young, the disabled, with black and minority ethnic groups – was striking, admirable and largely unknown or at least unappreciated. At the Royal Philharmonic Society Awards in May 2009, the award for public engagement went to Streetwise Opera, a group entirely devoted to opera with the unemployed. And the judges did not give it as a consolation prize for a well-meaning project. It was excellent by any standard. Much of the real heart of the arts world in Britain today consists of enterprises as particular and original as this. All start from a determination to be excellent before anything else.

THE NARROW VIEW

Yet a major obstacle in arguing the case for the arts is that too often funders, stakeholders and politicians know very little about what the arts really are, where they exist, what they do. Very recently, the finance director of a large arts funder complained of the problems of negotiating with the Treasury culture team. 'All they talk about is Covent Garden,' he protested. 'They think that the Royal Opera and a few suchlike are the arts in Britain! What I am going to do is hire a minibus, get the team out for a day and take them to a range of arts organisations that are NOT Covent Garden. They must get a better idea of what the arts world is really like!' How can arts policy at any level be sensibly devised and conducted if the basic position of the chief stakeholder is lack of understanding – or just plain ignorance?

The same or similar might be said of local authorities, many of whom fund arts activities of an extraordinary range. Do they understand what they are funding? From the recent evidence of the Clore Fellowship interviewees, many of whom work in local authorities, their masters are still wedded to instrumentalism, with many committed to reaching 'strategic agreements' of an explicitly instrumental kind over funding: 'We will pay you this but in return you must achieve the following targets connected with social and economic objectives.'

Recently, a local authority told its concert hall that further programming funding was available so long as it met the condition that road-safety figures improved in the town. When the board rejected the proposal as both wrong and impossible, the local authority first wriggled but then admitted that the only pot of available extra money they had lay in the road-safety budget! On further reflection, the authority gave the money and dropped the objective. If experience suggests that instrumentalism as a policy leaves a lot to be desired, the prospect of a strictly drawn local-authority 'strategic agreement' looks like a ball and chain.

Why does this matter? Doesn't dispensing public money demand that recipients be accountable for how they spend it? Of course, but it does not follow that the money is better, still less best spent if the donor or stakeholder determines beforehand what the desired results should be.

And locking arts organisers into prescriptive agreements brings another, even more damaging result. It creates an atmosphere, a culture, in which initiative, imagination and independence of thought are held back or even discouraged. The evidence from people working in local authorities is of bureaucratic inertia, restraint on independence and a formulaic response to leadership. This saps energy and demotivates ability and people at a distressing rate.

THE OBJECTIVES CULTURE

For many the root cause of so many ills, and not only in the arts, is the 'objectives culture'. You might have thought by now that experience of the distortions created by an insistence on and obsession with objectives was so well documented that the high-water mark of the 'objectives culture' had been reached and that the tide of 'compliance' would be on the wane.

Writing about the Stafford Hospital scandal, where the pursuit of targets by hospital trust managers was judged by the Francis report to lead to a possible extra 400 deaths in three years, the *Observer*'s Simon Caulkin, highly experienced in writing on business matters, could scarcely contain his anger. The general criticisms he made of the target culture in health provision apply to the arts world too, albeit without the same deadly consequences!

> The health service has been engineered to deliver abstract meta-goals such as four-hour waiting times in A & E and halving MRSA [the deadly hospital bug]—which it does, sort of—but not individual care, which is what people actually experience. Consequently, even when targets are met, citizens detect no improvement. Hence the desperate and depressing ministerial calls for, in effect, new targets to make NHS staff show compassion and teachers teach interesting lessons.

Or for arts organisations to be excellent — the similarities with the arts world need no labouring.

Caulkin's conclusion was severe:

> Targets make organisations stupid. Because they are a simplistic response to a complex issue, they have unintended and unwelcome consequences [...] Target-driven organisations are institutionally witless because they face the wrong way: towards ministers and target-setters, not customers or citizens.

As for hospitals, so for the arts.

In a devastating critique of the gobbledygook and cant of management theory in *The Times* in March 2009, Andrew Billen, the paper's leading cultural commentator, pointed out that at least four English police forces had decided to abandon officially imposed government targets and replace them with 'common sense'. The acting chief constable of Surrey dared to say: 'I want our officers to apply their professional judgement and discretion to do the right thing.' That, 'doing the right thing', appears to be as revolutionary a thought as committing arts leaders to delivering 'excellence'.

And Billen looked forward to a newly 'empowered' world – note the sarcasm involved in his deliberate use of management cant – where 'managers would be chosen not for their ability to bandy jargon with their superiors but for their empathy, pragmatism, experience and decisiveness with their staff'.

Apply any, all, of these observations to the arts world and what too many stakeholders are demanding, and the scale of the danger is clear. The risk is of demoralised, undermotivated and frustrated staff internally and underperforming organisations externally, a stupendous double whammy of failure. One word particularly expresses the dead end into which the objectives culture can lead, and it is 'process'. For, by its nature, and probably by its intention, 'process' never ends. In the classic managerial jargon, 'process' ensures the outcome of 'key deliverables'. It doesn't: it delivers more process. It doesn't actually do anything.

Following such nostrums slavishly, or being obliged to do so, can damage the effectiveness, the value, the very activity of the arts world. The argument is not about limiting the damage that flows from such attitudes, important as that is. It is about achieving the best possible art and not destroying what has been achieved.

The arts deserve special treatment – and a wise government will give it – because the sector by and large has not fallen into the trap of adopting the objectives culture wholesale. Rather it has shown how government social objectives can be adopted and adapted without disturbing the fundamental purposes of the arts. This is – or should be – a valuable lesson for much of government and the civil service to apply elsewhere.

For more than a decade, arts organisations have spent their increased funding well. They have not plunged into deficit. They have taken, faced and managed risk. They have transformed the way they are run. They offer strong and effective leadership models and release internal creativity.

They are focussed on doing what they should do – putting on operas, plays, concerts and exhibitions – not on processing objectives. They are international in their outlook. They have developed strong models of local involvement.

As Tony Blair said in March 2007:

> [The atmosphere of the culture of the country] feels different – more confident, more assertive, more creative and alive. This is an enormous achievement. One that we have done together. It serves our country well; will serve it further in the future. It is something we will and must cherish.

That remains today's challenge, as any government contemplates spending cuts of an unparalleled size. If the nation can't cherish its success stories, if it is indifferent to a decade of historic achievement in the arts, what hope is there?

15

THE ARTS AND CIVIL SOCIETY: FIRM FRIENDS OR DISTANT COUSINS?

May to November 2009

> *'Don't be burdened by inspiration. Do be burdened by a desire to be original.'*
>
> Kwame Kwei-Armah

> *'Art forms should not merge into one another. There should be a natural gap between them. The gap is where creation takes place.'*
>
> Siobhan Davies

The arts community never stops thinking about what it is, what it does, what it ought to do, what its obligations and responsibilities are. Occasionally the introspection becomes a neurotic twitch, as if constant self-scrutiny were needed. More often it is rather profound and plays an important part in the artist's own self-understanding. Such debate includes the way the arts do – or do not – connect with other parts of society such as the voluntary sector. That was one running theme for me during the second half of 2009.

A second was the intense debate about the nature of arts leadership stirred by my growing involvement in the Clore Leadership Programme.

A third revolved around the contrasting ways in which arts policy was practised in very different countries and cities, such as Brazil, Abu Dhabi and Beijing. The political debate about the value of the arts warmed up too as the election campaign became a real prospect.

In June 2009, the Clore open-day seminar set as its theme 'It's the art, stupid', a reference to the Clinton campaign slogan, reminding everyone that the state of the economy was the overriding political issue. In echoing that injunction we aimed to tug back our attention from the narrower if necessary obsessions with finances and political problems and turn instead to fundamental questions of the quality and the value of the art being created. We were not disappointed by the key participants. The playwright and actor Kwame Kwei-Armah warned the audience of the necessity of staying connected with the past: 'The present is not enough to sustain a human being.' The choreographer Siobhan Davies urged artists: 'Be destabilisers, reorganise your thinking, dismantle your previous learning.' These were tall orders. Where would she herself do this? 'I want a windy corner, a place of waking, of constant transfer.'

That was one vivid image. The ceramicist and artist Grayson Perry produced another. He offered a general warning about creativity: 'New ideas are like furry creatures at the edge of the forest. Don't frighten them away.'

These offered good lessons and demanding challenges facing actual or aspiring artists. In the case of entire nations, the lessons and challenges were rather different. In Brazil, a highly complex country memorably described as 'not a country for beginners', I discovered how the three-way split between the Portuguese colonialists, the descendants of African slaves and indigenous peoples produced a highly diverse culture or set of cultures linked together operationally by three guiding principles. The first was to use the arts for social remedies and improvement unashamedly and without apology. Brazilians were not burdened with anxieties about the implications of 'instrumentalism'; if the arts lifted kids out of social hopelessness and economic poverty, they were used for that purpose.

The second principle was crucially connected to the pragmatism displayed by the first. Brazilians did not neglect their European heritage from Portuguese colonial times, nor were they obsessed by fears that some might call them 'high arts'. The Brazilians fitted without angst into the brilliant, multicolour, multi-source tapestry that is their culture. For the third lesson was that arguments over distinctions and differences in the arts were a waste of time. Amazonian culture was very strong, Brazilian pop was distinctive, but the European heritage was theirs too. As one artist put it: 'We want to be Brazilian but not to sound Brazilian. We don't want to be mindlessly international either.' A Brazilian classical guitarist issued a chastening, almost traditionalist warning with a universal message: 'You can't overlook training, skill and knowledge. Just getting kids to dance a bit only achieves what it achieves. It is very important, essential, especially in the favelas, but we must not pretend that that is the end of the matter. Education is more than that!' Perhaps rigour is an ingredient in the Brazilian mix too. As discussions on these topics ended, a British colleague mused with heavy irony: 'What a disappointing event! We never talked of objectives, of metrics, of management at all.'

My international focus switched to Beijing in October, where a high-level party municipal official tried to impress me by saying that the city would build arts centres in every one of its 19 districts. This would enhance the arts and creativity. Such was and remains the Chinese traditional top-down approach to all cultural policy making. And from Abu Dhabi in the Gulf to the West Kowloon Cultural District in Hong Kong, the belief that culture, like concrete, is best poured from the top universally prevails among rulers, politicians and officials. I tried to persuade the Beijing official that buildings alone did not create good artistic activity; that available buildings, old theatres, disused warehouses, distressed spaces were a far better road. Art should spring from the availability of spaces and ideas rather than be overburdened by new buildings and venues. Good – or any – arts never sprang from con-crete alone; they had to stay embedded in it. I did not think he took the message one jot.

Meeting Chinese students of journalism in Beijing was far from reassuring too. While they appeared to reject the notion of party propa-ganda as undesirable – though their overt criticisms were inevitably muted – the students did not easily reveal their opinions about Chairman Mao's Cultural Revolution or the ravages of the Red Guards. As one student observed discreetly and realistically: 'My parents say the Cultural Revolution was very bad, but now we must live our lives.' Instead they found it easier to complain about the so-called 'misrepresentation' of China in the rest of the world. 'Our problem is the three Ts and the one F.' Which meant? 'Tibet, Taiwan, Tiananmen. And the F is the Falun Gong.' To find such a sense of defensiveness bordering on victimisation in China was a salutary reminder that the most powerful nations were also the most sensitive to external criticism.

Back in London, I was constantly refreshing and updating my thoughts on the nature of leadership in the arts. After one gathering with museums' staff I suggested this formulation: 'With leadership, you have a sense of direction, a story about an organisation which embraces its past, explains and contains its present and leads on to and points towards the future – a story that motivates staff, convinces stakeholders and inspires funders and supporters.' It was time to refine and put that first definition to the test.

And the political scene was warming up. By July, the simmering discontent with the way the Cultural Olympiad was being run – or not being run, according to your point of view – reached its climax. As the composer Michael Berkeley raged: 'It has been a complete and utter shambles.' Abruptly, a new committee, chaired by Lord Hall of the Royal Opera House and consisting of the leading London arts grandees, took over. Tony Hall began wisely by visiting people, places and organisations and asking them openly what they thought the Cultural Olympiad should be about. The answer was triumphantly revealed four years later, but only because the whole project had been ruthlessly and necessarily wrenched back on course.

Was the new Hall-led committee a coup against the previous steering group, I asked an insider innocently? She replied equally innocently: 'I think it was a north London dinner-party plot'! Plot or coup, it came in the nick of time to save the project. The Cultural Olympiad might be back on track administratively, but the sudden discovery of a £100 million 'black hole' in government spending that would have to be taken out of arts projects produced a furious outcry. An anonymous arts leader – and can you wonder why? – said: 'Everyone will blame the Culture Department for being hopeless and they are fairly hopeless, so it's not unjustified.' Twenty-one cultural organisations signed a letter: 'We believe that such a withdrawal of committed investment to our cultural life will be seen as a loss of nerve internationally.' The DCMS observed bleakly: 'Our capital budget is currently overcommitted'!

In October, the Arts Council's director, Alan Davey, set out to woo the Tory Party towards full-hearted support for funding the arts:

> In recent years a consensus has been building which acknowledges that the arts are a key part of our fabric as a nation; that they contribute to the creative life of the country which is itself a part of what creates our wealth. We're doing something right in this country [...] So let's not throw it away.

No doubt concerned that the Tories might gain some support at the election by adopting a supportive stance towards the arts, Labour's Ben Bradshaw tried to make the flesh creep and the blood curdle:

> This is a taste of what things would be like under a Tory government. Savage cuts combined with philistinism and political interference. Our cultural, creative and sports worlds and all those who love and value them need to wake up to this.

The arts were now a political football, prompting only the wry observation that at least some politicians thought they were worth kicking.

His shadow rival with the culture portfolio, the Tory Ed Vaizey, tried to show that, as an attentive listener, he was familiar with the New Labour's 'core script' for the arts: 'Within the overall framework of government spending, arts spending is a very small part. We're not going to save the economy by cutting the arts – but you could damage the arts by cutting the arts.'

Behind and beyond the arguments about funding, others appeared, almost as relevant to the future. Were the arts too isolated from other, like-minded parts of society? Would they be stronger if they stood together? Did they know how to cooperate with other sectors? When I was invited to speak to the National Council of Voluntary Organisations (NCVO) in November 2009 about the relationship between the arts and civil society, it seemed worth trying to answer those questions.

FINDING YOUR FRIENDS, IGNORING YOUR FRIENDS

Sometimes a question appears as a total surprise, such as the connection between the arts and the voluntary sector or, more broadly, civil society. When it did emerge, as raised it rang few bells in my curiosity. In many years of involvement in the arts, the desirability of such a connection had never been suggested. In a dozen years at the Barbican, there was no conscious involvement with the voluntary sector in any form. The possibility of associating an arts centre with any part of the voluntary sector seemed remote. It would not have struck us — had we thought about it — as potentially useful, necessary or indeed natural. The two sectors — the voluntary and the arts — sailed past one another like ships in the night, majestic but unheeding and indifferent.

Two random remarks from people in the voluntary sector unexpectedly hit home. 'The arts don't feel like part of the voluntary sector! They don't relate to other organisations!' What did this mean? That the arts were remote and stand-offish? Or that the arts were being actively excluded from the community of the voluntary sector? The next unexpected observation made the proposition impossible to ignore. 'The arts world,' observed an acquaintance, 'is not seen as part of civil society.' This deserved further examination. Was the arts world missing a trick in behaving so indifferently towards the voluntary sector? And if the arts were not recognised by some as part of civil society, then was there something wrong with the definitions or wrong with the arts? Was the arts world missing an opportunity to connect with others? Weren't connection and cooperation increasingly the watchwords of our times?

First, why should the voluntary sector think about the arts in this way at all? The first port of call is the UK Civil Society Almanac for 2009, the reference point for the sector. In all of the almanac's 152 pages the arts feature nowhere. There is no listing, no reference, no comment about the arts in this context. This is hard to explain logically. After all, the voluntary sector enjoys and is in part defined by having charitable status – just like the arts. Voluntary organisations are described in the almanac as 'making a vital social contribution to life in the UK' – so do the arts. Voluntary organisations – according to the almanac – are involved in 'social services, culture and recreation'! Yet if arts organisations are not involved in 'culture', what are they about? Does this confusion – accidental or deliberate – spring from a very narrow and particular definition of arts activity?

A decade ago, local-government cultural activities were clearly and precisely defined. London local authorities knew that 'culture and recreation' in their books and budgets were officially restricted to swimming, walking, parks, and other diversions and entertainment. Admirable as these activities were, the exclusion of museums, galleries, concert halls and theatres from the official local-authority cosmos was all too clear and all too inexplicable.

So too were the arts excluded from the cosmos as defined by the denizens of the voluntary sector. It could hardly be claimed that the use of the word 'culture' without addition, qualification or explanation automatically signalled the effective inclusion of the arts in definitions of the voluntary sector. It was neither an adequate description nor an account of the whole world of the arts. Besides, the suggestion that a single word of disputed definition – 'culture' – might be enough to include the arts was an empty notion. It left out far too much. The arts, for instance.

When it comes to defining 'civil society', the almanac generously and inclusively spreads its net very wide. It embraces housing associations, universities, independent schools, trade unions, political parties, cooperatives, social-enterprise activity and a diverse pot – or ragbag, possibly – that includes faith groups, sports and others that fall – according to the almanac – 'under the radar'. Yet all are comfortably swept up in what the almanac defines as 'civil society'.

Here too, there is no mention of the arts as a conceivable member of civil society, seemingly no awareness that they might be. This easily assumed exclusion produces a sense of puzzlement and confusion. To observe that there is no mention of the arts in the UK Civil Society Almanac is to identify a problem, not make an accusation.

Further puzzlement is raised by the definitions employed in the almanac. Civil societies, it asserts, share certain common values – such as a belief in voluntary association – and certain practices – such as the retention and application of surpluses for social purposes. The narrowness of definition and perception is now glaring. Attendance at an arts event of any kind is wholly voluntary – after all, audiences usually have to choose to part with money to attend, the truly 'voluntary act'. Hundreds of thousands of supporters give their time to the arts on a voluntary basis. All the resources arts organisations disposed of – few could make surpluses as such – are applied to social purposes. They are not distributed as profit, for there is none to distribute.

Yet one further part of the 'official' definition expresses the scale of the gap between the voluntary sector and the arts. The almanac defines 'civil society' as being about 'people acting together, independently of the state or the market, to make a positive difference to their lives and/ or the lives of others'. Amazingly, the arts are not – or are not seen by some – as part of a 'civil society' which behaves and acts in ways that appear indistinguishable. Why are the arts excluded from categories and definitions of which they appeared to be an organic part? Who benefits from such exclusion?

SAFETY IN NUMBERS

At this stage, the numbers merit a look. The Civil Society Almanac makes much of the sheer size of voluntary society – how many organisations, the numbers employed, the numbers who volunteer, the income earned, the size and value of assets. The numbers are undoubtedly large – huge even – and slightly give the impression of seeking to head off or bulldoze opposition to any possible criticism of the voluntary sector.

But how would they stack up against equivalent numbers from the arts world? The sample is limited, but it helps to tell or at least suggest a tale.

According to the Arts Council's 2008–9 'Taking Part' survey, no fewer than 79 per cent of adults had attended an arts event, been to a museum or gallery or actively participated in the arts in the previous year – that is 33 million adults. Total income from all sources adds up to £1.21 billion. The 850 regularly funded Arts Council organisations employ just shy of 70,000 people. Those numbers only relate to Arts Council-funded bodies, which are only a small part of the entire arts sector.

Add to those official numbers the scale of participation in the wholly voluntary arts sector. The National Operatic and Dramatic Association (NODA) – to take just one such body – has 2,500 societies on its books: these are the true amateurs. Typically, each society – and many are not even members of NODA – has 100 members doing everything from making the tea in the interval to music directing, singing, designing, and so on. At the very least, a quarter of a million people were involved in often tiny communities in such activities. And the audiences who attended? Over the last three years, total audiences for NODA events were estimated at between 5 and 7 million annually. These numbers reflect only a small, perhaps very small, part of the total arts world, its range, its scale, its base volunteering, its roots in what can only be called civil society. Why apparently do they not count?

Armed with those numbers, I shared my puzzlement with colleagues in the arts world. By and large, their responses to the proposition that the arts were not – or were not seen – as part of the voluntary sector were much like mine: first, the incredulity, followed by the bewilderment. Why this gap of comprehension exists, though, all found hard to explain. After all, the arts are charitable, just like the voluntary sector: they involve a large element of volunteering. The similarities go further: both sectors raise large sums of money from their supporters. Ninety-five per cent of their governance provisions and behaviour are identical. Both receive government funding for their core activities.

Perhaps the answer lies in a series of antitheses, contradictions or, possibly, paradoxes. Some reflect differences of behaviour, others involve misperceptions which exist on both sides. Whether they help to close the gap is another matter. They might explain why it exists.

First, the arts raise money from their core purposes and then use that money to pay for more of those core purposes. The activity is circular: put on art, raise or earn money, put on more art. The voluntary sector raises money from a wide variety of activities and then puts it towards its core purposes – helping or relieving need. Here the process is more of a straight line – from fund-raising straight through to the recipient. Recipients are not involved in fund-raising in the same way as the recipients in the arts – the artistes – are involved in performing them at the very outset.

Second, the arts' key relationship is with audiences of the performing arts or visitors to the visual arts. They attend, listen, view because they choose to do so. There is a choice as to whether they attend or not. For the most part, when they choose to attend – though not in the case of museums or galleries – they also choose to pay. The arts are there to meet that privately generated and driven demand. The voluntary sector's key responsibility by contrast is to beneficiaries. The beneficiaries are defined by need and circumstance, not by choice. The voluntary sector is there to answer, to relieve, to assuage that need. Demand and need, two different drivers resulting in two crucially different sets of relationships.

Third, a question of perception: the voluntary sector is identified with welfare and reform – the body; the arts world relates to creation and performance – the mind, heart and spirit. These are very different.

A further distinction looms. The implication of a world defined by demand is that there is choice. Do you want to hear classical music, to take your pick of repertoire, orchestras, venues and performers? It comes down to a matter of the individual's choice.

Think of a different question, no less or perhaps far more urgent. Do you need a roof over your head? If so, there are several charities to which to turn. The one best able to relieve need is determined not by individual choice but by the organisation's response to the scale of need presented and its ability to meet it. This amounts to a very different transaction.

But legal definitions obtrude too. The Charities Act asks the question: 'Who are your beneficiaries?' The answer from a charity is 'our clients', however defined and determined. How would the arts world answer such a question? Leave aside the fact that they are more accustomed to addressing the question: 'Who are your audiences?' any collective response to the wider question: 'Who are your beneficiaries?' would of course refer to audiences but would also have to include 'artists'. 'We raise money by employing artists so that we can satisfy audiences and employ more artists'! There's nothing wrong with that, it's just different from the voluntary sector.

At the end of the voluntary sector's road there is a particular type of consumer; at the end of the arts world's road stand not merely consumers but producers and creators – a more complex and diverse mix – all of whom have very different needs and demands to be met.

The differences between the sectors include questions of operational behaviour. The voluntary sector must demonstrate self-help, must raise money from shops, donations, individuals, foundations, local authorities and the government. It must maximise its earning capacity. The arts world too earns income from a very similar range of activities, the box office included.

But there is a practical and philosophical limit to the imperative of maximising income. No arts organisation – if it is wise – can risk jeopardising its core purpose – excellence in its chosen art form – by presenting exhibitions or productions purely because they might raise money. Such is the intrinsic limitation on the otherwise vital imperative to maximise earnings, but only up to a point and not at any reputational price.

ESSENTIAL RISK

Connected with this is a very different approach to risk. The voluntary sector has to be prudent and risk-averse in all financial matters. Even if an investment promises to yield wonderful returns and even more money for essential charitable purposes – see Icelandic banks – these may not be investments to be pursued because the risk involved in their failing is too great.

The arts, however, must take risks because innovation, experimentation and adventure are part of their core purpose and can only be realised through the taking of defined risks. Of course, the financial implications of taking artistic risk must be weighed carefully. But risk – sometimes high risk with real financial exposure – must be taken even if the consequences of failure are conceivable and might even be significant. For the voluntary sector, taking risk is principally financial and could damage your beneficiaries. For the arts, taking risk is an essential part of the artistic, the creative process. Not to do so would have reputational consequences and would damage the arts' beneficiaries, its artists and audiences.

By contrast, the end purpose and function of the voluntary sector is charitable, driven by a charitable mission. The arts too are charities, but their mission is not primarily charitable. They have an artistic purpose, an artistic mission. Charities must make money in order to spend it; arts may lose money because they must spend it. These are very different approaches.

The question of mutual perceptions between the sectors cannot be overlooked. Do the two sectors see each other straight or through some very refracting prisms? My arts friends and colleagues feel rather strongly about this. One observed: 'The voluntary sector has very old-fashioned ideas of what the arts do and how the arts are managed! Don't they know about our education programmes?' Another suggested: 'The voluntary sector might see the arts as the pastime of the rich, mainly taking place in the city. Don't they know that where a small town has an arts centre, with visiting arts activities, the quality and feel of life are different?' A third observed dryly: 'I suspect the voluntary sector sees the arts as a bit lacking in vocation, too much involved in pleasure, not sufficiently selfless, too indulgent!'

On the other hand, one arts friend offered a very different perspective: 'I don't think the arts are very good at joining in! Now, the heritage folk know to join in, but where are the arts in this conversation?' It is clear that some clarification of misconceptions, misperceptions even, would be a good idea.

Faced with such a tally of contrasts, misunderstandings and contradictions, two need to be approached with particular care. The first involves the notion of need. Who needs the arts? Who needs the voluntary sector? In the latter case, those who need help – with food, water, housing, liberty, freedom of speech, education. Such people don't need such services or commodities in a 'nice to have' way. They need because they need, because they do not have; because if they do not get, they might, no they would, be homeless, starve, die, be gagged intellectually or expressively or even lose their freedom. These are fundamental conditions of life beyond mere survival or existence.

Here the differences began to look like a chasm. In the voluntary sector, people come together to help; in the arts, they come together to share experience. Both are valuable, essential. Are they so different?

As for the arts? Does anyone need them in the same way as the voluntary sector experiences and services need? For a start, this difference between those two kinds of 'need' might explain some of the distance between the arts and the voluntary sector. Is the answer that they occupy rather different places in the hierarchies of need? How that hierarchy might operate and where the arts and the voluntary sector would respectively be assigned is a nice question. But it would be a mistake to allow these differences to explain and justify an unbridgeable difference.

But the question of 'Who needs the arts?' will not go away. Recently, a one-time Treasury knight was outlining in the friendliest and gloomiest way the nature of the funding catastrophe soon to strike. One remark struck home. 'Of course, essential spending will be protected,' he opined, 'but the discretionary budgets, such as the arts, will have to take their share of the cuts.' The warning lights began to flash. How can the arts be regarded, still less treated, as mere 'discretionary spending'? Are they to be funded only when every other conceivable social need has been met? Haven't we got beyond such crude views, especially in the Treasury?

The second area of delicate difference relates to how government support is treated. Recently, Nick Cohen argued in the *Observer* that as charities have become increasingly dependent on direct government funding – it has risen from 30 per cent of a typical charity budget to 70 per cent in a few years – so their capacity to act and advocate independently of government policy and priorities has been diminished and possibly undermined. Such was Nick Cohen's argument. By contrast it is true that the arts – and the BBC for that matter – have long practised and insisted on the 'arm's-length' principle. The government pays but avoids interfering in what it pays for except in the most general sense. It is a principle essential to police, to insist on and to maintain. Without such a principle, neither the arts nor the BBC would be what they are and must continue to be.

So can this maze be unravelled? Perhaps the best way to answer this is to move on to the direct question of whether the arts are part of the civil society or even the so-called 'wider civil society' as defined by the almanac. This states that civil society is about 'people acting together, independently of the state or the market, to make a positive difference to their lives and/or the lives of others'. It is impossible to understand how or why the arts should not be seen as an automatic, an intrinsic part of civil society – or should it really be called civilised society?

ANSWERING BACK

Certainly, the arts world feels strongly on the subject. This was one response from a leading arts practitioner: 'The arts are critical to civil society. They are the conscience of society; they reflect society back to itself; there are a myriad intersections where the arts act as a stimulus to make society think, learn, feel. Of course, the arts can be dangerous and unsettling, revolutionary even because they make people think critically about society.'

Another was even more direct in his response: 'It is nonsense to say they are not part of it. The arts define us as communities of people, they define aspects of us as a nation. If we don't use our imagination as citizens, we are immeasurably poorer. Where nations lack cultural expression through artists and through people, these places are significantly poorer, spiritually impoverished. We live,' he concluded, 'around cultural activity!' And what could be a more profound part of civil society?

A third colleague took a slightly different and deeply searching approach: 'The arts provide a neutral space between the state and the market. They are an auditorium for coming together. We need a new definition of the space in between, and surely the arts must be part of that definition.'

One further response from the arts moved into a slightly different area of civil society but a valuable one. 'You can't leave the arts out of civil society. Explicitly or implicitly they are into politics. For the arts have always been involved in the real world. The arts are both ordinary and extraordinary, they range from the everyday to the sublime, they provide us with wonder!'

Now it might appear obvious that a civil society – narrowly defined as it is at present – uninterested in wonder, communal dialogue, critical self-examination or discovery, isn't much of a civil society. But the case for including the arts in civil society for such reasons goes well beyond the merely rhetorical.

Every major arts organisation has an education and outreach programme, sometimes on a huge scale. There are hundreds in operation. To give one example only: twice in the last year, the British Museum had to close its doors as more than 30,000 people crammed into the building, first to mark Chinese New Year, then more recently to mark the Mexican Day of the Dead.

In the Barbican's education work, the limited group of local schools in the disadvantaged boroughs to the east of the City found that being part of the 'Adopt the Barbican' scheme, which gives them priority access to Barbican education projects, had a significant and measurable effect on their pupils' overall attainment.

At the Wigmore Hall, an alliance was formed with Action against Dementia to bring music to people with Alzheimer's or other deteriorating conditions of old age. Cut off, trapped even, as such people are, the experience of participating musicians and carers was invariably of an enhanced response and greater awareness from the individual during the musical performance.

In May this year, during interviews for the next group of 20 fellows of the Clore Leadership Programme, one candidate spoke of her work with teaching and performing dance with the severely disabled. This was her experience: 'I was really stretched recently. I was going to do a dance class with people suffering from advanced motor neuron disease. When I got into the room, I realised what I was up against. There were 20 people, severely disabled, in wheelchairs, accompanied by their carers. What on earth was I going to do? All I can say is that by the end of the session, every person had made some movement, given some reaction, however small, that showed that they had been aware of what I was doing and had responded to it.'

From 1997 the University of Liverpool ran a course called 'The Reader'. Literature was read aloud in and with groups, real literature: Milton, James Joyce, and suchlike. The response was excellent. The client group consisted of the elderly and the mentally disabled. The psychological impact, the improvement in well-being of the clients was such that the course became funded by Mersey Care, part of the city's welfare services.

Such surely is the core of the argument. If the presence of the arts in towns, villages and cities, doing what they do, from the sublime to the practical, does not qualify them to be part of civil society, then there has to be something wrong with the definition of civil society.

QUESTIONS TO ANSWER

Is there a way ahead? You might argue that the gap of comprehension and practice between the voluntary sector and the arts world does not exist; or that if it does exist, it doesn't matter. Or you might argue that such gaps do exist, that they are worth addressing and if possible closing. Either way, on the principle that if you can make a situation better you should try to do so, here are a few observations.

First, some questions for the arts to answer. Do they believe too much in their absolute excellence, an excellence deemed to be beyond question, beyond questioning, but deserving of support almost without reservation? Have the arts failed to reach out to the voluntary sector, demonstrating that they think there could be real benefits from doing so? Do they appreciate – as some observers do – that the voluntary sector is ahead of the arts world in the disciplines of assessment and gathering evidence of effectiveness, on the basis of which cases for funding could and should be made? ('They don't really do their homework!' as one foundation said.) Are the arts so 'frantically active' – another observation – in the business of creating art that they give themselves too little time to think? Do they accept that as a sector they are – according to one report – 'overstretched and undercapitalised'? All of which suggest that the arts world needs to take stock and reflect.

Might there be benefits to the arts from a closer, more reflective identification with the voluntary sector? Might the arts enjoy a different public profile as they face society and the political classes, local and national? The arts might be better understood, the full range of all their activities – artistic, social, economic, outreach – might be more deeply valued. The full complexity of the activities the arts undertake, the contradictions they resolve, might be better appreciated, valued and understood in the course of such a dialogue.

As a result, the arts could start to swing the debate more convincingly away from the widespread assumption that when it comes to public expenditure, support for the arts is discretionary, that is to say, non-essential. The case for arts funding might be stronger if presented in the wider environment of cooperation with the voluntary sector. And, as some believe, the arts might benefit from the more rigorous, evidence-based approach of need that the voluntary sector takes as a matter of course.

There could be benefits to both – the arts and the voluntary sector – from a coming together of such a kind. It would be a considerably larger sector, and Whitehall understands weight. It would carry a still stronger argument for funding. It would be able to make common cause over issues of tax reform for charitable giving – why fight two battles when interests are the same? It would mean the creation of a more consciously defined, cogently expressed new space, the one between the market and the state, the one where we live much of our lives, the one where – if we are honest – many of the best things in life take place. 'We are the people in between,' as one friend in the arts observed.

Perhaps a new name is needed, one that is more than a branding exercise! 'Third sector' is economist speak. 'Civil society' is social-scientist speak. Neither makes the heart beat warmly. The right name would be recognised once it is agreed what could best be done together. Actions first, definitions and categories afterwards.

So where might this leave the two sectors? Side by side yes, if they are wise and clearly and strongly aligned. Firm friends? Not yet; there are too many misconceptions on both sides. Distant cousins? Distant, surely: perhaps distant second cousins. Sooner or later, even they will discover that it is good to talk.

16

SMALL IS SIGNIFICANT: TAKING CARE OF THE ROOTS

January 2010 to October 2011

> *'Art can't change your life; it is not a diet programme*
> *or the latest guru; it offers no quick fixes.'*
>
> Jeanette Winterson

> *'[Art] doesn't educate or inform or make you a better citizen.*
> *We belittle art when we make it into information or luxury.'*
>
> Mark Ravenhill, playwright

There was only one matter to worry about throughout 2010. Who would win the general election? And, regardless of the result, how much would arts funding suffer as the next government – whatever its persuasion – attempted to retrench the public finances? Fear of cuts, the prospect of cuts, the actuality of the cuts: these were the running themes of the year.

But another was the endless capacity of the arts world to think about ways in which it could be better run and managed, better led, better able to make its case for public support. At a conference on the 'state of the arts' – hardly original as a topic! – one session explored the much touted notion that the arts needed a new 'business model' with the implication – hope? – that they should and could be less reliant on public funding, whether local or national. No such model was unveiled.

As my own contribution to new thinking, I suggested a formal 'incentive fund', where 'better than budget' performance in box-office, commercial, corporate and private support and/or a demonstrable improvement in efficiency would receive specific extra funding. The second thought was to take 'risk funding' seriously: box-office support for projects or activities that were identified beforehand as of special risk would kick in if the project were to lose money. My third suggestion was bureaucratically high-risk but worthy of consideration. It was that other departments whose activities actually benefitted from what the arts did – health, education, local communities, business – should contribute a (tiny) part of their huge budgets to supporting the arts. The big drawback would be the ghastly prospect of being accountable to several government departments. The big reward could be the realisation across Whitehall that the arts are constructive and relevant parts of government activity and not a private fad shared by the sheltered few.

There was more thinking on this subject, and on an international scale, at an event organised by the group Salzburg Global Seminar titled *The Arts in Lean Times: Opportunities for Reinvention*. There were ideas aplenty. Michael Lynch of the Southbank Centre jogged us into rereading the legendary French minister of culture, André Malraux: 'Art is what remains when the rest has vanished' – a reminder of the value and importance of what we do. Dick Penny of Bristol's innovative Watershed centre cast a new light on what it means to run an arts venue: 'You are custodians, not managers, of a shared cultural space held in shared ownership. You can start to trust the space because you are not in control.'

Another contributor explored ways of assessing an organisation's 'creativity', always a word to use cautiously. One scale to use might have 'creating' at one end of the spectrum and 'doing' at the opposite end, posing the question: 'Where does your organisation lie and are you happy with it?' An additional scale, it was suggested, might have 'anarchy' at one end and 'curation' at the other. A still more challenging notion suggested that arts organisations should subject themselves to a 'legitimacy' test, asking how far they served the needs of the arts, artists, audiences, community and stakeholders. A 'legitimacy register' could be a useful checklist of an organisation's place in its wider community. None of these ideas would add to bureaucratic processes; each might make them more self-aware, more self-analytical.

At another conference, on 'Globalisation and Identity', held by the International Society for the Performing Arts (ISPA) in Zagreb in June 2010, I tried to puncture some glib assumptions that globalised art is admirable and desirable. Some warned rightly that 'each art has its own authenticity; we should appreciate one another's art forms.' I added:

> Beware of globalisation taken uncritically; remember that 'globalisation' is an economic, a managerial and an American concept. National identity has been devalued by being merged, damagingly, with the notion of nationalism. Globalisation has little to say, less to offer, about tradition or history. So take globalisation with real caution.

July saw one of those happy occasions when one could bask in the sheer quality of the British arts scene. On 16 July, the BBC Proms opened with a suitably massive performance of Mahler's Eighth Symphony. This was followed on Saturday by a semi-staged version of Wagner's *Meistersinger* in the Welsh National Opera (WNO) production starring Bryn Terfel as Hans Sachs. On Sunday, the Royal Opera brought their production of Verdi's *Simon Boccanegra* to the Albert Hall, starring Plácido Domingo. Three classic blockbusters of the highest quality. I reflected that it represented a kind of pinnacle of British arts achievement, with three great institutions – the BBC, the Royal Opera and WNO – delivering outstanding quality, and that it represented a culmination of a striving to do the arts better than ever and to the highest international standards. I wrote in my diary:

> Glorious – but sad, because now, as the cuts fall, this quality will be threatened, weakened, undermined. Will we ever see the likes of this weekend again? Possibly not, and we will look back at what

was done, achieved in the glory days. Look back in sadness, regret, perhaps even anger.

And, inevitably, with the coalition government in office, all eyes were turned on where the cuts would fall on the arts and by how much. With the public-spending round due on 20 October, debating positions and battle lines had to be drawn up. Sir Nicholas Serota, director of Tate, was early into the fray at the start of the month, fearing what he called 'the greatest crisis in the arts and heritage since government funding began in 1940'. He warned of a 'ruthless blitzkrieg' threatening the successful way the arts were funded, 'a mixed economy of public and private support that has made Britain a civilised place to live, where all have an opportunity to enjoy the arts or celebrate our heritage and have been doing so in increasing numbers'. And Serota highlighted a particular fear that the cuts might damage the smaller organisations disproportionately with overall impact on the entire arts scene: 'You don't prune a tree by cutting at its roots.'

The spending axe duly fell, with Arts Council England facing a huge 30 per cent budget reduction and the major national museums receiving a 'mere' 15 per cent cut, no doubt because, as the Chancellor of the Exchequer George Osborne was quick to point out, 'we will continue to fund free entry to museums and galleries.' Museum charging remains a toxic option for any government.

The head of the National Campaign for the Arts, Louise de Winter, observed wryly: 'It's a rum day when cuts of 15 per cent can now be greeted with some measure of relief.' But she accepted that they would be 'more manageable than was previously feared'.

It was time for the arts to regroup, which they did. First Arts Council England managed to finesse their own deep cut of 30 per cent to a mere 6.9 per cent cut for their regular funded organisations (RFOs). Nicholas Hytner of the National Theatre praised the Arts Council to the skies and set a tone of determined realism: complaining was out, even in the face of the cuts. 'The challenges of the next four years will be tough and real but I hope that most of us will be determined and inventive enough to rise to them.'

Only days after digesting the impact of the 20 October spending round
on itself and its own organisation, 'the biggest cuts in [its] history', Arts
Council England unveiled a ten-year funding plan – because, according
to the chief executive, Alan Davey, it was determined to look ahead.

> Given that we have less money, we want to use it in the best way
> possible so we don't give up on the ambition, innovation and
> interestingness that arts groups deliver in this country. We can't
> enter that spiral of decline again.

What was significant in the response of the arts world was a highly professional combination of realism, determination and professional confidence
that it would be possible to manage the way through the cuts, that defeatism was unnecessary, that despondency was unbecoming, that imminent
dereliction of the arts estate was not imminent. In a sense this response
demonstrated how far the arts community had travelled in learning to
manage its affairs over a decade and a half. It had become stronger and
was undoubtedly more in control of its destiny.

The culture secretary, Jeremy Hunt, had only one tune to play, the
last one in his ministerial locker: private philanthropy, the last refuge
of the ministerially beleaguered. 'We have designated 2011 the Year of
Corporate Philanthropy,' he said, as if that could close the gaps looming
in arts budgets. It could not and would not. Designation came cheap;
realisation was another matter.

The year after the Conservative government's spending-round cuts,
2011, was the year for the arts to take stock and assess the future; after
all, the Arts Council's reduction of 6.9 per cent in its budgets for RFOs
was hardly a small matter. But the cuts would affect the following year's
funding; there was a 12-month period in which to review, plan ahead
and attempt to mitigate the damage. It was not a time for recrimination,
complaint or score settling. Public rhetoric always has a place, but not
immediately after decisions have been taken. The jobs to be done were
within every organisation.

For myself, that period – without direct executive responsibility – gave me the opportunity to think about the many ideas on offer about how the arts could be best – or at least better, and sometimes differently – run. The arts community seldom lacks different models of organisation. Lessons good and bad could be learned from other countries. In January, I took part in a seminar in the brand-new city of Shenzhen, a 'special economic zone' of China, just across the border from Hong Kong. The former British colony itself enjoys the status of one of China's 'special administrative regions': the Chinese are adept at such organisational and micro-ideological distinctions.

Thirty years ago Shenzhen consisted of just a small fishing port and many duck farms. Now it is literally a new city, with towering office blocks, garish hotels, long highways à la Beijing, and, to be fair, a huge amount of new-planted greenery, again in the Beijing manner. I said to myself, 'Canary Wharf – only ten times the size!' Remarkable, remarkable! Beautiful, no. Full of character, no. But it is not only about money. A grand municipal centre has a massive curving roof uniting its various elements, with a cylindrical scarlet tower at each end. The curving roof encloses a large municipal museum with a vast atrium – far too big, out of scale with the rest of the building, a residue of old communist instincts about the size of public space, perhaps. The displays covering Shenzhen's (short) history are striking and carry clear political messages, for it was and remains a political city founded on a political message. In 1979, the Chinese leader, Deng Xiaoping, descended in person and decreed that this muddy duck farm and fishing community should become the model for advanced, accelerated, socialist but market-based development to ape Hong Kong. It would connect with Hong Kong but would not be swallowed up by it. Shenzhen's 'special economic zone' status permitted, demanded even, speedy economic development without too many centralised restrictions from Beijing. Of course, it would remain 'socialist'! Because the leader said it would!

Shenzhen boasts other things, such as a concert hall, its architecture very reminiscent of Berlin's Scharoun-designed Philharmonie, all sloping, gold-encrusted, angled walls. There was very little music programmed when I was there, a very modern Chinese phenomenon. Which comes first, the creativity or the buildings to house them? And the city possesses the new title of 'city of design' because the government's central plan dictates that merely to be 'made in China' is insufficient; economic policy demands that mere manufacturing must be succeeded by the additional notion of 'designed in China'!

At a British Council-organised forum in Shenzhen on 'Cultural Leadership and the Creative Industries', the message from the 50 or so Chinese cultural administrators was abundantly clear. The country's cultural policy came from the top down – just like any other national policy. Did this represent real government support for the arts and culture? Not really, but they certainly told regional officials what to do. (This was the so-called 'double-edged sword' cultural policy – government dictation mitigated by indifference!)

In reality, cultural provision was very patchy throughout the country, the officials admitted. The government talked a lot about the creative industries, but there were very few of them. They lacked a creative professional core. In the arts themselves, what they rather oddly but revealingly called 'the consumption market' – the 'audience' to the rest of us – was very limited. But this absence of active public interest in and engagement with the arts was regarded as another problem of administration. 'We need a quality audience to consume and appreciate' was the official line – the order of those activities was significant.

When the discussion homed in on the heart of artistic policy making, the real gulf between the Chinese and the European experience yawned. The Chinese administrators were open and unashamed about, perhaps unaware of, their statement that 'the core of culture is to serve politics'! Surely it would be the opposite, everywhere else in the world: 'The core of politics is to serve culture.' After that, the next observation from Chinese administrators came as little surprise, though in other contexts it would have done: 'If artists follow government, they will not starve.' Perhaps they wouldn't starve, but neither would they produce art. The Beijing government's directive could not have been more clear: 'Be creative! Make creative industries grow and flourish!' But 'creativity' could not be created by top-down diktat.

Throughout the seminar, it was clear that the Chinese still needed to learn that there was no government-directed formula to achieve their desired aims. If there was a definable process that would lead directly to creativity, it involved intense individual independence of thought and work. It could not be delivered by a forced — 'long'? — creative march, which might be the only historical model the Chinese understand. The sheer depth of the differences between Europe and China in these matters was very salutary to observe.

Safely across the border into Hong Kong, through the elaborate checkpoints and metal fences and barriers, the language and terms of the arts debate could be more easily shared. It was a delight to hear Lars Nittve, the director of the planned Hong Kong art gallery 'M+', give this pithy definition of the various ways that Europeans approach museums. Answering the question 'Who are museums for?' Nittve observed that the Germans and Swiss would reply: 'We are for the artist.' The British maintain: 'We are for the public.' The Swedes say: 'We negotiate the moment when the public meets the work of art!' In those terse aphorisms whole worlds of museology and philosophy were concealed and revealed.

In March I tried to persuade the Arts Marketing Association (AMA) that the principles of good communication did not vary with the medium being employed. Whether old media — such as print or broadcast — or new, highly dispersed social media were in play, my 'seven principles of communication' held good. They are as follows.

First, keep control of your message, which may involve not being bullied into premature comment; always command what you say and when you choose to say it. Next, your message to the outside world must be the same as that to your internal audience — you cannot say one thing inside and another outside; it must be credible in both places and its credibility throughout depends on its consistency. Third, always be on the front foot: too much bad PR is defensive and if defensive will sound frightened. Fourth, don't fool yourself about the strength or weakness of your message — the chances are that it is neither as strong as you hope nor as weak as you fear, but somewhere in between. Fifth, never have a PR 'minder' in the room when you give an interview — you must trust

yourself and they must trust you. Next, build up contacts in the media –
you must know, and preferably like, the press and the media on a personal
basis. It is not difficult. Finally, speak English, cut the clichés, purge the
verbosity. If terms such as 'world-class' or 'cutting-edge' creep into your
press releases, cut them out at once.

At the Royal Philharmonic Society Awards dinner in May 2011, the
playwright Mark Ravenhill was characteristically provocative. Having
dismissed too many international cultural productions as being like
'life in an airport business lounge, surrounded by frills for sponsors,
pampered, luxurious and exclusive', he approached his serious core.
'Great art is made from a great paradox: it is grounded in the local,
the specific, the ephemeral, yet it achieves the metaphysical and cheats
time and place.' And for good measure, he added that great art was not
made in the 'floating worlds' of the business lounge but in the local
community. And a final Ravenhill challenge and admonition: '[Art]
doesn't educate or inform or make you a better citizen. We belittle art
when we make it into information or luxury.' All of which amounted
to a useful tug on the intellectual strings away from any flirtation with
relativism, instrumentalism or cosy beliefs that art makes people mor-
ally superior.

Getting artists to talk directly about the way they work can be a
treacherous and sometimes disappointing business. The Friends of the
Royal Opera House pulled off a coup in getting the three leading opera
music directors in one room at the same time to compare notes on how
they did their job. Perhaps it was because Tony Pappano from Covent
Garden, Ed Gardner from ENO and Vladimir Jurowski from Glyndebourne
liked one another that their conversation, which I chaired, was so open
and frank.

How different was opera conducting from the job in the concert hall?
Gardner pointed out that you have several weeks to rehearse an opera,
a few days – at best – to rehearse a concert programme. Jurowski was
more philosophical: 'In opera, every beat must be useful, very exact, it
must help somebody. You do not need to "be balletic", as you can be in
the concert hall!' Pappano was practical, in a self-disparaging way: 'The

big difference for me is that, in the concert hall, the orchestra can see me! In the opera pit, sometimes the chorus at the back of the stage can't see me properly!'

Were there operas they would never conduct? Jurowski: 'I will never conduct *Carmen* because it is so perfect and has been done so often, so successfully, so completely that I will have nothing new or better to say.' Gardner: 'I have tried *Salome* once or twice and every time it makes me feel ill, my head hurts!' Pappano: 'I have conducted *Salome* 50 times and my head hurts too!'

Were there operas they were actually afraid to conduct? Jurowski: '*La traviata* and Mahler's Eighth – I don't know how to do them.' Gardner: 'Monteverdi, there's nothing written down, in effect, so how do you approach it?' Pappano: 'I used to be terrified of *The Barber of Seville*. It seemed so difficult. It is so difficult. Then when I had to learn and play it, I realised what incredible fun it is.'

As they compared notes on their conducting techniques, it was Vladimir Jurowski who produced a definition of the activity with a deadly concision: 'So much goes into a single gesture. In the end just one beat must express everything you feel about an opera!'

It was undoubtedly a fascinating set of exchanges for any lover of music. But I reflected that for anyone who dismissed the arts as rather simple or as not like real work it should have been a reproach and would have been a revelation.

My own time during 2011 was focussed heavily on two lectures. One, to be given in Belfast in August, would focus on making the case for the arts a matter that could never be taken for granted and that needed constant renewal. The other, at Newcastle University in October, was about my 50 years in and around the BBC in a variety of roles and guises.

Although controversies surrounding the corporation were mild in this period compared to the Jimmy Savile scandal of 2012–13, BBC matters were seldom far from the news in 2011, whether the running sore of top salaries (far too high), the more immediate issue of the cuts being forced on the World Service (too large) or management's response to those cuts (too feeble). I ended by suggesting that if BBC leaders used words honestly and properly and turned those words into actions many problems would be solved. In such a context, I offered '13 antitheses' for the BBC to consider as it surveyed itself in those dark days of 2011 surrounded by challenge and controversy. The corporation should:

- restore the notion of trust in its working relationships (instead it demands accountability);
- rediscover and celebrate its long-held values: organisations will run on values and they are straitjacketed by systems;
- insist on programmes as programmes: they are not products, not 'units of resource' that are bundled up as programmes;
- rely on ideas as the yardstick for accepting programmes rather than judging them by genres, categories or even quotas;
- demand curiosity as the impulse for programmes rather than formulae;
- search for originality rather than mere distinctiveness, a lesser notion;
- believe in its audiences: they are demeaned by being treated as customers or consumers;
- be confident in publicity for its programmes: beware of the domination and rigidities of marketing;
- have ambitions rather than targets: have a strong sense of purpose rather than lists of objectives;
- know where it wants to go: ignore the direction of travel;
- accept responsibility: do not take refuge in compliance;
- use judgement in making decisions: it is far better than lists of risk analysis; and
- cling to quality: be suspicious of benchmarking.

And I concluded that if the true, human and rich vocabulary of trust, values, programmes, ideas, curiosity, originality, audiences, publicity, beliefs, ambitions, purpose, responsibility, judgement and quality was allowed to elbow out the dead, mechanical, reductive vocabulary of accountability, systems, process, genres, formulae, consumers, marketing, targets, objectives, distinctiveness, compliance, benchmarking and risk analysis, what a great organisation the BBC could be. I believe such a shift of thinking and vocabulary would lead to a huge upsurge of energy, originality and creativity that the staff would welcome and audiences would notice, respond to and love.

Over two years on, I see no reason to alter one word of that assessment. After the complex editorial and managerial disaster of *Newsnight* and the Jimmy Savile affair, and the deepening opprobrium over BBC top salaries and unjustified so-called 'redundancy' pay-offs, my recommendations are more relevant than ever.

In September 2011, the chief executive of Arts Council England, Alan Davey, much praised by the culture minister Ed Vaizey for his skill in handling the painful arts-funding cuts, set out revealingly the three points between which Arts Council policies needed to oscillate: between arm's length and interference; between London-centric and more regionally dispersed; between commitment to excellence and widening outreach. It struck me that this clear strategic awareness demonstrated the usefulness of having a theoretical basis – not an ideology – on which to work. It demanded and required flexible responses rather than rigid ones and permitted sensible adaptations as circumstances changed. It was a key to intelligent pragmatism. As a result, Davey's Arts Council had positioned itself where the arm's-length relationship was rather lengthy, where excellence was preferred to access but the latter was neither neglected nor ignored, and where the regions were not overlooked because of an innate preference for things metropolitan. This amounted to an effective redefinition of the way Arts Council England worked with its clients: principled, pragmatic, but not ideological.

By the autumn of 2011, the arts world was addressing agendas beyond the inevitable reduction of funding. Ruth Mackenzie, the new director of the Cultural Olympiad, announced the forthcoming programme and gave everyone a lift: 'This is my take on world-class excellence. These are exceptional, gold-medal talents. They are capable of producing experiences that are once-in-a-lifetime. Of course there is no guarantee – but exceptional talent is a great start.' The Cultural Olympiad could not make good arts reductions elsewhere, but it would showcase the sheer quality of the arts now available in the country. In the event it proved a brilliant success, organising a string of high-profile, high-risk events and occasions across the country, from light installations at Hadrian's Wall to mass dancing in London, that delighted huge audiences. In the process, it laid to rest the dismal banality of the Millennium Dome experience and demonstrated what Britain's arts could deliver when politicians did not interfere.

In October, it was time to organise my thoughts on the case for the arts in response to an invitation from Queen's University Belfast to give the first lecture in memory of the poet Louis MacNeice. I decided to avoid the usual agenda on such occasions and to delve both more deeply and more widely into why we need to make the arts matter in order to make the case for the arts.

BACK TO MY ROOTS

The poet Louis MacNeice, now honoured by Queen's University Belfast, was a fine poet, a great character and a notable figure in the BBC of the 1950s and the world of the arts. There is no question of his standing and reputation. As a fellow BBC man, I hope that he would approve of my interest in the arts and of the approach I take in viewing the future of the arts scene.

My old friend and colleague John Tydeman, long-time head of BBC Radio Drama, drew my attention to a poem by Anthony Thwaite – another BBC producer and poet – about MacNeice. When he joined the BBC as a trainee in 1959, Tydeman recalls MacNeice as a languid figure standing at the edge of parties looking like a lugubrious camel, with a trick of baring his teeth that only increased the resemblance. He was delighted that Thwaite observed the very same mannerism in his keenly observed poem. Thwaite catches MacNeice at the bar of the George pub – where else? – just around the corner from Broadcasting House in Portland Place, London.

There you stand
Aloof and quizzical, the long bar scanned
For friends and enemies, a scornful phrase
Poised to put down the parasite or bore;
But underneath that mask a lonely man
Looks out, lugubrious comedian
Or elegiac dandy, more and more
Driven into the corners of yourself.

I joined the BBC in 1960 as a general trainee, so when I was given a three-month attachment to the legendary Radio Features department, I briefly crossed the brilliant paths traced by MacNeice and the other creative giants of that department, people such as Douglas Cleverdon, producer of Dylan Thomas' *Under Milk Wood*, Terence Tiller, Rayner Heppenstall and David Thomson, author of that fine memoir of life in County Roscommon, *Woodbrook*. I had the privilege – one I hardly deserved – of being put in the same office as Heppenstall and Thomson. There was plenty of space there, as Heppenstall hardly ever appeared. David Thomson was remote and kind and obligingly pointed me to a cupboard full of recorded but long-unedited interviews with supposedly interesting personalities – such as Tennyson's grandson – that he was not personally interested in turning into finished programmes. That gave me plenty to do.

My main direct connection with those radio legends was in the previously mentioned George pub. It was a regular daily gathering ground for radio features producers, which fuelled many things, including creative ideas, not despite the intake of alcohol but because of it. Nothing could be more remote from today's austere, serious, prescriptive, formulaic, time-measured, objectives-driven, benchmarked approach to making programmes. It is not that the old times were obviously better, more creative, more adventurous, more original – though they were all of those things. But the fact that the behaviour of those BBC producers 50 years ago was sometimes too rowdy, too bohemian, even too self-indulgent, does not justify it being patronised, easily disapproved of or comfortably disparaged. We are not better today because we are

more stuffy and pretend to be more responsible, more accountable
than they were.

So with MacNeice and his generation arrayed behind me, let us take
stock of where the arts stand today. Put to one side public funding for the
arts – there is too little; ignore private support for the arts – there is too
little; keep a distance from government policies towards the arts – they are
too complex and too confused. What is left? A great deal, for it is a picture
based on how practitioners, administrators and leaders, great and small,
see and describe their world today. This picture will not concentrate on
the great institutions, the spectacular public buildings, the noisy public
rows that often characterise – or rather disfigure – most public accounts
of the arts. It will not exclude what the major institutions do because they
too are part of the scene. But they are not the only part of it.

FEEDING THE ROOTS

This is one of the times of the year when the front doormat resounds
with the heavy thump of glossy magazines from arts institutions great
and small – the Royal Opera, the Royal Academy, the British Museum,
the Art Fund, the Crafts Council, to name only a few. This is a heavily
London-centric experience, but the themes demonstrated spread widely
across the UK. Such glossy magazines lure the reader to the promised,
strongly anticipated delights of blockbuster exhibitions, dazzling performances, creative revelations beyond any conceivable greedy hopes. There
is something else. Each one of these organisations presents the high points
of creative achievement from its disciplines, as you would expect; but they
do far, far more. They bulge with details of the talks, discussions, debates,
lectures, films and study courses that the organisations assume they must
provide to their audiences. Such programmes of engagement reflect a
belief that the arts should speak as widely as possible to their audiences
and a sense that looking outwards is good for the organisation itself.

It goes further, with the belief that publicly funded bodies should be
more open to the people who fund them. Such beliefs hardly existed,
say, 15 years ago, or if so in very tentative form. They should not be taken

for granted even today. They add up to a remarkable transformation in the way that these organisations act and behave. Museums, galleries and concert halls are radically and wonderfully different places from those they were or thought they should be 15 years ago.

This dizzying buzz of arts programming – much of which can be enjoyed free – points to something else: the sheer weight of intellectual activity generated by, in and around the arts. In most discussion of the arts, it is easy to become fixated on the great exhibitions, the epic performances, the blockbuster projects, as if these were the only ones that really mattered. They are important, but we risk ignoring or underplaying the range and extent of arts activity if we look only on the peaks and judge the arts world by their height. Something else is going on; it is taking place in the foothills of the nation's creativity.

'Go to Peckham and Bermondsey,' a colleague advised, south London boroughs not instantly associated with high levels of arts activity. Here visitors will find many large, ugly, empty commercial buildings occupied by artists and impromptu galleries. This is, incidentally, an increasingly widespread international phenomenon. In Hong Kong, for instance, disused textile and consumer-goods factories have been infiltrated by the unofficial arts community, often to the intense irritation of city bureaucrats. The space is there, unregulated, cheap, available. As in Hong Kong, so in Peckham and Bermondsey. And there is more, according to my colleague. 'Do you know about the sculpture show in a car park there?' I didn't. 'Well, it is just an ordinary car park in Peckham, the show is called "Bold Tendencies", and by the time it closes it expects to have had 100,000 visitors!' Those would be numbers that any 'official' gallery would die for.

What did this represent? 'It's a fringe,' said my friend. 'But it's a fringe without a festival.' And why not? Arts colonise where business, industry and commerce have fled. Such arts need no permission, no policy, no theory, probably no public funding. They exist because they choose to exist. They are a sign of the depth and breadth of arts activity and experience all around us but that we pay insufficient attention to. Fortunately, the 'main' arts world is more aware than ever of the debt owed to and the importance of the taproots of creativity. Sir Nicholas Serota, director of Tate, warned the government as public-spending cuts loomed in the comprehensive spending review 18 months ago: 'You don't prune a tree by cutting at its roots.' If anyone listened, no one acted.

For the arts ecology – as it is and must be seen in practice – is intricate, rich and effective because of its very complexity. It was Charlotte Higgins, chief arts editor of the *Guardian*, who exposed the fallacy that arts funding is binary, that is to say, either publicly funded or privately supported; too often, too many, especially politicians, tend to assume it is. Higgins gave the example of Glyndebourne Festival Opera, in one sense the acme of privately funded arts. Its performances received no public-funding support. Did that make it an exemplar of privately funded arts? Not quite. Its pit orchestra, the London Philharmonic, is directly funded by Arts Council England. Glyndebourne Touring Opera takes the much-vaunted festival productions around the country to audiences for whom a visit to Sussex is beyond their reach physically and financially. The Arts Council funds Glyndebourne Touring Opera. Higgins concluded: 'The map, then, of our British arts landscape is impossibly, beautifully complex. Its pathways and routes are curlicued and winding – but they make sense.' Why are we so habitually, narrowly, destructively binary in our approach? Why do we resort to the false comfort – to some – and easy antagonism – for others – of the either/or, the public or the private? It does not reflect the arts world in reality, it does not help sensible thinking about positive solutions. The knee-jerk binary habit should be abandoned in favour of the joys, the rewards, the reality of creative diversity and funding complexity.

Those taproots of the arts exist in more formal ways too. Take the Museum of East Anglian Life in Suffolk, a first-class example of a place that captures, keeps, collects and sifts the objects, practices, beliefs and documents of the county's past. Under its director, Tony Butler, the museum totally recreated its aims, its purposes and many of its practices. Rather than abandoning its historic role as repository, Butler redefined the museum as a 'social enterprise' creating 'social capital'; this involved using the institution to work with the long-term unemployed, or engaging dementia sufferers through reminiscence programmes and many other suchlike activities. But Butler always laid down some crucial reservations. 'We are not a social service, tarred' – as he put it – 'with the pejorative "community" brush.' Community arts, he pointed out, were easily and often rejected as being remote from serious arts activity, the notion of 'community' front-loading the social values over those of the arts.

Butler insisted that his museum's projects worked – as he put it – 'high up the cultural pyramid'. So a project for young people in which they expressed their feelings and experiences of living in the country by putting it into music was developed and realised with the London Sinfonietta, Britain's premier contemporary-music ensemble. A dance project with eight schools to interpret the cycle of the grain harvest all around them was made with a professional dance group, DanceEast. The museum worked with the British Museum to help a Kenyan partner restore a historic site where tribal elders used to meet and turn it into an interpretation centre and a 20-acre location for teaching sustainable agriculture with traditional seeds.

Tony Butler insisted that these activities and projects were rooted in and sprang from the very nature of the museum as a museum. He rejected crude ideas of 'instrumentalism', the supposed prior need to be useful to society at the expense of being true to the arts. On this basis, he realised and released the potent, latent energies of a historical collection by abandoning old categories and daring to think of new ones that enhanced rather than diminished the museum. These lessons are available to all.

The local community museum in the North Yorkshire town of Ryedale is another case of an institution whose work, beliefs and functions relate first and last to the knowledge, experience and needs of its community. Until a few years ago, it was everything to be expected from such a small community museum, especially one where the community had lost its historical livelihood – mining. A former steel worker, Mike Benson, took over as the museum's director, perhaps a rather grand title for a place with just six staff and only £6,000 of public funding. Using his experience from the troubled days of British Steel, Benson applied two principles to the way the museum was to behave: people would work in teams in which responsibility and decisions were shared and individual talent was unleashed. Once Ryedale had been put back on its feet, leadership was shifted from Benson himself to the staff, with Benson thereafter acting more like a coach and less like a leader.

On this exiguous base, Ryedale created a turnover of £470,000, gained project funding of a further £200,000, attracted 40,000 paying visitors annually and recorded a further 70,000 visitors who used the museum in many different ways. As attendances increased and the collection grew, Ryedale cooperated with outside bodies in unexpected ways, such as the by working with the local probation service: the young probationers who participated achieved such positive results that the Home Office filmed the project as an example of best practice. Benson himself called his work 'heritage activism', making spaces for people or, as he put it, 'putting a human heart into a human being'.

To those who might assume that this reeked of conventional instrumentalism, Mike Benson placed the integrity of the collection and the purposes of the museum first. 'Don't fall between two stools,' he warned, 'don't try to put different hats on, or the whole sector wobbles.' In his openness to what others have to say, Benson used this phrase: 'You learn more from people who are outside the door.' And in answering how he knew that what he did was good, Benson declared simply: 'Something should speak for itself; if anyone comes in to evaluate you, then you have failed,' a wonderfully self-confident rebuke to the armies of accountability scrutineers who obstruct and disfigure the arts landscape.

Possible conclusions from places such as Ryedale and Suffolk are that they have flourished because they are needed by, wanted by, owned by and useful to their communities. They are headed by people who eschew conventional notions of leadership – but leaders they certainly are. They do not ape the great metropolitan museums or galleries; they are different, smaller but not lesser; that is why they matter. Their existence in the great pyramid of cultural life should not be overlooked. To understand today's arts environment adequately, the vitality at the base of the pyramid needs recognition and understanding as well as its towering peaks, the taproots as well as the lofty trunks.

GOLDEN AGE OR FAUSTIAN BARGAIN?

But excellent as the arts pyramid might be, it is time for a nagging doubt, for self-awareness, for a long moment of honest self-examination. How good is this national arts pyramid in reality? When Tony Blair gave one of his 'legacy' speeches shortly before leaving prime ministerial office in 2007 he noted with satisfaction that one arts leader had described the scene he was leaving behind as 'a golden age' for the arts. It had undoubtedly been a turbulent age, often a fractious one. Certainly the arts as a whole ended in a far stronger position in every sense than they had entered it a decade previously. But was it truly 'golden'? If so, whose achievement did it represent?

Earlier this year, a conference examined this proposition critically by putting a question mark firmly after the phrase 'golden age'. Was it truly such?

The New Labour decade included major tussles over terminology. The government of the period had been uneasy with, even downright hostile to, what it felt were 'arty' words and notions, never part of the New Labour lexicon. It never settled into its own comfortable vocabulary for the arts, comfortable either for the arts or for the party. The unease showed from the very top when the Department of National Heritage, created by the Tory government in 1992, was reconfigured and renamed the Department for Culture, Media and Sport (DCMS). While the previous title of 'heritage' was an undesirable, backward-looking starting point for any arts organisation, not to mention its traditionalist, right-wing connotations, it spoke of no interest in or involvement with the living arts as they existed in practice and in the present.

As the leading arts thinker and cultural entrepreneur John Newbigin noted in his contribution to the 'golden age' seminar, New Labour started with two disadvantages, both self-created and more problematical as a result. They had no vocabulary for the arts as such; indeed, they were extremely uncomfortable with the very notion of 'the arts', which they had predefined as coterminous with elitism, irrelevance and exclusiveness. So the initial policy emphasis was placed on the concept of the 'cultural industries'. It was of course obvious that the arts sector – however broadly defined – was in no way industrial, rather the reverse; so the successor term, the 'creative economy', soon took its place. 'Creative' was quite the buzzword of the time: everyone was creative, it was not a notion that could be claimed solely by elite arts practitioners; it was a democratic, inclusive notion, and once the word 'economy' was strapped on, you had shifted a long way from the definitions of the arts with which Labour so uncomfortably struggled.

However, further difficulties arose. If there was such an entity as the 'creative economy' it should be capable of measurement. If it contributed to economic and social well-being too, then an entire new vocabulary would be needed to explain the activity. Newbigin observed that what he called 'slippery terms, such as inclusiveness, cohesion, identity and well-being' – he could have added 'social exclusion' – were introduced and faced the identical problem that the arts did. What did they mean, and how could they be measured? And the terms proliferated – 'social capital', 'public value' – part of a process that Oscar Wilde would surely have recognised as 'the ineffable in pursuit of the indefinable'! As attempted definitions escalated they created a concatenation of evasion and confusion as New Labour simply ran away from any concept of 'the arts'.

There was yet one further definitional shift towards the end of the New Labour era, from 'creative economy' to 'knowledge economy', which Newbigin reasonably and somewhat wearily defined as 'an irresistible fusion of William Morris and silicon chips'.

Another contributor to the 'golden age' seminar, Robert Hewison, concluded: 'While the promotion of the creative industries and the economic contribution of culture strengthened the DCMS's hand in attracting resources, there was a price to pay in the form of auditing that proved ultimately hostile to creativity.' Hewison called it 'the arts world's Faustian bargain with government'. Everyone recalls what happened to Faust. If the arts collude – for tactical reasons – in pretending that they are like industry they have to expect to be treated like just another part of the economy. Mephistopheles – in this case the Treasury – always comes calling for his debts.

New Labour's urgent, often neurotic drive to pin down the arts by shifting descriptions and definitions, bullying them into anything and everything from 'creative industries' to the 'knowledge economy', ended – according to Hewison – in failure. 'More than a decade's worth of reports has failed to adequately define its parameters, establish its financial contribution, or satisfactorily work out the economic gearing between the expressively oriented arts and business-driven industry.' It was not only those who lived through the decade of lost definitions who sighed wearily at the sheer waste of time, effort and 'opportunity cost' that these activities led to.

In another corner of the ideological battleground, arms were taken up over the fundamental question of 'instrumentalism' – that the arts should be useful – versus the implied simplicities of 'arts for art's sake'! It lasted the full decade. Both sides overstated their case and tried to push the other into ever more extreme positions. As another seminar contributor, Eleonora Belfiore, observed: 'The spirit of New Labour policies for culture lay in the attempt to obfuscate matters of cultural value, which are characteristically controversial, in an effort to turn the arena of cultural policy making into an artificially neutral zone.' It failed. For a decade, culture, the arts, creativity and instrumentalism had been hotly contested.

THE PRICE OF PROCESS

Yet if the 'golden age' was a failure in ideological and party-political terms, by the end of the decade museum attendances had risen from 24 to 40 million, mainly due to Chris Smith's landmark achievement when culture secretary of getting the Treasury to concede free entry to museums. Regional-theatre audiences increased and the 'Renaissance in the Regions' programme invested heavily in local museum hubs. Overall arts funding was significantly increased. How could these successes be accounted a failure?

It might sound churlish to acknowledge the increases in funding yet describe the surrounding cultural policies as failures. It remains a fair description of what happened. Most of the myriad cultural policies and interventions of the decade were essentially diversionary tactics, displacement activities for politicians and civil servants. If, it might be argued, the use of terminology that the Treasury understood and tried to measure – 'creative economy', and so on – succeeded in prising out funds that they would otherwise not have released, who should complain? Yet good results do not emerge from weak, misleading or unsuitable notions, ideas and theories. Manipulating poorly conceived policies, getting round them, devising evasive stratagems, playing the Whitehall game – all were a waste of time but first were a waste of scarce resources. The Treasury and ministers should have understood that.

There was a further loss that sprang directly from the obsessive need for the arts to spend a decade fighting the cultural policy war. According to Eleonora Belfiore, the cultural sector 'has lost both the confidence and the vocabulary to articulate its own value to the public'. A damaging assertion if true, but how true was it? The arts were constantly speaking up for and about themselves, expressing their own value and justifying themselves.

FEARLESS DEFINITIONS

Sometimes such justifications needed to be expressed in negatives. At a dinner of the Royal Philharmonic Society, the ceramicist and Turner Prize-winner Grayson Perry startled his supposedly worldly audience by warning them that he was going to talk about the 'C word': yes, 'cool'. For art, he warned, could not be cool, should not aim at being cool, and anyone who tried to achieve that status was unlikely to be a true artist. More recently Perry spoke out against artists who were or sought to become 'global brands'. 'No names, no pack drill,' as the army used to say.

In similar vein, the playwright Mark Ravenhill warned of the dangers of the 'E word': yes, 'edgy', what he called 'the most vacuous bit of vocabulary in use'. And what was wrong with it apart from its glibness and its over-use? Ravenhill waded in: 'It allows everyone to feel that they are making exciting programmes without doing anything as audience-threatening as being innovative or highbrow. There's a warm glow of danger about edgy, but there's no real engagement with new or difficult ideas.'

Enjoyable and apt as those warning-off signs for today's modish language and behaviours were, were there positive statements about the real nature and value of the arts? The novelist Jeanette Winterson recently found herself confronted by a dinner guest who confidently told her that an arts degree was useless to society. It would have been wonderful to have been present. Winterson replied:

From where I was sitting, people who use phrases like 'monetise the brand' are insensitive to language and to life [...] Monetise is not a word. I am all for new coinings but ask that they have some value. Finance types don't seem to understand that language is not signage [...] We can't treat each other like something in the Inbox, because pretty soon the things we value end up in the Outbox.

Winterson then launched into her fearless and unapologetic credo:

Art can't change your life; it is not a diet programme or the latest guru – it offers no quick fixes. What art can do is prompt in us authentic desire. By that I mean it can waken us to truths about ourselves and our lives; truths that normally lie suffocated under the pressure of the 24-hour emergency zone called real life.

No hard-boiled Treasury official would understand such an observation, still less accord it any value. But it speaks from deep in the core of the arts experience. It is honest, it is true and it is a brave and wonderful place to start speaking up for what the arts do without pretence, concession or compromise.

The same Treasury mandarin might – or might not – respond in similar vein to Mark Ravenhill as he addressed the complexities of the world we live in and the ways the arts reflect them. Just what was the nature of the interaction between life and art? What should it be? This was Ravenhill's answer:

In a modern world that buys and sells information and luxury, the arts deal in something very different: wisdom, a complex, challenging, lifelong search that can make you happy and furious, discontented and questioning, elated or bored. It doesn't educate or inform or make you a better citizen. We belittle art when we make it into information or luxury. Wisdom can hurt, but human beings will always seek it out.

There was a further observation about the truly transformative nature of art from the philosopher and anthropologist Gregory Bateson. He asserted that there were only four phenomena with the power to undermine what he called 'the rash, rational, purposeful mind'. They were dreams, religious experience, art and love, and in his view the greatest of these was art. How could he justify this claim? Bateson's views were summarised by Tim Parks in the *Guardian* as follows:

> art enjoyed the special role of fusing different 'levels of mind' together: there was necessarily consciousness and purpose in the decision to create, but creativity itself involved openness to material from the unconscious, otherwise the work would be merely schematic and transparent.

While perhaps few would accept that as a complete justification for the special and distinctive nature of art, it is surely a subtle explanation of what its particular nature might be. Art needs and will always need the fearless, unapologetic definitions of the Wintersons, the Ravenhills, the Batesons.

It was greatly encouraging that the rising generation of arts leaders thought constantly about the fundamental purposes of the arts. In the 2010 cohort of fellows who joined Dame Vivien Duffield's Clore Leadership Programme, typically men and women in their mid thirties, these observations were typical of their approach:

'The arts are about the way a society feels about itself.'

'We are totally lost as a nation if we can't identify who we are.'

'Without culture, we are only survivors.'

So where does this leave the state of the arts? We should look at the arts ecology as a whole, as a broad-based pyramid or a massive tree with vast taproots; we should take more care of the base of that pyramid because the bodies it represents are inventive, original and dynamic, and have lessons for others to learn. Just because they are small does not make them worth less.

The last decade in the arts might have left organisations in a stronger position financially – albeit one that will now come under real pressure from budget reductions. But a decade of wrangling over policies, purposes, functions, objectives and outcomes has contributed little or anything to the quality of the arts produced. The arts have succeeded because they have stuck to their artistic purposes; the policy makers have only got in the way, then failed to make any contribution or any difference.

It is no glib assertion to claim that, as the result of the last decade of increased funding, sheer hard work and increased professionalisation, the arts ecology is more robust than it has been for a generation. Imminent, ill-considered and excessive funding cuts could only put all the ground painfully gained over a decade at serious risk.

A FUTURE AGENDA

Funding apart, is there a wider, more forward-looking agenda for arts organisations and government to adopt, one that will exist in good times and in bad? Conversations with a number of arts leaders suggest there is such an agenda and it could be one that significantly alters the way arts organisations behave in the future.

First, do they act like organisations or like institutions, the former containing the sense of something growing and changing organically, the latter implying a fossilised, arthritic body more interested in and adept at rules and procedures than permitting change?

Second, are museums, galleries and even performing-arts venues more like visitor attractions than centres of artistic excellence? How far are business plans and budgets skewed to the needs of the visitor attraction rather than to the prime business of the art, the collections and public engagement with them?

Third, how far is it true that the age of the gigantic – whether art gallery or concert hall – is over? If so how do arts organisations behave when the next capital plan is no longer a key part of their planning agenda?

Fourth, could the arts be truly and deeply inserted into schools' core curriculum? Could arts organisations cooperate and work together with universities instead of peering at one another with incomprehension and suspicion?

Fifth, can arts organisations respond to the possibility that policy and programme making should shift from being a mainly top-down process and instead acknowledge the power and potential of ideas that emerge from audiences?

Sixth, how will the arts adapt to a public that challenges more, questions more, knows more and wants more?

Finally, will the arts be stronger in standing up for their values against the usually mis-intentioned and misguided demands for results and accountability? If, as the academic Robert Hewison said, 'Audit destroys trust,' will the arts define, defend and develop their own notions of responsibility as a counter to the unsuitable demands of audit?

These amount to a significant agenda for the future, but it springs from the arts, belongs to the arts and will be delivered by the arts because it is owned by them.

The agenda for any future government is also searching. Will it place arts at the heart of education? Will government departments talk collectively about what New Labour once called 'cross-cutting agendas'? It was a common Whitehall observation that matters such as the arts – which in practice impinged on a dozen different ministries – tended to be ignored by all except the one with culture in its name. Will governments cling to the traditional funding model of a third, a third, a third – public, private, box office – which has served the arts so well? Will the Cameron government cease flirting with the fantasy that private giving and privately funded endowments are a more desirable way of funding the arts, setting aside their impracticability?

These are, as they ought to be, big questions. They could be answered but only if governments finally acknowledge that the arts are sufficiently broadly based, widely dispersed throughout the nation, generally used, highly valued and responsibly run, and that they deserve to be taken seriously as a core part of the economic and social polity. New Labour once promised to 'write the arts into our core script'. The time for that act of political inclusion has surely arrived.

INDEX